BEYOND POSTSTRUCTURALISM

BEYOND POSTSTRUCTURALISM

The Speculations of Theory and the Experience of Reading

Edited by

Wendell V. Harris

The Pennsylvania State University Press
University Park, Pennsylvania

Library of Congress Cataloging-in-Publication Data

Beyond poststructuralism : the speculations of theory and the experience of reading / edited by Wendell V. Harris.

p. cm.
Includes bibliographical references and index.
ISBN 0-271-01495-4 (cloth)
ISBN 0-271-01496-2 (paper)
1. Criticism—History—20th century. 2. Structuralism (Literary analysis) I. Harris, Wendell V.
PN94.B49 1996
801'.95—dc20 95-10930
CIP

Printed in the United States of America
Published by The Pennsylvania State University Press,
University Park, PA 16802-1003

It is the policy of The Pennsylvania State University Press to use acid-free paper for the first printing of all clothbound books. Publications on uncoated stock satisfy the minimum requirements of American National Standard for Information Sciences—Permanence of Paper for Printed Library Materials, ANSI Z39.48-1992.

Contents

II RECAPTURING THE VALUES OF READING LITERATURE

Acknowledgments

James Battersby's "Authors and Books: The Return of the Dead from the Graveyard of Theory" includes portions of "The Inevitability of Professing Literature," originally published in *Criticism, History, and Intertextuality (Bucknell Review)*, ed. Richard Fleming and Michael Payne (Bucknell University Press; Associated University Presses, 1988) together with material from "Conclusion: Worlds Without End" in *Paradigms Regained: Pluralism and the Practice of Criticism* (University of Pennsylvania Press, 1988). These portions are reprinted by permission of the Bucknell University Press, Associated University Presses, and the University of Pennsylvania Press.

Bernard Bergonzi, "Splendours and Miseries of the Academy." © Bernard Bergonzi, 1990. Reprinted from *Exploding English: Criticism, Theory, Culture* by Bernard Bergonzi (1990) by permission of Oxford University Press.

David Bromwich, "Literature and Theory," originally published as "Recent Work in Literary Criticism" in *Social Research* (autumn 1986). © *Social Research*. Reprinted by permission.

Christopher Clausen, "National Literatures," reprinted from *New Literary History* (winter 1994) by permission of *New Literary History.*

Gayle Greene, "Looking at History," slightly modified from *Changing Subjects: The Making of Feminist Literary Criticism,* ed. Gayle Greene and Coppélia Kahn (London: Routledge, 1993). Reprinted by permission.

Wendell Harris, "Adam Naming the Animals" from *Kenyon Review* (winter 1986). © Wendell Harris.

John Holloway, "Language, Realism, Subjectivity, Objectivity," from *Reconstructing Literature,* ed. Laurence Lerner (Oxford: Blackwell, 1983). Reprinted by permission.

Quentin Kraft, "Toward a Critical Renewal: At the Corner of Camus and Bloom Streets," from *College English* (January 1992). © 1992 by the National Council of Teachers of English. Reprinted by permission.

Richard Levin, "The Cultural Materialist Attack on Artistic Unity and the Problem of Ideological Criticism," from *Ideological Approaches to Shakespeare,* ed. Robert Merrix and Nicholas Ranson (Lewiston, N.Y.: Edwin Mellen Press, 1992). Reprinted by permission of the Edwin Mellen Press.

Virgil Nemoianu, "Literary History: Some Roads Not (Yet) Taken," from *Modern Language Quarterly* 54 (March 1993): 31–40. © University of Washington, 1992. Reprinted with permission.

Martha Nussbaum, "The Literary Imagination in Public Life," from *New Literary History* (November 1991). Reprinted by permission of *New Literary History.*

A. D. Nuttall, "Shaking the Concepts" (portions of this chapter) from *A New Mimesis: Shakespeare and the Representation of Reality* (London: Methuen, 1983). Reprinted by permission of Methuen and Co.

Robert Scholes, "An End to Hypocriticism," from *South Central Review* (spring 1991). Reprinted by permission of *South Central Review.*

John Searle, "Literary Theory and Its Discontents." *New Literary History* 25 (summer 1994). © John Searle. Reprinted by permission.

Raymond Tallis, "Literature as Textual Intercourse," from *Not Saussure: A Critique of Post-Saussurean Literary Theory* (London: Macmillan, 1988). © Raymond Tallis. Reprinted by permission of Macmillan Press.

Introduction

This collection of essays has two purposes. First, it brings together a set of variously focused but mutually reinforcing critiques of the more disabling exaggerations embedded in poststructuralist theorizing. Although in the last few years literary critics have turned from preoccupation with literary theory toward cultural issues, the examination of these fresher and, I believe, more important questions unfortunately remains cluttered and confused by the pressure of continuing modes of poststructuralist thought. While Barthes, Derrida, de Man, Culler, Miller, Foucault, Rorty, etc. no longer dominate lists of "Works Cited" so much as they once did, poststructuralist beliefs remain very much in circulation: it is widely if uncritically assumed that one must eschew the consideration of authorial intention; that meanings are undecidable; that there is no justification for seeking unity in a text; that all hierarchies of value are reversible; that history is no more than an open contest among competing narrative constructions; and that the very nature of language makes the falsifiability of statements about experience impossible. It need hardly be said that such assumptions set strong limits to the kinds of investigations, interpretations, and critical arguments regarded as acceptable. Whether or not explicitly asserted, these curiously hyperbolic doctrines, largely based on confusions about Saussure's views of language, continue to have currency even when they are incompatible with what the critics who cite them are actually trying to do. For instance, although the necessity of considering the historical context of a work of literature is again being recognized (and at times promulgated as though no one had considered such an approach before), discussions of context are apt to become badly muddled by failure to think through the relations between language, experiential reality, and authorial intention that must obtain if historical context is in fact significant. Similarly, if the language of the literary text actually were as self-referential as much poststructuralist theory asserts, literature would hardly be a site in which to explore the issues of race, gender, and class on which a great deal of critical discussion centers at present.

It seems to be one of the characteristics of the field of literary criticism that its practitioners hardly ever explicitly retract any of their previously stated positions. When a doctrine or approach proves unsound, or perhaps simply loses the interest of novelty, those who had adopted it, even those who had made a reputation advocating it, quietly abandon the position and move to pastures new. Quite often, however, residual corollaries of systems of thought no longer actively held, together with certain associated bits of vocabulary still carrying their original implications, continue to haunt critical discourse. The essays making up the first section of this volume have therefore been chosen for their aid in straightening out misconceptions and confusions that, although rarely explicitly defended nowadays, continue to insinuate themselves even though they often undercut the arguments in which they arc found.

The primary purpose of the second section of this collection is to suggest ways of regarding literature that emphasize its values in widening the sympathies and perspectives of readers. The essays that make up this section do not seek to promote a new generation of theories to replace those that dominated poststructuralism. Some critics, accustomed to reading literature through the lens of one or another intriguing theory, seem eagerly awaiting the advent of yet newer theoretical structures. However, it is highly likely that what is needed is not another pretentious all-embracing theory, not another attempt at making it all new, but a cleansing of the stables together with a return to thinking about what makes literature valuable, what makes it worthy of a place in the curriculum. Palpably in the air—that is, in the hallways, classrooms, and (perhaps as yet less strongly), in the professional journals—is a resurgence of the belief that literature has more important purposes than to serve as the subject of theorizing, especially theorizing the object of which too often has been the production of paradox and the demonstration of intellectual legerdemain. Also in the air is a newly revived pluralism—a pluralism that recognizes not only that there are a good many useful ways of talking about literature but that there are more kinds of literature worth talking about than traditional syllabi have recognized. The essays gathered in the second section seek in various ways to emphasize the role of literature in broadening understanding, providing new perspectives, and widening the range of available alternatives to what is threatening, unjust, fallacious, or absurd in social and cultural structures.

As will become apparent to the reader, the essays making up this volume share no single theory or perspective except that the study of literature is important and that it can be pursued more effectively than is often at present the case. I suspect every contributor would dearly like to argue one or more of the points made by almost every other contributor. That is as it should be. The authors of these essays believe in the importance of serious debate, the necessary existence of a variety of critical perspectives, and the value of literature for more purposes than the illustration of philosophical, psychological, or sociological theories. To which I add my own belief that if the case for the importance of the experience of reading poems, novels, plays, and personal essays is not made more convincingly than has been usual for the last twenty years, the study of literature is unlikely to remain a significant part of the university curriculum.

Part I

The Disabling Confusions of Current Literary Theory

1

From "Splendours and Miseries of the Academy"

Bernard Bergonzi

Bernard Bergonzi, emeritus professor of English at the University of Warwick, describes his 1990 Exploding English: Criticism, Theory, Culture *as "an account, from within, of a changing culture and form of life: the academic study of English Literature as I have been involved in it for the past thirty years, with a backward glance at its earlier history." Bergonzi, whose books have treated such diverse subjects as T. S. Eliot, H. G. Wells, Gerard Manley Hopkins, and the literature of the Great War, brings together in* Exploding English *a thoughtful and intriguing set of essays that blends his detailed knowledge of the history of the teaching of English literature in Britain with informed if informal analyses of the contributions and aberrations of current literary theories and institutional practices. Although his focus is on the British university, much of his commentary is equally applicable to the state of American literary studies.*

The following selections comprise sections I, II, and V of the chapter of Exploding English *entitled "Splendours and Miseries of the Academy."*

I

Traditionally, people who wrote criticism often also wrote poetry or novels, and engaged in the discussion of politics and public affairs. Things have been otherwise for some time now. As Frank Kermode has put it, "You won't find it easy to name an important critic who was a critic, and nothing else; that is, until quite recently. The world is now full of literary critics, some held to be important, who do nothing else but write literary criticism, and they all work in universities."[1] Kermode is referring to the demise of the man of letters, or the "bookman" as he became known in late Victorian England, and his replacement by the professionalized university critic. Kermode sees this change—which is at the heart of what I am writing about—as having radical implications for letters, comparable to such things as the advent, first of printing and then of cheap paper; the bourgeoisie's greater leisure for private reading; and the abandonment by circulating libraries of the three-volume novel, which had been the favored vehicle for fiction during much of the nineteenth century: Kermode exaggerates a little, I think; nothing in the establishment of university English is so important as the innovations in culture and technology that established the book in its modern form. But he is right in seeing the movement of criticism from literature to the academy as having large cultural implications. Kermode thinks that this process, with all that it implies, is a fact of life that has to be lived with, whatever we think of it. We may have no choice but to do so, though I believe that the change has been more damaging than beneficial. There is the further consideration that universities may not indefinitely be secure havens for literary criticism, in the market-dominated climate and rampant anti-intellectualism of a still largely Thatcherite Britain, and of many other parts of the world.

When English was established in British universities criticism played at best a minor part in it. There was a "critical paper" in the Oxford degree, but the emphasis was substantially on scholarship of a tough traditional kind, without much concession to the Arnoldian free play of mind. For a long time Oxford English was directed toward scholarship and was suspicious of criticism, and this attitude was reflected in its house organ, the *Review of English Studies*. Helen Gardner, for many years an Oxford luminary, did not believe that the purpose of "English" was to turn out critics, any more than it was to produce poets and novelists. The graduate in English was to be to some extent a scholar, insofar as he or she had a sense of the past and the capacity to understand literature in its historical contexts, particularly linguistic; beyond that, what was looked for was wide reading, an appreciation of masterpieces, and a capacity to write well, attend to evidence, and disentangle sense from nonsense in argument. It was not, in fact, a bad educational program, but it did not have the glamor of Cambridge English, where the idea of criticism was central, as instanced by the great success and influence of Richards's *Practical Criticism*. Gardner, like other Oxford Anglicans, resisted the religious and missionary approach to the study of literature evident in the Newbolt Report (on the teaching of English [1921]) and the Cambridge pioneers. She was not positively hostile to criticism; indeed, she produced a book called *The Business of Criticism*. But her concept of criticism was that it should be elucidatory and illuminating rather than evaluative. Her assumptions are broadly Crocean; value appeared in the individual's response to the particular work, but should not be erected into hierarchies, and the reader should cultivate "the receptiveness and disinterestedness which are the conditions of aesthetic experience."[2] Nonevaluative criticism, as propounded by the successive Merton professors, Gardner and Carey, has long been a popular ideal at Oxford. But another Oxford professor, John Bayley, sees things differently. Discussing a book on Dostoevsky, he remarks that while the author has much of interest to say about *The Idiot* "she does not quite persuade one that it comes off, indeed she does not really try, because like many scholars today she is concerned with showing how the thing works than with judging if it works well."[3]

From the beginning, academic literary study was divided between those who saw it as inevitably involved with making judgments and those who did not. Cambridge English represented the former: Richards and Leavis wanted an evaluative criticism, because they did not believe that literature was simply a matter of disinterested individual response; it was an index to the condition of civilization, which made judgments imperative. Wherever Leavis exerted an influence, either directly, on his pupils, or via *Scrutiny*, then criticism was emphatically evaluative. In practice this often meant that immature minds would take over Leavis's own evaluations without relating them to their own experience of literature, resulting in the diffusion of callow or inept judgments that has been condemned from the right by C. S. Lewis and from the left by Catherine Belsey. Although the New Criticism in its later American manifestations generally pursued a purely formal and elucidatory analysis, Gerald Graff reminds us that the original New Critics *were* evaluative, since they wrote as conservative Southerners who were much concerned with ideals of cultural health. They were also, for the most part, practicing poets and men of letters, who would want to make judgments. Similarly, Cambridge English was originally sustained by the achievements of literary modernism, which had a new agenda to write. In later academic criticism, it is only among Marxists and feminists that we find an overt evaluative pressure. Elsewhere the idea of a supposedly nonevaluative criticism has become general. I have remarked on its dominance in Oxford English, and a generation ago it was given magisterial expression in Northrop Frye's *Anatomy of Criticism,* which aspired to a "scientific" criticism where there would be no place for evaluation, since it is not nobler to study stars than earthworms. In the recent work of the global anglophone academy, evaluative criticism has largely disappeared. In its simpler, popularizing aspects the emphasis is on illumination and elucidation, and in its more advanced interpretative reaches the critic is concerned with tracing unnoticed patterns of coherence and unity or, depending on the critic's affinities, of incoherences and aporias. Yet vestigial gestures toward value persist, usually at the end of an exposition, where the critic in a final flourish claims, or at least hopes, that something valuable has emerged from the analysis; a revelation of the quality of the author's imagination; or of the inevitable tendency of all texts to be about their own processes of composition, or to come apart in the reader's hand; or of the aesthetic fascination of the patterns of imagery that have been revealed; or, at the very least, and least interestingly, that something "interesting" will have been said.

Most of this academic activity is not, in fact, criticism as traditionally understood but something else, which is fundamentally a form of technical description. Helen Gardner was aware of the problem, observing that the pursuit of image patterns, or of the ideas in a poem, can be useful to the interpreter, but cannot "be more than auxiliary in leading us to the true 'meaning' of the work, which is the meaning which enlarges our own imaginative life."[4] What Gardner calls "meaning" is, I take it, the work's unique expression of value, which we grasp intuitively. John Bayley, after the remark quoted above, goes on to complain about "the almost purely technical nature of this modern criticism, even more unsuited to how we actually respond to Dostoevsky than it is to most authors." Long ago, in the heyday of Cambridge English, Richards was making a similar distinction between the "critical" and the "technical": "All remarks as to the ways and means by which experiences arise or are brought about are technical, but critical remarks are about the values of experiences and the reasons for regarding them as valuable, or not valuable."[5] Geoffrey Thurley claimed that much modern criticism, so-called, was mainly concerned with "scansion," which is the description, often very close and attentive, of the structural, formal, and technical features of a text. Such criticism Thurley argued, very convincingly, never bridges the gap between description and interpretation, which for Thurley involves evaluation. In practice, much academic interpretation—whether New Critical, archetypal, deconstructive, or whatever—is really, in his terms, a more or less refined form of description or "scansion." He is very dismissive about the famous reading of a Shakespeare sonnet by Jakobson and Jones, which minutely analyzes its linguistic features, and emerges with a banal paraphrase that, Thurley remarks, "any schoolboy would scorn to produce."[6] If we take criticism out of its academic context and apply it to more things than literature, it is evident that comparisons of value are fundamental to it. Consider, for instance, informed discussions of sporting events, which are always displays of evaluative analysis: who played well, who disappointingly, and why and how; or whether a team has played better at home or away, this season or last. It is true that in such discussions the judgmental element does not exist in isolation, since it is interwoven with description, technical assessment of moves in play, and so forth, in ways suggested in Wittgenstein's lectures on aesthetics. But to remove this element results in, at best, a decaffeinated criticism.

It has been taken for granted for a long time that criticism and the academy go naturally together, and a large pedagogic and publishing industry has been built on that assumption. Nevertheless, I believe that the marriage, whatever its public appearance, is a difficult one, and results in bad faith and deception. Helen Gardner was not a deep thinker, but she saw certain things more clearly than many sharper minds. She was wrong to think that genuine criticism could be severed from evaluation, but right to think that there was no place for such criticism in the academy. The "criticism" that is copiously produced and read in literature departments eschews judgment for "scansion," technical analysis, and elaborate interpretations that nevertheless remain fundamentally descriptive. This state of affairs is not, I think, an aberration, but is inevitable in the structures of higher education.

The example of Leavis and *Scrutiny* may suggest otherwise. Leavis was a major critic and a very influential educator, who was convinced both that criticism was essentially evaluative and that it was at the heart of English studies. Yet Leavis was in many respects not a man of his time; though himself a dedicated university teacher, he was in spirit the last of the Victorian sages, who were men of letters and of affairs, not academics (prescinding from Arnold's and Ruskin's marginal tenure of chairs at Oxford). *Scrutiny* had an enormous influence on English studies, particularly in England, but its immediate model was the nonacademic *Calendar of Modern Letters,* and more remotely the great Victorian reviews, whose contents might be described as the higher literary journalism. In its early years *Scrutiny* was a fine embodiment of the spirit of criticism, literary and cultural. Leavis's judgments were very much his own, laboriously arrived at, and presented with subtlety and rigor. But these judgments were then taken over and prepackaged for pedagogic purposes, so one had the spectacle of the Leavisite schoolmaster or university teacher who presented his students with duplicated copies of, say, sonnets by Hopkins and Rossetti, which they were invited to compare and contrast in evaluative terms. There was no doubt that they were expected to admire the former and scorn the latter; anyone misguided enough to get the preference the wrong way round, would be regarded as at best naive and misguided, and at worst corrupted in sensibility. Denys Thompson's *Reading and Discrimination* (1934) is a collection of such comparative exercises. Leavisism assumed that its rewriting of the canon had a once-and-for-all quality, so that it was inconceivable that anyone could come to admire Shelley again, though this is precisely what has happened under the influence of Harold Bloom, who is dedicated to overturning the Eliot–Leavis version of poetic history. The attempt to enforce an evaluative criticism in the academy inevitably results in rigidity and dogmatism and, ultimately, a form of brainwashing. Leavisites, of course, claimed that they were committed to discussion, argument, the free play of mind; insofar as they were, it was contained within the enclosing form of life, not directed against it, rather like arguments within Marxist-Leninist ideology. It was this aspect of Leavisism that Oxford English, with its broad though often flaccid eclecticism, was most opposed to.

Venturing to propound a law of intellectual life, I suggest that evaluative criticism enters institutional literary study under the influence of practicing writers, or of critics who have a close discipular relation to them, but that in time it is rejected, like an alien organ. Writers, whose criticism arises directly from the problems and possibilities of their art, are inevitably evaluative; Baudelaire showed how being a poet also involves being a critic. Eliot's early and best criticism was what he called "workshop" criticism, an attempt to realign literary tradition in the interests of the kind of poetry he wanted to write. Leavis, at the beginning of his career a wholehearted admirer of Eliot, took over Eliot's tentative critical models and systematized them. Later he responded in a similar way to D. H. Lawrence's criticism, as well as to his creative achievement. In America, as I have remarked, the original New Critics were evaluative, in ways closely connected to their own poetic practice. Also in America there is the singular example of Yvor Winters, sometimes seen as an equivalent of Leavis, who was a poet of conservative but original talents, and a fiercely judgmental critic, who weirdly redrew the canons of English and American literature, so that T. Sturge Moore and Elizabeth Daryush emerged as major twentieth-century poets. Unlike Leavis's, Winters's deconstruction of tradition proved too extreme to have even a temporary lodgement in the academy, though his readings of sixteenth-century poetry have had some influence, and a theorist such as Gerald Graff acknowledges a debt to Winters, who was his teacher.

It remains to be shown why genuine criticism is not at home in the academy; or, more precisely, why it is irreconcilable with pedagogic practice. Criticism, I take it, is an activity that occurs between equals, whatever its object. The critic is an unusually acute and well-informed reader, but there should be equality of esteem between the critic and other readers. What he or she has to say is always open to comment, questioning, refutation. This is apparent in the correspondence columns of those publications where the tradition of public criticism continues, like the *Times Literary Supplement* and the *London Review of Books*. There is, of course, an immense amount to be learned from good critics, but the critic's role and tone are not those of a teacher. Critical seminars within the university may sometimes blur this distinction if they contain elements of genuine intellectual exchange. Leavis defined critical discussion as taking the form, "This is so, isn't it?" expecting the answer, "yes, but . . ." (though never, "I very much doubt it" or "No, in thunder!"). This formula may characterize the best form of discussion. But it is disingenuous for academics to pretend that they can participate in such discussion on terms of complete equality with their students, for there are questions of power and authority involved; at the end of the day, grades and marks, assessing and examining, come into the picture. Students do not forget these overshadowing realities even if academics, caught up in the euphoria of a "really lively discussion," sometimes do. The reality is often closer to that memorably described by David Lodge: "occasionally one feels, as a teacher, rather like a soccer referee who, having blown his whistle for the kick-off, finds the players disconcertingly reluctant to make a move and is reduced to dribbling the ball himself furiously from end to end, scoring brilliant goals in undefended nets, while the motionless players look curiously on."[7]

Not only should there be equality of esteem and status between critic and readers, though the former may appear as first among equals, they should all be in possession of the subject of discussion. They should all have read the book, in short. This is why reviewing is not properly speaking criticism, though it calls for critical qualities, and an extended review-article, looking at a whole *oeuvre,* may well be. This is true in all aspects of culture. If we are discussing a football match or a meal in a restaurant, then at the very least we should all have seen the match or eaten the meal. Furthermore, we should have a shared understanding of the rules of discourse about such subjects. A proper discussion of a football match cannot occur if one of the participants is quite ignorant of the rules of the game; and the kind of assessment of a restaurant meal that would involve the possible insertion of the establishment into a good food guide (or perhaps its deletion from it) will not get very far if one of the diners does not care for the meal because his idea of a gastronomic treat is a cheeseburger and french fries (though within the order of the burger discriminations are possible). The critical reader of a poem needs to have some idea of what a poem is, which need not be a theoretically sophisticated idea, and some acquaintance with poetry already.

In this context I want to refer to a brief but highly significant passage in Richards's *Practical Criticism.* In the latter part of the book Richards discusses the reports on the "protocols," the anonymous reports on the anonymous poems or extracts the respondents had been given to read. He examines their various kinds of failure in reading, arising from the reader's susceptibility to personal fantasy, dominance by dogma, overliteralness, careless construing, and so on. Most of these failures are in the order of mental operation, which is in accordance with Richards's dominantly psychologistic approach. This is still true when he says that some of the respondents lacked the emotional maturity to respond adequately to poetry. But he then goes on to remark that a further cause of inadequate response is the reader's unfamiliarity with poetry: "A lack of experience with poetry must be placed next to general inexperience of life in this list of deficiencies."[8] Here Richards switches from a psychological to a cultural factor. The remark has not been much noticed, but its implications must undermine the way in which "practical criticism" is often employed in literary education. It has long been common practice to give students isolated passages of poetry or prose, often but not always anonymous, to analyze, discuss, and respond to, in the manner of Richards's original undertaking. In this exercise students are urged to clear their minds of presuppositions, to concentrate on "the words on the page," and then to write down their responses. The reading is deliberately contextless, and the mind is assumed or encouraged to be a *tabula rasa*. (More traditional pedagogy went for appreciation rather than analysis, urging the reader to a direct experience of the poem, perhaps inhaling its beauty like the scent of a flower; but the underlying process was similar.) Such assumptions are quite contrary to what we know of how perception works. The practice of "practical criticism" in fact unconsciously takes it for granted that the readers already know enough about poetry to have a grasp of rules and conventions sufficient to make adequate sense of the passage. Richards had to acknowledge that what he called "the relatively cultivated youth of our age" were not very familiar with poetry. If that was true, then, how much more true is it now, given the vast changes in education, society, and culture that have ensued since 1929? I am not now going to engage in lamentations about the ignorance and lack of reading of present-day undergraduates, though I have done so in my time, and could be easily provoked into them again. I merely want to make the limited point that many of these students—who may be highly intelligent—do not have the existing familiarity with poetry, not to mention the general knowledge and cultural literacy, that would enable them to engage as equals in genuinely critical discussion.

Leavis held firm to the idea that any kind of responsible discussion of literature was a critical act, so that the academic was inescapably engaged in criticism when lecturing or conducting a seminar. In reality this is unlikely to be true, as student and teacher do not have an equal possession of the text. In other academic areas it is assumed that the teacher knows more than the student, and is there to convey this knowledge, whether as a corpus or a skill. The conveying need not, indeed should not, be done in an authoritarian way. In seminar teaching it should elicit feedback, questioning, the bringing out of implications or contradictions, and the opening up of fresh aspects of the subject. Nevertheless, teaching implies an imbalance of knowledge, otherwise it would not be necessary. The formal lecture, that archaic but strangely persistent mode, makes this apparent. In literature teaching the emphasis is on shared experience rather than the conveying of information; a lecture is supposed to provide knowledge, elucidation, or interpretation of texts on the assumption that the auditors have already read them. As anyone who has worked in an English department will know, many of those listening to the lecture will not have done the necessary reading, and are so reduced to hearing about and taking notes on something of which they have not had direct literary experience (even passing on their notes to friends who were absent from the lecture). In a Crocean or

Leavisite perspective this conveying of knowledge without experience is a useless activity. It is, however, a common one, and a kind of collective bad faith.

Attempts are still made to introduce an element of evaluative criticism into academic teaching, whether from a surviving Leavisism, or under Marxist or feminist auspices. My own efforts to do so have been instructive, but discouraging. Judgments made in the course of a lecture will be taken down in notes as if they were facts, whereas it is in the nature of critical judgments that they cannot be taken over by others; it is on this dilemma, I believe, that Leavisism ultimately foundered. In the habitual contexts of English Literature teaching, students assume that if a work is on a reading list then it must be of approved quality, otherwise why is it there? Attempts to provide adverse judgments on canonical works tend to be resented as "finding fault with" or "picking holes in" these works of established merit, the result of a tiresome foible on the part of the teacher, and leading to disorientation if persisted in. In these matters, I think the students may have a more realistic sense of the situation than the teacher. There has been much discussion of the nature of literary canons;[9] university teachers of English are seen as both initiators and guardians of the canon (as, for instance, by Kermode in his essay, "Institutional Control of Interpretation").[10] The academic institutionalizing of literary study inevitably leads to the establishing of canons (made necessary, among much else, by the logistic requirements of reading lists and bookshop orders), and where there are canons evaluation is, in the context of pedagogy, either impossible or unrewardingly difficult, since canonization implies merit. And what is true of undergraduate teaching in England is equally true, *mutatis mutandis,* of the high-pressure environment of American graduate schools. Furthermore, the great mass of academic critical writing produced in the United States is elucidatory, analytical, descriptive, scansional, not evaluative. What is everywhere assumed, if not always made explicit, is that literary judgment has no place in the academy. This is a correct assumption, since the institutional conditions preclude its effective existence.

Academics can still write evaluative criticism of course, and insofar as they do they are producing the kind of criticism practiced by men of letters. John Bayley provides an interesting instance. Remarking that Dostoevsky's *The Idiot* does not altogether "come off," he is making a coherent and discussable point, whether or not one accepts it. Samuel Johnson might have said something similar, though in a very different idiom, about some accepted masterpiece of European literature. But it is possible that the

Dostoevsky scholar whose book prompted Bayley's comment might not have understood it—how could an acknowledged great novel, worth writing about at length, be said not to "come off"? Bayley is a senior academic who has kept his distance from institutional pressures and writes in the manner of the traditional man of letters.

The despised belletrist criticism of an earlier day could make radical judgments in an offhand manner; those articles, for instance, with titles like "On Rereading Stendhal," which come to the conclusion that Stendhal has been much overrated. An established professor of French literature might nowadays privately believe as much, but would probably think it unprofessional or damaging to argue the case publicly. Leavis, who notoriously had no hesitation about attacking canonical figures, was closer to this tradition, however much he detested the belletrist spirit, than he was to later developments in academic criticism. His iconoclasm about Milton, for instance, was anticipated by Walter Bagehot. Conversely, men of letters have always been ready for exciting literary discoveries. The young T. S. Eliot, coming across Laforgue as a Harvard undergraduate is a celebrated instance; there is André Gide, well on in middle age, registering his delight and astonishment at James Hogg's *Confessions of a Justified Sinner.*

Donald Davie, in a dispirited essay called "Criticism and the Academy," ruefully acknowledges that the belletrist criticism of men of letters such as Edmund Wilson and Cyril Connolly (unequal figures, these, one has to remark) might have more to be said for it than he, as a lifelong academic, would be happy to acknowledge:

> Edmund Wilson and Cyril Connolly were as ready to talk of Ovid as of the memoirs of Ulysses S. Grant, and indeed ready to illuminate the one by shafts of light thrown from the other. . . . Connolly and Wilson, we may agree, lived dangerously; they took risks, knowing full well that they were not *au fait* with the latest scholarship, had not mastered "the secondary material." And we tell our graduate students that they must never take such risks, construing as scruple what in fact is timidity.[11]

Davie himself provides the example of a dedicated university teacher, who is at the same time a fine poet, a practitioner of rigorously evaluative criticism, and a judicious reviewer. He is, in fact, a rare surviving embodiment of those long-vanished ideals of the 1950s, when it briefly seemed that University English might provide a terrain where all these practices could converge.

Morris Dickstein has contributed an excellent essay to the collection in which Davie's piece appears, called "Journalism and Criticism." Acknowledging the apparent opposition between these two terms, he goes on to argue, and to show from historical evidence, that throughout the nineteenth century, and into the early twentieth, much of the central function of criticism was carried by literary and cultural journalism, most of it, admittedly, of a more spacious and literate order than is common today. It is to this tradition, I have suggested, that *Scrutiny* was indebted. At the present time, it has become attenuated but not extinct, and it continues in the long review-articles in the *New York Review of Books* and *London Review of Books,* and a few other periodicals. Academics contribute to it, certainly, but writing as critics, not academics, for it involves judgment as much as elucidation. To take a particular instance, Martin Amis's *The Moronic Inferno,* published in 1986, is a collection of reprinted journalistic pieces on life, literature, and culture in contemporary America, a country for which he has mixed feelings of attraction and repulsion. It is the work of a novelist and journalist, not an academic, and notwithstanding the sometimes excessive brightness of the prose and the shortwindedness of the articles it seems to me a brilliant late embodiment of the Anglo-American tradition of literary and social criticism.

A central figure in Dickstein's essay is Henry James, a great critic, who could be subtly descriptive, elucidatory, analytical, and judgmental within the same piece of writing. As Dickstein points out, much of James's critical writing was produced according to the exigencies of journalism and magazine publication; nevertheless, as now brought together in two large and handsome volumes in the Library of America series, it must be the finest body of literary criticism in English from a single author. The whiggish notion that such writing might be somehow improved on or even supplanted by the critical mass-production of the anglophone academy is quite self-delusory.

II

Richards, as we have seen, thought that in order to be a good reader of poetry one must already be a reader of poetry. This is true, to a lesser extent, of all forms of imaginative writing, but poetry is the most obviously governed by convention and genre, and in the eyes of both the Russian Formalists and of nonliterary readers the most likely to display linguistic deformation. In many academic disciplines no prior knowledge is required or assumed. It is possible for sixth-form students in British secondary schools to take the Advanced- ("A"-) level examination for school-leavers in such subjects as philosophy or economics or sociology, but it is not at all common, and incoming university students of these subjects usually begin at the beginning, with open minds but with the necessary commitment to learning. In principle it would be quite possible for the study of English poetry to begin in a similar *ab initio* fashion, except that it would be fruitless for someone to embark on it who did not have at least some familiarity with poetry and a wish to read more. This is because the study of poetry *as* poetry—rather than as historical or cultural material—is a matter of intuitive and affective response, not just of willingness to accept an intellectual discipline, as might be the case with philosophy, economics, and so forth. (I grant that the difference is not absolute, and there may be elements of the affective and the intuitive in the pursuit of any intellectual discipline, but they are likely to be marginal.) It could be a rewarding form of teaching to help an uninformed but well-motivated student to come to terms with poetry, but it would involve time and leisure. The student would need to read as widely as possible in different kinds of poetry, to learn something about literary history, genre, and convention, and to acquire the practical-critical skills of close reading. All this might well be accomplished in the comparatively open-ended context of adult or continuing education, which is not dominated by the teleology of the examination system. In the high-pressured and directive context of undergraduate teaching it may be desirable, but is not practically possible. Too often, even the desirability is not recognized.

It is my experience that many students of English Literature with good A-level results dislike poetry, or at least feel baffled by it, and can go through a three-year degree course without this attitude being radically changed. There are elements of a vicious version of the hermeneutic circle involved: people don't like poetry because they haven't read enough to come to terms with it, and they haven't read enough because they don't like it. Several factors are involved in this unhappy state of affairs: a general decline in cultural literacy, and in skill and practice in reading. Poetry demands a form of reading that, though rewarding, is unusually intensive, and it is often avoided in sixth-form English teaching. Work for the A-level examination in English Literature means a narrow concentration on a limited number of texts, and curricular pressures do not leave time for the undirected contextual reading that would provide broader literary experience. Furthermore, I suspect that many sixth-form English teachers have acquired an Honors degree in the subject without ever coming to like or appreciate poetry, and they pass on their incapacities. Hence the concentration on plays and novels, often modern ones, which is made increasingly possible with A-level syllabuses governed by the specious lure of relevance. There are, of course, complex social and cultural factors to consider. It is a common leftist belief that poetry is an "elitist" mode, precisely because of the cultural literacy it presupposes, which gives an unfair advantage to students from middle-class homes with books. The advantage is undeniably there; but what of the ever-increasing number from middle-class homes without books? The grammar schools once provided the necessary culture of learning, as well as specific instruction, for students from underprivileged homes, as we see in Judith Grossman's novel *Her Own Terms* (1988), or Anthony Burgess's autobiographical recollection of reading English at Manchester University[12] in the late thirties (some twenty years before I started teaching there myself). Many things have changed since then. Not only have the grammar schools disappeared, but the number of students going into higher education to read English has greatly increased, the social catchment is wider, and reading has come to seem more difficult.

It was a recurring motif in the Newbolt Report, echoed by Leavis, that English was not just another school or university subject, to be placed alongside geography or geology. There is some truth in this, but not altogether in the sense that was there intended. Unlike other academic disciplines, English in higher education presupposes both an existing knowledge and an existing competence, which in practice is often lacking. As I have suggested, up to a generation ago a common form of life united sixth-form and university English, regardless of whether their orientation was "Oxford" or "Cambridge," since the latter made much the same assumptions about literacy and competence as the former. That shared culture has gone, though its traces have persisted for a long time, at least among those unworldly older academics who assume that students of English will have read the whole of Shakespeare in the sixth form, or that they can readily identify classical or biblical references. The belated realization that these things are no longer so leads to the embittered and baffled reaction that they *ought* to be so. However, that is a declining reaction; the experience of regularly interviewing would-be entrants to an English degree course soon induces a sense of realism. In the state of affairs that still obtained when I entered the profession in 1959 the grammar school teacher and the university teacher of English were not radically different kinds of person; indeed, contingent or accidental factors might have determined which career path was followed. Since then there has been a marked divergence between school and university; students have become less well equipped, and academics, particularly young ones, have become more high-powered, ambitious, and professionalized. I am convinced that many students often do not understand what is being said in teaching situations, though they become adept at pretending to, as they do not wish to lose face. There is a further factor that feminists have drawn attention to, which is that the majority of students of English are women, whereas the majority of academics teaching it are male, and that the female students have a built-in deference to male teachers and to the minority of male students. This is broadly true, and has long distorted the group dynamics of seminars, though I have the sense that things are changing as women become more self-confident (the arrival in increasing numbers of female mature students has been helpful). At the same time, I have noticed that women academics can be ruthless bullies of girl students, with the possibly laudable motive of giving them the equivalent of a good shake.

David Lodge, whose experience as novelist, critic, and professor of English has given him many insights into the situation I am describing, provides in his novel *Nice Work,* a neat instance of the gap between students and teacher. Dr. Robyn Penrose is a recognizable type of advanced young academic, leftist, feminist, poststructuralist:

> She probably knows more about the nineteenth century industrial novel than anyone else in the entire world. How can all that knowledge be condensed into a fifty-minute lecture to students who know almost nothing about it? The interests of scholarship and pedagogy are at odds here. What Robyn likes to do is to deconstruct the texts, to probe the gaps and absences in them, to uncover what they are *not* saying, to expose their ideological bad faith, to cut a cross-section through the twisted strands of their semiotic codes and literary conventions. What the students want her to do is to give them some basic facts that will enable them to read the novels as simple straightforward reflections of 'reality', and to write simple, straightforward, exam-passing essays about them.[13]

In an American context, E. D. Hirsch has remarked on a similar conflict of interest between students who want to know the basic meanings of texts, in their historical contexts, and junior academics who believe there are no basic meanings, only a multiplicity of interpretations.[14] Such divisions are not, so to speak, purely academic. They lead to confusion on the part of students, and it may be too glib to say, as one sometimes hears, that such confusion and disorientation are an inherently desirable part of the educational process. It does not always work like that, for they can lead to real difficulties in study, and sometimes to pastoral problems.

V

No discussion of institutionalizing of literary study in higher education would be complete without a mention of the academic publishing that exists in a close, indeed symbiotic relation with it. "Publication" is increasingly important, not just to secure advancement in an individual academic's career, but as a sign of an institution's status. I think it true to say that at the present time it is not at all difficult for academics to appear in print. I am not thinking primarily of the well-established learned journals, which have high editorial standards and a long queue of articles waiting to appear. (In the pursuit of performance-indicators, publication in "refereed journals" counts for much, though I am not sure if I have ever appeared in a refereed journal in my life.) However, new academic journals are regularly launched, devoted to one or other of the many specialisms into which English is fragmenting, and in their earlier issues, at least, are likely to be looking for contributions. It is, however, in the vastly expanded world of academic book publishing that the greatest opportunities lie. I do not claim to understand the economics of this system, which depends on small print-runs and numbingly high prices, and the assumption that institutional libraries will "want," or need, to buy these books. But it is evident that publishers, to stay in business, need to bring out a large number of titles every year. This is true in other academic areas, of course, but English is one of the largest earners, since books in this area can be hopefully addressed to "general readers," in a ritual recognition that there is a world elsewhere, as well as to students (though I suspect they are mostly read by teachers). University teachers of English are regular recipients of visitations from hopeful, fresh-faced publishers' editors trawling for new titles. Even

Ph.D. students can be approached before they have finished their theses, though the publication of unrevised theses seems to me undesirable, common though it has become: a thesis is written, as a rule, for two examiners, whereas a book, however specialized, should have a rather wider readership in mind.

Certainly, any academic who wants to write a book on a canonical author, topic, or period, is likely to get a contract without very much formality (particularly if it has to do with "women" or "theory," or ideally both). This is not the case, though, if the proposed subject is outside the catchment area of school and university examinations, as Terry Lovell discovered when she offered to write a book on Gissing for a left-wing series, which had asked for one on Jane Austen.[15] There is, I have found, some gentle entertainment to be had in discussion with publishers' representatives, observing the wide-eyed eagerness with which they greet potentially salable ideas, and their clenched, wary, glazed-eyes response to proposals they feel negative about, or perhaps do not understand. The discussion may be restricted to impeccably intellectual topics, but the play of market forces is going on all the time just below the surface. In one sense, everyone benefits from the buoyancy of academic book publishing. The academic gets the publication record that leads to tenure or advancement, and his or her name becomes known in the profession; the institution gains performance-indicators; and the publisher keeps a full and interesting list. It is hard to speak against a situation that makes everyone happy, but one has to say it represents a form of intellectual inflation that is just as pernicious in its way as monetary inflation. Far too many inferior or unnecessary academic books are published each year. Some publishers maintain traditionally stringent standards, but others, in a competitive market, are relaxed about quality control. It is far from unknown for an expert reader who provides an unfavorable report on a book in manuscript to find it nevertheless being published a year or so later.

The book from its invention has been a commodity, dependent on patronage or the market for its circulation, and this is a fact of history that there is a little point in complaining about. But in the present economic state of academic publishing the encounter between market forces and intellectual value tends to subordinate the latter to the former. This situation is common in many academic areas, as I have discovered talking to colleagues, and it may be that this state of inflation and overproduction is economically unavoidable, that many inferior books have to be published in order to let the good ones appear. But what is unavoidable may still be undesirable, and one might as well say so. Where literary criticism is concerned, we are faced with the depressing reality that this is now just one more academic specialism, a large specialism, admittedly, produced by and consumed within the academy. The price of books of academic criticism indicates that they are not aimed at the educated general reader (once they cost about the same as a bottle of whisky; now they cost three to four times as much). So many books, to pick up a point once made by Malcolm Bradbury, are published primarily to be stored, moving smoothly from publishers' warehouse to library stacks without arousing much disturbance on the way, and are discussed, if at all, only in scholarly journals.[16] Forty years ago, when criticism still occupied a traditional place as part of public discourse, the first books of a distinguished generation of British critics—Bayley, Davie, Hoggart, Kermode, Wain, Williams—were reviewed in the daily and weekly press.

At the present time, interpretation, often of a narrow and unrewarding kind, flourishes, usually though falsely claimed on publishers' blurbs to be saying something completely new and important. Many interesting works of English literature of the past remain unedited and unavailable, and it is a pity that the ingenuity and assiduity that goes into the labor, or play, of interpretation could not be directed to the truly useful work of editing these texts. Meanwhile the publishers' catalogues arrive regularly, with their copious listings not just of new titles, but of new series, aimed to appeal to the collecting instinct. I dutifully read through them with sinking feelings and, sometimes, a touch of nausea. I do not seem to be alone in this response. The writer of an admirable article on research in the humanities published in the *TLS* in 1987 wrote, "I believe passionately in the value of those activities we call 'the Humanities,' yet when I see a compilation like the British Library's *Current Research in Britain (1986): The Humanities* . . . I feel sick."[17]

Notes

1. Frank Kermode, "The Decline of the Man of Letters," *Partisan Review* 52 (1985): 203.
2. Helen Gardner, *The Business of Criticism* (Oxford: Clarendon Press, 1959), 13.
3. John Bayley, *The Order of Battle at Trafalgar* (London: Collins Harvill, 1987), 80.
4. Gardner, 148.
5. I. A. Richards, *Principles of Literary Criticism* (London: K. Paul, Trench, Trubner, 1925), 23.

6. Geoffrey Thurley, *Counter-Modernism in Current Critical Theory* (London: Macmillan, 1983), 38.

7. David Lodge, *Write On: Occasional Essays '65–'85* (London: Secker and Warburg, 1986), 40.

8. I. A. Richards, *Practical Criticism* (London: K. Paul, Trench, Trubner, 1929), 311.

9. Robert von Hallberg, ed., *Canons* (Chicago: University of Chicago Press, 1984).

10. Frank Kermode, *Essays on Fiction, 1971–82* (London: Routledge and Kegan Paul, 1983), 168–84; published in the United States as *The Art of Telling* (Cambridge: Harvard University Press, 1983).

11. Donald Davie, "Criticism in the Academy," in *Criticism and the University*, ed. Gerald Graff and Reginald Gibbons (Evanston: Northwestern University Press, 1985), 175.

12. Anthony Burgess, *Little Wilson and Big God* (Harmondsworth: Penguin, 1988), 167ff.

13. David Lodge, *Nice Work* (London: Secker and Warburg, 1988), 35–36.

14. E. D. Hirsch, Jr., "Back to History," in *Criticism in the University*, ed. Gerald Graff and Reginald Gibbons (Evanston: Northwestern University Press, 1985), 189–97.

15. "I was recently asked to contribute a monograph on Jane Austen to a radical series whose object was to re-analyze the canon from a left perspective. I offered to take on Gissing instead, and received the rather shamefaced response that Gissing was not to be included in the series. The acid test seems to be whether or not the writer was studied at A-level. Even demystification of the canon must stay strictly within its boundaries." Terry Lovell, *Consuming Fiction* (London: Verso, 1987), 172–73n.

16. Malcolm Bradbury, *The Social Context of Modern English Literature* (Oxford: Blackwell, 1971), 218.

17. Stefan Collini, "Viewpoint: Research in the Humanities," *Times Literary Supplement*, 3 April 1987.

Relevant Publications by Bernard Bergonzi

Wartime and Aftermath: Literature and Its Background, 1939–60. New York: Oxford University Press, 1993.

Exploding English: Criticism, Theory, Culture. Oxford: Clarendon Press, 1990.

The Myth of Modernism and Twentieth Century Literature. Brighton, Sussex: Harvester, 1986.

"Bernard Bergonzi." Interview. In *Conversations with Critics*, edited by Nicolas Tredell, 94–110. Manchester: Carcanet Press; Riverdale-on-Hudson: Sheep Meadow Press, 1994.

"Theorists and Postmen." *Literature and Theology* 6 (March 1992): 80–85.

"A Quiet Place: 'Readers' vs. 'Students.' " *Encounter* 69 (July–August 1987): 40–45.

"Marvels of the Micro-Critic: Ricks and the Reading of Poems." *Encounter* 64 (February 1985): 39–42.

"Experts and Readers: Recent Literary Criticism." *Encounter* 63 (July–August 1984): 46–51.

"Modern Metamorphoses: From Ovid to Ezra Pound." *Encounter* 61 (July–August 1983): 79–82.
"A Strange Disturbing World: The Conflicts in Criticism." *Encounter* 59 (June–July 1982): 58–67.
"The Foundling and the Bastard: Theories of Fiction." *Encounter* 57 (July 1981): 64–70.

2

Language, Realism, Subjectivity, Objectivity

John Holloway

John Holloway's reputation as a literary critic and scholar was first established by his study of Carlyle, Disraeli, Newman, George Eliot, Arnold, and Hardy in The Victorian Sage *(1953). Since then he has written such influential essays as those collected in* The Charted Mirror *(1960),* The Proud Knowledge, Poetry, Insight, and the Self, 1620–1929 *(1977), and* Narrative and Structure *(1979). Although he is known as a highly perceptive critic rather than as a theorist in the current sense, he has frequently developed explanatory frameworks for the literary phenomena he has studied. Thus his reflections on the disabilities of much of the kind of theorizing that has been most influential over the last twenty-five years come from a scholar-critic who is very much at home with the pursuit of overarching patterns and generalizations. The questions he raises, which return to the basic theses out of which the greater portion of poststructuralist theorizing has grown, are nonetheless salient for their modest phrasing. John Holloway, a fellow of Queens' College, Cambridge, is also the author of seven volumes of verse, including a book-length poem on Cambridge,* Civitatula, *published in December 1993.*

I

In this discussion I shall, in a modest way, examine certain general ideas about literature that began to come to prominence in the late 1960s and, while undergoing various degrees of metamorphosis, continue to be influential. More particularly I shall seek to examine the bases or underlying foundations of these ideas. The ideas in question may be indicated by mentioning the name of Roland Barthes in France, or certain American writers like Fredric Jameson. Barthes, Jameson, and others more or less like them have on the whole sought to establish their views along one line rather than another. They have based them, with one notable exception, Barthes's *S/Z,* not so much upon detailed empirical study of individual literary works, as upon generalized and far-reaching inquiries or opinions relating to the fundamental nature of language, communication, thought, the individual, society, the historical process, indeed civilization in general. These literary conceptions in the end take us back to Freud, to Marx or thinkers who followed Marx, and in particular to the French linguist Ferdinand de Saussure.

The body of work that I take stock of is large. I had better say frankly that I have read in this field (not, doubtless, so extensively as I might) more because there is widespread interest in it and it has become influential, than because I have found it exceptionally congenial. On the contrary, I have often had to strive against feeling to some extent out of sympathy with it, and I begin by saying why. One reason is that this body of work seems sometimes to suggest that the study of literature is not, or is no longer, a real subject of study at all. Thus Jameson writes of how "literature in our time [is] essentially impossible";[1] and Catherine Belsey, at the end of her book *Critical Practice* (1980), a popular account of the whole field, and one to which I shall revert, raises "the question whether we should continue to speak of *literature* at all."[2] I hope I am ready to follow an argument where it leads, but it is natural that I should sooner find such doubts and beliefs ill-founded rather than the reverse, and natural too I suppose that I should begin with a certain skepticism with regard to general, theoretical arguments that reach conclusions quite contrary to repeated and for me important aspects of my own experience over many years.

Moreover, there are certain other aspects of this body of writing, so far as I have explored it, that have left me less than ardently sympathetic. To begin with, we are dealing with entirely new conceptions of literature and literary criticism, which (so we are told) follow from new conceptions of the individual and of the individual's relation to society. These new conceptions, in their turn, follow from what at least the exponents of the views I discuss see as new and transforming conceptions of the nature of thought and of language itself. One cannot easily conceive of an intellectual enterprise more ambitiously fundamental and far-reaching; and to someone like myself, such a program calls for certain qualities. It calls for self-caution and intellectual modesty, and for habits of mind that seek the greatest exactitude and cogency in argument, the greatest care to foresee and to meet objections and difficulties. That strikes me as far indeed from the spirit of inquiry I have encountered in these writings. On the contrary, they seem to emanate from exceptional self-assurance; and from a conviction, often enough, that what they have to say is obvious, once one frees oneself from preexisting prejudice. I concede, as a matter of principle, that that may quite possibly be true in the case in question; but all the same I find myself in difficulty when someone whose thought I am trying to follow addresses me in what I find a high-handed style.

I also have another difficulty: some of the more seminal writers in these fields seem repeatedly dogmatic and obscure, and sometimes the thought even enters my mind that they are being half-deliberately obscure. Those on the other hand whose main effort has been to popularize and elucidate the work of the seminal figures seem to me often to write vaguely and loosely, and with signs of what, in many different contexts, I have come perhaps unfortunately to associate with an overconfident and untrained mind. Catherine Belsey gives some attention to such matters in her book, and perhaps she would respond to that unamiable word "untrained" by claiming that I wanted to "recuperate for common sense" what she and others had to say specifically in condemnation of common sense; or at least, what they believe common sense has had to say to us in the past: "recuperating" it by translating it "back into the discourse of every day" (6). But unfortunately, I remain unsure that this defense is adequate.

We are familiar, in ordinary terms, with what "recuperation" means: rephrasing something meaningful and controversial so that it is made to seem commonplace and self-evident after all. It occurs to me, though, that such rephrasing is not simply into plain language (the "discourse of every day," no doubt) but into *vague* plain language. For example, someone says, "communism—oh yes, you mean everybody should have their fair share," or "religion—you mean, there's something higher than just material reality." It is not the case that new and surprising convictions cannot be stated lucidly; as witness Hume, or Mill on the subjection of women, or Keynesian or Marxian economics. If lucidity is exactly synonymous with "simplicity," then of course when Catherine Belsey quotes the phrase "the tyranny of lucidity" (4) with approval, she is doing something all can support. But that is not quite the end of the matter. Aristotle, Saint Augustine, Saint Thomas Aquinas, Spinoza, Kant, and indeed Marx and Freud, certainly do not write simply. But they all leave the reader with a sense that they are conscious of the difficulty of the questions they raise, and are striving to express their ideas, however intricate, with exactitude, and to argue precisely and conclusively. The more novel and difficult their ideas, the greater the sense of this kind of effort that they leave as one reads them. Something similar is also true of writers like Kierkegaard or indeed Hegel. Sometimes they write enigmatically, even vaguely; but their work still leaves a sense of great effort to be as clear as they can about concepts that are fluid and elusive as well as new and puzzling. They are altogether remote from leaving an impression that they do not mind if they mystify the reader, which I must admit to finding in Roland Barthes; or that perhaps they could not think lucidly and rigorously about anything whatever, which I must admit to finding in some of the popularizers.

II

There is however one writer in this field, Saussure himself, who does not create such difficulties. Saussure's thinking (as reproduced for us, one must remember, merely from the notes of some who were in his lecture audiences)[3] was indeed intricate and specialist, as well as highly original in certain respects. But the record we have of it is in a terse, dry style, a style that indeed seems to seek the kind of exactitude and lucidity possible for such thinking, and for which the introduction of technical terms is of course perfectly acceptable. All the more interest attaches therefore to one crucial area of Saussure's thought, the area that has meant so much to those who see him as having veritably transformed the totality of human self-understanding.

This crucial area concerns Saussure's account of how words have meaning. I shall discuss it in some detail, but perhaps it will be helpful if as a preliminary to that, I show why it is worthwhile to do so. Let me state first of all, and in Saussure's own words, the conclusion he comes to. "A word" (or linguistic sign), he begins, "unites . . . a concept and a sound-image."[4]

The key question for him then becomes, How does the meaning of the concept get determined? In brief, his final answer is expressed in his words, "it is quite clear that initially the concept is nothing, that is only a value determined by its relation to other similar values, and that without them the signification would not exist" (117). That, at least, is the English translation, which is all that our popularizers refer to. The French in the original edition reads, "il est bien entendu que ce concept n'a *rien d'initial*"; and in another version, "le schéma idée:image auditive *n'est donc pas initial* dans la langue" (my emphasis).

One could barely assert that those words in the English edition, as they stand by themselves, are perfectly self-explanatory. But before discussing them more closely, it is to the point to see how much has been made to hang upon them, and upon the general Saussurian position which they express. In brief, Saussure's remarks there have led to a strong tradition in language-theory that—to put the matter loosely—thought consists in using language, and language is a self-defining system. The words in a language, that is, derive their meaning from each other, not through any relation to objects in the world. Thus Roland Barthes, in 1964: "this 'something' which is meant by the person who uses the sign . . . being neither an act of consciousness nor a real thing . . . can be defined only within the signifying process, in a quasi-tautological way."[5] Fredric Jameson, eight years later, was more emphatic: "the traditional concept of truth itself becomes outmoded, because the process of thought bears rather on the adjustment of the signi*fied* to the signi*fier*"[6]—not, notice, the other way around. Barthes, Jameson adds, has replaced truth by "internal coherence." Terence Hawkes writes: "We thus invent the world we inhabit";[7] though he seems immediately to retract that in part, by adding "we *modify and reconstruct* what is *given*" (my emphasis). Language gives "not *given entities* but *socially constructed signifieds,*"[8] writes Catherine Belsey. I take that to mean that what it reflects is the "invented" world that it constitutes. Given the likeness between these views, and the "coherence theory of truth" in writers like Bradley and Bosanquet, it is remarkable that for Belsey the term "idealist" (in the expression "empiricist-idealist," in fact) is a term of condemnation (7).

The second stage in what has been drawn from Saussure's position extends into certain central matters in the study of literature; and Roland Barthes, in 1970, enunciated something like the principle upon which this extension rests. "The structure of the sentence, the object of linguistics, is found again, homologically, in the structure of works."[9] We may compare

Tzvetan Todorov: "The concept we have of language today . . . if this perspective is followed, it is obvious that all knowledge of literature will follow a path parallel to that of the knowledge of language: moreover these two paths will tend to merge."[10] Structuralist criticism, wrote Jameson, is "a kind of transformation of form into content . . . literary works are about language"; and he quotes from an article of 1967 in which Todorov said that every work tells the story of its own creation: "the meaning of a work lies in its speaking of its own existence."[11]

It is not difficult to see how all these observations hang together. No one thinks that the structure of a *sentence* is a matter of its content. We refer to its structure by the categories of traditional grammar, the "tree" diagrams of linguistics, or whatever it may be. Also by tradition, however, the structure of the literary work is seen in other terms; and those terms do make reference to content, at least in large part. If the analogy between work and sentence (see particularly the quotations from Barthes and Todorov above: again, assertions not proofs, be it noted) holds good, that would be a fundamental error. The structure of literary works would be constituted entirely by their language-features, without reference to what, conventionally, they are taken to be "about." Perhaps some of those concerned would wish to go further, indeed, and deny that it was a matter of analogy at all. Perhaps they would claim that it was a matter of literal truth: a novel could be studied profitably simply because, and insofar as, it was an extended sentence (in some sense) with the grammar of a sentence.

From this conception of the literary work (and it must be remembered that the above is only a brief outline of it, because the purpose of this part of the discussion is to indicate the momentous consequences that have been made to follow from Saussure), there have been further momentous extensions. One I have referred to already. "Literature, in our time," writes Jameson, "is essentially an impossible enterprise" (158). He goes on to say that as a possible exception to that, certain kinds of writing now might be "charged with the absolution of the guilt inherent in the practice of literature." One will recall how Catherine Belsey, not unlike that, questioned "whether we should continue to speak of *literature* at all," because of "the case for primacy of the signifier," and I think also because there is something objectionable in the value-judgements frequently implicit in the term"[12]—the term *literature,* that is.

What then should be the position of fiction? Fiction being, as Jane Austen put it, a "work in which . . . the most thorough knowledge of human nature, the happiest delineation of its varieties . . . are conveyed to the world";[13] while George Eliot likened fiction to "a painting of the Dutch School," and said of her own work, "my strongest effort is to avoid any arbitrary picture, and to give a faithful account of men and things as they have mirrored themselves in my mind."[14] George Eliot added, of course, "the mirror is doubtless defective . . . the reflection faint or confused."

Those who follow Saussure will not be overmuch impressed by such claims. Barthes, in *Writing Degree Zero,* said that the main linguistic indicator of realistic narrative fiction in French, the past definite tense, was "the expression of an order, and consequently of a euphoria."[15] "To tell the truth," he goes on, the actions that constitute the narrative "can be reduced to mere signs," and for "all the great story-tellers of the nineteenth century, . . . reality . . . is subjected to the ingenious pressure of [their] freedom." The narrative past tense is therefore "part of a security system for Belles-Lettres . . . one of those numerous formal pacts between the writer and society for the justification of the former and the serenity of the latter . . . it . . . has a reassuring effect." The narrative past is something that allows the "triumphant bourgeoisie of the last century" (39) in a sense to have it both ways: to assert its values in a form in which, all the same, it did not have to defend them.

Generalizing, later in *Writing Degree Zero,* Barthes asserts that the whole style of expository prose and its "clarity" such as we find in "classical writing" (and in the nineteenth century in the realist novel, he implies) is a "class writing," the invention of a bourgeoisie that became dominant in the mid-seventeenth century. But by the mid-nineteenth century, that dominance had come to be called in question, bringing "the definitive ruin of liberal illusions" (66). The idea of realist fiction, and its characteristic style, no longer presented itself to writers as self-evidently valid. Hence the multiplicities, and the crises, of modern literature.

Somewhat similarly, Belsey speaks of "expressive realism" as belonging to "the last century and a half, the period of industrial capitalism," and as based ultimately on ideas familiar to us ("genuinely familiar semes"): and so "a predominantly conservative form" in that it will "largely confirm the patterns of the world we seem to know."[16] In its stress on individual characters it confirms and reinforces the idea of individualism that is an attitude necessary to capitalism; and in constituting something by way of a message from the personal character of the author, personally to the reader, "classic realism constitutes an ideological practice in addressing itself to readers as subjects" ("the reader's existence as an autonomous and knowing subject"); and the passage concludes, "in order that they freely accept their subjectivity *and their subjection*" (69; my emphasis).

According to this writer, however, there is another and noncapitalist manner in which to read the literary work. This is to recognize that the "coherence and plenitude" of the text of classic realism is "masquerading" on its part; and that if we examine the "process of its production," we may pinpoint the real nature of the text, which is its partaking of what is "inconsistent, limited, contradictory" in the ideology that gave it birth and that it has itself been sustaining (104). In this case, the reader is no longer a "consumer" (the word presumably has overtones of capitalism) of the text, and the idea is like that of Barthes in *S/Z:* "the goal of literary work (of literature as work) is to make the reader no longer a consumer, but a producer of the text."[17] Conventional criticism, Belsey adds, makes "departments of literature . . . function like consumers' associations . . . advising readers on the best (spiritual) buys." The deconstructionist reader will be able to "foreground the contradictions" in the text "and so to read it radically."[18]

Perhaps that "deconstructionist" conception of criticism might simply replace the author-reader, capitalist-consumer mythology in regard to "classic realism" with a model in which critics and readers were all capitalist producers together; or perhaps the capitalist critics should go, as much as the capitalistic authors, and readers be left alone to enjoy a sort of neolithic-peasant status. But I do not now have in mind to embark upon a critical examination of this ambitious and far-reaching body of work. I have hitherto simply been expounding its conclusions briefly, because the point of interest here is to see how this vast edifice of thought has been erected, by the writers from whom I have quoted (and also by others) upon that central and decisive line of discussion in Saussure. It is Saussure's own argument at which I propose to look closely, and I select him because his work is the key to all the rest. I shall not attempt to prove, and there is no need to prove, that any of Saussure's conclusions were false; but if he did not succeed in establishing them beyond question, two things follow: first that the views of those who have simply based their work on his are (whether false or true) unproved; and second, that if they relied confidently and unquestioningly on Saussure when his argument was in fact an inconclusive one, that speaks ill of their capacity to argue at all.

III

I begin by saying that Saussure's work also deserves such close examination because it is worthy of, and from myself it certainly enjoys, deep respect. Saussure tries to argue and elucidate his position as fully as the difficulty of its subject matter will allow. If it transpires that he did not quite clinch his case, that is not the same as saying that his conclusions are false. But it reflects adversely upon his followers in the two ways I have just mentioned. First, their own vastly more sweeping conclusions (for Saussure had nothing to say in the *Cours* about literary works, realism, capitalism, ideology, and so forth) remain dubious. Second, since in most cases Saussure's followers have simply accepted his conclusions and been content to paraphrase them and to insist on them as preliminary to their own wider opinions, but have done nothing to seek out the weak points in Saussure's work and to remedy them, it does not speak well of their own powers of logic or scruples about carrying readers along with them unjustifiably. One conspicuous exception to that should however be noted: Culler's short introduction to the 1974 English edition of the *Cours,* in which certain very fundamental difficulties in Saussure are touched on briefly but effectively.

I suggested earlier that the crucial area in Saussure's thought was his account of how words have meaning. There is no need to emphasize that that has been found an area of difficulty, perhaps supreme difficulty, since Plato. Saussure does not consider the Nominalist tradition of thought about this problem, save very briefly and generally in a discussion (*Cours,* part 1, chap. 1: "Nature of the Linguistic Sign") which alternates the words "thing" and "idea" ("choses," "idées toutes faites") with a somewhat disquieting ease. But that matter aside, Saussure goes on to say, as I mentioned, that the right way to think about a linguistic sign is to see it as uniting a sound-image (the word, that is, in spoken language) and a concept. Saussure is perhaps not perfectly explicit and consistent at this point, but on the whole his position is clear enough: the sign "carries the concept." "I mean by sign the whole [*le total*] that results from the association of the signifier with the signified." He goes on to say that linguistic signs are arbitrary in that an "idea" is not "linked by any inner relationship [*rapport intérieur*] to the succession of sounds . . . which serves as its signifier" in any particular language; and that "no one disputes the principle of the arbitrary nature of the sign."[19]

The term "inner relationship" is perhaps not clear to us today, and it may be that in using it, Saussure was consciously or unconsciously recalling the use of the term "internal relation" in certain Idealist philosophers of the late nineteenth century. Be that as it may, Saussure is surely right if what he means is that no word for a certain something in English (or French, let us say) will be intrinsically better than the word for it in any other language; and right also to say that no one would dispute that opinion. By way of elucidation he adds, "the signifier . . . is arbitrary in that it actually has no natural connection with the signified" (69). It is fair to add that in the vast majority of cases—words like "hiccup" might be different—it is not easy even to see what a "natural connection" would be; and self-evident that there is no actual need to have a "natural connection" in any particular case, "hiccup" or anything else.

As part of his explanation of the difference between diachronic and synchronic language studies, Saussure likens "a state of language" at a given point in its history to a "state of a set of chessmen" at a given point in a game of chess. In some respects this is a helpful comparison, but in one respect it is not self-evidently so. This is the way in which the comparison seems to introduce the term "values" *(valeurs)* as something to some extent analogous to "meanings" in the field of language. These new terms play key roles in Saussure's argument as a whole, yet I cannot avoid the conclusion that Saussure uses the term "value" ambiguously in regard to the game of chess. "The respective value of the pieces depends on their position on the chessboard" (88), he says, referring to the state of a game at a given point in it: and this is what is compared to the state of a language as studied, at a given point in time, by synchronic study. Yet almost immediately he adds: "values depend above all else [*surtout*] on an unchangeable convention [*une convention immuable*] the set of rules that exists before a game begins and persists after each move." But in this sense, the value of this or that chesspiece, so far as I can see, in no way "depends on [its] position on the chessboard"; nor is there any analogy between values depending on rules that "exist before a game begins," and linguistic values (however that expression is to be explained), which can and do change steadily over the history of a language, and cannot possibly be formulated before that history begins, because they do not exist. Saussure said that a given state of the chess-game "corresponds closely" *(corréspond bien)* to a given state of the language at a certain point in history; but in the course of his remarks he has in effect gone beyond the limits of that "close correspondence."

Perhaps it was a pity that Saussure ever introduced the comparison with chess: it provided him with a title for part 2, chapter 4 of the *Cours*, "Linguistic Value"; this chapter is both key, and in some ways especially disquieting. Here, Saussure begins by asserting that "psychologically our thought—apart from its expression in words—is only a shapeless and indistinct mass" *(une masse amorphe et indistincte)*. I hesitate to comment upon this, because I am unsure of what wordless mental activities would generally be allowed as "thought." Does someone steering a bicycle, or an observer at sea, watching two distant ships, and estimating their relative speeds and courses—or indeed, mentally rehearsing such an activity—engage in thought which is "only a shapeless and indistinct mass?" I am much disposed to doubt that. What about cases such as those where we realize that we have expressed ourselves ambiguously and rephrase our remarks, or recognize that an argument, as we follow it in reading a book, contains an as yet unidentified logical fallacy? My own experience is that such reactions or intuitions do not take the form of verbal thinking. They are preliminary, of course, to fresh verbal thinking; but the "something has gone wrong" intuition (though not, I believe, in those words, nor any others) precedes that. On the other hand, it is barely satisfactory to say that the first stage in identifying an inadequacy in verbal thought, and so correcting it, is not thought at all; as also, to say that the first step toward making verbal thought more exact is itself wholly without exactitude, because, in Saussure's words, part of "a shapeless and amorphous mass." If on the other hand I am told that these and all other such activities are "really" performed in words, then I have to admit that I have no knowledge of wordless thought; but then, I can neither agree nor disagree with Saussure's assertion about it.[20]

Saussure goes on, at this point, to raise a most important question. Let us concede that it is language that in many cases, or no doubt easily most, makes it possible for us to think in a "distinct" way. How do the units of language acquire their distinctness? Earlier, he has rightly pointed out that words as units of significance are made up of individual sounds—let us briefly say, vowels, consonants—and that these individual sounds are not vehicles of meaning by virtue of their absolute and exact quality, as some phonetician might record them for some given speaker at a given time. They are adequate vehicles of meaning, in that speakers consistently maintain certain recognizable differences within the whole system of sounds that they employ in speech. If one lisps all one's *r*'s, from this point of view it hardly matters. If one lisps some of them, however, and trills the others, hearers may think that the lisped *r*'s were intended for *w*'s and confusion will result. The sounds one makes in speech, then, have their meaning-values (that is, the ways in which they can contribute to the meanings of the words they enter) from the whole system of sounds that meaning depends on, in a given language, not from their intrinsic phonetic quality. Just as Saussure said, "no one disputes the principle of the arbitrary nature of the sign"—though from how his disciples labor the point, you might think they had forgotten that—so he could have said, "no one disputes" his assertion that individual sounds gain their meaning-values in language from the system of differences in which they occur.

IV

There then comes a crucial step in Saussure's discussion. In examining the relation between signs as wholes (not simply the individual sounds that are joined together to make signs) and their own distinctive kind of meaning, Saussure extends the principle that he enunciated for individual sounds. In doing so, he may seem to contradict what he had said earlier:

> to consider a term as simply the union of a certain sound with a certain concept is grossly misleading [*une grande illusion*]. . . . [I]t would mean assuming that one can start from the terms and construct the system by adding them together when, on the contrary, it is from the inter-dependent whole that one must start and through analysis obtain its elements.[21]

Saussure seems inclined to say that "significance" is the counterpart of a sound-image, while "value" is what a term has "solely from the simultaneous presence of the other [terms]." That is an interesting distinction, and he illustrates it with the English words "sheep" and "mutton." "Sheep" can have the same significance as the French word "mouton" ("*Le français* mouton *peut avoir la même signification que l'anglais* sheep"); and so, I suppose, what you may have on your plate for dinner is indeed, in a certain sense, "sheep stew." It is impossible to say that the meat in it is not sheep, with the implication that it is some other animal. But the word "sheep," in English, does not have the same *value* as "mouton" in French. We cannot, in our language, combine it like that with "stew." Saussure adds that the same thing is true about "grammatical entities" (as, for example, tenses).

I cannot but ask myself whether Saussure's discussion, at this point, is altogether self-consistent. To begin with, he distinguishes very clearly between the "signification" of a word and the "value" that attaches to that word: "this is something quite different" (115) *(c'est tout autre chose).* Then he draws attention to several quite distinct features of language, apparently in amplification of that distinction. First, he observes that in a given language, groups of words with related meanings "limit each other reciprocally." An example in English, possibly, would be "beautiful, handsome, pretty, attractive." Learning fully how to use each of those four words is in part anyhow a matter of learning when not to use the other three. That is certainly a reasonable suggestion. Second, Saussure mentions how words in two languages that are loosely called "synonyms" are often not entirely so. "Louer une maison" in French will be the equivalent in English of both "to let a house" and "to rent a house." "There is obviously no exact correspondence of values," he writes; and he claims that this shows how words do not stand for "pre-existing concepts" *(concepts données d'avance)*—a claim that on that evidence, by the way, is valid only on the additional premise that the relation between word and concept should in all cases be a one-one relation. Third, Saussure draws attention to how "grammatical entities" are not constant as between languages. "The value of a French plural does not coincide with that of a Sanskrit plural, even though their signification is usually identical." What he means there, I believe, is that a French plural usually "means the same" as the corresponding Sanskrit plural, but that Sanskrit plurals cannot be used to translate French ones in the particular case where the French plural is for two items only; in Sanskrit the dual must then be used. He also offers further examples, about tenses of verbs or about verbal "aspects" as in Russian. Finally he says, "We find in all the foregoing examples *values* emanating from the system" *(au lieu d'idées données d'avance, des valeurs émanant du système).* The concepts to which these values may be said to correspond are defined "by their relation with other terms in the system. Their most precise characteristic is in being what the others are not." It might have been better to say "relation with other concepts," but that is a detail.

But now comes the most crucial state in Saussure's argument. He produces once again the diagram that he initially made use of to illustrate the signified/signifier or concept/auditory-image basis of the "sign"; and it is now that he says, "it is quite clear that initially the concept is nothing [*n'a rien d'initial,* remember], that is only a value determined by its relations with other similar values, and that without them the signification would not exist" (117) (*sans elles la signification n'existerait pas*).

At this point, one wonders whether Saussure should not have written "without them the *value* would not exist," instead of "the signification." That, after all, is what he has proved; and he has already told us that "value" and "signification" are quite different. If so, how can he simply replace the word "value" by the word "signification" in that passage, as if the two were not "quite different" but just the same?

We may concede that there are certain cases where the "value" of a term, in Saussure's sense, is determined, even exclusively so, by its relations with other terms in a group of terms. "Certain cases": Saussure actually specified these cases, speaking of "all words used to express related ideas," of "words enriched through contact with others," and third, of words that do not have exact equivalents in meaning "from one language to another." It is no good, of course, to claim at this stage that *all* words in every language belong to these classes. If that were so, the whole enterprise of opening a further stage in the discussion, distinguishing the three classes, and offering examples of each, would have been otiose and indeed profoundly misleading. One must therefore ask whether Saussure shifted, in his conclusion as above, from "some" to "all"; and whether he was perhaps led into doing so, by his momentary identification of "signification" and "value." I admit freely that I do not know quite for sure whether this stage in Saussure's argument is definitely defective, or whether it could be salvaged. I know of no follower of Saussure who has tried to resolve the difficulty. If one turns, for example, to section II.5 of Roland Barthes's *Elements of Semiology,* all one finds is a statement that value and signification are not the same, and that Saussure "increasingly concentrated" on value. That is to rehearse what may be a weak link in the train of thought in a style that identifies weakness with strength.

In this connection, there seems to be a a fundamental problem that Saussure fails to discuss. Suppose we concede that the "value" of, say, the term "mutton" is that it is the proper term to use when "sheep" would not be so, but "mouton" would. Is it possible to go further, to the extent of saying that *all* terms are of this kind, and may be "defined negatively by their relations with the other terms in the system"? Can that process of "negative definition" be maintained indefinitely, round and round as it were, so as to cover, in the end, the language as a whole? It is easy to see how certain terms may be defined, even must be so, in this manner. The term "miscellaneous" in budgets of income and expenditure is an obvious example. In the Cambridge University Library there is a small group of relatively unimportant nineteenth-century books with the class-mark "LO": so far as I recollect, I once found a cataloguer's note in one of them, which indicated that "LO" in fact stood for "left over". But could *all* the items in a budget, or a catalogue, or any other such system, be so defined? If "mutton" is defined negatively, merely through its relation to "sheep" and to "mouton" (let us say), can we then go on to define "sheep" negatively in relation to "mutton"? If so, how would we distinguish that pair of words from "pig/pork" or "cattle/beef"? Or should we say that "sheep" means something like "not pig, not cattle . . ." and so on indefinitely, which is exactly how we define a word like "miscellaneous"? Such questions call for answers from those who insist on this kind of account; and in the absence of such answers, I remain inclined to wonder (this is putting it mildly) whether there is not some absolutely basic distinction between the system of language-*sounds,* and the system of language-*words* or terms. I am too much numbed by my reading of Saussure's followers, and their self-emancipation from the "tyranny of lucidity" to say quite what that distinction is; and it does not fall to someone in my position to say what it is, because it falls to them to prove that it does not exist. In this context, moreover, I begin to imagine how, given leisure, one might as a kind of enormously elaborated "consequences" game build up something like an imaginary language (not, though, for communication in the ordinary sense) where all the terms one invented had "values" determined negatively, in reference to their fellow terms. In such a language, it could be as much against the rules to say things like "mutton is cooked pig," or "sheep moo" as it is in English to say things like "mutton is cooked neither" or "sheep whenever." The question remains, though, whether such an invented system would not be something fundamentally different in kind from English or French, and so on. One reason for that is that given more leisure and nothing much to do with it, one could invent not one but fifty such "languages," using the same "dictionary" of terms in each case; and the "values" of the terms could be totally different in each case, because there would be total liberty in setting up the rules of the system every time. But there is something, something that does not enter into activities of that kind, that prevents us from playing, as we might put it, variations in our own language in this way; and that something is not merely the social group that speaks it. Something else prevents us from saying "cows moo" and also "sheep moo," something that brings it about that, while of course language in the abstract is collectively manipulable to any extent, this is like saying that if we want we can turn our real language into a game-language. Language is not so manipulable, if what it enables us to do is to be preserved.

V

It is not my purpose to resolve these difficulties. I wish only to indicate that there is good reason to think that Saussure did not resolve them: and if he did not, what becomes of the work of those who have treated his as we now see dubious conclusions as their starting point? But I am not optimistic that (assuming my attempt to show Saussure did not settle all these matters has been successful) what I have said will cause some of his followers either to modify their views or to strengthen their arguments. Reading their work has left the impression of writers who are confident about their findings in such fields as theory of language, psychology, philosophy, literary criticism, literary theory, for a particular reason. That reason is, their findings are in accordance with—though I strongly believe, not necessitated by—certain wider convictions. These are political and historical convictions, of a "Marxist" kind, which they appear to hold already (though I should myself contrast the intense intellectual concentration and vigor, and sometimes the splendid writing, of *Capital,* with their own work, but that is by the way).

Perhaps one thing that might happen is that the writers in question would attempt to "recuperate," not for capitalist-liberal-bourgeois ideology but for Marxist ideology, such criticisms as one might make of their work. Jameson writes, "the traditional concept of truth itself becomes outmoded":[22] possibly that implies that the requirement of proving, as against declaring, becomes a symptom of bourgeois myopia. Complaints about vagueness of expression and lack of definition will perhaps be reinterpreted as the responses of a bourgeois subjectivity in "subjection" (we have already encountered this ingenious pun) to the "tyranny of lucidity." When Hawkes writes, of the sort of criticism he advocates, that it is "aiming, in its no-holds-barred encounter with the text, for a coherence and validity of response, not objectivity and truth,"[23] it will be no good to reply that any fantasy may be coherent, while only objectivity and truth give intellectual positions validity. That will easily be recuperated too. Nor, doubtless, will it be persuasive to point out that all these authors presumably claim objective truth for their own works, and would not allow that Hawkes's accounts of the "most important feature" of the kind of criticism he proposes: "it offers a new role and status to the critic. . . . The critic *creates* the finished work as he reads. . . . [He needs] not humbly efface himself. . . . None of these readings is *wrong,* they all add to the work"—that that kind of criticism would enable us, if we apply it to their own works, to see these as fantasies, gifted and entertaining if hubristic and a little strident. Likewise when Catherine Belsey advocates in literature the "interrogative" text that "does literally invite the reader to produce answers to the questions it implicitly or explicitly raises," what chance is there that she might allow us to read her own book in that sense, and to her questions produce our own answers that (if truth were not an outmoded concept) would be contradictory of hers? Rather than an "interrogative" text, however, Belsey seems to be writing, in her own terminology, a "declarative text" as in "classic realism" itself: one that is "imparting 'knowledge' to a reader whose position is thereby stabilized." At the same time, though, she is perhaps also writing an "imperative" or "propaganda" text: "propaganda thus exhorts, instructs, orders the reader, constituting the reader *in conflict with* what exists outside"[24]—the conflict in her case being with Western bourgeois civilization of the past three centuries, and with literary criticism as it has been understood hitherto.

Those three categories, declarative, imperative, interrogative, are taken by Belsey from an address by Benveniste entitled "Levels of Linguistic Analysis."[25] But in his piece Benveniste is writing about "propositions" (in the French text); and he gives his discussion no bearing on literature, history, or politics. Belsey supplies those connections herself. Likewise when, elsewhere, she takes up the matter of subjectivity, saying that its "obviousness" has been challenged by post-Saussurean "linguistic theory." She again utilizes an article by Benveniste, this time to reach the conclusion that "if language is a system of differences with no positive terms, 'I' designates only the subject of a specific utterance."[26] Benveniste, however, argues that human subjectivity is constituted "in and through language," as against the view that human language is constituted by human subjectivity. His discussion implies nothing depreciatory in general of subjectivity. The argument is analytical and exact, though there of course remains something speculative, perhaps overspeculative, about it. But Benveniste speaks of "l'unité psychique qui transcende la totalité des experiences vécus . . . et qui assure la permanence de la conscience"[27] (the psychic unity that transcends the totality of actual experiences . . . and that makes the permanence of the consciousness). In another essay on a related subject, published two years earlier, entitled, "The Nature of Pronouns," Benveniste left it quite clear that he had in mind something other than a *grammatical* subject only, by the fundamental contrast he drew between the functioning of "I" or "you" as against "he." "I" is the "*individu* qui énonce la présente instance de discours" (the individual who utters the present instance of discourse); or again, "c'est en s'identifiant comme *personne unique* prononcant *je* que chacun des locuteurs se pose tour a tour comme 'sujet' "[28] (it is by identifying himself as a unique person pronouncing "I" that each speaker sets himself up in turn as the "subject"). The word "individu" recurs several times. Benveniste offers a sophisticated explanation of the ground of subjectivity; Belsey then recruits (or it could be, recuperates) Benveniste, so as to reach conclusions like "ideology interpellates [i.e., in brief, "addresses, challenges"] concrete individuals as subjects, and bourgeois ideology in particular emphasizes the fixed identity of the individual."[29] What Belsey writes of "ideology" is: "It is a set of omissions . . . smoothing over contradictions, appearing to provide answers to questions which in reality it evades, and masquerading as coherence" (57). Well, those are words that perhaps give the reader more food for thought than the author intended.

In Hawkes also, the writing seems sometimes to proceed under a kind of impetus which means that, for some unstated reason, conclusions of certain kinds may be reached on easy terms. One example is the following: in this quotation I have omitted Hawkes's italics, and inserted those that show how the argument, one can only say, is *slid* forward: "any observer is bound to create *something* of what he observes. Accordingly, the relationship between observer and observed achieves a kind of *primacy.* It becomes the *only* thing that can be observed. It becomes the stuff of reality itself."[30] From "some" to "most" (primacy) to "all" (only). That is simply not going to convince anyone who wants, or is capable of benefiting from, a serious treatment of the subject.

Another similar example comes later. Hawkes, quoting an American anthropologist, adds: "*in short,* a culture comes to terms with nature by means of encoding, through language. And it requires *only a slight extension* of this view to produce the implication that *perhaps* the *entire* field of social behaviour . . . *might* in fact also represent an act of 'encoding.' . . . In fact, it *might itself be* a language" (my emphasis).

Barthes's arguments sometimes run in the same style: "We see culture *more and more* as a general system of symbols. . . . Culture, in *all* its aspects, *is* a language";[31] or again (here the far-reaching conclusion precedes the more modest, and in fact perfectly trite, assertion), "writing is *in no way* an instrument for communication, it is not an open route through which there passes *only* the intention to speak."[32] Once again, "some" can turn into all, or for that matter be simply jumbled up with it, and no harm.

If I may be allowed a more personal remark, I should like to say, with the greatest emphasis, that I know no reason why Marxist thought, in any field, should not be as disciplined, lucid, and rigorous as any other kind; and I think Marx himself, for whose dedication and for whose intellectual eminence I have had deep respect for a very long time, is done a disservice by writings that I am not willing to characterize generally, in the terms I think it would be just, if harsh, to use. I am also sorry not to have accomplished more in this discussion. In a field where others have found themselves able to promulgate how everything under the sun ought, and almost self-evidently, to be stood on its head, all I have done is to argue that certain lines of thought in Saussure, that have been taken by many to be like the Rock of Ages, probably need to be reconsidered and either strengthened or amended; as perhaps also, that certain lines of thought in the work of some of his followers may not deserve that level of attention. I have even failed, probably enough, to subject my subjectivity to the tyranny of lucidity at all times; but at least I am among those who can say, if that is so, they are sorry for it, and would not seek to escape condemnation of it.

Notes

1. Frederic Jameson, *The Prison-House of Language* (Princeton: Princeton University Press, 1972), 158.
2. Catherine Belsey, *Critical Practice* (London: Methuen, 1980), 144.
3. Ferdinand de Saussure, *Cours de Linguistique Générale.* The most informative text is the multiple *édition critique* by Rudolph Engler (Wiesbaden: Harrassowitz, 1967). Hawkes cites only the first French edition (1915); Belsey, only the 1974 English translation.
4. Ferdinand de Saussure, *Course in General Linguistics,* rev. ed., trans. Wade Baskin (London: Fontana, 1974), 66. Subsequent quotations are from this edition if in English. Quotations in French are from the *édition critique* (see note 3).
5. Roland Barthes, *Elements of Semiology,* trans. Annette Lavers and Colin Smith (London: Jonathan Cape, 1967), 43.
6. Jameson, 133.
7. Terence Hawkes, *Structuralism and Semiotics* (Berkeley and Los Angeles: University of California Press, 1976), 107. Subsequent quotations are from this edition.

8. Belsey, 44.
9. Roland Barthes, "To Write: Intransitive Verb?" in *The Structuralist Controversy,* ed. R. Macksey and Eugenio Donato (Baltimore: Johns Hopkins University Press, 1970), 136.
10. Tzvetan Todorov, "Language and Literature," in *The Structuralist Controversy,* 126.
11. Jameson, 199.
12. Belsey, 144.
13. *Northanger Abbey,* chap. 5.
14. *Adam Bede,* chap. 17 paras. 2, 6.
15. Roland Barthes, *Writing Degree Zero* (1953), trans. A. Lavers and C. Smith (New York: Hill and Wang, 1968), 37.
16. Belsey, 7, 50–51.
17. Roland Barthes, *S/Z* (1970), trans. Richard Miller (New York: Hill and Wang, 1975), 4; quoted in Belsey, *Critical Practice,* 125.
18. Belsey, 129.
19. Saussure, 67.
20. It may be worth noting that Saussure's belief in wordless thought as "a shapeless and indistinct mass" (with his diagram, like a stormy sea, to represent it), seems to have been held by other writers in his own time. See C. Spearman's "a general course of cognition like that of the present writer, surging on like a deep, dark, formless sea" (*The Nature of Intelligence,* 1923, chap. 12); or F. Aveling, *The Consciousness of the Universal* (1912). I refer to these matters from another standpoint in *Language and Intelligence* (1951), 38ff.
21. Saussure, 113.
22. Jameson, 133.
23. Hawkes, 156.
24. Belsey, 90–91; my emphasis.
25. Emile Benveniste, *Problèmes de linguistique générale* (1966), trans. M. E. Meek (Coral Gables, Fla: University of Miami Press, 1971).
26. Belsey, 59.
27. Benveniste, "De la subjectivité dans le langage" (1958) in *Problèmes de linguistique générale,* 260.
28. Benveniste, "La nature des pronoms" (1956), in *Problèmes de linguistique générale,* 252, 254.
29. Belsey, 64.
30. Hawkes, 17.
31. Barthes, "To Write: Intransitive Verb?" 136.
32. Barthes, *Writing Degree Zero,* 25.

Most Relevant Publication by John Holloway

The Slumber of Apollo: Reflections on Recent Art, Literature, Language, and the Individual Consciousness. Cambridge: Cambridge University Press, 1983.

3

Adam Naming the Animals

Wendell V. Harris

Wendell Harris, professor of English at Pennsylvania State University, taught and wrote primarily about nineteenth-century English literature until 1983 when concern over structuralists' frequently exaggerated extrapolations from the work of Ferdinand de Saussure led to articles entitled "On Being Sure of Saussure" and "Contemporary Criticism and the Return of Zeno." The essay reprinted here, which emphasizes the importance of the context of an utterance, of parole, *includes advocacy of approaches to literary interpretation derived from speech-act theory, discourse analysis, and the earlier (nonmetaphysical) tradition of hermeneutics. Although the essay was first published in 1986, the approaches it commends remain largely ignored by theorists who nevertheless must employ the interpretive strategies these modes of analysis explore in order to have anything to say about a text.*

For some time now I have felt a curious discomfort in reading fashionable contemporary criticism, especially the deconstructionist variety in its uneasy alliances with Marxist, neo-Freudian, feminist, and Bloomian approaches, but only recently have I recognized the true source of that discomfort: acute claustrophobia. For all the talk of interminable deferment, open texts, and infinite decentering, most "revisionist" criticism seems too barricaded behind a specialized argot, too dependent on the axioms of particular philosophies, ideologies, or faiths, too circumscribed in method, too reductive in result, and too bound to the present decade. We require a larger, broader perspective to see what the stakes are, what larger patterns there may be, and what alternatives may be available. Fortunately, if one steps back far enough to see how language is now understood in a variety of disciplines related to literary criticism, an alternative does in fact emerge, one that validates the possibility of interpretation and at the same time recognizes the centrality of language and the power of extratextual contexts. I want to point out some converging paths that lead to an intellectual overlook that commands a more comprehensive view of language. First, however, I will offer a version of how currently fashionable criticism came to occupy the ground it does.

I

Let us begin at a beginning, Genesis 2:19. "And out of the ground the Lord God formed every beast of the field and every fowl of the air; and brought them unto Adam to see what he would call them: and whatsoever Adam called every living creature, that was the name thereof." This scene has been imagined for centuries pretty much as follows: Adam sitting on a pleasant green slope while orderly animals file slowly past under a clear and sunny sky. By extension one can equally well imagine the naming of particulars in the vegetable and mineral kingdoms with angels of the lower orders bringing samples of each kind to Adam.

My point is that for centuries even those who regarded Genesis as a fable would hardly have quarreled with the general concept of language figured forth by such a scene. Despite debates over such matters as the status of universals, the reality of secondary qualities, and even the real existence of anything outside the mind, language was in general regarded as a transparent means of referring to whatever reality a thinker thought was real (to sum up the matter in a tautology). Certainly literary study until recently had no questions about the adequacy or instrumentality of language. In the late nineteenth century, the debate about making a place for vernacular literature and literary theory in the university revolved not around the powers and peculiarities of language, but around how to study literature "in itself," how to exclude gossip about the author, literary history, cultural history, philology, and the like. The academy in England and America not untypically tried to settle the issue by affirming the value of teaching vernacular literature before it decided what was to be taught or how—which explains why the New Critical recipe for close analysis of the text brought relief to so many professors of literature.

Then along came the Swiss linguist Ferdinand de Saussure, whose cogent analysis of the nature of language, first published in 1915, slowly percolated beyond a select circle of linguists. Since his ideas pervade modern critical theory, it is hardly necessary to trace his argument once more. I need only say that the Saussurian principle that has had the greatest impact is that language is made up of sounds or their written equivalents (signifiers) arbitrarily related to concepts (signifieds) that somehow divide up raw sense data. Just as the sounds that constitute individual words partition the continuum of sound possibilities, concepts break apart the continuum of sensory flow and mental activity. Language can no longer be seen as simply labeling discrete objects-in-the-world but as dividing up the most primitive data available to the mind—to which some philosophers give the unhappy but accurate term "raw feels"—according to a human frame of reference.

Now, a good Saussurian would have to picture that scene in the Garden of Eden rather differently. Adam would be looking from some distance at a disorderly gathering of creatures dimly illuminated by wavering torchlight and perhaps raising a dust that conspires with the night to obscure them. Adam's task is to pick out as many kinds as he can, never being sure that two that look alike should bear the same name or that he has given names to all. Nor can there be anything final about the process: once he is expelled from Eden, the creatures he encounters will no longer be simply pleasant companions, but potentially harmful or useful, and therefore new groupings will suggest themselves. In short, there is no transcendental order of elephants or Platonic Idea of grasshoppers. Whether we distinguish between crickets and grasshoppers or even between grasshoppers and elephants is a matter of our own purposes.

Such a scene is, I think, an accurate enough translation of Saussure's view. He denies that concepts exist, waiting to be named—rather they are given their boundaries by the way language divides preconceptual chaos. As I read his *Cours de linguistique générale,* he in no way questions that there is a reality beyond language toward which language points and which language in fact allows us to manipulate. Nothing in Saussure requires us to fall into linguistic idealism, to regard reality as wholly language-dependent.

That which we identify in the realm of sense stimuli by the name "cricket" would sing on the hearth whatever name we gave it, while that source of stimuli given the name "grasshopper" would not. And though an Adam might give the same name to grasshoppers and elephants (they are both gray green, herbivorous, and ungainly), there is a real difference in who can step on whom.

But it has proved possible to regard language in a much more radical way. If one emphasizes the synchronic dimension, the meaning—or to use Saussure's less loaded term, the "value"—of a word cannot be fixed by direct reference to an extralinguistic reality. On the other hand, if one emphasizes the diachronic dimension, clearly the value of a word will have been different at different times, varying as the total synchronic system has varied. Finally, if one tries to think of the status of word values under the aspect of synchrony and diachrony simultaneously, meaning appears even more necessarily to roll darkling down the torrent of indeterminacy. Thus language as a whole comes to seem autonomous, and individual words anarchic. The concept of language as a system of signs with known values may be an illusion; possibly language is not a vehicle with which one can communicate about reality. Or is it the other way around? Perhaps only language exists and there is no reality beyond language about which to communicate. Though I think very few people really believe that the experiences we call birth, death, pain, pleasure, solidity, and motion are purely linguistic constructs, it is surprising how many talk as though they did.

Back to Genesis once more. It is as if angel or devil—I prefer Derridevil—came to Adam after the Fall arguing that there had never been a Garden of Eden: Adam had never been cast out but was always absent from it, for if it had ever been present to him he would not have required language, the signature of absence. Such an argument would finally arrive at the conclusion that there are no animals to name, and no Adamic self to name them—only language "inhabiting" a hillside. And of course if Adam had challenged: "How can you be explaining this to me since in naming me and allowing me to name you, you are deferring the possibility of our presence," the answer would have been, "Right, we are merely two traces confronting each other across the uncanny abyss."

Or, alternatively, the Derridevil might have argued: "Well, now, in addition to losing your happy habitation, I've come to tell you that you believe in something you never had: language. It isn't really possible, you know. How could God have told you to create language by doing things like naming animals without Himself using language? You can't really imagine an origin for language, can you? Besides, look at the absurdity: here a snake, there a snake—but they are not the same snake. Even this snake is not the same as the one you looked at a minute ago—because the one you looked at a minute ago was not the one you had looked at a minute earlier. Moreover, when you tell Eve about this snake, the snake you are talking about will be absent, whereas this one is present. You won't even be thinking of the same thing: she obviously responds to snakes rather differently than you." And who can doubt that if Adam had asked the Derridevil, "How is it you can explain all this to me if there's no language," the answer would have been ready. "I'm only speaking under erasure; I'm allowed that under diabolic license."

I trust the kind of argument I have put in the mouth of my demon is familiar enough; he or she speaks not only for deconstruction but for the larger movement that I follow Geoffrey Hartman in calling "revisionist."[1] As a typical example I would cite Hillis Miller's well-known analysis of Wallace Stevens's "The Rock."[2] Miller notes that the word "cure," which appears centrally in the poem, includes among its meanings "caring for," "securing," "solidifying," "banishing," "scouring," and—by echoing "curologia"—"naming or copying." Having called in these meanings from all points of the etymological and historical compass, Miller announces that they are "incompatible, irreconcilable." One may then "borrow from the French an untranslatable name for this enigma of the nameless, this impasse of language, '*mise en abyme.*'" The exploration of such an abyss by what Miller calls the "uncanny" or deconstructive critic proceeds as follows: "The deconstructive critic seeks to find . . . the element in the system studied which is alogical, the thread in the text in question which will unravel it all, or the loose stone which will pull down the whole building" (341).

But such criticism, though it seems at first altogether liberating in its freedom to pursue homologies, analogies, homophones, metonomies, etymologies, and lexical history in any direction they may lead, finally comes to seem claustrophobically constricting because it cannot move in the one direction that will take it out of the abyss, across the aporia, beyond deferment. That is, it finds no interest in the willed communication of determinate statements about human experience. The question then becomes: Is it possible, first, to accept the interdependence of language and reality as we conceive it and, second, to admit the Protean shaping pressures of synchronic structure and diachronic history and yet still validate the communicative powers of language upon which we depend?

Fortunately the answer is yes, even on Saussure's terms. Whereas to concentrate on language as a structure of differences in the abstract is to enter a house of mirrors, to consider how language is used in the concrete instance (hereafter referred to as *parole* or discourse) is to recognize not only that language is in constant interaction with sensory reports of the physical world but also that its very mode of existence is social. Saussure states that language "is the social side of speech, outside the individual who can never create nor modify it by himself; it exists only by virtue of a sort of contract signed by the members of a community."[3] In effect, members of a community use language as though the meanings of words were agreed upon at the moment of use. Curiously, in Genesis the animals are created and named before Eve is created—the biblical account thus allows language to exist for a brief time unshared. But once Eve is on the scene, the mutual interdependence of language, "reality," and society begins. The signifier (say "tree," in whatever language) and the tall, branched plant (the object of the senses) are linked arbitrarily in one sense, but within a linguistic community, even of two, the link is not arbitrary in the sense of being individually willed; it is agreed upon, shared.

It begins to seem, then, that meaning exists through the interaction of several dimensions or, I would prefer to say, contexts: sensory reports generated by physical reality, linguistic forms, and a community that shares those forms. These in turn lead to more complex contexts derived from shared experiences that combine language and reality. For instance, after the Fall the signifier "tree" will have an additional signified or reference. Adam, sweatily delving the soil, can complain, "If you'd only had the sense to stay away from that tree" and be fairly sure that Eve knows what tree he is talking about. The contextual interaction I have been sketching makes it equally possible to share (that is, for one person to understand and accept another's) linguistic creativity. One remembers, for example, that the fruit of the tree that gives knowledge of good and evil is without a specific name in Genesis. I do not know when that fruit became identified with the apple, but let us imagine that Adam shunned the naming of the fruit that brought all that woe into the world, and recognizing some sort of physical similarity, referred to it as "the fatal apple." Thenceforth he and Eve would know that within certain shared contexts the signifier "apple" had a unique additional reference. Thus, to carry our imaginary analogy a step further,

Jacob and Esau would know the special meaning of "tree" and metaphorical meaning of "apple" only if told the story of the Fall.

I am not trying to extrapolate from Saussure (nor, certainly, from Genesis) a total theory of how discourse is interpreted. I simply wish to suggest that the Saussurian revolution implies rather than denies that the meaning of the individual *parole* results from the interaction of shared contexts: the language system, sensory reports, experience, cultural tradition. There are three important corollaries of such a view: first, the user of language assumes that the reader will share certain contexts, and the reader assumes that the user makes that assumption; second, interpretation consists of identifying the contexts with which the *parole* fits and rejecting those with which it clashes. The unity or consonance for which the interpreter searches is not then simply an artificial critical assumption but the result of the "contract" Saussure places at the base of language; third, interpretation is essentially probabilistic (though our routine success in conveying what we intend and responding to what others say and write indicates that the probability of adequate interpretation is high).

The view of discourse that I have sketched here is hardly intended to stand by itself. Rather, it is offered as a propadeutic simplification of the practices and theories of discourse that are developing in a variety of disciplines. I know of no umbrella term for these approaches. "Contextualist" is possible, but since "contextualism" has already been employed in more restricted senses, and moreover since "context" suggests a passive situation rather than an interactive set of fields, I prefer "ecological" to suggest that each text must be interpreted in a complex, interactive environment.

The convergence of ecological models of discourse that are being developed by initially quite diverse starting points is, I think, immensely exciting. However, this broad-based movement is as yet hardly recognized *as* a movement even by the scholars who are contributing to it. Nor has its role as an alternative to revisionist, deconstructionist theory been generally recognized. It offers, nevertheless, a competing formulation, one of language-in-use, including, of course, literature. Revisionist criticism delights in considering possible meanings of specific words of concepts in isolation from both text and external contexts and in setting up abstract theories of language and then teasing out paradoxes and contradictions that undercut whatever deductions might be made from them. Ecological approaches begin with the fact that we communicate more or less satisfactorily about something we are satisfied to call "reality," and ask how such communication occurs, given the undoubted ambiguity, frequent indirection, and the lack of assured correspondence with any nonlinguistic reality.

II

I. A. Richards and Kenneth Burke anticipated the ecological approach, though we have not fully recognized our debt to them in this area. I refer not to the Richards of *The Meaning of Meaning* (1923) or *Principles of Literary Criticism* (1924), but the Richards of *The Philosophy of Rhetoric* (1936), who by that time had given up the notion for which he has unfortunately remained best known, the distinction between language that is referential and literary language that is simply emotive. Though Richards does not cite Saussure in *The Philosophy of Rhetoric*—he had dismissed him earlier—he is by this time recognizing that language partially creates reality and is taking into consideration what Saussure had called the "associational" (now usually termed "paradigmatic") dimension, which extends the concept of meaning to include associational fields. Thus he is now able to say that "a phrase may take its powers from an immense system of supporting uses of other words in other contexts" and that meaning depends not only on the context in which a word appears but on "*unuttered* words in various relations which may be backing it up."[4] What Richards adds to Saussure is the importance of the existential situation in which a word is used as well as the specific linguistic context. That is, we will take the meaning that seems most relevant to the total set of contexts: thus the difference in immediate perception of the word "bridge" heard as one drives down a road, sits by the fire after dinner, or waits in the dentist's office.

For Kenneth Burke, too, the importance assigned to the ecology of a text or spoken utterance is patent. Consider the opening of *The Philosophy of Literary Form:*

> Let us suppose that you ask me: "What did the man say?" And that I answer: "He said 'yes.' " You still do not know what the man said. You would not know unless you knew more about the situation, and about the remarks that preceded his answer.[5]

Burke continues, "Critical and imaginative works are answers to questions posed by the situations in which they arose. They are not merely answers, they are *strategic* answers, *stylized* answers." In that opening lies not only the main thrust of that long essay but a direction that leads right on to the "dramatism" of *A Grammar of Motives*.

However, what has now become the fullest statement of the ecological movement, speech-act theory, began independently of either Richards or Burke. Growing out of J. L. Austin's seminal lectures in 1955 on the uses to which language may be put *(How to Do Things with Words)*, the theory's special interest for us lies in the way speech-act theorists have come to analyze indirection in discourse. If someone says, "It's cold in here," he or she may be requesting that the window be closed, or suggesting that the thermostat be turned up, or recognizing hostilities between those in the room, or asking for sympathy, or perhaps commenting on the decor. How does one know? The intriguingly simple answer given by H. P. Grice ("Logic and Conversation," *Syntax and Semantics*, III) is that we relate any text or utterance to a whole set of contexts: social conventions, our knowledge of what is generally regarded as true, our acquaintance with institutional facts (marriage laws, the political system, the rules of football), and the immediate nonlinguistic situation (arriving late at a cocktail party, changing a tire in the rain, attending a seminar).

Grice's simple but essential assumption is that we expect discourse to conform to certain general maxims or principles—it should be as relevant, perspicuous, and true as possible, and no more nor less detailed than the situation demands. When we perceive that any of these expectations is violated, we look for a nonliteral interpretation. But context is all-important at both stages. We know what is an appropriate utterance only by juxtaposing it against contexts, and when we move from what we call a "literal" interpretation we do so by moving from one context to another. When "He's a little child" is said of an adult, or the question, "Did you enjoy the party last evening?" is answered by "It's time to go to lunch," we look for the contexts in which such apparent violations of truth, informativeness, and relevance would become appropriate. To take a literary example: "Old Marley was dead, to begin with. There is no doubt whatever about that." We are two sentences into "A Christmas Carol" and we know there is to be some question about Marley's death or survival or reappearance simply because in general there is no question about whether a given person is dead or alive; the maxim of quantity (of information given) has been violated.

A different starting point, vocabulary, and set of interests seems to put E. D. Hirsch's well-known argument for the possibility of valid interpretation of an author's intentional meaning at some distance from speech-act theory, but in fact the differences (though I don't believe Hirsch would agree with me) are not essential ones. I can hardly trace the whole of Hirsch's argument here—which in any case is generally well known—but much of it turns on the following principles: (1) "an author's verbal meaning is limited by linguistic possibilities but is determined by his actualizing and specifying some of those possibilities"; (2) such limitation occurs through the author's determination of contexts and their reconstruction by the reader;[6] (3) interpretation can only be probable, never certain, because contexts other than the immediate situation in which an utterance is spoken or a text is published are consciously chosen in the first instance and reconstructed in the second; (4) the understanding of an author's *meaning* must be distinguished from a reader's quite legitimate pursuit of *significances,* which depend on the reader's own imposition of purposes and frames of reference.

Thus, to simplify, both Hirsch and Grice take as given that the author and reader mutually assume a range of shared knowledge and experience that would allow the recognition of the intended contexts and thus the construction of the appropriate textual ecology.

The roads taken by speech-act theorists pursuing questions of the philosophy of language and by Hirsch in pursuing hermeneutic problems are paralleled by that still shaggy new endeavor, discourse analysis, which attempts to understand how strings of sentences, rather than the strings of words that make up sentences, relate to each other. We find the same basic principles, as for instance in Michael Stubb's *Discourse Analysis:* "However odd the utterance, hearers will do their utmost to make sense of the language they hear, by bringing to bear on it all possible knowledge and interpretation" and again, "On the one hand there is no use of language which is not imbedded in the culture; on the other hand, there are no large-scale relationships between language and society which are not realized, at least partly, through verbal interaction."[7] The terminology differs from that of speech-act theorists, but the central principle is the same: we assume a discoverable, intended meaning and we further assume that any violation of the usual rules of discourse, any apparent contextual incongruency, is purposeful, that it implies an indirect interpretation achieved by transferring the text to a context in which it is appropriate.

More elaborate is the form of discourse analysis that seeks to determine how the mind processes language. George Dillon's *Language Processing and the Reading of Literature* examines how readers fit together both the parts of a sentence and groups of sentences: we first identify the structure of a proposition, then integrate that provisionally into the structure of the whole as understood to that point, then provisionally relate this to the author's intention. Such construction is of course probabilistic at each level, and the context becomes increasingly complex as one moves to the second and then to the third level. But at each level we make use of acquired competence that we are hardly aware of. Dillon points out how much reading competence depends on syntactic rules that are rarely explicitly stated: "descriptive material following a verb of perception is to be taken as specifying what was perceived" and "if there is an initial noun phrase preceding the verb and if it is congruent semantically as the subject of the verb, assign it the function of subject" and "the first eligible noun phrase to the left of the pronoun should be the antecedent."[8] There is a direct parallel between these syntactic conventions and literary and cultural knowledge at the higher levels. The writer assumes the reader knows these rules; the reader assumes the writer knows the rules; both assume that violations are purposeful.

The development of a more and more fully ecological set of principles will also be found in recent theories of metaphor. So active is the current discussion of metaphor that no one individual theory adequately suggests the parallels with other kinds of ecological interpretation. As a shortcut, I will cite the three philosophical issues explored in Mark Johnson's introduction to his collection of essays on metaphor (*Philosophical Perspectives on Metaphor*). The first is the question of how is recognized. Attempts to identify either syntactical or semantic deviance seem to have failed, and again the promising direction now appears to be contextual. Johnson approvingly quotes Ina Loewenberg: "Metaphorical utterances are identifiable only if some knowledge possessed by speakers which is decidedly not knowledge of relationships among linguistic symbols can be taken into account."[9] In other words, the placing of the relevant sequence of words against external contexts is a necessary condition for our recognizing metaphor. (To take a standard outrageous example, Shakespeare's "she was a morsel for a monarch" would not necessarily be a metaphor among cannibals.) In speech-act terms, when such juxtaposition against routine external contexts tells us that one of the Gricean maxims is being violated, we attempt to interpret the word sequence by finding a way to make it appropriate to some possible set of contexts—and one of the things we may discover in this process is that we are dealing with metaphor. Max Black's summary of how metaphor is recognized is very close to Grice's explanation of how we recognize any violation of the Cooperative Principle: "The decisive reason for the choice of interpretation may be, as it often is, the patent falsity or incoherence of the literal reading—but it might equally be the banality of that reading's truth, its pointlessness, or its lack of congruence with the surrounding text and non-verbal settings."[10]

The second question is how the mind processes a metaphor. Is it by simply perceiving similarities, by moving from denotation to connotation? The most promising notion seems to be that of an interaction not simply between individual words or even sets of connotations but between fields of association or gestalts. Thus "He attacked the weak point in my argument but I successfully defended it" is, like most such metaphors which are neither noticeably vivid nor entirely dead, related to overarching metaphorical patterns or gestalts—here the pattern is "argument is war." Such an understanding of metaphor leads to the view that the projection of a gestalt structure like war onto one like argument produces a third gestalt that is part of the way we structure "our experience, thought, and language." This view brings us back from a different direction to the ecological principle of the mutual structuring of language, cultural modes of thought, and perforce, our understanding of reality.

The third question, the cognitive status of metaphor, has already been partially addressed in answering the question of how metaphor works. Metaphors can either reinforce or realign fields of associations, and thus alter accepted contexts by which we interpret language on the one hand and experience on the other. As Johnson argues, the question of whether metaphors are reducible to literal paraphrase is now seen in a more fundamental way. "The underlying issue is whether 'reality' is objectively given, so that, as knowers, we can only stand apart and comment on it, or whether we have a 'world' only by virtue of having a language and system of value-laden concepts that make experience possible for us."[11] The answer assumed by the most interesting contemporary theorists of metaphor is one shared by the ecological mode of thought: brute reality, the source of "raw feels," must exist independently of thought, but what we call experience, that which we can think and talk about, is mediated by concept-formation, which in turn is at least partly interdependent with language.

Turning from metaphor to the theory of argument, we note developments inaugurated by Stephen Toulmin's distinction between "the standards and values of practical reason . . . and the abstract and formal criteria relied on in mathematical logic and much twentieth-century epistemology." Though he is not directly concerned with how language is interpreted, Toulmin argues in part that "language as we know it consists, not of timeless propositions, but of utterances dependent in all sorts of ways on the context of occasion on which they are uttered."[12] Chaim Perelman's *The New Rhetoric* (1958, English trans. 1969), presents an argument very much like Toulmin's. The most recent further development of the Toulminian revolution of which I am aware is Charles Willard's *Argumentation and the Social Grounds of Knowledge*. Though Willard is not at all concerned with literary theory, his comments on language square with the ecological movement: "Ordinary utterance is intended toward, given meaning by, the definition of the situation; it is context embedded. To understand a particular argument is to understand the intentional defining activities of the speakers."[13]

Additional endeavors I find generally compatible with the essential principles of ecological interpretation are the literary theory of Charles Altieri, which combines elements of Wittgenstein and speech-act theory; the "linguistic criticism" of Roger Fowler; and at least that much of Paul Ricoeur's hermeneutic theory, which develops the distinction between semiotics and semantics. See Altieri's *Act and Quality* (Amherst: University of Massachusetts Press, 1981), Fowler's *Literature as Social Discourse* (Bloomington: University of Indiana Press, 1981), and Ricoeur's *Interpretation Theory* (Fort Worth: Texas Christian University Press, 1976).

III

Let me try to sum up the relations between the theories I have been exploring and so derive a set of general ecological principles. Having conscientiously tried to avoid as much of the high-flying vocabulary of contemporary criticism as possible, I hope I shall be forgiven indulgence in whimsically grand shorthand in naming these.

(1) The multitudinous possibilities of interpreting single words in isolation acquire limits in actual language use not only through the internal context (the order and syntax of the text itself) but from numerous external contexts. Since the overlapping of these contexts both suggests and sets bounds to meaning, this principle may be called the *multicontextual bounding of interpretive possibilities*.

(2) The external contexts are experiential, cultural, and linguistic. Not

only extrapolation from Saussure, but contemporary philosophical arguments, investigations into the psychology of perception, and Kuhnian arguments about science all assure us that our experience of brute reality, the system of cultural norms, conventions, and institutions, and the structure of language are mutually defining. Thus we have the principle of the *interpenetration of language, culture, and sense experience.*

(3) What mediates among language, culture, and sense experience (or raw sense response) is the fact of human purposiveness. Our Adam might have had real difficulty in developing language while still inside the Garden of Eden, where reasons for naming would have been largely aesthetic, but postlapsarian Adam, condemned to earn his bread by the sweat of his brow, would need to distinguish harmful from innocuous, friendly from unfriendly, useful from destructive. To grant purpose admits the relativity of the way we grasp language without making that relativity arbitrary or capricious. Purpose thus mediates between language and both physical and institutional facts. We have the principle of *the mind's purposive observation and manipulation of its own linguistic usages.*

(4) The writer constantly assumes certain responses in the reader, who in turn is assuming certain intentions in the relations between the text and external contexts. The complexity of that process can hardly be overstated. Writing and reading thus both require *continuous strategic calculation.*

(5) Such calculation on the author's part includes using language in such a way that we are routinely able to recognize implied meanings—often by supplying additional, perhaps unanticipated, contexts in order to discover indirection, irony, metaphor, and complex implicatures. Such maneuvers generally imply a comment or evaluation on the matter they imply; we may say then that discourse very frequently depends on *implied extrapolation.*

(6) Because as readers we assume that the author has constructed a set of textual/contextual relations that will allow us to reconstruct it, as readers we will try all possible strategies to arrive at a comprehensible interpretation. The unity we expect somehow to discover or impose on a text is not grounded in a metaphysical system but rather in an *heuristic assumption of unity.*

(7) But because our reconstructions are always the result of provisional adjustments of text and contexts, of interpretive tactics that are only partially rule-governed because the "rules" are always subject to violation, interpretation can never be other than probable. In fact, most of the time we are satisfied with our probable interpretations. That gives us our seventh principle, that of the *necessary sufficiency of probability.*

IV

The overarching interdisciplinary perspective that lies beyond the inwardly spiraling walls circumscribing the revisionist critics' alleged new freedom, then, is this. The deconstructionists and revisionists are right in denying the possibility of wholly determinate linguistic reference, incontestable interpretations of texts, and indeed access to an unmediated reality. The belief that humans ever participated in such absolute knowledge in the past or can ever achieve it in the future is almost certainly as much a myth as the Garden of Eden—in which, I have tried to suggest, Adam might well have found language problematic enough anyway. But the alternatives for literary critics are not simply somnolent dozing by dying New Critical fires or the following of deconstructive paradox into that critical night where all cats are indeterminately black. One can simply recognize that language, mind, culture, and that brute reality which is what it is and will be what it will be (to paraphrase the good Bishop Wilson) interlock in the same precarious, ecological way as the human body, the physical, material enterprises of civilization, and the natural world.

If Adam's naming was necessarily tentative, incomplete, and humanly purposeful, his and our use of language must be creatively shifting, dependent on context, problematically related to extralinguistic reality, and interpretable only through probabilistic construction. Ecologial interpretive theory tells us that language, whether in a sonnet, novel, newspaper, or instruction book for a new appliance, is able to serve our purposes because it is controlled by our purposes, even while our purposes are partly its products.

Notes

1. Geoffrey Hartman, *Criticism in the Wilderness* (New Haven: Yale University Press, 1980).

2. J. Hillis Miller, "Stevens' Rock and Criticism as Cure," *Georgia Review* 30 (1976): 5–31, 330–48.

3. Ferdinand de Saussure, *Course in General Linguistics,* ed. Charles Bally and Albert Sechehaye, trans. Wade Baskin (New York: McGraw-Hill, 1966), 14.

4. I. A. Richards, *The Philosophy of Rhetoric* (London: Oxford University Press, 1965).

5. Kenneth Burke, *The Philosophy of Literary Form* (New York: Random House [Vintage ed.], 1957), 3.

6. E. D. Hirsch Jr., *Validity in Interpretation* (New Haven: Yale University Press, 1967), 47, 48.

7. Michael Stubbs, *Discourse Analysis* (Chicago: University of Chicago Press, 1983), 5, 8.

8. George Dillon, *Language Processing and the Reading of Literature* (Bloomington: University of Indiana Press, 1978), xix–xx, 4, 69.

9. Mark Johnson, *Philosophical Perspectives on Metaphor* (Minneapolis: University of Minnesota Press, 1981), 22, 170.

10. Max Black, quoted in Johnson, 22.

11. Johnson, 41.

12. Stephen Toulmin, *The Uses of Argument* (Cambridge: Cambridge University Press, 1958), 181.

13. Charles Willard, *Argumentation and the Social Grounds of Knowledge* (University: University of Alabama Press, 1983), 21.

Relevant Publications by Wendell V. Harris

Dictionary of Concepts in Literary Theory and Criticism. Westport, Conn.: Greenwood, 1992.

Interpretive Acts: In Search of Meaning. Oxford: Clarendon Press, 1988.

The Omnipresent Debate: Empiricism and Transcendentalism in Nineteenth-Century English Prose. DeKalb: Northern Illinois University Press, 1981.

"Canonicity." *PMLA* 106 (January 1991): 110–21.

"Bakhtinian Double Voicing in Dickens and Eliot." *ELH* 57 (summer 1990): 445–58.

"Romantic Bard and Victorian Commentators: The Meaning and Significance of Meaning and Significance." *Victorian Poetry* 24 (winter 1986): 455–69.

"Toward an Ecological Criticism: Contextual Versus Unconditioned Literary Theory." *College English* 48 (February 1986): 116–31.

"Adam Naming the Animals: Language, Context, and Meaning." *Kenyon Review*, n.s., 8 (January 1986): 1–13.

"Contemporary Criticism and the Return of Zeno." *College English* 45 (October 1983): 559–69.

"On Being Sure of Saussure." *Journal of Aesthetics and Art Criticism* 41 (summer 1983): 387–97.

4

From "Shaking the Concepts"

A. D. Nuttall

A. D. Nuttall is professor of English and chair of English, New College, Oxford. The first sentence of the preface of his 1983 A New Mimesis *is "This book is an attempt to show that literature can engage with reality." Further into the opening paragraph Nuttall sums up what he opposes:*

> *My argument is directed against formalism, that is, against the resolution of matter into form, reality into fiction, substance into convention. Where structuralism is formalist, I am antistructuralist; otherwise not. I am conscious that my target is unreal; no one can really live with the kind of fundamental, epistemological formalism which this book attacks. But current critical discourse has adopted a certain style. This style admits or even welcomes metaphysical absolutes, and these absolutes themselves directly imply a wholly disabling conclusion.*

Much of the book centers on mimesis in Shakespeare's plays, but the opening chapter, "Shaking the Concepts," is directed against four of the five following "theorems" of structuralism and poststructuralism:

1. *The world consists not of things but of relationships.*
2. Verum factum: *Truth is something made.*

3. *The ultimate goal of the human sciences is not to constitute man but to dissolve him.*
4. *Language is prior to meaning.*
5. *Verisimilitude is the mask in which the laws of the text are dressed up.*

The selection from that chapter that follows addresses the first two of these theorems.

Relationships, Not Things: *Verum Factum*

In the eighteenth century the word "nature" carried an automatic credit; to use it was to be absolved from any necessity to argue or demonstrate and the approval one received seems to have come equally, so far as one can now tell, from the learned and the unlearned. The five propositions I have given have a similar quality but with an important difference. They carry a charge of automatic credit; they are immediately congenial to the intelligentsia. But they are not congenial to anyone else. To the man in the street each is either unintelligible or else obviously false.

Atomist objectivism has been thoroughly overthrown. It does not follow, however, that one must instantly fly to the polar opposite and affirm that only relationships are real. Something is obviously badly wrong with the first theorem, "The world consists not of things but of relationships." The notion of a relationship presupposes the notion of things that are related. A world consisting of pure relationship, that is, a world in which there are no things, is *ex hypothesi* a world in which no thing is related to any other and in which there could therefore be no relationship. The proposition is thus fundamentally incoherent and one can watch it dismantle itself, like a self-destructive work of contemporary art.

We may choose, then, to withdraw for a moment from the full metaphysical denial of "things" and instead assert a more modest claim: that it is the relationships between things that make for meaning and intelligibility. After all, whenever we say anything about an individual person or thing we find that we cannot avoid saying something about other persons and things at the same time. If I say that Margaret is generous I say (at the same time) that she gives more than other people do and so directly imply that they give less than she. If I say that a book is red I have said that its color is like that of a pillar box and unlike that of a clear sky. The impulse to drop the endless comparisons and talk instead about the individual itself turns out to be one that can never be satisfied. Only by trusting relationship can we establish our understanding of things.

This truce enables us to proceed to the second theorem, which is that all these patterns of relationship (than which human knowledge has no better material) are themselves the work of the human mind. This immediately generates an extreme consequence. So-called knowledge is really fiction: *verum factum, verum fictum* (truth made is truth feigned).

Vico himself would have welcomed the jingle. Tacitus's cynical observation (*Annals* v, 10) *fingunt simul creduntque*) (They feign and at the same time they believe), struck him, somewhat oddly, as "noble."[1] Vico, we must grant, did not consider that all knowledge was a human construct. He distinguished between *scienza* (which comprehended mathematics and "the human sciences") from *conscienza,* which was of physical objects.[2] Only the first is constructed by human beings. But the concession is less than it seems. For only God has knowledge of physical objects.[3] What we know is the civil world, and this is ourselves. Thus "in a sense men have made themselves."[4] It remains difficult to judge how absolute Vico's thesis really was. He seems as time passed to have hesitated over the example of mathematics but at the same time to have felt more and more strongly that history was the fundamental, typical form of human knowledge, and history, he is clear, is construct. Max H. Fisch says that in *La nuova scienza* history essentially replaces mathematics as the exemplary science of what is "humanly true."[5]

The implicit conclusion that knowledge is fiction is to some extent obscured by the structuralist emphasis on impersonality and convention. Something that is not made by you or me but is rather the work of *Homo Sapiens* or *Homo Occidentalis* may seem a little firmer or stronger than a mere fiction. In fact, however, though it may thereby have a greater claim to stability, it has no greater claim to truth. If one says "But that is what truth *is,*" one merely concedes the reduction of truth to the status of a cultural fiction. A story which three people agree to tell is not ipso facto truer than a story told by one person.

To be sure, there is in philosophy no position so untenable but that some intrepid spirit will be found occupying it. B. F. Skinner in his *Verbal Behaviour* seriously declared that proposition to be most true which is enunciated most loudly and most often by most people.[6] Chomsky in an annihilating review[7] mildly suggested that Skinner might try to make his theories true by training machine guns on large crowds of people and forcing them to chant the basic propositions of Skinnerian psychology. More commonly the question of truth is simply dropped. Jonathan Culler proposes without a tremor that we cease to pretend that the ordinary world is real: "First, there is the socially given text, that which is taken as 'the real world.' "[8] Notice that Culler places quotation marks around *the real world* but none around *text*. The traditional relation of object and representative is silently reversed.

Thus, the fact that a given "truth" is a construct of a whole society rather than an individual, though that may seem to confer a saving "otherness" or independence on the supposed truth, cannot begin to confer veracity. Structuralism is clamorously opposed to Cartesian subjectivism of the individual; but that which is subjective to an individual culture it eagerly accepts and indeed accords an uncontested authority.

Another sort of screen is provided by the fact that anthropology commonly treats the practices and discourse of remote peoples. The idea that the "truths" honored by these peoples are a fiction is subliminally reinforced by the reader's sense of the grasp on fact afforded by his own culture. It is easy to diagnose cultural fiction in the story that the world rests on the Great Tortoise when one "knows" privately that the earth is located in space. It is thus fairly easy to postpone the moment when the principle of *verum factum* is retorted against oneself. But its ultimate application to oneself is unavoidable, as long as the principle is maintained as a metaphysical absolute. Tell your structural anthropologist that his structural anthropology is a subjectively generated myth (subjective, that is, to his culture) and he or she will often commit the highly venial sin of resistance, will show signs of wishing to claim objective truth, of the old-fashioned kind, for structural anthropology if for nothing else. And at once the trap closes. Either the absoluteness of *verum factum* must go, or else must its claim to be believed.

For if the anthropologist did not claim objective truth, did not avail himself of the usual twentieth-century stratagem whereby the expert exempts himself from the noncognitive determination that enslaves all the rest, we should once more be confronted by the spectacle of a self-dismantling philosophy. If the truth of a given system inheres solely in certain arbitrary, collectively agreed conventions and patterns, once we perceive this, our innocence is lost and we realize that there is no reason to believe statements made within that system to be true; they may be consistent with the rest of the system, but not true. But what tells us that all reference has this purely conventional and contextual character? Structural anthropology, say. And what is structural anthropology? A cultural system of patternings like any other. So the contention that "truth" and "falsity" are functions of an imposed system of patterning may be consistent with other elements in the patterning system known as structural anthropology, but there is no reason to regard it as true. But in that case we need not have set out on this journey at all.

The picture is familiar. It is, as I have suggested, characteristic of modern thought in its more philosophically daring moments to see all human culture as merely epiphenomenal to a set of factors available only to the investigator. But the "self-exemption of the expert" can produce some oddly contorted sentences. For example here is Terence Hawkes:

> A wholly objective perception of individual entities is therefore not possible: any observer is bound to *create* something of what he observes. Accordingly the *relationship* between observer and observed achieves a kind of primacy. It becomes the only thing that *can* be observed. It becomes the stuff of reality itself.[9]

Notice first the relative modesty of "a *wholly* objective perception . . . is not possible," which might imply some sort of meager enclave for objectivity, for a *verum* that is not *factum* but merely *est*. But then, note, this modesty is abruptly replaced by stark assertion: the relation between observer and observed is the *only* thing that can be observed. Which is flat contradiction. If the relation is the only thing that can be observed, what does "observer" mean in the first sentence? Obviously not the enlightened watcher of relationships. Logically we are back in the desolate landscape of "pure relation" where no thing is related to any other. The "accordingly" of the second sentence is especially piquant. The cynic observed that the English phrase "as a matter of fact" is normally used to introduce a lie. "Accordingly" here denotes inconsequence. What is implied is nothing less than a collective cultural solipsism. This is at first sight horrifying but at second glance absurd since it can advance no claim upon our assent. The monster has no teeth.

Where, then, do we go from here? The philosophy of brute facts or still more brutal *things* has been dislodged and its replacement, apparently, can never establish itself as a replacement. But we have not exhausted the possibilities. It is necessary to distinguish two meanings of the phrase "objective truth." If "objective truth" means "truth which, so to speak, states itself, without regard to the nature and interests of the perceiver," we must grant at once that objective truth has been superseded. If, on the other hand, "objective truth" means "truth which is founded on some characteristic of the material and is not invented by the perceiver," there is no reason whatever to say that the notion of objective truth has been superseded. Indeed its supersession would mean the end of all human discourse, not just Newtonian physics but even *Tel Quel*. Objective atomism is dead but objectivity is unrefuted.

The distinction, however, is not often observed. It is as if people had noticed that all vision is perspective and then (because of some rhetorical color in the word "perspective") had forthwith slid into the very different contention that the visual world is subjective to the individual.

In fact, as anyone who reflects on the history of European painting will realize, the iron rules of perspective combine the admission of an individual viewpoint (for no two people in a room does the furthest corner make the same angle) with a fully comprehensible objectivity (if one of them changed places with the other, the angle for the second would be the same as the angle for the first, so long as they were the same height and neither was astigmatic).

Indeed, it is not so much that Renaissance perspective somehow ingeniously combined these things. A firmly predictable objective reference is actually derived from the preliminary specification of viewpoint. Thus in the work of a Renaissance artist like Domenico Veneziano we can infer securely what a person on our right would see, but no such foundation for inference is available in an iconographically parallel work by a much greater artist—the last great artist of the Gothic Middle Ages—Jan Van Eyck. It is not that Van Eyck is incapable of visual realism. His command of varying texture, fur, gold, linen, velvet, skin, is breathtaking and perhaps still unmatched. But his command of perspective is uncertain, and in consequence the world presented in his pictures is spatially infirm and not fully intelligible. Thus, although individuality of viewpoint is more carefully pointed in Domenico's work, it is to his painting rather than to Van Eyck's that we tend to attach the cool adjective, "impersonal." Instead of "although" we should really say "because."

It may be objected that my parenthetical concession that astigmatics may see differently betrays my entire case. In fact, it is not that astigmatics *may* see differently; they *do* see differently. We should not know this if the facts of visual perspective had not first been ascertained. Pathological divagation from a norm cannot be demonstrated if there is no demonstrable norm.

Radical or "Cartesian" subjectivism, whereby it is suggested that each individual may inhabit an utterly private universe, is an entirely separate issue, and can never be corroborated by particular demonstrations of idiosyncrasy any more than it can be refuted by apparent cases of agreement. The astigmatic does not embarrass the visual objectivist.

Again, it may be objected that the classical perspective employed by Renaissance artists is at bottom a convention. Not all societies have represented the world in this manner. Meanwhile, "what we actually see" is itself quite separate. The objection is plausible.

In *Art and Illusion* E. H. Gombrich quotes a story told by the Japanese artist Yoshio Markino of his father.[10] To follow this story it is necessary to understand that in the art practiced by Markino's father a rectangular object would be shown by parallel, not converging lines, that is, by axonometric perspective rather than by the classical perspective laid down for the Renaissance by Leon Battista Alberti in his *Della pittura*. Apparently, when the father was first shown a picture that employed the converging lines of classical perspective, he thought the box in the picture must be irregularly shaped. Readers seize on the story as illustrative of the conventional or arbitrary character of classical perspective. But in fact the latter part of this story suggests a somewhat different state of affairs. I quote Markino's father: "I used to think this square box looked crooked, but now I see this is perfectly right."

Of course he may have meant only that he had adjusted to a different visual game with different rules. But the phrase "Now I see" strongly suggests that he noticed how classical perspective approximates better to the facts (I deliberately omit the now almost compulsory quotation marks) of visual perception. The image obtained by a primitive camera exhibits all the characters (with certain very minor differences) of Albertian perspective. The history of trompe l'oeil painting tells the same tale. A perspective view of a room painted on a wall would not deceive the eye were it not that we do indeed see perspectivally.

It may be said that it deceives *our* eyes merely because we are so habituated to the graphic convention that we project it back upon the ordinary world, and that a Japanese would be similarly deceived by an axonometric representation, since he sees axonometrically.

But what can it mean to say that someone sees axonometrically? If you draw a picture with Albertian perspective and then try to draw the same picture with axonometric perspective, one clear difference emerges at once; in the second picture more of the background is occluded by the foreground. In the first picture nine little trees show in their entirety; in the second only six show.

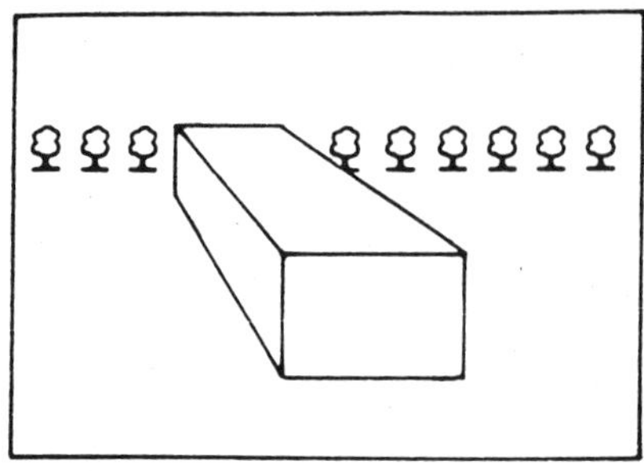

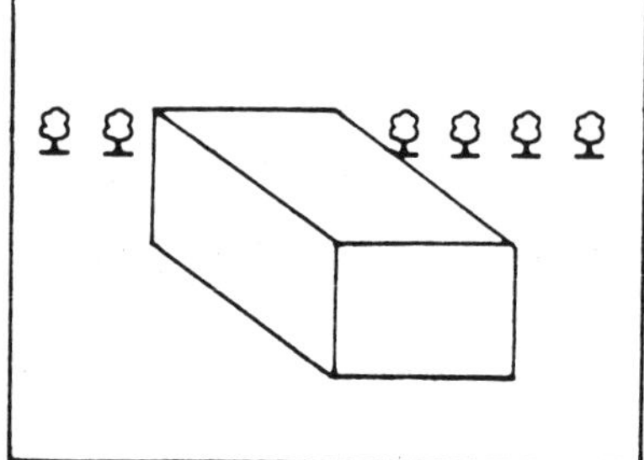

Do the Japanese see six trees, in real life, where we see nine? I think not. Indeed, if we are to be really strict, the trees should not be small in the second picture since the law of diminution by distance is precisely what is denied in axonometric perspective. The full application of this austere denial has extraordinary consequences. We would not see trees against a background of distant hills, since if the hills were represented on the same scale as the trees we should not see the hills at all, but only a portion of them. It is perhaps very revealing that Japanese or medieval pictures that approximate to axonometric perspective often do so in a piecemeal fashion, treating particular objects axonometrically, but subjecting the recessive planes of the picture to a brisk series of summary reductions in scale. Once again one suspects that they are compelled to do so because perception does so systematically and continuously.

It might be thought, however, that my distinction between visual facts and conventions is much too cut and dried. It is well known that if another person stretches out a hand toward one's face, that hand does not look so large as it ought to according to the laws of classical perspective. However much of the background it occludes, it obstinately retains the known size of a hand and does not look three times as big as the face which is two and a half feet behind it. The great painters of the Renaissance tactfully accommodated this factor when they refused to represent foreshortened recumbent bodies in full perspective.

That such involuntary modification of the datum does happen was shown clearly by R. H. Thouless in an admirable series of experiments carried out fifty years ago.[11] Thouless asked subjects to look at a disc set at an angle to the field of vision so that its retinal image was (as in classical perspective) a narrow ellipse.[12] He then asked the same subjects to choose from a series of ellipses varying from the very narrow to the almost circular that which most nearly resembled the shape the object had presented to the eye. Pretty consistently the subjects chose an ellipse that was thicker than the retinal image; that is, they chose a compromise shape, somewhere between the retinal shape and the known circular shape the disc presented when viewed directly.

Thouless, commenting on this, remarked that when a child is taught to draw in strict perspective, it is wrong to say that he is being taught to draw the way he really sees: "his drawing response is on the contrary being reconditioned to the stimulus object instead of to the phenomenal object."[13] But in fact Thouless makes it clear that what he somewhat misleadingly calls the stimulus object is in fact phenomenally available—that is, available *as an appearance*—to the subject. One does not have to cut open a subject's head to view the retinal image. "The way the subject sees" is in fact an ambiguous phrase and can with equal propriety be applied to the datum (which with an effort of concentration can be accurately reported on) or to the *modified* datum. We therefore do not have a simple contrast between a retinal stimulus and a phenomenon available to the subject. Rather the contrast is between a "hard" given phenomenon and a phenomenon that has been involuntarily modified.

The modification occurs only when subjects know that the object is really circular. Unconscious modification to the real shape was less in art students who had been trained in perspective. Thouless notes that in practice a draftsman can preserve the "retinal stimulus character" (or, as I would say, the hard phenomenal datum) by holding a pencil at arm's length and measuring the size of objects against it (this test is exactly parallel to my "occlusion" test). Thus the final implication of Thouless's work (contrary to that whole panic-stricken movement of the twentieth century that sought to deny the very existence of *sensa,* but in line with the more recent work of philosophers like Frank Jackson)[14] is that the classical perspectival shape is available to the subject *and* that it is unconsciously modified. That modification occurs he shows very clearly; but by the same token he shows that there is a datum that is modified (otherwise modification, or, to use Thouless's term, "regression," simply would not apply to the case). The entire demonstration that an unreflective person might take to corroborate conventionalism in fact does no such thing. The perspectival facts of perception are alive and well.

Gombrich himself (my source for the anecdote about Markino's father) recorded his warm appreciation of Thouless's work but subjoined a curious criticism. It is the word "real" that worries him:

> A penny is not more real when seen from above than when looked upon sideways. But the frontal view happens to be the one which gives us most information. It is this aspect which we call "the characteristic shape" of the object, the one (or sometimes two) which exhibits most of those distinctive features by which we classify and name the things of our world. It is on these distinctive features . . . that primitive art will concentrate, not because it draws on knowledge rather than sight, but because it insists on clear classification. Now this same insistence on distinctive features also influences our reaction in real life whenever we are confronted with an uncertainty. It is therefore inexact to speak of our knowledge which influences our perception of the oblique penny. Rather, it is our search for knowledge, our effort after meaning. . . .[15]

Of course it is true that a penny viewed directly is no more real than a penny viewed indirectly. But it by no means follows that Thouless was wrong to call the shape presented in direct viewing the real shape. He meant by this that it was round, as a penny is round. A penny may be described as "really round" if every point on its circumference really is equidistant from the center. This (with microscopic variations) actually is the case with pennies.

Gombrich implicitly admits as much when he says that the direct view gives us more information and exhibits those features on which our classification is based. "Information" and "features" are here implicitly objectivist terms. Yet he nevertheless smarts under a mysterious pressure to withdraw terms like "real" and "knowledge." The prerational influence of the Zeitgeist was never more evident. Moreover, its next move can be confidently predicted. Gombrich is visually sophisticated enough, or nervous enough, to shy away from any confident ascription of reality to the shape. But he can still write the words "in real life" without quotation marks. It is on this phrase that the modish reader can now be expected to pause and ask, "Does he not know that 'real life' is a problematic concept?"

Gombrich has shifted the level of our discussion from the reality of the phenomenon *qua* phenomenon to the reality of the physical object. It is easy to be tripped by a confusion of these levels. Dreams are both real and unreal. They are real *qua* dreams but their contents are not real outside the dream. My dream that a lion was driving the bus was real in that I actually had such a dream, but unreal in that the lion did not really drive the bus. Phenomena are not the same as the physical objects of which they are phenomena. A percept of a penny is not a real penny, though it is a real percept.

Plato made use of the necessary gap between object and percept to decry the validity of the senses. In the *Republic* (598A) Socrates extorts from Glaucon the wholly undamaging concession that a bed viewed from different angles presents different shapes. He concludes, correctly, that the appearance is different from the physical object and, incorrectly, that the artist who adheres to such an appearance is a liar. In fact, because the range of variations in apparent shape is systematically related to the real object and this relation is intuitively intelligible to the observer of the picture, truth may be preserved in a picture organized according to appearance.

In an admirable study, *The Curious Perspective: Literary and Pictorial Wit in the Seventeenth Century,*[16] Ernest B. Gilman tells how perspective, proudly presented by Alberti in his *Della pittura* as a source of truth, gradually became as the years passed an instrument of deception. Gilman tells his story well, with a running implicit suggestion that the initial claim upon truth was somehow "found out" or exposed by those who came later. Here as elsewhere it is necessary to distinguish between the formal modifications that are essential to perspective as such and those that are exploited to produce a disturbing effect. In Albertian perspective no less than in Dubreuil a round wheel may be represented by an oval. The Renaissance artist must have been clear about this or he could not have drawn his perspective picture. So far from being untruthful such forms are a means of accurate representation. No one who has assimilated the language of perspectival art (and, for certain reasons to do with the way our eyes actually work, it is easy to assimilate) is deceived by an oval representation of a wheel. On the contrary, as we have seen, he is able to infer roundness with a certainty never before available. Just as in ordinary perception we are rarely given a precise, frontal presentation of a wheel but can nevertheless see, in terms of the visual organization of the context, when a thing is round and when it is not, so Albertian art can confer relative certainty, where older "conceptual" art, with its literalist method of conveying shape (a square-in-fact must appear as a square-on-paper) frequently leaves the viewer bewildered. Gilman writes as if the claims of Albertian perspective are somehow overthrown when the fact of "distortion" ("systematic modification" might be a better phrase) is honestly acknowledged. The fact that the defense against such attacks was occasionally mismanaged (as by Filarete) does not mean that the attacks were truly formidable.

The use of perspective to deceive is another matter. Borromini's diminishing colonnade in the Palazzo Spada deceives because in it representation is doubled with reality. Borromini, in order to make the colonnade look longer than it really is, used actual columns of decreasing height, knowing that they would be taken for columns of equal height. It is only because like columns in a single structure are normally the same height and in ordinary perception a line of equal columns diminishes as it recedes that Borromini's deception works. The fidelity of perspective art to the facts of visual perception is nowhere more evident than in such jeux d'esprit. Clearly, it is fidelity to the laws of spatial perception rather than to a particular concrete place that is claimed in the (usually ideal) scenes of Albertian perspective. Again and again, the so-called deceptions of perspective turn out to be deceptions as to what is concretely real and what representation. The room that seems to continue is really a painted wall. Only a language capable of veracity can be used for deception.

The Platonic condemnation in the *Republic* is thus doubly absurd. Not only are the modifications by which percepts or representations differ from their objects reconcilable with veracity, the distinction between vehicle and tenor is actually essential to every act of representation. Here as elsewhere it is Augustine who streaks ahead of his peers: *unde vera pictura esset, si falsus equus non esset?* (How could it be a true picture, unless it was a false horse?)[17]

Meanwhile the cardinal truth stands: specific demonstrations of subjective or ideological modification always presuppose an objective referent against which they are plotted. One may show subjectivity in musical taste by the fact that Jane likes Tchaikovsky though Jill does not. But this demonstration presumes that in the "hard phenomenal" sense they are hearing the same thing. For, if we were to allow that, if Jane were to hear Tchaikovsky the way it sounds to Jill, she would say "But this is awful!" their *tastes* could be identical; Jane's smiles and Jill's frowns would then be appropriate, by identical canons of taste, to the differing private displays confronting them. If you want to say that their tastes diverge, you have to be able to say that their perceptions do not.

Here I can imagine a structuralist objection that might run as follows:

> Your musical example is trapped in the old metaphysical assumptions of subjective privacy and objective publicity which have now been swept away. You presume that there is a distinctive, individual "sound" called Tchaikovsky for each individual perceiver, and devoutly *hope* that it is always the same. The characteristic sound which language calls "Tchaikovsky" is really a node, a point of intersection of thousands of relationships; its "identity" is constituted, for example, by the fact that Tchaikovsky lies somewhere between the Russophile music of Glinka, Balakirev, and Mussorgsky on the one hand and what he himself spoke of as southern or Italian influences on the other. When a person "hears" Tchaikovsky this intersection of relationships *is* what he hears. It is therefore not just practically impossible but inconceivable that a person, admitted to another's experiential field, should say "That's not Tchaikovsky, that's William Boyce!" The most that could occur would be a momentary disorientation followed by a "twigging" of the usual system. Take the analogy of color perception. Suppose that *A*, admitted to *B*'s visual field, sees a pillar box and says, "Well, well, that's what *I* call 'blue.' " This reaction is perhaps conceivable but it cannot survive for long; he will rapidly lose any sense of cerulean distance in the color (I am striving to catch what might seem to be the intrinsic phenomenal "affect" of blue) but, as he learns that it is now the color of hot coals and blood, will associate it with heat and urgent danger. At the same time language will lead him to call the pillar box "red." So with a musical transference of consciousness: even if we were to allow that the entire relational field of music were somehow represented for each subject by different primal sounds, the auditory character, the auditory *identity* of any musical experience, before we get on to such secondary questions as its aesthetic impact, would be determined by the rest of the system. An initial puzzlement followed by a recovery of the usual system is perhaps conceivable. A wholesale *inversion* of auditory characters that are themselves dependent on the pre-personal system is utterly inconceivable.

Such is the objection. My answer is that I do not intend the idea of a radical transfer of one mind into another's experience as a serious possibility. I say only that, if *per impossibile, per contradictionem,* it were to occur, it would at once prevent any inference of subjectivity in taste. Meanwhile, as long as we do infer that tastes are subjective, we implicitly commit ourselves to the existence of common objects of perception (which may indeed be richly structured). The disquiet expressed above is merely an elaboration and a particular sort of comment on a difficulty already acknowledged in my phrase *per impossibile.* In fact the general tendency of such an argument, the tendency to rule out the idea of *radical* subjectivism, is welcome to me, but its credentials would require separate scrutiny. Perhaps the most obvious difficulty in the counterpicture here proposed by structuralism is the psychological one; if identity invariably depends on context, so that the nature of a context will depend on the context of that context, and so on, where is the point of entry? How does one begin to learn if one must know everything before one knows anything?

The problem is especially acute in aesthetic perception as opposed to practical perception, because the urgent hints and pushes supplied by practical reality are largely absent when, say, we are listening to music. Yet, in my own personal recollection, Elgar's music had its distinctive "taste" or quality most vividly of all when I first heard it as a small child in a state of pretty complete musical ignorance, so that for years afterwards it always rose unbidden in my mind as an obvious example of a translinguistic individual.

Meanwhile, what might be called "the objectivist correlative" remains inescapable. If you want to say that a society imposes its cultural forms on reality, you must have a conception of the reality with respect to which the imposition is detected. The alternative is a Derridian flux of *écriture.*

Much of what I have been discussing can be traced to one or other of two philosophical sources; first, relationalism, according to which identity can always be resolved without remainder into relationship. This theory became prominent in English philosophy with criticisms of Locke's doctrine of substance. People observed knowingly that seemingly solid objects were really mere bundles of qualities (as if solidity were not itself a quality, and as if an object so qualified were not solid!). This was the first of my "brief theorems" and evidently stands squarely behind structuralism, though most structuralist inquiry can function just as effectively with a less absolute metaphysical underpinning.

The second doctrine, which underlies my second "brief theorem," *verum factum,* is the romantic doctrine that the imagination may actually be *constitutive* of the objects of knowledge. This doctrine, if taken in its full rigor, implies that knowledge is not really knowledge but a mode of fiction:

verum factum, verum fictum. The doctrine of the constitutive imagination is certainly not proved by the demonstrable element of interpretation or "configuration" present in all perception, since, as I have tried to show, all the excellent demonstrations of configuration presuppose independent access to visual facts, otherwise we should not know that configuration had occurred. We understand the common example of the lines that can be interpreted either as an overhanging cornice or a set of steps because we can *see* that the lines remain the same while our interpretation varies.

Certainly Bacon was wrong in suggesting that we could put our notions to one side and attend to "things" in themselves; "thing" is a normative concept; we decide what counts as a thing or it is decided for us by our inherited perceptual apparatus. The question, "How many things are there in this room?" is a nonsense question. Do we include the neutrinos? Do we include twinges of nostalgia? But the fact that we are "set" to register other human beings very swiftly and miss utterly the blictris that so engross the eyeless Alpha Centaurians does not mean that we *make* the other people we see.

The shapes we bring to bear on the world are interrogative rather than constitutive. We trawl with the human net and therefore catch only what can be caught in its mesh, but it does not follow that we are the sole inventors of the catch. I and the history of my species may decide what counts as a chair, but if I then "trawl" for chairs in this room I shall find so many, and no more. Human astronomy is perspectival in the sense that it is from a given point of view, but this does not imply that the knowledge so gained cannot be objective. A whale would, I imagine, be unlikely to notice my ears, but may conversely be aware of gradations in the character of seawater of which we are unconscious, but this does not mean that my ears are an anthropocentric fiction or conversely that the gradations of the sea are a myth of the whale race, a phallaenocentric fiction. In this book the word *object* will occur frequently, without apologetic quotation marks. This, inevitably, will "smell of" Locke and the benighted epistemology of the seventeenth century. But in fact I shall be using the word in a "baptized" sense, that is, with full acceptance of the fact that human needs condition the schemata by which we elicit certain characters from the world. As I use the term, there is no implication that the universe will admit no other organization than that implied by human language, or that other intelligent beings with different needs and therefore different perceptual equipment would nevertheless obtain the same set of "things." But there is an implication that reality is such that our terms can be used referentially in a fruitful manner, which is the kind of cumbersome metaphysical periphrasis that can be dispensed with in practice. If reality is such that *horse* can be used referentially, there are horses. This we ought to have learned from the hiccup in seventeenth- and eighteenth-century philosophy over Primary and Secondary Qualities. The matter is most easily explained by a short dialogue:

A: There is no Red without eyes.
B: Then color is a subjective phenomenon.
A: But some objects are so constituted that they appear red to our eyes, and others are so constituted that they do not.
B: But in that case "Being so constituted as to appear red *is* 'Being red'; those are the red objects, and they *are* red."

The reader is invited to construct a similar dialogue, beginning with, "There are no horses without human beings to conceptualize (or say) 'horse.' "

Orthodox Darwinians agree that biological adaptation is the product of natural selection, not design, yet they freely use teleological language among friends, where it will not be misconstrued; for example, "That tooth is for rubbing, not cutting." My use of *object* is in certain respects like their use of *for.* There remains the difficult question, "What does it mean to say that reality is *such* that it can be referred to in our language?" Can that "such" be unpacked further? Some writers have tried to describe phenomenally the reality that lies beyond our concepts, calling it a "darkness" or a (positive) "Nothingness" or "*Néant.*" But how could we know that what lies outside our conception is "dark"? The alternative is to construe "dark" as merely a picturesque way of repeating the fact that we do not know its nature, but in that case the purported description collapses into tautology. But the open word *reality* makes no pretense of description, yet at the same time its proleptic openness greatly assists the whole business of *extending* our conceptions, the work of *learning*. The presumption that talk of the darkness that lies beyond our concepts is fundamentally honest while talk of specific objects carries a taint of falsehood can and should be reversed. Meanwhile, however, the idea that transconceptual reality corresponds structurally to our concepts seems to involve an immediate metaphysical absurdity; the terms of the supposed correspondence are *ex hypothesi* unavailable. Facts are not hypostatized propositions (hypostatized for us by an accommodating deity). But facts are not mere propositions either. When language successfully describes reality, it is not that the relation between the two is something *less* than structural correspondence. It would be truer to say that it is *closer* than mere correspondence. We do not say "That corresponds to 'duck' "; we say, "That is a duck." We can only describe the world, phenomenally, in terms of our current colonization of it. Thus far, it has proved to be richly structured, relational and full of marvels. Obviously, we do not know what we do not know; who, then, is to say whether the unknown is a mess of shadows or a fabric of inconceivable richness? Meanwhile that which we know *is* as we know it, or else the knowledge is not knowledge.

Notes

1. Giambattista Vico, *La Nuova Scienza,* 376, in *Opere,* ed. Fausto Nicolini (Milan, 1953), 503; in the English translation by T. G. Bergin and M. H. Fisch, *The New Science* (Ithaca: Cornell University Press, 1948), 105.

2. See Isaiah Berlin, "A Note on Vico's Concept of Knowledge," in *Giambattista Vico: An International Symposium,* ed. G. Tagliacozzo and H. V. White (Baltimore: Johns Hopkins University Press, 1969), 371–78.

3. Vico, 331, in *Opere,* 479; in Bergin and Fisch, 85.

4. Vico, 367, in *Opere,* 497; in Bergin and Fisch, 100.

5. Max H. Fisch, "Vico and Pragmatism," in *Giambattista Vico: An International Symposium,* 401–24, esp. 414.

6. B. F. Skinner, *Verbal Behavior* (New York: Appleton-Century-Crofts, 1957), 425–29.

7. Noam Chomsky, review of Skinner's *Verbal Behavior,* in *Language* 35 (1959): 26–58, esp. 35.

8. Jonathan Culler, *Structuralist Poetics: Structuralism, Linguistics and the Study of Literature* (Ithaca: Cornell University Press, 1976), 140.

9. Terence Hawkes, *Structuralism and Semiotics* (Berkeley and Los Angeles: University of California Press, 1977), 17.

10. E. H. Gombrich, *Art and Illusion* (London: Phaidon, 1962), 227.

11. See R. H. Thouless, "Phenomenal Regression to the Real Object, I," "Phenomenal Regression to the Real Object, II," and "Individual Differences in Phenomenal Regression," in *British Journal of Psychology* 21 (1931): 339–59; 22 (1931): 1–30; and 22 (1932): 216–41 respectively.

12. Thouless seems not to have noticed that, strictly speaking, the perspectival shape is not a regular ellipse, but an ellipse slightly flattened on the side that is further away. The modification is so slight that it can hardly affect his findings.

13. Thouless, "Phenomenal Regression to the Real Object, II," 28.

14. See Frank Jackson, *Perception: A Representative Theory* (Cambridge: Cambridge University Press, 1977).

15. Gombrich, 255.

16. Ernest B. Gilman, *The Curious Perspective: Literary and Pictorial Wit in the Seventeenth Century* (New Haven: Yale University Press, 1978).

17. Augustine, *Soliloquies,* II.x, in *Patrologia latina,* ed. J.-P. Migne (Paris: J.-P. Migne, 1844), vol. 32 (1861), col. 893.

Relevant Publications by A. D. Nuttall

A New Mimesis: Shakespeare and the Representation of Reality. London: Methuen, 1983.

Dostoevsky's Crime and Punishment: Murder as Philosophic Experiment. Edinburgh: Scottish Academic Press for Sussex University Press, 1978.

A Common Sky: Philosophy and the Literary Imagination. London: Chatto and Windus for Sussex University Press, 1974.

"The Sense of a Beginning." In *Addressing Frank Kermode: Essays in Criticism and Interpretation,* edited by Margaret Tudeau-Clayton and Martin Warner. London: Macmillan, 1991.

"Power Dressing: On Greenblatt, *Shakespearean Negotiations.*" *Comparative Criticism, A Yearbook* 12 (1990): 265–72.

"Personality and Poetry." In *Persons and Personality,* edited by A. Peacocke and Grant Gillett. Oxford: Basil Blackwell, 1987.

"Solvents and Fixatives." *Modern Language Review* 82 (1987): 273–85.

"Loam-Footed English Empiricism." *Renaissance* 37 (spring 1985): 193–97.

"Realistic Convention and Conventional Realism in Shakespeare." *Shakespeare Survey* 34 (1981): 33–38.

5

Literature as Textual Intercourse

Raymond Tallis

Although Raymond Tallis's academic connection is with the University of Manchester, his name will not be found in the lists of members of literature departments there: a medical doctor who trained at the University of Oxford and St. Thomas's hospital, his professorial appointment is in the Department of Geriatric Medicine. He is the editor of Reviews in Clinical Gerontology, *and the author of more than one hundred medical publications, including two major textbooks. However, his startlingly wide range of knowledge and interest includes literature, linguistic theory, and philosophy. In addition he is a poet (the most recent of his four volumes of verse is* Fathers and Sons, *1993) and a writer of short stories. Two books on the nature of human consciousness, and forthcoming volumes on the "two cultures" and contemporary theory are listed in the selected bibliography. In his own words, his "major literary preoccupation,* De Luce, *a fictional essay, has been on the stocks in various guises since 1967"; his hope is "to finish it by the millenium."*

Tallis's 1988 Not Saussure, *which has recently been issued in a new edition, is subtitled "A Critique of Post-Saussurean Literary Theory." Although he raises questions about certain of Saussure's conclusions, Tallis's sharp critique is aimed much less at Saussure than at what he regards as the impossible conclusions drawn from Saussure's work and certain other reasonable starting points through modes of argument. Chapter 2 from that book, "Literature as Textual Intercourse," is reprinted here. The chapter follows an analysis of various modes by which recent and contemporary theorists mislead readers (for instance, the "Body of Evidence Gambit" and the "Promissory Note Ploy") and precedes an extended critique of arguments that reality is actually intralinguistic. Tallis goes on in later chapters to challenge the primary principles of Derrida and Lacan.*

Introduction

> A text . . . is a multidimensional space in which a variety of writings, none of them original, blend and clash. The text is a tissue of quotations drawn from innumerable centres of culture.[1]

> Influence as I conceive it means that there are no texts but only relationships between texts.[2]

> The meaning of a work lies in its telling itself, its speaking of its own existence.[3]

Like many of the more startling ideas developed by literary theorists, the thesis that a work owes its origin to, and primarily refers to, other works has its roots in common sense.

No one, I think, would wish to claim that writers are entirely original; that a novelist, say, is the "absolute origin" of his novels. After all, he creates neither the genre within which he writes nor the language he uses. Much is, inevitably, owed to predecessors who, at the very least, shape his literary responses to the world around him. Indeed, they make it possible for the writer to have *literary* responses: the production of literature is, after all, a socially mediated form of behavior rather than a personal, or an impersonal instinctive, reaction to the world. Moreover, many, perhaps most, writers have to work their way through an apprenticeship in which they consciously or unconsciously imitate or borrow from predecessors whose work they admire, though of course a real writer does not stop there.

We tend to underrate the role of influence in shaping a new work and to overrate the originality of the individual artist. We pay disproportionate attention to what is new in a new work. In consequence, we imagine that a genre is undergoing rapid change when in reality the underlying tradition and the basic assumptions are changing only very slowly. Even revolutionary literature has more similarities to than differences from the orthodox or traditional writing that precedes it. The pathbreaking new work puts out only a little from the mainland of the already said, the already written. Real change is inevitably rather gradual because of the "boxed in" situation of literature. Its production and consumption belong to a rather specific form of human behavior: literature is a subgenre within the wider genre of "prepared communication"; this in turn is a subspecies of verbal communication; and the latter is itself only one mode of human interaction. The very process by which a work is perceived as literary—makes literary sense—depends upon its being more or less explicitly located within a comparatively narrow universe of discourse whose coordinates have been established by previous works of literature. The new work owes part of its intelligibility to being situated with respect to, or within, a tradition it for the most part continues even while repudiating aspects of it. "Literary meaning depends on codes produced by the prior discourses of a culture"[4]—and many of these codes will be specifically literary traditions, habits, and principles. Insofar as tradition shapes the form of a work, earlier writing is the latter's implicit framework; or (to use the fashionable terminology) the context of individual texts is, to this extent, more text.

It is easy to see how these observations apply to form—how at the level of form, literary works imitate, hark back to and hence implicitly refer to, one another. But they are equally applicable to content. For previous writing will in some degree determine what is worthy of *literary* notice, even what is noticeable—and hence writable—not only at the level at which "suitable" themes are identified for literary treatment but also further down, in the manner in which they are handled and even in the selection of empirical detail. The poet's choice of "daffodils" as a theme will be fully intelligible only in the context of a tradition of "simple pastoral" verse, even though such a tradition may have been renewed by the poet's personal dissent from, say, a more consciously sophisticated urban verse devoted to social, satirical, or abstract philosophical themes. The subgenre of "lyric poetry" will be a major influence in determining that there shall be a literary result of the encounter between the poet and the flower—that the latter should count as the theme of a poem. Moreover, the selection of detail, once the theme has been established, is never governed purely by an unmediated openness to the topics and objects that form the overt subject of a piece of writing. What is included in the poem about daffodils will not be fixed solely by the poet's personal experiences and private memories of daffodils. He is talking about daffodils, yes; but in a way that no mere daffodil sensation or daffodil feeling could have triggered or organized. And other things besides the structure and properties of daffodils and the poet's personal experiences of them will influence what is excluded from as well as what is included in the poem. The contemporary idea of "a poem"—the current rules of the game—will make it unlikely, if he is, say, Wordsworth writing in the first decade of the nineteenth century, that his poem will make reference to recent modifications of the position of daffodils in the Linnaean classification or to the primitive biochemical observations of his botanist contemporaries. And the rules of the game will also ensure that when he writes he will forget much of what he has himself seen—for example, the blackbird droppings on the specimen he looked at yesterday.

The example comes from poetry; but other literary discourses, though less deliberately offset from the wider realm of everyday communication, are also written to or against—at any rate in relation to—a generic prescription. Just as no one's memories or feelings fall naturally into iambic pentameters, so the soul does not spontaneously secrete its hoarded experiences as novels. To adapt what La Rochefoucauld said of falling in love: no one would write novels unless he had read about them first. The sense of genre within or against which he is writing exerts both conscious and unconscious constraints upon the writer. But it also establishes the space into which he can write. If genre is a prisonhouse, it is one that the writer can escape only at the price of abandoning literature altogether.

Tradition is as potent an influence upon how we read as it is in determining what is written. What seems to be offered to us when we confront a particular work is at least partly determined by the silent presence of other works belonging to the genre to which we assign the one we are actually reading. The wrong "mental generic set" will prevent us from being able to assimilate or even make sense of it. Anyone who reads, say, *Philosophical Investigations* under the impression that it is a detective story or *The Red and the Black* in the hope of learning the rules of snooker will simply read past what is essential in these works or find them incomprehensible. Likewise, it is the "generic mental set" of the reader that makes, say, William Carlos Williams's jottings count as more than banal diary entries unaccountably chopped up into lengths. The verse-like form of his fragments means that they can command, or commandeer, a readerly attention, an intensity of noticing, that they would not otherwise receive and certainly do not warrant. (The freedom of much "free verse" is bought at the cost of the enslavement of the reader to the ideas of genre and the different forms of attention owing to different genres.) As E. D. Hirsch has written (with an exaggeration that is only too typical of literary theorists): "an interpreter's preliminary generic conception of the text is constitutive of everything that he subsequently understands, and . . . this remains the case until the generic conception is altered."[5] The consumption, as well as the production of literature, then, is an activity that takes place within internal traditions of form, content, and genre. Extraliterary reality, the manifest theme of the work, is by no means the exclusive determinant of its shape or content; its extralinguistic referents are not its only referents.

So much would be accepted by anyone not under the spell of semimystical ideas about the feelings, perceptions, and inspirations of authors. But this is a far cry from some of the claims that have been advanced under the banner of "intertextuality." It will shortly become apparent that the term "intertextuality" is sufficiently ill-defined for it to mean all things to all critics. Its infinite elasticity makes possible the conjuring tricks whereby the rabbits of paradox ("texts refer only to other texts," "there are no poems only inter-poems," "literature is about itself") are pulled out of the hat of common sense ("no one writes in isolation," "the poet is influenced by other poets, as well as by his own experiences"). The reader, acquiescing in a fairly unexceptionable claim about the nature of literature, takes "intertextuality" on board. Once safely installed, "intertextuality" undergoes spectacular metamorphoses. Its scope expands enormously until it can license almost any conclusion about the nature of literature, of language or even, as we shall see, human consciousness itself.

The Intertextuality of Literature

At its least ambitious, the "intertextuality" thesis is about literature. Noncontentiously, it takes its rise from the obvious fact that many literary works are explicitly or implicitly allusive. Scholarly references, quotations, echoes, reworkings of traditional themes, deliberate employment of established styles, and retelling of classic or archetypal "literary" stories, the deliberate contrivance of ironic effects by the juxtaposition of disparate and incompatible styles—these intertextual features have been the very stuff of literature since ancient times. Some writers—David Jones and T. S. Eliot are typical instances—create much of their oeuvre out of echoes and the ironies of cultural dissonance. Successful literary composition has often involved the conscious recovery of formal archetypes; while, at a lower level, second-order and second-rate writers have created an oeuvre out of a largely unconscious reiteration of stereotypes.

The contemporary obsession with "intertextuality," however, goes much further than acknowledging those aspects of literature that make it necessary to read one text in the light of or context of another. A prestructuralist critic would read even David Jones's great poem "In Parenthesis" as being primarily about the catastrophe of the First World War and subsume its densely allusive style under the poet's attempt to render that bottomless event thinkable. But intertextuality for many modern critics is a concept used to undermine both the idea that the author is the source of "his" works—or that he even personally intends them—and the belief that they refer to extratextual reality. The author-creator and external reference are to be classed along with the "true voice of (unmediated) feeling," and "direct transcription of empirical, sensory reality" (by a pen seen as a neutral, handheld camera) as simply parts of a now-discredited mythology of literature. In other words, contemporary concern with intertextuality takes the argument beyond the obvious fact that literature is in conversation with other literature to the conclusion that a work of literature is *only* about literature—either about itself or other works. We are asked to believe that the relations between one work and others eclipses the relations between any work and an extraliterary world; and to infer from the fact that, say, poems refer to one another that other poetry is the only reference (or occasion) of all poems. To accept, in short, that literary writing is shaped entirely by literary, textual forces and that it reflects neither extraliterary reality nor the experiences, feelings, and conscious intentions of their authors; that literature is "contextualized" from within rather than being governed at least in part by nonliterary or even nondiscursive influences.

Theories about the nature of poetry provided one of the more important roads to both the French and American acceptance of the more contentious ideas about the scope of intertextuality. In fact it is probably neither a simplification nor an exaggeration to say that "intertextualism" began life as a specific thesis about poetry, though it did not rejoice under that name. More precisely, it was about the proper function of verse and about defining the poetry that certain critics—and, indeed, practitioners—approved of. It arose, that is to say, out of normative principles.

The history of Symbolism—Mallarmé's famous remark about poetry being "made with words rather than ideas," Valéry's claim that poetry stands to prose as dancing does to walking, and so on—is too well known to require potted rehearsal here. It is sufficient for our present purposes to note Jakobson and Sartre as important intermediaries between symbolism and modern French "intertextual" poetics. Both cordoned off poetry from other discourses by asserting that poetry was nonreferential. For Sartre, a poem was an opaque object without external reference that invited the reader to look at, rather than through it. Opaque poetry stood to transparent prose as a jewel to a window.[6] Jakobson's views on language, "literariness," poetry, and referentiality will not be discussed in detail here. Suffice it to say that his pronouncements were influential in popularizing the idea that poetry, or the poetic parts of literature, or language in its essential poeticalness, were nonreferential.

As for the American critical scene, Lentricchia convincingly argues that there is a continuity between the present popularity of post-Saussurean ideas about literature and the theoretical ideas associated with the New Criticism that flourished in the middle decades of this century.[7] A brief glance at the New Criticism will show how it prepared the ground for the massive extension of the critical conception of literary influence, imitation, and tradition that subsequently took place under the cover of the term "intertextuality."

Lentricchia makes only passing reference to I. A. Richards, though he is generally acknowledged as one of the founding fathers of the New Criticism. His early belief that poetry was distinguished from other modes of discourse by being essentially emotive rather than informative[8] was crucial both for the development of the New Criticism and for its eventual displacement by post-Saussurean theory. If, Richards maintained, poetry sometimes seemed to convey information, this was either illusory (apparently factual statements were "pseudo-propositions") or incidental to its central purpose. Poetry is not about "extraliterary" reality. Its meanings are nonreferential and as such they are a more suitable subject for psychological measurement—by a kind of "affective calculus"—than for empirical verification or logical investigation. A poem is not empirically true or untrue—it is not in that sense open to the world—rather it is powerful or weak, affecting and effective or feeble and inert.

Richards's ideas about the true nature of poetry imperceptibly became a prescription for true poetry; they changed from a theory about what poetry was to a theory about what poetry should be. At about the same time, Archibald MacLeish was declaring (in a poem) that a poem should be "palpable and mute / As a globed fruit":

> A poem should be equal to:
> Not true
>
> A poem should not mean
> But be.[9]

A poem should be an object in itself; for objects, unlike factual statements, are not hollowed out by reference; nor do they live or die by their truth values; they simply are. Such ideas are similar to those Sartre was advancing twenty years later in *What is Literature?*

Cleanth Brooks was one of many critics who accepted the essential nonreferentiality of verse and he elaborated the more specific thesis that a poem should *be* what it asserts. It would achieve the required nonreferentiality by referring only to itself. Donne's "The Canonization" is satisfying as a poem because it *is* itself the "well wrought urne" that it invokes at its climactic moment. "We'll build in sonnets pretty roomes" the poet writes, as he builds his pretty sonnet-room.[10] Insofar as "The Canonization" has a reference, it *is* that to which it refers and, as such, is exemplary. Contemporary poets should follow Donne's example and refuse to write poems that are about anything other than themselves. Poems that attempt to be other than self-referential are defective, contaminated; in short, nonpoems. To use verse as a medium for talking about one's feelings, one's beliefs, one's sufferings or about any aspect of the world outside of the poem, is to show that one has misunderstood the name and nature of true poetry. It betrays one's insufficient sophistication. The ideal poem is "above the battle" and the true poet is a disinterested virtuoso playing with (rather than asserting) ideas, assuming voices, creating in the space of the poem unique harmonies out of phonetic, tonal, and stylistic dissonances. (The poem as a "space" is another metaphor favored by the New Critics.) Since true verse is not about anything other than itself, any attempt to explicate its meaning, to say what it is "about" is to traduce it, to commit "the heresy of paraphrase." The critic should instead pay close attention to verbal and formal features of poetry and ignore as far as possible its biographical, historical, and philosophical contexts. (It is not, of course, possible to do this, as was discovered at a more fundamental level by those linguists who tried to develop a comprehensive semantics-free grammar.) And so it came about that, as Gerald Graff has noted, "the key principle of the New Criticism [became] its hostile (or at best equivocal) view of the referential powers of literature."[11]

From the idea that real *poetry* is non- or self-referential it is but a step to the position that real *literature* should have no external reference; that literature in its essential "literariness" does not stoop to the representation of external reality but rather aims to be a fragment of a second, perfected, reality where all is "luxe, calme et volupté," to realize that Utopia of language where feelings, ideas, and images are subordinated to the creation of a linguistic site composed explicitly of none of them. Such literature has no external, nonliterary origin: like the ideal poem, it is a series of little closed universes that have no other occasion than themselves or each other. By these standards most of fiction and prose nonfiction could be safely disregarded as subart, unworthy of serious critical attention.

It is interesting to speculate how the lack of an external referent changed from a New Critical criterion of good literature to the inescapable condition of literature itself. Lentricchia makes a convincing case for the major influence of Northrop Frye's *Anatomy of Criticism* in this regard. For Frye, literature is a closed universe of order, outside of which there is only chaos. Literature does not emerge out of, nor does it reflect, extraliterary reality: "poems can only be made out of other poems." Being without external origin or external reference are not only necessary features of good verse but the inescapable condition of all literature, which is uniquely intelligible and ordered in an unintelligible and chaotic world. The sheer inclusiveness of Frye's scheme, which brought all literature within a single system—so that any given work could claim to have been foreseen, occupying a predetermined position in a closed literary universe—must certainly have been influential in carrying his larger quasi-metaphysical claim that the individual work is not about the real world (which is chaotic and formless) but is merely a figure, a position in a map that has already been drawn. The artist will struggle in vain against the curse by which literature is cut off from the world: the price of making a work that has an intelligible order is conformity to a genre and the inturning of reference. The primary relation of the poem or novel is to the genre to which it stands as token to type and not to a world that it expresses or reflects. And the fundamental critical task is not to mediate between literature and extraliterary reality—adjudicating the extent to which the one is true of the other—but to develop a sensibility and a critical apparatus that permits an ever more refined and precise allocation of works to genres discriminated within a system that is at once rigorous and all-inclusive.

The stage is set for the full acceptance of a critical approach that treats the work as an intertextual construct. It will be evident from what has been said so far that this is a position that will prove difficult to evaluate. Defining a counterposition will require that one should be able to draw the boundaries that separate internal from external reference in literature. Few people can command the necessary erudition to determine the extent to which *all* writers are consciously or unconsciously influenced by other writers. Besides, it is not merely a matter of (encyclopedic) knowledge but also one of interpretation. It is possible, for example, to argue that all literature is characterized by such a degree of inturned intertextuality as to be really about the difficulties that lie in the way of its being written. Todorov, in a much-noticed passage, tells us that "every work, every novel, tells through the fabric of its events the story of its own creation, its own history. . . . The meaning of a work lies in its telling itself, its speaking of its own existence."[12] So every novel is guaranteed to be, if not "a well wrought urne," at least "a well cooped hoggesheadde." Several critics have claimed that inturned, indeed ingrown, intertextuality, is a feature of even the most apparently naive and outgoing of realistic novels. We shall discuss this (self-defeating) position elsewhere; for the present, it is sufficient to observe that, if it can be argued that the *central* theme of the novels of Dickens, Conrad, and Thackeray is a meditation on the art of fiction,[13] then no one is so placed as to be able to assess the extent of the presence of intertextuality in literature.

One method of counterargument would be to look at actual cases. Supposing we compare two artists operating under roughly the same generic constraints and find that they have apparently two quite different attitudes, topics, themes, and referents—would this not then undermine the argument that all works have, say, their genre as their primary, or even sole, referent? For identical genre should mean identical reference. Or, even more tellingly, suppose we compare several pieces by the same writer, again operating under the same generic constraints—say, Shakespeare writing sonnets. A thoroughgoing textual analysis could dissolve much of the content of these sonnets into a play of allusions, and read them as highly formalized exercises typical of the style of the Renaissance sonnet. But how well does this stand up when we look at the verses themselves? Compare this:

> What is your substance, whereof are you made,
> That millions of strange shadows on you tend?
> (Sonnet 53)

with

> Farewell! thou art too dear for my possessing,
> And like enough thou know'st thy estimate.
> (Sonnet 87)

and

> Th'expense of spirit in a waste of shame
> Is lust in action; and till action, lust
> Is perjured, murd'rous, bloody, full of blame,
> (Sonnet 129)

No one reading these three sonnets could surely doubt that within the very closely circumscribed limits of the Renaissance love sonnet totally different messages may be transmitted and different referents discriminated. The enawed sense of mystery experienced by the lover contemplating his beloved in Sonnet 53, his resigned grief in Sonnet 87, and his anger—directed at his lust and, by implication at his lust's object in Sonnet 129—are all, of course, stylized; but they are nevertheless also highly differentiated and make sense in relation to the widely divergent experiences, attitudes, and postures they invoke and thus refer to. Although it would be absurd to deny the formal elements that run through the sonnets, it would be perverse to see them as being solely designed to draw attention to themselves, to earlier sonnets, or to the sonnet form itself. This is emphasized even by those scholars who consider that the formal element of the sonnets has been underestimated. "Attentiveness to Shakespeare's handling of form" generates

> the discovery that the greater the immediate effect of the sonnet, the more surely does it prove, upon examination, that the effects rest no less surely upon form than upon the appeal of the sentiments or of the imagery. . . . A close study of the language of *The Sonnets* makes it clear that, great as was Shakespeare's ability to use imagery not

> only for its beauty but also for its integrating power, he possessed in even greater measure the power to make the formal elements of language express the nature of the experience with which the language deals.[14]

There are some who would remain unimpressed by the fact that, although the genre exerts constraints upon both form and content, it does not determine the referent of a work of art because the latter can vary enormously even within the tightest of generic constraints. They would be unmoved by being reminded that assigning the work to its correct pigeonhole is consequently not the same as making sense of it and identifying its reference; so that even if every work could be assigned a place within such a schema, and an individual novel or poem were an instance of a preestablished type, it would not follow that the type was the only or even the primary reference of the work. For there is nothing to prevent the committed intertextualist from claiming that, notwithstanding the variety of referents available to a writer working within even the most narrowly defined genre, the range of referents is still internal to literature; and that apparently different, apparently extraliterary, referents merely represent different positions within a closed universe of literary discourse.

Such a claim will again render radical intertextualist theses immune from testing against external evidence. Or perhaps not entirely immune. And it is appropriate at this juncture to mention Barthes's famous attempt to construct a "rhetoric" of love, in which the experiences and adventures and reflections and strategies of the lover were read as figures, tropes, as scenes of language, nodes in a network of amorous discourse.[15] Apart from certain isolated insights, the project was not a success. This is admitted as much in the subtitle of *A Lover's Discourse:* "Fragments." The reason for Barthes's inevitable failure to transcribe all the lover's experiences from content to form—to make of "being in love" a matter of differences without positive terms—can be stated very simply. It overlooks the element of accident, of particularity, and ultimately the irreducible *haecceitas* of being there, that constitutes *all* experiences, not just amorous ones.

But we hardly need to turn to empirical evidence to test the ideas of extreme intertextualists. We can usually rely upon advanced critics to provide us with internal or self-refutation. In the case of certain prominent intertextualists, our expectations are generously fulfilled. In some instances, the theory contradicts itself; in others, the theory is contradicted by the critic's own interpretive practice. A few critics—among them Harold

Bloom—manage to pull off both forms of self-contradiction, showing how the business of adhering consistently to dubious ideas requires constant vigilance.

For Bloom, intertextuality is the key to the artist's inner struggle and creative power.[16] A poet is concerned not so much to write about the world, or about the things that happen to him, but to write poems that are different from other poems—more specifically from the poems written by those whom he has identified as his precursors: "poems . . . are neither about 'subjects' nor about 'themselves.' They are necessarily about *other poems;* a poem is a response to a poem, as a poet is a response to a poet."[17]

Becoming a poet consists essentially of falling in love with and being engulfed by a precursor, falling out of love with him, and then fighting against his influence. The "strong" poet is one who successfully overthrows those who, by virtue of being his forerunners, count as father figures. The motor of the poet's creativity is not excitement about the world, anger or astonishment at the way things are, delight at the discovery of a talent not possessed by others or even a desire to save a bit of reality, but the "anxiety of influence" which causes him to launch a parricidal attack upon his unsuspecting precursor. This, rather than any personal angle on things or the happy accident of being gifted, is what generates his poems. It is perhaps fortunate for the luckless ephebe that his precursors are few in number and that the influence that preoccupies him emanates only from one or two forebears rather than the whole of preceding literature. It is not clear why he should alight upon those few rather than experiencing the whole of literature weighing down on him as incubus. I suspect, to judge from some of the examples Bloom has given, it is because they are usually found together in the college syllabus. Yeats cannot abide Shelley, nor Whitman Emerson because they have spent too much time together in Subsidiary 289. (This is not entirely just. Some of the lines of influence that he traces seem convincing and illuminating: Spenser as Milton's "massive precursor," for example.)

The first thing that strikes one about Bloom's thesis is that it is an astonishingly candid example of the common critical vice of attributing one's own preoccupations to the writer one is studying. Critics have been most typically concerned with the provenance of works and establishing who influenced whom in the history of literature; and so, according to Bloom, influence is the central concern of artists. In order to render this more plausible, Bloom develops the thesis that the artist *is* a critic and, of course, vice versa: "As literary history lengthens, all poetry necessarily becomes verse-criticism, just as all criticism becomes prose-poetry" (3). The conflation of the artist-critic and the critic-artist is inevitable in an age of latecomers when all but the strongest artists feel an insuperable sense of belatedness. (Latecoming began after Homer.) Both artist and critic, poet and teacher of poetry are present at the Primal Scene of Instruction, at first as ephebes or pupils and later as precursors or teachers. This Primal Scene of Teaching is anterior even to the Primal Scene of Writing: intertextuality antedates textuality; or the text is born of intertextuality.[18] No wonder, then, that artists are, like critics, more interested in the influences upon works than the works themselves; for there *are* no works: "influence as I conceive it means that there are no texts but only relationships between texts" (see note 2). The meaning of a poem is another poem or, perhaps, another poet. There are no poems, only inter-poems.

This is, of course, a comparatively restricted version of the intertextuality thesis. In Bloom's scheme of things, the work does not refer to the outside world, true; but at least it does not dissolve into an infinite nexus of other works, into a comprehensive schema corresponding to the closed universe of literary discourse or into the great mass of literature itself. The text refers to other texts, but to a finite number of texts: it is possible to identify the corpus upon which the artist is committing his necrophobic revenge. And there in part lies its vulnerability. For the evidence Bloom adduces for his lines of influence is sketchy indeed; and at times almost laughable. It is necessary to read the original texts to appreciate the full weakness of Bloom's argument but the reader may deduce the irresponsibility of his scholarship from his claim—without further evidence—that Shelley's reference to

a deep, autumnal tone,
Sweet though in sadness

alludes both to Wordsworth's "sober colouring" in "Intimations of Immortality" and to the "still, sad music" of "Tintern Abbey." It is upon this kind of evidence that ephebe-precursor relations are established and the key to the inmost penetralium of the great poet's soul found. At this level, everything alludes to everything else and any reference to autumn or its colors could be seen to be an interreference to any other reference to autumn and its colors. Bloom, however, is not anyway too worried by the quality of his evidence: "Poetic influence, in the sense I give to it, has almost nothing to do with the verbal resemblances between one poet and another.

Hardy, on the surface, scarcely resembles Shelley, his prime precursor, but then Browning, who resembles Shelley even less, was yet more fully Shelley's ephebe than even Hardy was" (19). No, true resemblance lies in the identity of spiritual forms: "at once the aboriginal poetic self and the True Subject"; and here we have to take Bloom's word since spotting this kind of thing lies beyond ordinary critics. And, indeed, beyond poets themselves: "The theory . . . has encountered considerable resistance. . . . I take the resistance shown to the theory by many poets, in particular, to be likely evidence for its validity" (10). Even making allowances for the rueful irony of one who may have received a bruise or two on the podium and the endemic Freudianism of Bloom's world, this is unconvincing.

The most obviously implausible aspect of Bloom's vision of the vengeful artist-son (the ephebe) murdering the father figure (precursor) is that it overlooks the process whereby someone becomes a poet in the first place (rather than, say, a doctor or a race-track owner) and the long personal evolution that antecedes the identification of themes and hence of rivals and forerunners. A lengthy chapter of accidents, decisions, self-interpretations, encounters with canonical texts, and so on will predate the moment when an individual decides to dedicate himself to verse and then emulates those who become his precursors. Bloom's defense that he is fully aware that "even the strongest poets are subject to influences not poetical" but that he is concerned only with the poet as a poet, "the aboriginal poet," is weak. It leads one to suspect that, for Bloom, the essence of a poet is that part of him that confirms Bloom's theories.[19]

The sincerity with which Bloom holds his views may be judged from his practice when he deals with particular poets. Take Hardy, a writer whom he reveres above all the moderns: "In Hardy's best poems, the central meter-making argument is what might be called a sceptical lament for the hopeless incongruity of ends and means in all human acts. Love and the means of love cannot be brought together, and the truest name for the human condition is simply that it is loss."[20] This sounds very much like a vision of the world, rather than a vision of a poetic precursor, an anxiety about life rather than an anxiety of influence. So what happened to the central criticism-making argument advanced by Bloom earlier, that poems are not "about subjects," that they are necessarily about *other poems*? It seems to have been put to one side: "but whether the theory is correct or not may be irrelevant to its usefulness for practical criticism, which I think can be demonstrated" (10).

What Bloom in fact demonstrates is that his theory can be usefully—and quietly—laid to one side when he settles down to practical criticism and becomes one of the most moving and exciting critics writing today. Which shows, perhaps, that one can go a long way as a literary critic even when one is in the grip of foolish notions. Perhaps the sign of the true critic is that he can find his way into the interstices between his own—and anyone else's—ideas. He has (to parody what T. S. Eliot said of Henry James) a mind so fine that even when it has been thoroughly violated by the least plausible of ideas, he can still talk excitingly and even sensitively about literature.

Bloom is his own straw man; he lacks the guile of other intertextualists. He is foolish enough to allow his assertions to be testable—at the least against his own practice. But if we are to avoid the charge of merely tilting at windbags, we must confront the more diffuse and slippery intertextualists. For reasons given earlier, however, the intertextualist position as a thesis, or group of theses, about literature as a whole is quite simply beyond evaluation. It is only when it is seen to imply larger claims about *all* writing, *all* language or *all* consciousness, that it can be evaluated, though even then it is not available to formal verification or refutation. Many critics already subscribe to the view that intertextuality is not merely a literary affair; it might seem then that the job has already in part been done for us. But we shall have to redo this work in order to bring out the fact that the essential invulnerability of the appeal to intertextuality—and the claim that the context of a literary text is only more text—lies in its infinitely extendable scope. But in this extendability resides its downfall. For once the theory is extended to the limit, it is seen to have all but lost specific content.

The Intertextuality of Consciousness

> There is no unmediated experience of the world; knowledge is possible only through the categories and laws of the symbolic order. Far from expressing a unique perception of the world, authors produce meaning out of the available system of differences, and texts are intelligible only insofar as they participate in it.[21]

> Some scholars glibly mistake the intertext for sources and seem to think that intertextuality is just a newfangled name for influence or imitation. We must be clear that intertext does not signify a collec-

> tion of literary works that may explain the text or its influence on readers, nor one that may be used as a basis of comparison to point out the author's originality. An intertext is a corpus of texts; textual fragments, or textlike segments of the sociolect that shares a lexicon, a syntax with the text we are reading (directly or indirectly) in the form of synonyms or, even conversely, in the form of antonyms.[22]

Those who are not convinced of the special or unique intertextuality of literature will point out that there are many "intertextual" features in everyday discourse. Much of what we say is consciously allusive; indeed, there are certain people—especially in adolescence—whose conversational output consists almost entirely of jokey references, quotations, assumed voices, deliberate collisions of dissonant linguistic registers, and so on. But even such people are able to maintain this only when the engine is idling: camp evaporates in a crisis, when life, livelihood, or comfort is threatened. The argument against the unique intertextuality of literature could be pressed further, however, by correctly observing that even "serious" or "straight" conversation is shaped by a framework of expectation as to what is appropriate in the oral subgenre that is being engaged in. A unique situation is always seen under a general aspect. This is implicit in the very fact that it is *intelligible* to its dramatis personae; *particulare sentitur; universale intelligitur.* Thus apprehended, it makes a finite range of conversational choices available: a certain "user area" (to use the computer terminology) within the thesaurus of catchphrases is opened up; the transitional probabilities between themes, between phrases and between individual words within phrases are set and are, in theory at least, calculable by social linguists or discourse analysts. Between the stereotyped aperture and the stereotyped closure, the conversation will take a familiar course across citations, clichés, platitudes, and other conversational ready-to-wears. The entire discourse is pervaded by oral intertextuality. Does it, however, follow from this that its only, or even the primary, reference is other discourse rather than the outside world?

I think not. Consider this example. During the course of a conversation, I tell you that my child is sick. My account of the situation utilizes words that have high intrinsic and transitional probabilities. I employ no nonce words or *hapax legomena* and the content and course of my report could have been at least in part predicted by a computer and, as the conversation proceeded, Bayesian logic could be employed to this end with increasing precision. Your sympathetic response is equally stereotyped. Even so, after we have met, you make a *particular* journey to the shops and buy a particular toy that you know that my child has had his eye on for some time. Endemic oral intertextuality has not prevented our conversation from having specific reference to extradiscursive reality and being governed by, and projected upon, nondiscursive grounds. Despite its intelligibility, it has (to invoke the terms of Duns Scotus's dissent from Aquinas) *haecceitas* as well as *quidditas*.[23]

The splendid scorn that Joseph Weizenbaum poured upon the artificial intelligentsia for their naive response to his ELIZA program[24] is relevant to the naive believers in the omnipotence of textual forces. The limitations of computer predictions or simulations—obvious to all but the besotted—apply equally to the belief that the course of a discourse can be predicted/explained by reference to textual forces. No "dialogue programs" could take into account the fact that the interlocutors in any normal conversation are open to a world not defined or circumscribed by the theme of the discussion. As you are expressing a stereotyped sympathy, a dog runs across the road. A calculus of probabilities will not have predicted the transition from "I am sorry to hear that he is unwell. It must be a terrible worry for you" to "Just look at that stupid animal!" But then neither computers nor discourses as viewed by certain literary critics are open to the exigencies of the moment. Nor do they contain deictic reference to spatial and temporal coordinates. In short, they are not *there* in the way that real people or real discourses are.

Let me take the counterargument further by considering this more dramatic example.[25] I am on call for emergencies in the hospital. The phone rings and I receive this terse, prefabricated message: "Cardiac arrest, Ward 6A." My acting upon this message will depend upon my interpreting it within the context of my situation as an on-call medical practitioner. Moreover, it is a piece of discourse that belongs to a highly specialized genre of utterances, to a discursive formation that will have been governed by the history of technology, of our conception of the human body, of duty and salaried labor, as well as by the development of certain institutions such as a National Health Service and by various other discourses that influence, and guarantee, the meaning of statements made within the context of professional medical discourse. It is, in other words, contextualized by more text. None of this will prevent the message from referring to an extratextual reality—in this instance a dying man in a hospital ward—and from carrying a truth value that may be ascertained by empirical observation. It is governed by nondiscursive grounds. The textual context of "Cardiac arrest, Ward 6A" does not prevent it from being true and (on this occasion) "No cardiac arrest, Ward 6A" or "Cardiac arrest, Ward 2A" from being (disastrously) untrue. Textual forces are *always* at work; but they are not omnipotent and they never act in isolation.

The intertextuality of the oral text does not cut it off from the world, from society, from the suffering, living human being. From which it follows that intertextuality per se does not itself close the text off from eternal reality, bending reference in exclusively upon itself. So the intertextuality of literature does not enclose the individual work within a sealed universe of literature. Or at least it does not unless one takes the further step of claiming that *all* texts, even the oral texts of everyday conversation, are somehow sealed off in a closed textual universe. In order to sustain that claim, it is necessary to take the final step of asserting that the real referents of ordinary conversation are themselves textual.

There are many prominent critics prepared to do this and to maintain that the world, the society, the suffering human beings to which discourses—ordinary conversation as much as allusive or highly stylized literature—refer and in which they are operative, are themselves huge and boundless texts. The relation between the conversational text and the apparently extralinguistic reality to which it refers is simply another mode of textual intercourse—between a small text and a big one. The world outside of the text is itself a text, as are the consumers and producers of the texts. If the literary text reaches outside of itself, by virtue of which it appears to have verisimilitude, this is because it is grafted on "to another general and diffuse text which might be called 'public opinion.' "[26] Public opinion is something held by texts about texts. According to Barthes, for example,

> this "I" which approaches the text is already itself a plurality of other texts, of codes which are infinite or, more precisely, lost (whose origin is lost). . . . Subjectivity is a plenary image, with which I may be thought to encumber the text, but whose deceptive plentitude is merely the wake of all the codes which constitute me, so that my subjectivity has ultimately the generality of stereotypes.[27]

As for the codes,

> the code is a perspective of quotations, a mirage of structures . . . they are so many fragments of something that has always been

> *already* read, seen, done, experienced; the code is the wake of that *already*. Referring to what has been written, i.e. to the Book (of culture, of life, of life as culture), it makes the text into a prospectus of this Book. Or again: each code is one of the forces that can take over the text (of which the text is the network), one of the voices out of which the text is woven . . . these voices (whose origin is "lost" in the vast perspective of the *already-written*) de-originate the utterance: the convergence of the voices (of the codes) becomes *writing*, a stereographic space where the five codes, the five voices, intersect. (20–21)

Julia Kristeva speaks of "the notion of intertextuality" coming "to have the place of the notion of intersubjectivity."[28] The intersubjective world becomes an inter-text and each text is contextualized by the boundless text (or inter-text) of a culture or society.

This at first appears to be a more radical position that will save the less radical one. It goes far beyond the valid claim that much of the outside world is mediated to us via stories to the suggestion that outside world itself *dissolves into* those stories. Nevertheless, the wider intertextuality claim deradicalizes the intertextuality thesis as a specific thesis about literature. Literature again seems to be open to the world at large. Or rather, literature has no less access to extraliterary reality than our daily conversations have. As Riffaterre expresses it:

> An intertext is a corpus of texts, textual fragments or textlike segments of the sociolect.
>
> "Sociolect" . . . is language viewed not just as grammar and lexicon but as the repository of society's myths, commonplace phrases and descriptive systems (stereotyped networks of metonyms around any given lexical nucleus). (see note 22)

The context of literary, as of nonliterary, discourse is apparently boundless. Meaning is context-bound but the context in question is boundless: it is the boundless text of society. This much is conceded even by Derrida;[29] and Culler, drawing out the implications of intertextualism, tells us that "to understand the language of a text is to recognise the world to which it refers"[30]—which represents a considerable retreat even from the position of some New Critics.

Toward Nonreferentiality

We have seen how the scope of "intertextuality" is extremely variable: it may be interpreted as a property of certain highly abnormal literary texts that seem to refer primarily to themselves, to the genre to which they belong or to other literary texts; or it can balloon to encompass the whole of reality. We begin with the claim that literature is closed off from the world outside of it, is nonreferential in the ordinary sense, because individual works are shaped by and/or refer to other works or to themselves. When it is pointed out that nonliterary texts—such as conversations—can refer to one another without apparently becoming nonreferential, the response is to widen the scope of intertextuality enormously. Ordinary statements in fact, we are told, refer primarily to other statements and if they seem to be contextualized by the real world and by real people it is because that world and those people are themselves texts. The outside world to which all statements refer is simply a boundless intertextual construct. There is an outside of texts but that outside is composed solely of text. The thesis that literature is a closed system thus expands until it changes imperceptibly into the thesis that language is a closed system—so that it does not refer even in ordinary daily life to an extralinguistic reality. This in turn shades into the position that there is no extralinguistic reality. Consciousness, reality, and society become conterminous with language. The constraints of genre reflect the prisonhouse of language that in turn constrains consciousness. Consciousness, the world, reality, society become a single closed system. At its limit, where there is nothing but language—"wall-to-wall text" in Edward Said's striking phrase—intertextualism becomes a linguistic version of neo-Kantian idealism. At this limit, it is scarcely surprising that "Il n'y pas de hors-texte" because, as *texte* is defined, it is coextensive with all that there is. But before that position can be earned, the advocates of extreme intertextuality must demonstrate that reality is intralinguistic.

Notes

1. Roland Barthes, *The Death of the Author,* in *Image—Music—Text,* selected and trans. Stephen Heath (London: Fontana; Glasgow: Collins, 1977), 146.
2. Harold Bloom, *A Map of Misreading* (New York: Oxford University Press, 1975), 3.

3. Tzvetan Todorov, quoted in Terence Hawkes, *Structuralism and Semiotics* (London: Methuen, 1977), 100.

4. Jonathan Culler, *Barthes* (London: Fontana, Modern Masters; Glasgow: Collins, 1983), 81.

5. E. D. Hirsch Jr., *Validity in Interpretation* (New Haven: Yale University Press, 1967), 74. A yet more exaggerated version of this claim, originating from Pleynet, is quoted by Jonathan Culler in *Structuralist Poetics* (London: Routledge and Kegan Paul, 1975), 136: "It is indeed this word (novel, poem) placed on the cover of the book which (by convention) genetically produces, programmes or 'originates' our reading. We have here (with the genre 'novel,' 'poem') a *master word* which from the outset reduces the textual encounter, by making it a function of the type of reading already implicit in the law of this word."

6. Jean-Paul Sartre, *What Is Literature?* trans. Bernard Frechtman (London: Methuen, 1970). See especially chap. 1, "What Is Writing?"

7. Frank Lentricchia, *After the New Criticism* (London: Methuen, 1980).

8. I. A. Richards, *Principles of Literary Criticism* (London: Routledge and Kegan Paul, 1925). See, for example, 267: "A statement may be used for the sake of the *reference,* true or false, which it causes. This is the *scientific* use of language. But it may also be used for the sake of the effects in emotion and attitude."

And poetry was distinguished by being predominantly emotive and hence nonreferential, of aesthetic rather than utilitarian value. Richards subsequently regretted the simpleminded way in which his early doctrine was applied and developed more complex schemes of analysis; but it was the early distinction that was influential.

9. From *Ars Poetica,* first published in 1926. This poem, although enjoyable, seems to me to have meaning rather than being, to be more like a statement than a globed fruit, audible and visible rather than mute and palpable.

10. Cleanth Brooks, *The Well Wrought Urn* (New York: Harcourt Brace, 1947).

11. Gerald Graff, *Literature Against Itself: Literary Ideas and Modern Society* (Chicago: University of Chicago Press, 1979), 10.

12. Todorov, quoted in Terence Hawkes, *Structuralism and Semiotics* (London: Methuen, 1977).

13. Michael Boyd, *The Reflexive Novel: Fiction as Critique* (Lewisburg: Bucknell University Press, 1983); William E. Cain, ed., *Philosophical Approaches to Literature: New Essays on Nineteenth- and Twentieth-Century Texts* (Cranbury, N.J.: Associated University Presses, 1984).

14. W. M. T. Nowottny, "Formal Elements in Shakespeare's Sonnets: Sonnets I–VI," *Essays in Criticism* 2 (January 1952): 76–84.

15. Roland Barthes, *A Lover's Discourse,* trans. Richard Howard (New York: Hill and Wang, 1978).

16. Harold Bloom, *The Anxiety of Influence: A Theory of Poetry* (New York: Oxford University Press, 1973).

17. Bloom, *A Map of Misreading,* 18.

18. Bloom, *A Map of Misreading,* chaps. 2 and 3.

19. It aligns him with Jacques Derrida as one of the great modern heirs of Mr. Pickwick. Bloom's recent encomium of Robert Penn Warren in the *New York Review of Books* relates that writer's poetic impulse and choice of themes to the accident by which Warren caused his brother to lose an eye in childhood. In other words, Bloom seems to have forgotten the irrelevance of extrapoetic influences in a poet's oeuvre. It appears that he no longer believes his own unbelievable thesis.

20. Bloom, *A Map of Misreading,* 20.

21. Catherine Belsey, *Critical Practice* (London: Methuen, 1980), 45.
22. Michael Riffaterre, "Intertextual Representation: On Mimesis as Interpretive Discourse," *Critical Inquiry* 11 (1984): 141–62.
23. See, for example, Frederick Copleston, *Mediaeval Philosophy,* part 2, *Albert the Great to Duns Scotus* (New York: Doubleday, 1962), esp. chap. 46.
24. Joseph Weizenbaum's famous ELIZA program is discussed in his *Computer Powers and Human Reason* (San Francisco: Freeman, 1976).
25. This example is also discussed in R. C. Tallis, "The Realistic Novel versus the Cinema," *Critical Quarterly* 27, no. 2 (1985): 57–65.
26. Jonathan Culler, *Structural Poetics,* 138.
27. Roland Barthes, *S/Z,* trans. Richard Miller (New York: Hill and Wang, 1974), 10.
28. Quoted in Culler, *Structuralist Poetics,* 138.
29. Jonathan Culler, *On Deconstruction: Theory and Criticism after Structuralism* (London: Routledge and Kegan Paul, 1983), 125.
30. Culler, *Structuralist Poetics,* 135.

Relevant Publications by Raymond Tallis

Not Saussure: A Critique of Post-Saussurean Literary Theory. London: Macmillan, 1988; second edition, New York: St. Martin's Press, 1995.
In Defense of Realism. London: Edward Arnold, 1988; re-issue, London: Ferrington, 1995.
The Explicit Animal: A Defence of Human Consciousness. London: Macmillan, 1991.
The Pursuit of Mind (coeditor, with Howard Robinson). Manchester: Carcanet, 1991.
Newton's Sleep. London: Macmillan, 1995.
Enemies of Consciousness. London: Macmillan, forthcoming.

6

Literary Theory and Its Discontents

John Searle

John Searle, professor of philosophy at the University of California–Berkeley, has been a primary opponent of the excesses of poststructuralist thought, and especially deconstruction, since his 1977 "Reiterating the Differences," a reply to Jacques Derrida's "Signature Event Context," in which Derrida sought to find in J. L. Austin's How to Do Things with Words *the kind of evasions and contradictions deconstruction assumes to be lurking in all discourse. Much the greater part of Searle's writing, however, has not been specifically directed to the debates over poststructuralist theorizing but rather to the development of speech-act theory (a central early statement is Searle's 1969* Speech Acts: An Essay in the Philosophy of Language*) and the exploration of questions in the philosophy of language. His latest book is* The Rediscovery of Mind *(1992). The present essay is one of the most polemic in this volume; its virtue here is that it focuses not only on questions about the broad metaphysical ramifications of deconstruction and poststructuralism generally, or the political and cultural tendencies of poststructuralism, but on the more primary question of the*

The first version of this essay was delivered as a Romanell–Phi Beta Kappa lecture at the University of California–Berkeley in 1987. Several people made helpful comments on earlier drafts and I am especially indebted to Isabelle Delpla, Hubert Dreyfus, Jennifer Hudin, Stephen Knapp, Dagmar Searle, Charles Spinosa, and George Wilson.

legitimacy of the forms of argument taken by many poststructuralist theories.

I

I want to discuss literary theory, and it is important to say "literary *theory*" and not "literary *criticism*." I will discuss, not in great detail, three different approaches to questions concerning textual meaning: Stanley Fish's claim that the meaning of a text is entirely in the reader's response;[1] the claim made by Stephen Knapp and Walter Michaels that meaning of a text is entirely a matter of the author's intention; and the view of Jacques Derrida that meaning is a matter of, well, what? Meanings are "undecidable" and have "relative indeterminacy," according to Derrida. Instead of fully determinate meanings, there is rather the free play of signifiers and the grafting of texts onto texts within the textuality and the intertextuality of the text.

It is an odd feature of the extensive discussions in contemporary literary theory that the authors sometimes make very general remarks about the nature of language, without making use of principles and distinctions that are commonly accepted in logic, linguistics, and the philosophy of language. I had long suspected that at least some of the confusion of literary theory derived from an ignorance of well-known results, but the problem was presented to me in an acute form by the following incident. In a review of Jonathan Culler's book, *On Deconstruction,* that I wrote for the *New York Review of Books* (27 October 1983) I pointed out that it is not necessarily an objection to a conceptual analysis, or to a distinction, that there are no rigorous or precise boundaries to the concept analyzed or the distinction being drawn. It is not necessarily an objection even to theoretical concepts that they admit of application *more or less*. This is something of a cliché in analytic philosophy: most concepts and distinctions are rough at the edges and do not have sharp boundaries. The distinctions between fat and thin, rich and poor, democracy and authoritarianism, for example, do not have sharp boundaries. More important for our present discussion, the distinctions between literal and metaphorical, serious and nonserious, fiction and nonfiction and, yes, even true and false, admit of degrees and all apply *more or less*. It is, in short, generally accepted that many, perhaps most, concepts do not have sharp boundaries, and since 1953 we have begun to develop theories to explain why they *cannot*. Indeed, in addition to examinations of the problem of vagueness, there have been quite extensive discussions of family resemblance, open texture, underdetermination, and indeterminacy. There has even developed a booming industry of fuzzy logic whose aim is to give a precise logic of vagueness.

When I pointed out that Derrida seemed to be unaware of these well-known facts, and that he seemed to be making the mistaken assumption that unless a distinction can be made rigorous and precise, with no marginal cases, it is not a distinction at all, he responded as follows: "Among all the accusations that shocked me coming from his pen, and which I will not even try to enumerate, why is it that this one is without doubt the most stupefying, the most unbelievable? And, I must confess also the most incomprehensible to me" (*Limited Inc.*, 123). He goes on to expound his stupefaction further:

> What philosopher ever since there were philosophers, what logician ever since there were logicians, what theoretician ever renounced this axiom: in the order of concepts (for we are speaking of concepts and not of the colors of clouds or the taste of certain chewing gums), when a distinction cannot be rigorous or precise, it is not a distinction at all. If Searle declares explicitly, seriously, literally that this axiom must be renounced, that he renounces it (and I will wait for him to do it, a phrase in a newspaper is not enough), then, short of practicing deconstruction with some consistency and of submitting the very rules and regulations of his project to an explicit reworking, his entire philosophical discourse on speech acts will collapse even more rapidly. (*Limited Inc.*, 123–24)

I shall gladly yield to his authority when it comes to "the taste of certain chewing gums"; but, alas, I have to disappoint him and not "renounce" his "axiom," for the reason that, logically, in order to renounce something you must first have believed it, and I have never believed it. Indeed he is perhaps the only living philosopher I know who still believes this "axiom" for he writes: "It is impossible or illegitimate to form a *philosophical concept* outside the logic of all or nothing" (*Limited Inc.*, 117). Further, he writes:

> I confirm it: for me, from the point of view of theory and of the concept, "unless a distinction can be made rigorous and precise it

> isn't really a distinction." Searle is entirely right, for once, in attributing this "assumption" to me. (126)

And then he continues (somewhat more plaintively),

> I feel close to those who share it. I am sufficiently optimistic to believe that they are quite numerous and are not limited, as Searle declares, with rather uncommon condescension, to "audiences of literary critics" before whom he has "lectured." (126)

It is clear from this discussion that Derrida has a conception of "concepts" according to which they have a crystalline purity that would exclude all marginal cases. It is also clear that in his view intentional states also have this feature, and they even have what he calls "ideal self-presence."

He is mistaken in supposing that these views are widely shared. In fact I cannot think of any important philosophers of language who now hold such views and it is not surprising that he gives no examples. The very opposite has been more or less universally accepted for the past half-century, and I shall shortly give some reasons why Derrida's conception of "concepts" could not be correct. For reasons I will explain at the end, when Derrida makes remarks like this he reveals not only his ignorance of the history of the philosophy of language, but his commitment to a certain traditional pre-Wittgensteinian conception of language.

I believe that Derrida's ignorance of the current philosophical commonplace that concepts are in general quite loose at their boundaries is typical of a more widespread ignorance of certain fundamental linguistic principles. In what follows, I argue that if you get certain fundamental principles and distinctions about language right, then many of the issues in literary theory that look terribly deep, profound, and mysterious have rather simple and clear solutions. Once you get the foundations right, many (though of course, not all) of the problems are solved. So what I am going to do, rather tediously I fear, is to state about half a dozen principles, all but one of which are taken for granted by people who work in linguistics and the philosophy of language, as well as in psychology, psycholinguistics, and cognitive science generally; but which are not always well appreciated in literary studies.

Now let me say in advance that, of course, there is nothing sacred about these principles. Perhaps we can refute all of them. But I also have to tell you in advance that there are certain rules of the investigation. The first is this: If I say, for example, "There is a distinction between types and tokens," it is not enough to say "I call that distinction into question." You actually have to have an argument.

II

So much by way of introduction. I shall now list half a dozen principles, and then I shall conclude by applying these very general principles to literary theory and to questions concerning the nature of textual meaning.

(1) *The Background of Interpretation.* The first point that I want to mention is the most controversial, and though I have been arguing for this thesis for almost twenty years, many people whose opinions I respect still disagree with me about it. I call it the thesis of the Background:[2] The functioning of meaning in particular and intentionality in general is only possible given a set of background capacities, abilities, presuppositions, and general know-how. Furthermore, in addition to the preintentional background the functioning of meaning and intentionality generally requires a rather complex network of knowledge, beliefs, desires, etc. Speech acts in particular, cannot be fully determined by the explicit semantic content of a sentence or even by the speaker's intentional content in the utterance of the sentence, because *all meaning and understanding goes on within a network of intentionality and against a background of capacities that are not themselves part of the content that is meant or understood, but which is essential for the functioning of the content.* I call this network of intentional phenomena, the "Network," and the set of background capacities, the "Background."

The utterance of any sentence at all, from the most humble sentences of ordinary life to the most complex sentences of theoretical physics, can only be understood given a set of Background abilities that are not themselves part of the semantic content of the sentence. One can appreciate this point if one thinks of what is necessary to understand utterances of simple English verbs. Consider, for example, the utterance, "Cut the grass." Notice that we understand the occurrence of the word "cut" quite differently from the way we understand the occurrence of "cut" in "Cut the cake," (or "Cut the cloth," "Cut the skin," etc.) even though the word "cut" appears univocally in both sentences. This point is illustrated if you consider that if I say to somebody, "Cut the cake," and he runs a lawnmower over it, or if

I say, "Cut the grass," and he runs out and stabs it with a knife, we will, in each case, say that he did not do what he was literally told to do. How do we know, as we do know, which is the correct interpretation? We do not have different definitions of the word "cut," corresponding to these two occurrences. We understand these utterances correctly, because each utterance presupposes a whole cultural and biological Background (in addition to a Network of beliefs, etc.). Furthermore, for some simple occurrences of "cut" we simply do not understand the sentence at all, because we lack a Background that would fix the interpretation. Suppose I hear the sentence, "Cut the mountain." I understand all the words, but I do not understand the sentence or the corresponding speech act. What am I supposed to do if told to "cut the mountain"? To put the point generally, both literal meaning and speaker meaning only determine a set of conditions of satisfaction—that is, they only determine what counts as, for example, obeying an order, what counts as a statement's being true, what counts as a promise being kept—given a set of Background capacities.

I believe, furthermore, that it is impossible, in principle, to put the Background presuppositions into the literal meaning of the sentence. You can see this point if you consider actual examples. Suppose I go into a restaurant for a hamburger. Suppose I say "Give me a hamburger, medium rare, with ketchup and mustard, no relish." That utterance, we may suppose, is intended almost entirely literally. I have said more or less exactly what I meant. But now suppose they bring me the hamburger exposed in a solid block of concrete. The block is a yard thick and requires a jackhammer to open it. Now did they do what I literally asked them to do? My inclination is to say "No."

One might object: "Well, you didn't tell them everything, you didn't say 'no concrete.'" But this objection starts one down a road one does not wish to follow. Suppose I go in next time and I say "Give me a hamburger, medium rare, (and so on), and this time NO CONCRETE." There are still an indefinite number of ways they can misunderstand me. Suppose they bring me a three-thousand-year-old, petrified, Egyptian hamburger. They might say, "Oh, well you didn't say it had to be a *new* hamburger. This is a genuine King Tut hamburger. What's wrong with that?"

It will not be adequate for me to say, "Well, I'll block that—next time I'll say 'No concrete and no petrified hamburgers.'" There will still be an indefinite number of possible ways to misunderstand my utterance. Next time they might bring me a hamburger that is a mile wide so that they have to knock down a wall of the restaurant and use a lot of trucks and cranes to get the edge of it near me. And so—more or less indefinitely—on.

I am not saying that perfect communication is impossible and we cannot fully say what we mean. On the contrary, our communications are often perfectly adequate; and we can, at least in principle, say exactly what we mean. What I am saying is: Meanings, concepts, and intentionality *by themselves* are never sufficient to determine the full import of what is said or thought because they only function within a Network of other intentionality and against a Background of capacities that are not and could not be included in literal meaning, concepts, or intentional states. In my technical jargon: intentionality, intrinsic or derived, only determines conditions of satisfaction within a Network and against a Background.

I said earlier that many valid distinctions are not rigorous and precise, but it is a consequence of the thesis of the Background that in the traditional Fregean sense according to which a concept is a kind of pure crystalline entity that allows for no marginal cases, there simply cannot be any such concepts. Any use of any concept is always relative to a Background, and consequently a concept can only determine its conditions of satisfaction relative to a set of Background capacities. What goes for concepts and meanings also goes for intentional mental states. If I am right about the Background, there are no such things as intentional states having the kind of purity they were alleged to have by the traditional authors on Intentionality in the "phenomenological" tradition, such as Husserl.[3]

I think several philosophers who have become dimly aware of the thesis of the Background find it very disconcerting, even threatening. They correctly see that it renders a certain type of context free account of meaning and intentionality impossible, and so they mistakenly conclude that any theory of meaning is impossible. This is especially true of those who see the *contingency* of the Background.[4] Our ways of acting do not have to be the way they in fact are; there is nothing transcendentally necessary about them. But it is a mistake to conclude from this that theorizing is thereby rendered impossible. The Background does not make theory impossible; on the contrary, it is one of the conditions of possibility of any theorizing, and where language and mind are concerned it is one of the chief objects of the theory.

At the beginning of our discussion it is important to get clear about (a) the basic idea of the Background and (b) the distinction between meaning as representational content on the one hand and Background as nonrepresentational capacity on the other, because all of the other principles and distinctions I am going to make depend on these points.

(2) *The Distinction Between Types and Tokens.* I believe the distinction between linguistic types and linguistic tokens was first formulated by Charles Sanders Peirce. If, for example, I write the word "dog" on the blackboard three times, have I written one word or three? Well, I have written one *type* word, but I have written three different *token* instances of that word. That is, the token is a concrete physical particular, but the type is a purely abstract notion. We need this distinction because the identity criteria for types and tokens are quite different. What makes something a case of "the same token" will be different from what makes it "the same type." You might think that this is such an obvious distinction as to be not worth making, but in fact a fair amount of the confusion in literary theory rests on a failure to get that distinction straight. Derrida introduces a notion that he calls *"iterabilité,"* the idea that linguistic forms are, in his sense, iterable. But the notion is very ill-defined in his work. He is unable to say clearly what the domain of its application is; that is, what entities exactly are iterable. He speaks of "marks" and "signs," but actual marks and signs, that is actual physical tokens, are precisely not iterable. It is, rather, the *type* of mark that can have different instantiations. This is one way of saying that it is types and not tokens that allow for repeated instances of the same. Derrida lacks a clear answer to the question, "What is it that gets iterated?" in part because he seems to be unaware of this distinction.

The distinction between types and tokens, by the way, is a consequence of the fact that language is rule-governed or conventional, because the notion of a rule or of a convention implies the possibility of repeated occurrences of the same phenomenon. The rules of syntax, for example, have the consequence that the same type can be instantiated in different tokens. There are further type-token distinctions within the type-token distinction. Thus, for example, when Hemingway wrote *The Sun Also Rises,* he produced a token, which inaugurated a new type, his novel, of which your copy and my copy are two further tokens.

(3) *The Distinction Between Sentences and Utterances.* A third crucial distinction is that between a *sentence,* or any other linguistic element, and an *utterance* of a sentence or other linguistic element. A sentence, type or token, is a purely formal structure. Sentences are defined formally or syntactically. But an utterance of a sentence is typically an intentional action. To utter a sentence is to engage in a piece of intentional behavior.

We need this distinction, in addition to the distinctions between types and tokens because, though every utterance involves the production or use of a token, the same token can function in quite different utterances. To take an example from real life, there is a man who stands on a street corner at a school near my house, and every so often he holds up a sign which says STOP. He is protecting small children from passing motorists. Each time he holds up the stop sign, he is making a separate utterance and thus is performing a separate speech act. But he uses one and the same sentence token for each different utterance. Thus, the identity criteria for the elements of the sentence-utterance distinction do not exactly match the identity criteria for the domain of the type-token distinction. Once again, we need this distinction between the sentence or other symbol, on the one hand, and the intentional utterance of that sentence or symbol, on the other, because the identity criteria are quite different.

(4) *The Distinction Between Use and Mention.* A fourth distinction, common in logic and philosophy, is that between the use of expressions and the mention of expressions. If, for example, I say "Berkeley is in California," I use the word "Berkeley" to refer to a city. If I say " 'Berkeley' has eight letters," I am mentioning the word "Berkeley" and talking about it. It should be obvious that the use-mention distinction allows for the fact that one can sometimes both use and mention an expression in one utterance. Consider for example the occurrence of "stupid" in the following utterance: "Sam is, as Sally says, 'stupid.' "[5]

Now, when Derrida speaks of what he calls *citationalité,* one would think that he is talking about the use-mention distinction, but, as with *iterabilité,* he does not give a coherent account of the notion, and this leads him to say things that are obviously false. For example, he thinks that when a play is put on the actors in the play do not actually use words, they are only citing them. The production of a play is a case of *citationalité.* This mistake reminds me of the freshman student who liked Shakespeare well enough, but was dismayed to find that Shakespeare used so many familiar quotations in his plays. In the standard case of producing a play, the actors produce the words written by the playwright, they actually *use* the words, they do not *mention* or *cite* them.

(5) *Compositionality.* A crucial principle in understanding language is the principle of compositionality. Syntactically, the principle says that sentences are composed of words and morphemes according to grammatical formation rules. Semantically, the principle says that the meanings of sentences are determined by the meanings of the elements and by their arrangement in the sentence. Thus, for example, we understand the sentence

"John loves Mary" differently from the way we understand the sentence "Mary loves John," because, though each sentence has the same morphological elements, they are combined differently and thus each sentence has a different meaning.

Both the syntactical and the semantical aspect of compositionality are crucial to any account of language. If you have certain sorts of rules[6] for combining linguistic elements, then the syntactical aspect of compositionality has the consequence that with a finite stock of words and a finite list of rules for combining them into sentences, you can generate an infinite number of new sentences. The semantic consequence is that you can take familiar words with familiar meanings and get completely new semantic units, new meaningful sentences, whose meanings you have never encountered before, but will understand immediately given that you understand the meanings of the words and the rules for combining them. Most of the sentences you hear, by the way, you have never heard before. One can easily produce a sentence that one has never heard before, and that one is unlikely ever to hear again. For example, if I now utter the sentence, "I just found a Chevrolet station wagon at the top of Mount Everest," I have uttered a sentence that you are unlikely to have heard before and are unlikely to ever hear again; but it is easily recognizable as an English sentence, and you have no difficulty in understanding it. This is an important principle because, among other reasons, it has the consequence that any attempt to define the meaning of a sentence in terms of the *actual* intentions of actual speakers is bound to fail. There is an infinite number of meaningful sentences that no actual speaker ever has or ever will utter with any intentions at all.

(6) *The Distinction Between Sentence Meaning and Speaker Meaning.* It is crucial to distinguish between what a sentence means (i.e., its literal sentence meaning) and what the speaker means in the utterance of the sentence. We know the meaning of a sentence as soon as we know the meanings of the elements and the rules for combining them. But of course, notoriously, speakers often mean more than or mean something different from what the actual sentences they utter mean. That is, what the speaker means in the utterance of a sentence can depart in various systematic ways from what the sentence means literally. In the limiting case, the speaker might utter a sentence and mean exactly and literally what he or she says. But there are all sorts of cases where speakers utter sentences and mean something different from or even something inconsistent with the literal meaning of the sentence.

If, for example, I now say, "The window is open," I might say that, meaning literally that the window is open. In such a case, my speaker meaning coincides with the sentence meaning. But I might have all sorts of other speaker's meanings that do not coincide with the sentence meaning. I might say, "The window is open," meaning not merely that the window is open, but that I want you to close the window. A typical way to ask people on a cold day to close the window is just to tell them that it is open. Such cases, where one says one thing and means what one says, but also means something else are called "indirect speech acts." Another sort of case where there is a split between the sentence meaning and the speaker meaning is the case where the speaker utters a sentence, but does not mean what the sentence means literally at all, but means the utterance metaphorically. So, for example, somebody in a diplomatic context might say, "The window is open," meaning that there are opportunities for further negotiations. In yet another sort of case, a speaker might utter the sentence ironically. If all the windows were closed, somebody might utter that sentence ironically meaning the opposite of what the sentence means. In all of these sorts of cases there is a systematic set of relations between speaker meaning and sentence meaning. *It is crucial to understand that metaphorical meaning, ironical meaning, and indirect speech act meaning are never part of sentence meaning.* In a metaphorical utterance, for example, none of the words or sentences change their meanings; rather, the speaker means something different from what the words and sentences mean.

Now it is tempting to think—and especially tempting to think when one is analyzing literary texts—that there must be an answer to the question, "Which is prior, literal sentence meaning or speaker meaning?" But as usual, one has to be very careful about these questions. The answer depends on what one means by "prior." If by the question one means, "What are the conditions of possibility of being able to communicate with sentences at all?" well then, of course, sentences have to have standing, conventional sentence meanings in order that we can use them to talk with. In that sense, communication in actual natural languages requires standing sentence meanings in order that there can be particular speaker meaning in particular utterances.

On the other hand, in any actual speech situation, what matters for the identity of the speech act is the speaker meaning, and that is what sentences are for. Sentences are to talk with. A sentence type is just the standing possibility of an intentional speech act. So in one fundamental sense, speaker meaning is prior, since the speech act is the basic unit of communication, and the identity criteria for the speech act are set by speaker meaning.

However, having said that, one does not want to give the impression that one can just say anything and mean anything. Furthermore, for any complex thought it will not in general be possible to have, much less communicate, that thought, unless there is some conventional device, unless there is some conventional sentential realization of the possible speaker meaning. For example, suppose I want to say to somebody the equivalent of

> If only Roosevelt had not been so sick at the time of the Yalta conference in 1943, no doubt the situation in the Eastern European countries in the postwar decades would still have been unfortunate in the extreme, but it seems reasonable to suppose that the sequence of disasters and catastrophes that overcame those countries would at least have been less onerous than it in fact was.

Now try to imagine what it would be like to think that thought, only without any words, or to try to communicate that thought to someone without any words, but just by gestures. The point I am making here is that there is an extremely complex set of relations between the conventional sentence meaning and the realized or articulated speaker meaning. In one sense, speaker meaning is primary, since the main purpose of the whole system is to enable speakers to communicate to hearers in the performance of intentional speech acts. But it would be a mistake to conclude that communication can be separated altogether from conventional sentence meaning. It is only possible to communicate, or even to think, complex thoughts given a structure of sentence meanings.

I have already said in passing what I now want to make fully explicit. Sentence meaning is conventional. Only given a knowledge of the conventions of the language can speakers and hearers understand sentence meanings. The relationships between sentence meaning and speaker meaning depend on a set of principles and strategies by means of which speakers and hearers can communicate with each other in ways that enable speaker meaning to depart from sentence meaning. I gave several examples of that earlier: metaphor, indirect speech acts, and irony. In all these cases, there is a systematic set of relations between the conventional meaning of the sentence and the particular historical speaker's meaning, as determined by the speaker's intentions on particular historical occasions.[7]

What, then, is the role of the hearer? The speech act will not be successful unless the hearer understands it in the way that the speaker intended it. And sometimes, of course, the speaker fails to communicate, and hearers understand his utterance in ways that are quite different from the way that he intended. Anyone who has ever written or spoken on a controversial subject knows this to be the case. And it is, of course, impossible to correct or prevent all of the potential misunderstandings. There will always be some ingenious ways of misunderstanding that you could not have foreseen. Any teacher who has ever read students' examination answers will know that there are ways of misunderstanding your views that you would have thought inconceivable if you did not actually find them there on the final exam. The role of the hearer, then, is crucial for the successful performance of the speech act. In the ideal speech situation, the speaker says something, he has a certain speaker meaning that may or may not coincide with the sentence meaning, and the hearer understands that meaning; that is, he understands the illocutionary intentions of the speaker.

In the previous sentence I say "illocutionary intentions" because, although speaker meaning is entirely determined by speakers' intentions, not just any old intention with which a sentence is uttered is relevant to meaning. For example the intention to speak loudly or to annoy the hearer are not illocutionary intentions and therefore are not meaning intentions. It is a very tricky task to try to identify meaning intentions precisely. For a recent attempt see my *Intentionality,* chap. 6.

(7) *The distinction between ontology and epistemology.* I promised half a dozen claims, but there are two more. It is crucial to distinguish questions of what exists (ontology) from questions of how we know what exists (epistemology). The failure to make this distinction was the endemic vice of logical positivism, and such a failure is built into any form of verificationism. Where language is concerned, often we cannot know what someone meant, or intended by an utterance, but this has no relevance to the question whether there was a definite meaning and intention in his utterance. Epistemic questions have to do with evidence, and though they are immensely important to biographers, historians, and critics, they are of very little interest to the theory of language. Roughly speaking, as theorists we are interested in the ontology of language, and the epistemological question—How do you know?—is irrelevant.

This purely theoretical distinction between ontology and epistemology is immensely important for the practice of textual criticism for the following reason. If we are having difficulty in interpreting a text because of lack of evidence, say about the author's intention, we are in an epistemic quandary and can reasonably look for more evidence. If we are having difficulty with a text because there is simply no fact of the matter about what the author meant we are dealing with an ontological problem of indeterminacy, and it is fruitless to look for more evidence. The standard mistake is to suppose that lack of evidence (i.e., our ignorance) shows indeterminacy or undecidability in principle. I have been amazed to see how often this mistake is made, and I will give examples later.

(8) *Syntax is not Intrinsic to Physics.* One last point: Though every sentence token is indeed a physical entity, it does not follow that syntactical categories are physical categories. Every sentence token is physical, but "sentence token" does not identify a physical natural kind. There are, for example, no acoustic, chemical, gravitational, electromagnetic properties that all and only sentences of English have in common, and that could therefore serve to define the class of sentences of English. This has the consequence that the relations between textuality and intentionality can become complex, as we shall see.

III

I now want to use the apparatus that we have developed in these eight principles and distinctions to demonstrate that many of the controversial issues in literary theory have clear and simple solutions, once these principles are kept in mind. I begin with a simple example. Knapp and Michaels's claim that a sequence of marks found, say, on a beach could not really be words or even examples of language unless produced intentionally. They make this claim as the first step in their attempt to show that all meaning is intended speaker meaning, and that in consequence the meaning of any text is necessarily what the author or authors intended it to mean.

Suppose you found on the beach a set of marks that looked exactly like this:

A slumber did my spirit seal
I had no human fears:
She seemed a thing that could not feel
The touch of earthly years.

Now these marks certainly look as if they constituted a sentence composed of English words, but according to Knapp and Michaels ("Against Theory") there are no words, sentences, or even language unless the marks were produced intentionally. Naturally, they agree, one would seek an explanation of the marks but there would be only two possibilities: "You will either be ascribing these marks to some agent capable of intentions (the living sea, the haunting Wordsworth, etc.), or you will count them as nonintentional effects of mechanical processes (erosion, percolation, etc.). But in the second case—where the marks now seem to be accidents—will they still seem to be words?" Clearly not. They will merely seem to *resemble* words (728). And later: "*It isn't poetry because it isn't* language" (728; my emphasis).

So, according to Knapp and Michaels, what look like words and sentences are not such and are not even language! They announce this remarkable claim as if it were a discovery of considerable theoretical significance. But if what I have said is correct, there cannot be any substance to the issue as to whether or not a given formal structure is a string of words or a sentence and thus an example of *language*. The answer must follow trivially from the definition of wordhood and sentencehood. In linguistics, philosophy and logic words and sentences are standardly defined purely formally or syntactically. That is, words and sentences are defined as formal types that can be instantiated in different physical tokens. It could not be the case that the formal sentence types require the intentional production of tokens in order to be sentences, because there is an infinite number of formal types, and only a finite number of actual human intentions. But from the definition of formal types, it follows trivially that a formal type can be instantiated in a concrete physical token, independently of the question whether or not that token was produced as a result of human intentions. So, on the standard definition of wordhood and sentencehood, it is simply not true that in order for a physical token to be a word or sentence token it must have been produced by an intentional human action.

On the standard definition, in short, Knapp and Michaels's claim is simply false, because they are confusing sentences with utterances. However, they might be proposing an alternative definition for these notions. In that case, the issue cannot be a substantive one: it can only be a question of whether or not one wants to make an intentional utterance part of the criterion for wordhood and sentencehood. So, it follows from what I have just said that what they say is either just a confusion (that is, they are confusing intentionally uttered tokens with tokens); or, if it is not a confusion, then it amounts to a proposal for altering our standard definitions.

Thus, what they present as a *discovery* amounts to either an obvious *falsehood* or a proposal for a *redefinition*. Notice, in this case, that once the distinctions are made clear, the other points fall into place; it then becomes an easy question whether or not some object that has the structure of a word or sentence really is a word or sentence token.

This same criticism of Knapp and Michaels was made by George Wilson in "Again, Theory." In their reply to Wilson, Knapp and Michaels claim that they were not interested in such general issues in the philosophy of language but only in the interpretation of texts, and that they never intended to deny "that the physical features of a set of marks intrinsically determine whether that set of marks is a token of a sentence type in a given language" ("Reply to George Wilson," 188). This answer to Wilson will not do. First, because it is inconsistent with everything they say in "Against Theory"; and, second, because it cuts the ground from under their thesis that all textual meaning is necessarily speaker meaning.

To see these points let us go back to the beach and examine the marks in the sand. In the passages quoted above Knapp and Michaels explicitly deny that the marks in question, unless produced intentionally, constitute words and they even deny that they are an instance of language. They are not poetry because a fortiori they are not even language. Such claims are made throughout the article: "For a sentence like 'My car has run out of gas' even to be recognizable as a sentence, we must have already postulated a speaker and hence an intention" ("Against Theory," 727). And about the sentences on the beach: "what had seemed to be an example of intentionless language was either not intentionless or not language" (728). Again: "Our point is that marks produced by chance are not words at all but only resemble them" (732). So what are we to conclude? Are the intentionless marks on the beach really a sentence of English regardless of how they were produced (as they admit in "Reply to George Wilson"), or are the marks not even words at all, but only resemble words (as they claimed roundly in "Against Theory")? Whatever the answer, the two accounts are inconsistent.

In "Against Theory," as part of their general attack on intentionless meaning, they attack me precisely because I make the distinction between the conventional meaning of a sentence and the intentional meaning of a speech act, between sentence meaning and speaker meaning. I argue in numerous works that the meaning of a speech act is determined by the author's illocutionary intentions, in contrast to the meaning of a sentence, which is determined by the rules of the language of which the sentence is a part. They take some pains to reject this distinction and to argue that I did not go far enough. According to them I was correct in stating that something was only a speech act if produced with illocutionary intentions, but I failed to see that something was only a word, language, and so forth, if it was also produced with speaker's intentions. Indeed, I debated Walter Michaels on precisely this point when he lectured to the Berkeley Cognitive Science Group. A relevant passage in "Against Theory" is worth quoting in full:

> Even a philosopher as committed to the intentional status of language as Searle succumbs to this temptation to think that intention is a theoretical issue. After insisting, in the passage cited earlier, on the inescapability of intention, he goes on to say that "in serious literal speech the sentences are precisely the realizations of the intentions" and that "there need be no *gulf* at all between the illocutionary intention and its expression." *The point, however, is not that there need be no gulf between intention and the meaning of its expression but that there can be no gulf* (my emphasis).
>
> Not only in serious literal speech but in *all* speech what is intended and what is meant are identical. In separating the two Searle imagines the possibility of expression without intention and so, like Hirsch, misses the point of his own claim that when it comes to language there is no getting away from intentionality." Missing this point, and hence imagining the possibility of two different *kinds* of meaning, is more than a theoretical mistake; it is the sort of mistake that makes theory possible. It makes theory possible because it creates the illusion of a choice between alternative methods of interpreting. (729–30)

This passage makes it crystal-clear that they are denying that there can be a gulf between the speaker's intended meaning and the meaning of the sentences that the speaker uses to express that meaning, and thus they are denying that there are "two different *kinds* of meaning," sentence meaning and speaker meaning, just as the earlier quoted passages from this same article make it crystal-clear that they denied that a string of marks found on the beach but produced without any intentionality is a string of "words" or even "language" at all. They cannot consistently say that Searle is wrong to distinguish between the identity criteria of speech acts in terms of speakers' meaning and the identity criteria of sentences in terms of the conventions of a language and at the same time argue that they have accepted this distinction all along.

Nor will it do to retreat from "word" and "language" to "text," as they do in "Reply to George Wilson"; the same sort of problem arises for "text" and even "literary text" that arose for "sentence." That is, if "text" is defined in such a way that the author's illocutionary intentions are essential to the identity of the text and the "meaning of the text" is defined in such a way that it is identical with the author's intentions in the production of the text, then their thesis follows trivially. This is an acceptable definition, and one I used in *Expression and Meaning*[8] but the point I am making now is: However defined, a text consists of words and sentences and they continue to have a *linguistic* meaning, whatever the intentions of the author. Furthermore, it is also possible to define "text" syntactically, as a set of words and sentences, however produced. And in that case the meaning of a text can be examined quite apart from any authorial intentions, because the meaning of the text consists in the meanings of the words and sentences of which it consists.[9]

They announce: "At the center of our account of interpretation is the view that an interest in the meaning of any text—when it really is an interest in the text's meaning and not in something else—can never be anything other than an interest in what the text's author or authors intended it to mean." Construed one way this is trivially false, construed another way it is trivially true. It is possible to regard any text as a collection of words and sentences and to examine its meaning as such. So construed, their view is trivially false. It is also possible—and, I have argued, really essential—to regard a text as the product of speech acts and to insist on understanding the author's intentions in understanding the text. So construed, their view is trivially true. *But once they concede, as they do in "Reply to George Wilson," that "the physical features of a set of marks intrinsically determine whether that set of marks is a token of a sentence type in a given language," then they have already conceded what they claim to be denying; namely, that there are at least two types of meaning, the conventional sentence meaning and the intentional speakers' meaning.*

For this reason, they are mistaken in criticizing E. D. Hirsch for recommending the course they adopt. They criticize him for recommending that interpreters of literary texts should look for the author's intentions, because they claim that "the object of inquiry is *necessarily* the author's intended meaning" ("Reply to George Wilson," 187). They criticize Hirsch for recommending what they regard as inevitable, but on their own account it is not inevitable. They recognize that a set of marks can be a *fully meaningful* token of sentence type in a given language without any intentionality by way of which those marks were produced. But to say that implies that the meaning of such sentences can be examined independently of any intentionality of speakers. This allows for precisely the possibility that they have been claiming to deny; namely, that a text can be regarded as either as a string of sentence tokens and its meaning examined independently of any authorial intent, or a text can be regarded as a product of an intentional speech act and its meaning examined in terms of the intentions of the author.

Many critics interested in textual meaning have been concentrating on the meanings of words and sentences for decades. This may produce bad criticism, but it is not a logical impossibility; or, rather, it is only a logical impossibility given a certain definition of "text." Nor will it evade these inconsistencies to say that they are only interested in the problems of literary theory as an "attempt to govern interpretations of particular texts by appealing to an account of interpretation in general" ("Against Theory," 723), and that they were not interested in these abstruse questions about language in general. This will not do for two reasons: first, they do in fact make claims about language in general and not just about literary texts. Indeed, they even criticize other authors (me, for example) who are not especially concerned with literary texts, and they use examples ("My car ran out of gas") that have no special connection with literary texts. In short their claims about literary interpretation in "Against Theory" were a consequence of more general claims about language. And second, it is impossible to be interested in questions of texts, meaning, interpretation, and so forth, without making certain theoretical assumptions, because all of these notions are defined in terms of certain theoretical principles and distinctions. Once you get the principles and distinctions straight most of the conclusions fall out trivially and unproblematically. Unless they are made explicit, confusion is almost bound to ensue, as I hope their example illustrates.

To summarize, in "Against Theory," Knapp and Michaels make three claims relevant to our present inquiry:

1. Marks are only words, language, sentences, etc., if produced intentionally.
2. Linguistic meaning is entirely a matter of speakers' intentions. There

are not two kinds of meaning—sentence meaning and speaker meaning. There is only intentional speaker meaning.

3. For this reason interest in the meaning of a text is necessarily an interest in the author's intention. There is no other possibility.

I have argued as follows: on the standard account of linguistic meaning as articulated in the first half of this article all of these claims are obviously false. It is important to see, however, that once Knapp and Michaels concede, as they do in "Reply to George Wilson," that it is possible to construe something as a sentence token, even though it has not been produced intentionally (contrary to claim 1), then claims 2 and 3 collapse; once you concede that something is a sentence token, you concede that it has a linguistic meaning. But then once you allow that sentence tokens have linguistic meaning independently of their intentional production, then you allow that any literary text can be construed as a set of sentences and these sentences have a linguistic meaning. Like Hirsch's claims, their claim amounts to a recommendation that we should concentrate on the intended author's meaning. But they have not shown that any such concentration is necessary or inevitable.

Though claim 1 of Knapp and Michaels is not acceptable as it stands, there is a much deeper truth underlying it. From the fact that every syntactical token is a physical entity, such as an acoustic blast or a physical mark, it does not follow, nor is it the case that, syntactical categories are categories of physics. Notions such as "sentence of English" cannot be denied in terms of, for example, acoustics or mechanics. There are no acoustic properties, for example, that all and only English sentences have in common. There is a deep reason for this, and that is that the entire system of syntax only exists relative to human intentionality, including the Network and the Background. It is only given a knowledge of the rules of the grammar and the Background ability to use that knowledge that there can be such a thing as a formal or syntactical definition of sentencehood in the first place. So, though Knapp and Michaels are mistaken in thinking that every sentence token requires an intentional production in order to be a sentence, they are right if they think that intentionality is crucial to the existence of syntax as a system.

IV

I now want to use the results of my discussion of Knapp and Michaels to draw some general conclusions regarding issues in literary theory. A recurring controversy in literary theory has been over the question "What is the role of the author's intention in determining the meaning of a text?" In the history of this subject, a series of competing answers has been proposed to this question, sometimes giving rise to polemical disputes about the relative merits of the different answers. What I want to suggest is: In many cases the different answers are not competing answers to the same question, but noncompeting answers to quite different questions. So, for example, if the question is, "Does the author's intention determine the meaning of the text?" the answer will depend on what criteria of identity we adopt for "the text." Do we count the sequence of sentence tokens that instantiate particular sentence types as constituting the text? If what constitutes a text is simply a sequence of sentences, then the answer to the question has to be no. It does not matter what intentions the author had when he produced particular tokens of those types, because if we are just looking at the tokens as instantiations of sentence types, and if sentence meaning is conventional, it follows, again trivially, that the sentences of the text have a meaning that is quite independent of any authorial intention. Once the question is made precise in this way, it is easily answered.

But of course, there is another question, and that is, "Does the author's illocutionary intention determine what speech acts he or she is performing; that is, what intentional speech acts he or she is performing in the production of the text?" Does authorial intention determine speaker's meaning? To this question, I hope it is obvious that the answer is yes. The author's intention determines which intentional act the author is performing. So the answer to this question has to be trivially and obviously yes in the same way that the answer to the previous question has to be trivially and obviously no. And of course, there are still further questions that we could ask.

A third question could be "Does the author's intention determine how the text is interpreted; does it determine the meaning that the hearer understands?" I hope it is obvious that the answer to this question is no. Notoriously, authors are understood in ways that are quite different from what they actually intended.

Now these three different claims—that meaning is a linguistic property of the text, that meaning is a matter of authorial intention, and that meaning is in the reader—certainly look like competing theories. The first view says that the meaning of the text is strictly a matter of what the words and sentences mean in the language. This, I take it, is the formalist view of the New Critics. The second view says that the meaning of the text is entirely determined by authorial intention, and this is the view of Knapp and Michaels in "Against Theory." The third view says that the meaning of the text is entirely a matter of the reader's response to it, and this is (or was) the view of Stanley Fish *(Is There a Text in This Class?)* and the so-called reader-response theories of criticism.

Now, these certainly look like competing answers to the question "What is the meaning of the text?" And in particular, they look like competing answers to the question "What is the role of authorial intention in determining the meaning of the text?" But if what I have said is correct, the appearance of disagreement is at least partly an illusion. Once this question is made sufficiently precise, it will be seen that there are three different questions to which three different answers are being offered.

Well, one might say, "So much the better. We welcome this ecumenism and perhaps everybody can go home happy." The problem, however, is that in the literature on this subject, very strong claims are made on behalf of these different answers, and these claims tend to exceed what has in fact been proved. For example, Fish in *Is There a Text in This Class?* makes the following statement, "Whereas I had once agreed with my predecessors on the need to control interpretation lest it overwhelm and obscure texts, facts, authors, and intentions, I now believe that interpretation is the source of texts, facts, authors, and intentions" (16). I am afraid that this sentence contains an exaggeration. From the correct observation that the effect that a text has on a reader or hearer is not always determined either by the literal meaning of the sentences or by the intentions, conscious or unconscious, of the speaker or author, it does not follow that, for example, texts, facts, authors, and intentions have their source in interpretations. The claim is absurd. The fact that, say, Mount Everest has snow and ice near its summit, is in no way dependent on anybody's interpretations. And as far as texts and authors and intentions are concerned, I have on frequent occasions been an author, I have created texts, and I have had intentions. Often communication broke down because, to a greater or lesser extent, I failed to communicate my intentions, or they were unclear even to me, or my intentions were poorly expressed. But the interpretations were the source of neither text nor author nor intention. My existence as an author and the existence of my texts and intentions were in no way dependent on the understandings and misunderstandings that my readers my have experienced in encountering my texts.

Similarly, it seems to me Knapp and Michaels make claims that are much too strong. They claim to have shown that the meaning of a text is entirely determined by the intentions of the author. But, as we have seen, the meaning of the speech act performed in the production of the text should not be confused with the meaning of the actual sentences that are constitutive of the text. The sentences have a conventional meaning independent of whatever authorial intentions they may have been uttered with.

V

I now turn to the most obscure of these cases, Derrida's attempt to "deconstruct" the notion of meaning that occurs, for example, in the theory of speech acts, and in particular the idea that the intentions of the speaker suffice to determine the meaning of the utterance, and hence the identity of the speech act. The argument is not easy to summarize. In part, at least, it is the mirror image of the claim made by Knapp and Michaels. They claim that something is not even a text unless it is produced with authorial intention. Derrida claims that since the very same text can function totally detached from any authorial intention, the author cannot control the meaning of his utterance. Because the sign is subject to "iterability" and "citationality" the horizon of the author's intention is insufficient to control the free play of the signifiers.

The "argument," if I may so describe it, occurs at various places in his writings but since it is never stated clearly as an attempt to present a valid argument, the best way to convey it is to quote some representative passages and then summarize its drift.

> The sign is constituted in its identity as mark by its iterability. ("Signature," 180)

> The possibility of its (the mark) being repeated *another* time—breaches, divides, expropriates the "ideal" plenitude or self-presence of intention, of meaning (to say) and, a fortiori, of all adequation between meaning and saying. Iterability alters, contaminating parasitically what it identifies and enables to repeat "itself"; it leaves us no choice but to mean (to say) something that is (already, always, also) other than what we mean (to say), to say something other than what we say *and* would have wanted to say, to understand something other than . . . etc." (*Limited Inc.,* 61–62)

Again,

> My communication must be repeatable, iterable, in the absolute absence of the receiver or of any empirically determinable collectivity of receivers. (*Limited Inc.*, 7)

Such passages raise two questions: First, why does Derrida suppose that intentions have what he calls " 'ideal' plenitude or self-presence"? In my view intentions could never have such mysterious properties, because intentions can never function in isolation. Intentions—along with other biological phenomena such as beliefs, desires, and so forth—function only within a highly contingent Network of other intentional states and against a preintentional Background of capacities. So for the purpose of this discussion, which has to do with his criticisms of my views, we just have to ignore the claim about ideal self-presence. He simply misunderstands my position. The second question is, What does he mean by "iterability"? Here is part of his answer,

> Let us not forget that "iterability" does not signify simply, as Searle seems to think, repeatability of the same, but rather alterability of this same idealized in the singularity of the event, for instance, in this or that speech act. (*Limited Inc.*, 119)

Furthermore, he writes,

> The iterability of the mark does not leave any of the philosophical oppositions which govern the idealizing abstraction intact (for instance, serious/non-serious, literal/metaphorical or sarcastic, ordinary/parasitical, strict/non-strict, etc.). Iterability blurs a priori the dividing-line that passes between these opposed terms, "corrupting" it if you like, contaminating it parasitically, qua limit. . . . Once it is iterable, to be sure, a mark marked with a supposedly "positive" value ("serious," "literal," etc.) can be mimed, cited, transformed into an "exercise" or into "literature," even into a "lie"—that is, it can be made to carry its other, its "negative" double. But iterability is also, by the same token, the condition of the values said to be "positive." The simple fact is that this condition of possibility is structurally divided or "differing-deferring" [*différante*]. (*Limited Inc.*, 70).

These passages occur in a polemic that Derrida wrote against me, as well as against J. L. Austin. The argument is so confused that for a long time I could not believe he was actually advancing it. But such passages as those quoted exhibit his confusions clearly. Here is the argument in summary:

> There are a series of distinctions made by analytic philosophers, the distinction between metaphorical and literal, between true and false, between meaningful and meaningless, between felicitous and infelicitous, between parasitical and nonparasitical, etc. All of these distinctions are undermined ("corrupted," "contaminated") by the phenomenon of iterability. Here is how it is done. Any mark or sign must be iterable, but because of this iterability, the sign or mark can always be disrupted from its point of origin and used for some completely different purpose. What was true can be false. What was literal can be metaphorical. What was felicitous can be infelicitous. What was meaningful can be meaningless, etc. Therefore, all of the original distinctions are undermined. Furthermore, this undermining cannot be avoided since iterability is the condition of possibility of something being a mark in the first place.

What is wrong with this argument? Roughly speaking, everything. Most important, from the fact that different tokens of a sentence type can be uttered on different occasions with different intentions; that is, different speaker meanings, nothing of any significance follows about the original speaker meaning of the original utterance token. Nor does anything follow that contaminates the basic distinctions which I have mentioned earlier. None of these distinctions are "contaminated" or "corrupted" or anything of the sort by the possibility of producing different tokens of the same type with different speaker meanings. Since the issues are of some interest and since Derrida's argument reveals a neglect of the distinctions I cited earlier, I shall go through it slowly by stating my views in contrast to his.

On my view, if I say, "It is hot in here" or "Give me a hamburger," it is up to me, *modulo* the Network and the Background, what I mean. If I say, "It is hot in here," and I mean, "It is hot in here," then that is a matter of my illocutionary intentions. If I say "It is hot in here," and mean ironically that it is cold in here, that is up to me as well. Of course, on my view I can't say just anything and mean just anything. There is a complex set of relations between sentence meaning and speaker meaning, and all meaning and intentionality depend on relations to the Network and the Background.

It is a consequence of my view that meaning and intentionality have a much more radical form of indeterminacy than is conceivable to Derrida, because they have no independent functioning at all: they only function relative to a nonrepresentational Background. However given a set of Background capacities and a Network of intentionality, including a shared mastery of a common linguistic apparatus between speaker and hearer, meaning and communication can be completely determinate. When I complain about the heat or order a hamburger, I am, in general, able to do so without ambiguity or vagueness, much less indeterminacy. Within the constraints set by the condition of the possibility on the speech act, I can say what I want to say and mean what I want to mean.

This account preserves intact the basic distinctions between metaphorical/literal, true/false, etc. Derrida thinks that iterability refutes this account. He thinks that because marks and signs are iterable, that is repeatable and alterable on subsequent occasions, that somehow or other the original speaker has lost control of his utterance and that he therefore has no choice "but to mean (to say) something that is (already, always, also) other than what we mean," etc, etc. I believe that his argument is a massive tissue of confusions, and that if we apply the distinctions that I have been trying to elucidate, his various points simply dissolve. Suppose I say, "It's hot in here," meaning: it's hot in here. Now what follows about my speaker meaning from the fact that the sentence type, of which my utterance was a token, is, in his sense, iterable and citable? Nothing whatever follows.

I uttered a sentence token that exemplified a particular sentence type. My utterance had a sentence meaning that is determined by the operation of the principles of compositionality operating over the conventional elements that composed it, including such structural elements as intonation contour, word order, and sentence boundary. My utterance had a particular speaker's meaning, which in this case coincided with sentence meaning. All of this apparatus functions within the Network and against the Background. If communication is successful, I will have succeeded in performing a serious, literal, nondefective speech act. What follows from the fact that I or somebody else might take a completely *different token* of the same sentence *type* and do something completely different with it? To repeat, nothing whatever follows. The intentionality of the speech act covers exactly and only that particular speech act. The fact that someone might perform *another* speech act with a *different* token of the same type (or even another speech act, with the same token) has no bearing whatever on the role of speaker's utterance meaning in the determination of the speech act.

Derrida holds the bizarre view that speech-act theory is somehow committed to the view that the intentionality of the particular token speech act must somehow control every subsequent occurrence of tokens of the same sentence types. Since the idea that speakers' intentionality might achieve such a thing is quite out of the question, he thinks he has uncovered a weakness in the theory of speech acts. But speech-act theory—my version or anybody else's—is not committed to any such view and his failure to grasp this derives from his failure to grasp the type-token distinction, the sentence-utterance distinction, and the speaker meaning–sentence meaning distinction. It is just a simple confusion to suppose that from the fact that I say something and mean something by what I say, and somebody else might use other tokens of those very words and sentences to mean something completely different, it follows that somehow or other I have lost control of my speech act.

I will give one more example. Someone once wrote a poem that began, "A slumber did my spirit seal . . ." Now suppose I decide I want to use that line to call my dog with. "A slumber did my spirit seal!" I shout around the neighborhood until my dog comes home. Is that supposed to show that Wordsworth has lost control of *his* meaning, of *his* speaker meaning?

There are lots of places where Derrida makes this mistake, but one of the clearest is in his book *Spurs*. There he discusses the following example. The German for "I have forgotten my umbrella," with quotation marks around it, was found in Nietzsche's *Nachlaß* (i.e., among his unpublished manuscripts). The discussion of this token occupies several pages of Derrida's book. I shall not quote all of it, but enough, I hope, to give the flavor of the text. He begins with an epistemic claim.

> It might have been a sample picked up somewhere or overheard here or there. Perhaps it was the note for some phrase to be written here or there. There is no infallible way of knowing the occasion of this sample or what it could have been later grafted onto. We will never know for sure what Nietzsche wanted to say or do when he noted these words, not even that he actually wanted anything. (*Spurs,* 123)

So far, this seems correct. But so far, it is merely an epistemic point. There are facts of the matter for which we lack evidence, and consequently, we cannot know them for sure. But Derrida tries to derive ontological conclusions from this epistemic point. He writes:

> The reminder [*restance*] that is this "I have forgotten my umbrella" is not caught up in any circular trajectory. It knows of no proper itinerary which would lead from its beginning to its end and back again, nor does its movement admit of any center. Because it is structurally liberated from any living meaning [*vouloir dire vivant*], it is always possible that it means nothing at all or that it has no decidable meaning. There is no end to its parodying play with meaning, grafted here and there, beyond any contextual body or finite code. It is quite possible that that unpublished piece, precisely because it is readable as a piece of writing, should remain forever secret. But not because it withholds some secret. Its secret is rather the possibility that indeed it might have no secret, that it might only be pretending to be simulating some hidden truth within its folds. Its limit is not only stipulated by its structure but is in fact intimately confused with it. The hermeneut cannot but be provoked and disconcerted by its play. (*Spurs,* 131–33)

It is not surprising that the "hermeneut" is disconcerted, because the hermeneut in question does not know enough philosophy of language to give an intelligent account of the fragment. There are a rather large number of mistakes in the passage, and I will simply list the three most obvious.

1. The German sentence type has a conventional meaning in German. Given the Network and the Background, the interpretation of sentence meaning is quite determinate. In a different Background culture, where all umbrellas were made of chocolate and eaten for dessert after use in rainstorms, the literal sentence meaning could be understood differently (it might mean: I have forgotten the taste of my umbrella); but given the existing cultural, biological, and linguistic situation in the late nineteenth century, the literal interpretations are unproblematic. (Do I have to go through them?) It is, by the way, only because we know the meaning of the German sentence that we are so confident of its translation into French and English.

2. The sentence token actually found in Nietzsche's *Nachlaß* exemplifies the type, and consequently, shares with it this conventional meaning. It is just a mistake for Derrida to say, "it is always possible that it means nothing at all." Or rather, it is more than a mistake, because he has no idea what the "it" is of which he says that it might "mean nothing at all" (type? token? utterance? speech act?) At the very least he is confusing sentence

meaning with speaker meaning. That is, from the fact that Nietzsche might not have meant anything by the production of the token (speaker meaning) it does not follow that the token might "mean nothing at all" (sentence meaning).

3. For accidental historical reasons, we do not know what if anything, Nietzsche intended by this sentence token. In particular, we do not know if he intended it as a speech act or if he was simply considering the sentence itself. But from the epistemological limitations, from our lack of evidence, nothing whatever follows about the ontology. If Nietzsche had a determinable speaker's meaning, then he had it. Whether or not we can know it is of biographical rather than theoretical interest. To put this point quite simply, the lack of empirical evidence has no bearing whatever on the issue of indeterminacy or undecidability in principle. Indeterminacy and undecidability in principle are problems that arise *given perfect knowledge,* given that all of the epistemic questions have been solved. It is simply a confusion to apply these notions in an epistemic fashion.[10] Derrida is here confusing epistemology with ontology.

In short, Derrida fails to show that the occurrence of this fragment in Nietzsche's *Nachlaß* is of any theoretical interest whatever. Once all the distinctions are brought to bear, the only remaining difficulties are epistemic; consequently, though they may be of practical importance to biographers, historians, and critics, they are of no theoretical interest in developing a theory of language. The idea that there is some mystery or some tremendously obscure and difficult point that will disconcert the hermeneut only shows that the hermeneut is confused to begin with.

My impression is that a fair amount—not all of course, but a fair amount—of what passes for passionate controversies and deeply held divisions within literary theory is in fact a matter of confusions having to do, as I said earlier, not with competing answers to the same question, but with noncompeting answers to different questions, different questions that happen to be expressed in the same vocabulary because the authors are not making the distinctions that I am urging. In the most extreme cases, it seems to me that a lot of what passes for profundity and enormous obscurity and insight into deep and mysterious matters is in fact dependent on a series of rather simple confusions. These confusions derive in turn from the lack of a theoretical apparatus within which to pose and answer the questions that preoccupy us. No doubt the apparatus I have proposed is in various ways inadequate, but without some such apparatus we cannot clearly pose or intelligibly answer the questions. Once those confusions are sorted out, then much of the pretension dissolves like so much mist on a hot day.

VI

I have suggested that a good deal of confusion in literary theory derives from a lack of awareness of familiar principles and results. How is this possible? Well, partly it derives from the hyperspecialization of contemporary intellectual life. It is not easy for someone specializing in twentieth century American literature, for example, to become knowledgeable about the invention of the predicate calculus by Gottlob Frege in Germany in the late nineteenth century, for example. But the normal ignorance due to disciplinary boundaries is aggravated by the fact that among the people in literary studies who have written on issues in linguistics and the philosophy of language and have been taken as authorities on these issues, there are some that don't seem to know very much about these subjects. I earlier cited some mistakes that Derrida seems to be making, and I believe these are typical of deconstructionist authors. I believe the mistakes derive not only from neglect of the principles I have mentioned but also from a general lack of familiarity with the recent history of the philosophy of language, as well as recent linguistics. "The philosophy of language," as we now use that expression, only begins in the late nineteenth century with Frege, and continues through the works of Russell, Moore, Wittgenstein, Carnap, Tarski, Quine, and others right up to the present day. Earlier philosophers often wrote about language, but their contribution to contemporary discussion in the philosophy of language is minimal, unlike their contribution to most other areas of philosophy. As far as I can tell, Derrida knows next to nothing of the works of Frege, Russell, Wittgenstein, etc.; and one main reason for his incomprehension of Austin's work, as well as of mine, is that he does not see how we are situated in, and responding to, that history, from Frege to Wittgenstein. When Derrida writes about the philosophy of language he refers typically to Rousseau and Condillac, not to mention Plato. And his idea of a "modern linguist" is Benveniste or even Saussure. All of these are important and distinguished thinkers, and their work should certainly not be neglected, but you will not understand what is happening today if that is where your understanding stops. Derrida is himself a very *traditional* philosopher in a sense that one can state briefly but precisely by saying that his work proceeds from assumptions that are pre-Wittgensteinian. For example, only a pre-Wittgensteinian philosopher could have made those remarks I quoted at the beginning of this article about the purity of concepts.

The fact that he is a traditional philosopher in this sense has three consequences for the present discussion. First, when he sees the failures of the traditional assumptions, he thinks something is lost or threatened. He thinks for example, that the possibility of misunderstandings creates some special problem for the theory of speech acts beyond the commonsense problem of trying to figure out what people mean when they talk. Furthermore, in desperation, he invents new jargon to try to deal with the failures of the old. "Iterability" and "différance" are just two examples. But this jargon does not enable him to overcome the foundationalist assumptions of the philosophical tradition. At best they provide a temporary disguise for its failures.

Second, in all of his quite lengthy attacks on speech-act theory, both mine and others', he still cannot grasp that this work does not proceed from his traditional philosophical assumptions. He finds it literally incomprehensible ("stupefying" is his word) that I do not accept certain traditional assumptions. For example, he thinks that if I use the notion of intentionality I must be engaged in some Husserlian foundationalist project; he supposes that where I make distinctions, the very enterprise must exclude the possibility of marginal cases; and he has nothing to say about my theory of the Background and its importance for the philosophy of language. Since he appears to know next to nothing of the history of the philosophy of language over the past hundred years he has not grasped that in everything I write I take these works, and especially the works of the later Wittgenstein, *for granted.* One of my many problems is: Given that certain traditional foundationalist approaches to problems in philosophy are now more or less out of the question, how does one now, in a post-Wittgensteinian era, construct a theory of mind and language? Derrida, working from assumptions that are pre-Wittgensteinian, seems unable to comprehend what it would be like to construct a post-Wittgensteinian theory of speech acts or intentionality. He thinks any such theory must be traditional in the way that, for example, Husserl was a traditional philosopher. For these reasons, perhaps the best way to answer Derrida would be not to provide a list of his mistakes, misunderstandings, and omissions, but to expose the traditionalist assumptions that make them inevitable.

Third, because of their lack of familiarity with the advances made and the distinctions drawn during the past century or so, Derrida and other deconstructionist authors tend to lack credibility in contemporary philosophy and linguistics. In deconstructionist writing in general and Derrida in particular, the intellectual limitations of the background knowledge does not prevent a certain straining of the prose, an urge to achieve a rhetorical effect that might be described as the move from the exciting to the banal and back again. The way it works is this: Derrida advances some astounding thesis, for example, writing came before speaking, nothing exists outside of texts, meanings are undecidable. When challenged, he says "You have misunderstood me, I only meant such and such," where such and such is some well-known platitude. Then when the platitude is acknowledged, he assumes that its acknowledgment constitutes an acceptance of the original exciting thesis. I conclude by illustrating this rhetorical move with three examples.

The first and most obvious is his claim that writing ("archewriting," which "communicates with the vulgar concept of writing") comes before speech, that written language precedes spoken language. "I shall try to show later that there is no linguistic sign before writing" (*Of Grammatology,* 14), he promises. But the claim that writing precedes speaking is obviously false, as any historical linguist can attest. However, of course, Derrida does not mean this. What he means in large part is that many of the features of written speech are also features of spoken language. When this point is acknowledged, he then supposes that he has demonstrated the original thesis. From the exciting to the banal and back again.

A second case concerns his discussion of meaning. Derrida is notorious for the view that meanings are unstable. He even uses words such as "undecidable" and "relative indeterminacy" (*Limited Inc.,* 144–45) in these discussions. This view has the consequence, for example, that all readings are to some degree misreadings, that all understandings are misunderstandings, etc. But when challenged he tells us that he did not mean any of that at all. Now he says that he meant to remark only that "the essential and irreducible *possibility* of *mis*understanding or of "*in*felicity" must be taken into account in the description of those values said to be positive" (*Limited Inc.,* 147). So the original daring thesis now amounts to the platitude that misunderstandings and infelicities are always possible. But this does not seem to prevent him or his followers from continuing to use the original formulations.

A third example of the same rhetorical maneuver is his claim that nothing exists outside of texts: "Il n'y a pas de hors-texte." Here is what he now says about it:

> *Il n'y a pas de hors-texte* "means nothing else: there is nothing outside contexts." (*Limited Inc.*, 136)

So the original preposterous thesis that there is nothing outside of texts is now converted into the banality that everything exists in some context or other. As Austin once said, "There is the part where you give it out and the part where you take it back."

Notes

1. I gather that Fish no longer believes this. But it doesn't matter for my present discussion, which is designed to use this and other examples to illustrate certain general themes.

2. I have discussed these points in much greater detail in other writings. See especially my "Literal Meaning," "The Background of Meaning," "The Word Turned Upside Down," *Intentionality,* and *The Rediscovery of the Mind.*

3. For brevity I state this position baldly. I argue for it in more detail elsewhere, especially in *Intentionality.*

4. The first philosopher known to me who had something like the idea of the Background was Hume. He saw that rationality depended on custom, practice, habit, etc. The philosopher most impressed and most unhinged by the radical contingency of the Background was Nietzsche. An important text on the Background is Wittgenstein's *On Certainty.*

5. There are different ways of characterizing this distinction. The standard characterization in the logic textbooks is to say that when a word is mentioned and not used, the word itself does not actually occur at all; rather, its proper name occurs. So, for example, if I write "Berkeley" with quotes around it, I have produced the proper name of the word and not the word itself. I think this characterization is mistaken. I think that the quotation marks do not create a new word, but rather indicate that in the quoted occurrence the word is being mentioned and not used. In my view, the word does not suddenly get swallowed up into a proper name of itself just by my writing quotation marks around it. But many respectable philosophers (Quine, for example) think that the word "Berkeley" no more occurs in this sentence than the word cat appears in the word "catastrophe." They would agree that the sequence of letters occurs, but the word itself does not occur; only its proper name occurs. I do not accept this part of the standard textbook account of the use-mention distinction, but in any case, it is crucial to make clear that there is a distinction between the use and the mention of expressions. For further discussion, see my *Speech Acts,* especially chap. 4.

6. The rules have to be recursive. By itself, compositionality does not imply generative capacity.

7. My *Expression and Meaning* is in large part devoted to explaining these relations.

8. In analyzing the status of *fictional* texts, I wrote: "There used to be a school of literary critics who thought one should not consider the intentions of the author when examining a work of fiction. Perhaps there is some level of intention at which this extraordinary view is plausible; perhaps one should not consider an author's ulterior motives when analyzing his work, but at the most basic level it is absurd to suppose a critic can completely ignore the intentions of the author, since even so much as to identify a text as a novel, a poem, or even as a text is already to make a claim about the author's intentions" (*Expression and Meaning,* 66).

9. In "Against Theory 2," Knapp and Michaels consider the possibility of defining textual identity on syntactical grounds alone, but reject it for the strange reason that "if this criterion of textual identity were applied consistently, then any text could mean anything; indeed, any text could mean anything any other text could mean" (58). This is not true. If the syntax of a sentence is defined relative to a language construed synchronically, it is simply not true that, for example, the sentence "The cat is on the mat" could mean anything. In some other language it might mean something else, but in present-day English it has a quite definite meaning.

10. It is no accident that Gödel's famous incompleteness proof is given in a paper about undecidable *sentences* ("Über formal Unentscheidbare Sätze der *Principia Mathematica* und Verwandter System, I," 173–98) because he shows that in *Principia*-type systems there are true assertions that are not theorems. The point has nothing to do with lack of evidence.

References

Culler, J. *On Deconstruction, Theory and Criticism after Structuralism.* Ithaca: Cornell University Press, 1982.

Derrida, J. *Limited Inc.* Evanston: Northwestern University Press, 1988.

———. *Of Grammatology.* Baltimore: Johns Hopkins University Press, 1976.

———. "Signature Event Context." In *Glyph.* Baltimore: Johns Hopkins University Press, 1977, 172–208.

———. *Spurs Nietzsche's Styles.* Chicago: University of Chicago Press, 1978.

Fish, S. *Is There a Text in This Class?* Cambridge: Harvard University Press, 1980.

Gödel, K. "Über formal Unentscheidbare Sätze der *Principia Mathematica* und Verwandter Systeme, I." *Monatshefte für Mathematik und Physik* 38 (1931): 173–98.

Knapp, S., and W. B. Michaels. "Against Theory." *Critical Inquiry* 8 (summer 1982): 723–42.

———. "Against Theory 2: Hermeneutics and Deconstruction." *Critical Inquiry* 14 (autumn 1987): 49–68.

———. "Reply to George Wilson." *Critical Inquiry* 19 (autumn 1992): 186–93.

———. "A Reply to Our Critics." *Critical Inquiry* 9 (June 1983): 790–800.

Searle, J. R. *Speech Acts.* Cambridge: Cambridge University Press, 1969.

———. "Literal Meaning." *Erkenntniss* 13 (1978).

———. *Expression and Meaning.* Cambridge: Cambridge University Press, 1979.

———. "The Background of Meaning." In *Speech Act Theory and Pragmatics,* edited by J. R. Searle, F. Kiefer, and M. Bierwisch. Dordrecht, Holland: Reidel, 1980.

———. "The Word Turned Upside Down." *New York Review of Books* (27 October 1983): 74–79.

———. *Intentionality: An Essay in the Philosophy of Mind*. Cambridge: Cambridge University Press, 1983.
———. *The Rediscovery of the Mind*. Cambridge: MIT Press, 1992.
Wilson, G. "Again, Theory: On Speaker's Meaning, Linguistic Meaning, and the Meaning of a Text." *Critical Inquiry* 19 (autumn 1992): 164–85.

Relevant Publications by John Searle

The Rediscovery of the Mind. Cambridge: MIT Press, 1992.
Foundations of Illocutionary Logic. Cambridge: Cambridge University Press, 1985.
Minds, Brains and Science. Cambridge: Harvard University Press, 1984.
Intentionality: An Essay in the Philosophy of Mind. Cambridge: Cambridge University Press, 1983.
Speech Act Theory and Pragmatics (editor). Lancaster: D. Reidel, 1980.
Expression and Meaning: Studies in the Theory of Speech Acts. Cambridge: Cambridge University Press, 1979.
The Campus War. New York: World, 1971.
The Philosophy of Language (editor). Oxford: Oxford University Press, 1971.
Speech Acts: An Essay in the Philosophy of Language. Cambridge: Cambridge University Press, 1969.

"Literary Theory and Its Discontents." *New Literary History* 25 (summer 1994): 637–65.
"Consciousness, Unconsciousness and Intentionality." *Philosophical Topics* 17 (1989): 193–209.
"Meaning, Communication and Representation." In *Philosophical Grounds of Rationality, Intentionality, Categories and Ends*, edited by R. Grandy and R. Warner. Oxford: Clarendon University Press, 1986.
"The Word Turned Upside Down." Review of J. Culler's *On Deconstruction*. *New York Review of Books* (27 October 1983).
"Reiterating the Differences: A Reply to Derrida." *Glyph* 1 (1977): 198–208.
"The Logical Status of Fictional Discourse." *New Literary History* 6 (1975): 319–32.

7

The Cultural Materialist Attack on Artistic Unity and the Problem of Ideological Criticism

Richard Levin

Both the no-nonsense style and incisive strategies of critique employed by Richard Levin, professor of English at the State University of New York, Stony Brook, have made him a controversial figure. These qualities can be found in many an essay on contemporary critical trends that extend the kind of questioning he initiated in the 1979 New Readings vs. Old Plays. *Although a political liberal (a title he explicitly claims along with membership in the ACLU and NOW), he has especially been seen as a political conservative by a number of those critics who have committed themselves to one or another contemporary theory because of its presumed efficacy as a weapon against real social evils. However, if one of Levin's principles stands above the others, it is the insistence that political utility is not a criterion of truth and that theories that assert the way things are must be based on evidence that they are in fact that way—at least as viewed from a specific perspective. The corollary to this is that theories that do not correspond to human experience, however convenient for the purposes of a particular argument, are unlikely to produce the beneficial effects their wielders envisage. Levin's essays thus tend to ask, in one way or another, What reason is there to accept such and such an assertion? What would one also have to believe to accept this proposition? Where would strict adherence to this theory lead? One direction in which such critiques of ideologically motivated critical theories leads is toward the reasoned pluralism this essay champions.*

I should begin by defining the term "ideological" in my title since it now has several different meanings. In the most common usage, "ideology" refers to a consciously held set of beliefs or creed, usually in the social or political realm. In this sense an ideological approach to Shakespeare would be one that is deliberately constructed from such a creed in order to serve it, and the two most important examples today are Marxist and feminist criticism. But Marxist and feminist critics often use the term in another sense to refer to people's perception of themselves and society, which usually reflects beliefs that are not consciously articulated; in this second sense of course all human beings have an ideology, whether they are aware of it or not, and therefore all critical approaches are ideological, including (as these critics never tire of telling us) those that claim not to be.[1] Some Marxists have gone even further to argue that, since ideology in this sense is a "false consciousness," a misperception of reality serving the class system, while the Marxist perception of reality is "scientific" and true, then all critical approaches except their own are ideological. But my purpose here is not to deal with these questions in the abstract. Instead I shall limit myself to one of the most prominent groups of ideological critics in the first sense, the new Marxists or cultural materialists and feminists associated with them, and will focus on one of their most prominent projects, the attack on artistic unity, drawing most of my examples from their criticism of Shakespeare. But I believe many of my remarks will also apply to other fields of literature and to other aspects of cultural materialism, and even to other ideological approaches, and in my conclusion I shall address what seems to be the most basic problem posed by the role of ideology (in this first sense) in literary criticism.

Now anyone who has been imbricated with or only interpellated into the current ensemble of hermeneutic theorizing and praxis must be aware that the concept of artistic unity is in very serious trouble. For about ten years it has been subjected to a sustained attack by a large number of critics loosely grouped under the name "poststructuralist," with the cultural materialists in the van; and because their arguments have gone virtually unchallenged, there now seems to be a widespread impression, even among critics of other persuasions, that the concept has been invalidated and can no longer be used if one does not wish to be considered hopelessly out of date. It would seem, then, that the time has come to subject this attack itself to what is now called an interrogation, which will result in a qualified defense of the concept of unity. This interrogation of the cultural materialists' attack on unity must begin by recognizing that it is part of a much larger attack that they, along with other poststructuralists, have mounted on what they refer to as the "formalist" approach—primarily the old New Criticism—and on the philosophy of "liberal humanism" that is supposed to underlie it. Indeed they often define themselves in terms of their opposition to a catalogue of fallacious beliefs attributed by them to this approach and its philosophy, which invariably includes the belief in unity (or "organic unity").[2] Before closing I will also present a qualified defense of the formalist approach itself; but now I want to turn to the attack on artistic unity.

Most commonly the cultural materialists assert that this unity is a fraud perpetrated by formalist criticism. According to Terry Eagleton, for example, its "arbitrary prejudice" that "literary works form organic wholes" is imposed on the text: "many suggestive frictions and collisions of meaning must be blandly 'processed' by literary criticism to induce [the texts] to . . . constitute harmonious wholes."[3] Francis Barker and Peter Hulme insist it is "meaningless to talk about the unity of any given text—supposedly the intrinsic quality of all 'works of art,' " since materialist criticism "demonstrate[s] that, athwart its alleged unity, the text is in fact marked and fissured by the interplay of the discourses that constitute it"; and in their reading of *The Tempest* they find that "the play's unity is constructed only by shearing off some of its . . . complexities and explaining them away," which conceals "the text's actual diversity."[4] "If new criticism would see *Macbeth* as a seamless web of images," says Peter Stallybrass, "we may note that, on the contrary, it is constructed by montage. . . . Unifying the play's images, then, tends to efface the play's conflicting registers."[5] Malcolm Evans calls textual unity "the fetish of humanist criticism," and claims it is a "fictional unity" that must be "torn apart" to show "the discourses and social contradictions that constitute the text."[6] Graham Holderness contrasts "orthodox criticism" of Shakespeare's plays, which seeks to "ratify the seamless unity of [their] ideology rather than analysing its innate incoherences," with "a materialist criticism [that] will discover, not . . . a serene harmony, but the stresses and tensions, the discords and contradictions" within them.[7] Jean Howard explains that literary texts are not "organically unified wholes," since "only when their heterogeneity is suppressed by a criticism committed to the idea of organic unity do they seem to reveal a unitary ideological perspective," and so recommends "the project of fracturing the unified surface of the text to let the multiplicity of its social voices be heard."[8] In formalism, Catherine Belsey says, "the quest is for the unity of the work, its coherence, a way of repairing any deficiencies in consistency . . . [and] smoothing out contradiction, . . . thus effectively censoring any elements in [it] which come into collision with the dominant ideology."[9] Jonathan Dollimore asserts that the formalists' "appeal to this notion of structural coherence [in Jacobean plays] has in practice neutralised the destabilising effect of contradictory dramatic *process*" by "effacing it," and thus "Brecht's claim that bourgeois theatre aims at 'smoothing over contradictions, at creating false harmony' . . . surely applies equally" to these critics.[10] Other statements of this sort could be cited.

Sometimes the perpetration of this fraud of artistic unity is attributed not to formalist criticism but to the literary text itself. (Anyone who wonders why the blame should be placed on these texts rather than their authors obviously has not yet heard of The Death of the Author, which occurred twenty years ago in France under the auspices of Roland Barthes and Michel Foucault; the belief that literature is written by "autonomous individuals" is now another major item in the catalogue of formalist/humanist fallacies.) The second passage quoted from Jonathan Dollimore shows that he subscribes to both of these explanations, and so do Jean Howard and Catherine Belsey: according to Howard, in "many of Shakespeare's comedies, the ending . . . attempts to smooth over, or erase, the contradictions or fissures which have opened in the course of the play";[11] Belsey claims "the strategies of the classic realist text divert the reader from what is contradictory within it," from "the play of contradictions which in reality constitutes the literary text," requiring the deployment of "a scientific criticism" (i.e., cultural materialism) that "distanc[es] itself from the imaginary coherence of the text" and "recognizes in the text . . . ideology itself in all its inconsistency."[12] Toril Moi says we can show that the text is not "what it pretends to be" by "look[ing] for underlying contradictions and conflicts as well as absences and silences in [it]."[13] And Pierre Macherey and Etienne Balibar tell us why materialist criticism rejects the "illusory semblance of *unity*" of a literary work, which they call a "mythical unity": "The text is produced under conditions which represent it as a finished work, displaying an essential order. . . . Yet, in itself, the text is none of these; on the contrary, it is materially incomplete, disparate and incoherent, since it is the conflicted, contradictory effect of superimposing real processes which cannot be abolished in it except in an imaginary way."[14]

Although these two explanations differ in their location of the blame, they yield the same result: a literary work that appears to be unified—whether this appearancc is produced by formalist error or by the work itself—but that actually turns out to be disunified when interpreted correctly. We should notice that this conception of correct interpretation is remarkably similar to the one employed by the old New Critics, who regularly divided each text they encountered into an apparent or surface meaning, which has misled previous commentators, and a real or deep meaning that they themselves just discovered. It is therefore hard to understand why the cultural materialists should include in their catalogues of formalist/humanist fallacies the idea that the meaning of literary texts is "transparent" and "self-evident," for if the New Critics believed that, they would not have undertaken those elaborate "close readings" to discover the real meaning that lurked beneath the apparent meaning. This division is in fact fundamental to the two approaches adopted (and sometimes combined) in most of the New Criticism: the thematic approach, where the apparent subject of the work, the particular characters and actions presented there, is distinguished from the real, abstract subject embodied in the central theme; and the ironic approach, where the apparent values, or "face value," of the work (which usually seemed to call for a sympathetic response to the main characters) are distinguished from the real, ironic values that undercut those apparent values and apparently sympathetic characters. The cultural materialists' strategy is of course much closer to the latter approach; indeed, it seems to be based upon the same formula with only a change in terminology. The functional equivalents of the real meaning or values of the work are those "fissures" and "conflicts" and "contradictions," and they invariably undercut the apparent meaning or values, now become the "dominant ideology," which, as in the old New Critical version, was erroneously taken at face value by earlier commentators. But there is a crucial difference between the two strategies: New Critical ironists claimed that they were interpreting the author's intention, that he deliberately subverted the apparent, "face value" meaning in order to convey the ironic meaning, which was the real meaning because he meant it (and which therefore gave us a unified work), whereas the cultural materialists, as was just noted, eliminate the author and hence his intention, so that their distinction between the apparent and real meanings must rest on other grounds.

It is not at all easy, however, to determine what those grounds are, since the cultural materalists' basic line of argument seems to be fissured by one of those internal contradictions that they like to find in other texts. For they, along with most other poststructuralists, reject the idea that a literary work has a "real" or "objective" meaning; in fact, that idea figures prominently in their catalogues of formalist/humanist fallacies. They maintain, on the contrary, that we cannot know the "real" work in itself, and that what we call its meaning must therefore be determined, not by anything intrinsic to it, but by the ideology of the interpreter, who is never objective or disinterested. " 'Disinterestedness' is always, at best, an ideological flag of convenience," according to Evans, who asserts that "all reading [is] an intervention and a production rather than a simple decoding" of the text, since "there is no such thing as the object as in itself it really is."[15] Holderness states that meaning is never "simply inherent in the text itself," and warns against any "reversion to an unprovable objectivity of the text."[16] Howard asks that we "decisively break with [the humanists'] fundamental assumptions about the nature of interpretation as the uncovering of 'what is already there' "[17] Dollimore and Sinfield assure us that "cultural materialism does not, like much established literary criticism, attempt to mystify its perspective as the natural, obvious or right interpretation of an allegedly given textual fact."[18] Belsey explains that "as a scientific practice [cultural materialism] is not a process of recognition but work to produce meaning"[19] (compare the quotation above where she says this approach "recognizes" the ideology "in the text"). McLuskie rejects the "spurious notion of objectivity,"[20] and Barker says that anyone who believes in it is guilty of "hubristic objectivism."[21] Yet in all the passages quoted earlier these critics seem to be claiming that the disunity is actually and objectively there in the work, and that the unity is not (which is of course one reason why I selected them). The unity of the work is always stated in terms that deny its reality: "surface," "supposedly," "pretends," "seem[s]," "alleged," "false," "fictional," "imaginary," "mythical," "illusory semblance," "arbitrary prejudice," "fetish." It can only be created by diverting us from, repairing, smoothing over (and out), explaining away, processing, neutralizing, censoring, erasing, effacing, shearing off, suppressing, or abolishing the disunity, that must therefore really be in the work prior to any critical activity (thus it is "discovered" or "recognized" by materialist criticism). This disunity is always affirmed in the language of real presence: it is "actual," "underlying," "innate," "within" the text; it is how the text "is constructed," it characterizes "the text . . . in itself"; it "in fact mark[s]" the text; it "in reality constitutes the literary text"; and so on. Yet according to their own principles they should be saying that the disunity is not more real than the unity: if the latter is "produced" by formalist criticism (or by the text itself), then the former must be "produced" by their own approach.

If we turn from these theoretical considerations to actual critical practice, I think we can see that this alleged disunity is even more dependent upon the cultural materialist approach than the alleged unity was upon formalism. While it is certainly true that formalist critics always looked very long and hard for unity in each work they examined, and that they could adopt some very questionable expedients in order to get what they were looking for, they did not always claim to find it; in fact, they would sometimes object that a work was disunified or inadequately unified.[22] Thus the quoted passages are simply wrong in saying that formalists assumed "literary works form organic wholes," or that they were "committed to" this idea, or that they regarded unity as "the intrinsic quality of all 'works of art' "; on the contrary, they thought of unity as an attribute of superior works but not of inferior ones. The materialists, of course, always seek disunity in the work, just as the formalists sought unity, but the difference is that they never fail to find what they are seeking, which leads one to suspect that this disunity really inheres in their approach rather than in the work itself. And this suspicion is strengthened by some of their own accounts of their methodology that we have seen, which describe it as a "project of fracturing" wherein the work is "torn apart," for then those fissures and contradictions would be created by the approach, which seems to operate on the text like a sledgehammer. And if these critics have difficulty producing fissures and contradictions in the text by this method, their approach allows them to demonstrate its disunity by finding "absences and silences" in it, as Moi explains.[23] Since any work must be silent about a great many things, they can always assert that there is some subject (usually a contemporary situation) that it should refer to but does not, so that this silence becomes evidence of evasion or suppression and therefore of disunity. While the formalists claimed to know what is really in the text, these materialists know, not only what is really in it (i.e., fissures and contradictions), but even what is really left out of it (i.e., absences and silences). Talk about hubristic objectivism!

I think it is fair to conclude, then, that the materialists' attack on artistic unity does not stand up under interrogation. It is self-contradictory and proves nothing except that their approach can create disunity (or the appearance of it) in *any* work, so that this disunity turns out to be no more "real" than the unity they claim to be refuting. I now proceed from this negative refutation of their refutation to the positive defense of the concept of unity, but that requires an interrogation of the concept itself. The materialists never attempt this; they seem to assume that unity has a single meaning that is transparent and self-evident, that they are attacking the same kind of unity that their opponents are affirming. But artistic unity comes in several varieties, for there are different senses in which a work may be—or may be said to be—a complete whole. Most New Critics, we noted, were concerned with thematic unity, where all parts of a work are subordinated to and unified by an abstract "central theme," usually formulated as a general proposition. I have written some unkind words about the use of this concept of unity, and I am not taking back any of them now, but it does describe one possible way authors could integrate their works.

There is another quite different kind of artistic unity (also recognized by some New Critics)[24] that is located not in an abstract thematic idea but in the concrete structure of the plot. This is of course what Aristotle has in mind in his famous definition: "the plot . . . must represent a single piece of action and the whole of it; and the component incidents must be so arranged that if one of them be transposed or removed, the unity of the whole is dislocated and destroyed. For if the presence or absence of a thing makes no visible difference, then it is not an integral part of the whole."[25]

Like the New Critics, he clearly does not regard this unity as an attribute of all literary works, for in the same chapter he faults some of them that lack it (8.1451a20–23). Coleridge has another conception of what he calls "organic unity," which influenced the New Criticism, and there are still others. I am not going to survey them all here; I only point out that there are a number of different ways of viewing the unity of a literary work—many more than are dreamt of in the cultural materialist attack. For the purposes of this argument, however, I am grouping them all under the formalist label because, despite their important differences, they resemble the New Critical conception in two crucial respects: they regard unity as something that is intended by the author, and also as something that is not always attained, so that it can be employed both as a working hypothesis for interpreting works (which, like all such hypotheses, may later have to be modified or discarded), and as one of the criteria for judging them. And from this it follows that they all treat unity in relative rather than absolute terms, since literary works—or their authors, if one suspects that those recent obituaries have been somewhat exaggerated—will be more or less successful in achieving this goal. Few people would maintain, for instance, that the Clown in *Othello* makes a significant contribution to the play (in fact, he is usually dropped in performances), so we would have to acknowledge that his presence detracts from its unity.[26] But this does not mean that the play is disunified or that the concept of unity cannot be fruitfully applied to it, because unity is not an all-or-nothing proposition, as the cultural materialists seem to think. Indeed it is possible to make use of this conception (in any of the versions just discussed) to interpret and to judge literary works without believing that it has ever been achieved completely, or ever will be.

It is certainly true that many New Critics asserted that many plays possess the "highest possible unity," which integrates "every word of the text," and so on. But while such claims might be justified in dealing with short lyric poems (which of course is where the New Critical enterprise began), when applied to works of greater magnitude and complexity they clearly overstate the case, and so render the conception of unity itself vulnerable to the sort of attack we are examining. Aristotle also seems to be guilty of this kind of hyperbole when he says that the plot of an epic should be "whole and complete in itself . . . like a single living organism,"[27] for it is most unlikely that something "made" by art could actually attain the degree of unity found in something "grown" by nature. But this does not mean that the idea of organic unity is not applicable in the realm of art. Like the idea of happiness in the *Nicomachean Ethics,* it is presumably to be regarded by authors as "a target to aim at,"[28] and therefore by critics as a criterion for judging their relative success.

This conception of artistic unity as an intended goal of authors—not the only such goal, obviously—seems to be confirmed by actual experience. There is good evidence, for instance, that Renaissance dramatists thought of their plays as unified wholes, because they objected to "unauthorized" additions to or deletions from them. Thus Shakespeare has Hamlet insist that clowns should "speak no more than is set down for them, for there be of them that will themselves laugh to set on some quantity of barren spectators to laugh too, though in the mean time some necessary question of the play be then to be consider'd" (3.2.39–43). And a number of dramatic quartos and folios contain statements by the author (or publisher) complaining that the plays were cut in performance and assuring the reader that they have now been printed in their "perfect" or "original" form.[29] We have much more evidence, of course, that most modern authors feel the same way about the unity of their creations. Moreover, if audiences then were anything like us, they assumed that the play they were witnessing was meant to provide a complete, unified experience. That is why we try to get to the theater before the opening curtain and return to our seats when the intermission is over, because we do not want to "miss anything."[30] We also read the printed text of a play (or novel) with the same expectation, which Renaissance readers presumably shared; and if some pages are missing, we demand another copy that contains the "whole" work. And after seeing or reading a play, even those of us who are not practicing critics will object if we feel that it "didn't hang together," or that an episode in it was "irrelevant," or that some important matter was "left dangling." It would appear, therefore, that the conception of artistic unity was not invented by the New Critics or by Coleridge or even by Aristotle; it seems rather to be the normal assumption that underlies both the producing and the consuming of most literary works in our culture.

We might ask then why the cultural materialists have not taken these facts into account in their attack. The answer seems clear enough: what they are actually talking about, as several of those quotations indicate, is not this formalist kind of unity at all but another kind that is *ideological,* in the second sense defined at the outset. This may seem similar to the thematic unity of the New Criticism, but it is really quite different because it is not propositional and, we noted previously, is not intentional, for ideology in this sense is a construct of society that the author need not even be conscious of, which is one of the justifications given for The Death of the Author. In that respect, the cultural materialists' approach is much closer to another historical mode of interpretation, preceding the New Criticism, which was based on the idea of an aesthetic Zeitgeist. In the memory of people yet living, including myself, the plays of the Renaissance were regarded as sites of a fundamental conflict between two Zeitgeists called classicism and romanticism, which were also ideologies in this sense (although we did not use the word in those benighted days). And since that conflict, like those sponsored by the cultural materialists, was supposed to be incapable of resolution, all the plays in which it was fought out were always disunified. Thus students were required to seek—and to find—traces of romanticism in plays that seemed to be wholly classical and vice versa (much like the projects recommended in some of the passages quoted earlier, which tell us to "search for underlying contradictions and conflicts" in an apparently unified text, to "fractur[e] the unified surface of the text to let the multiplicity of its social voices be heard," and so on). The New Criticism changed all that by positing an authorial artistic intention that could integrate, more or less successfully, these romantic and classical adversaries, or any others. It could also integrate the kinds of conflicting ideologies favored in cultural materialism. In *King Lear,* to take an obvious example, we find an opposition between the organic or "feudal" view of nature espoused by Lear (1.4.275–89), Gloucester (1.2.103–14), and Albany (4.2.29–36), and the atomistic or "capitalist" view espoused by Edmund (1.2.1–22); but formalist critics could argue that this was deliberately set up by Shakespeare as part of an overall unified design, and so could the pre-poststructuralist Marxists, who were also intentionalist.[31] The cultural materialists, however, having killed off the author and hence the possibility of such a design, only see the opposition, which then becomes proof of the play's disunity. And any other conflict of this sort can be treated by them in a similar fashion, because what they are really asking for is not ideologial *unity* but ideological *uniformity*—or, putting it another way, without the concept of an authorial design, the only possible meaning of ideological unity would be uniformity. And since no play shows such a uniformity, which would require the elimination of all dramatic conflict, each one turns out to be "disunified."[32] But the kind of unity that these critics are denying in the work is not the kind that anyone has ever affirmed.

Although this may explain how the cultural materialists are able to demonstrate the disunity of each work they deal with, it does not account for their assertions, found in many of the initial quotations, that this disunity is a necessary condition of all literary works, nor does it answer the question still hanging over us concerning the ground for their assertions that in all literary works this disunity is real while the unity is only apparent. For such assertions depend, not on inductions from individual works, but on deductive reasoning from universal laws. And here we encounter another fissure or contradiction in the cultural materialist approach itself, because these critics (again in company with most other poststructuralists) reject the belief in "universal truths" or "eternal verities," which they regularly include in their catalogues of formalist/humanist fallacies. It is surprising, therefore, to find that in their essays terms such as "all," "always" (or "always already"), "inevitably," and "never" appear with a very high frequency—much higher than in any formalist criticism I have seen. Apparently they themselves have a pipeline to some verities that sound pretty eternal (and hence their real objection to the formalists must be that they subscribe to the wrong ones). And one of the most eternal of these is that all societies—except a truly socialist society, of course—are fissured by irreconcilable contradictions (this is treated as a single linguistic unit, like "damnyankee" in the old South). From this it follows that the ideologies that are produced by and produce these societies must always be fissured by those contradictions, and therefore those contradictions must always fissure the literary works that are produced by and produce those ideologies. What we have here, then, is that familiar Marxist dyad of the "base" and the "superstructure," the former embodying the real cause and the latter its less real effects. That is why these critics know in advance that all literary works will actually be disunified, even though they may appear unified. (They do not have to face the question of whether the literary products of a truly socialist society are also disunified, since apparently no such society exists.) This aspect of their treatment of unity most closely resembles that of the Freudians, who also operate deductively from a universal law of causation that bypasses the artistic intention of the author, although here the basic cause is located not in the author's society but in his or her psyche: since all psyches—except those of therapized Freudian critics, of course—are fissured by deep conflicts, these conflicts must always fissure the literary works produced by those psyches, no matter how unified the works may appear (in fact, as in the Marxist version, the apparent or surface meaning of the work will often attempt to conceal the real conflicts underlying it).[33] But we would have to maintain, again, that the kind of unity that is disproved in either of these deductive systems is quite different from the unity treated in formalist criticism.

What conclusions, then, can we draw about this question of artistic unity? If the question is whether unity is really a characteristic of all literary works, then the answer must obviously be negative. No one, not even the most hopelessly irredeemable formalist/humanist, has ever claimed this, despite what the cultural materialists say. If the question is whether any particular literary work is really unified, the answer must be that there is no answer, since this depends on how one looks at it. Instead of trying to discuss what the work really is, I would like to resurrect the very useful little word *qua,* which signifies this crucial role of perspective. If we adopt the formalist perspective and look at a literary work qua artistic product—that is, as something consciously designed by an author to evoke a coherent and pleasurable experience in an audience—then it will turn out to be more or less effectively unified, as we found, and the concept of unity can therefore be applied both as a working hypothesis in interpreting it and as a criterion in judging it. The cultural materialists, however, along with most other poststructuralists, claim that this formalist perspective itself is no longer tenable because the work of Barthes, Foucault, Lacan, Althusser, and Derrida has invalidated the "humanist" assumptions (of a unified and autonomous author as the origin of meaning, etc.) on which it rests.[34] And this claim is now often accepted, which explains why there is a widespread impression that the concept of artistic unity is out of date, as I noted at the beginning, and why those humanist assumptions have become fallacies. But we have seen that most audiences in our culture (and apparently in the Renaissance) did expect a play to be unified, and that is because they viewed it as a product designed to create a coherent effect that gave them pleasure, which is why they bought their theater tickets (or the play text) in the first place. (I refer to lay audiences—to people, that is, who will not write about or teach or take a test on the work they are seeing or reading.) And it is the formalist approach that can account for their expectation and their pleasure,[35] since it proceeds from the same basic perspective that underlies the experience of these audiences, so we must conclude that its conception of an artistic work, and therefore of artistic unity, cannot be invalidated by the attack we are examining or by any other, regardless of the latest advances of "theory." It will continue to be valid, although it may slip in and out of fashion in the academy.

It is essential to add, however, that this is not the only valid way of looking at literary works and hence at the concept of unity. For the work itself cannot tell us how we should regard it, and that is why we need the term *qua*. Any work, in addition to being a product designed by an author for an audience, is also inevitably a product of its society and of the psyche of its author, and therefore can be viewed qua either of these perspectives. From this it follows that what might loosely be called the historical and the psychological approaches—which include, but are by no means limited to, Marxism and Freudianism—also have, and will continue to have, their own validity, although they too may slip in and out of fashion. And from their perspectives, it was shown, the concept of unity takes on meanings very different from the formalist concept, so that their answer to the question of whether any given literary work is unified could always be negative. But that answer does not really contradict the one given previously, since it results from another way of looking at the object. This also applies to many of the other alleged formalist/humanist fallacies we have encountered in the course of this interrogation. Is the author or what is now termed the "subject" really unified and autonomous? The answer again is that it depends on our perspective (which is also true of the unity of "living organisms" that Aristotle refers to). Qua atomic structures, humans have neither unity nor autonomy; we are simply a concourse of particles with no clear boundaries, since these particles are continually entering and leaving us. But qua biological structures, we possess a high degree of unity and autonomy; when I return to my seat in a few minutes, I will not leave parts of my body here at the podium, nor will parts of the podium come along with me. And in the realm of literature we would say that, qua the formalist approach that views a literary work as the conscious product of an author, this author can be relatively unified and autonomous, while qua these other approaches he or she may never be unified or autonomous or even relevant, which is what The Death of the Author proclaims. Thus this qua gives us the basis for critical pluralism, the recognition of an irreducible plurality of valid critical approaches, which enables us to live together and talk to each other because we can understand and respect our different perspectives. To adapt the immortal words with which Touchstone ends his speech on quarreling, "Your *qua* is the only peacemaker; much virtue in *qua*."

The trouble with this solution to the problem is that the cultural materialists also reject critical pluralism, which to them is another formalist/humanist fallacy. Many of their essays include at least one passing attack on pluralism, where it is often bracketed by ironic quotation marks and preceded by some adjective like "naive" or "urbane" (an interesting pairing) or "liberal" or "benign," which are all bad words in their vocabulary.[36] And the reason they are against it is that, unlike Touchstone, they are not seeking peace but victory. They do not want cultural materialism to be regarded as one among several valid approaches to literature: they want it to be the only valid approach, as can be seen in Belsey's references to it, in the passages quoted earlier, as "scientific criticism" (meaning that all other approaches are unscientific), and in the final chapter of Eagleton's *Literary Theory,* which argues for that claim. And they see pluralism as a devious strategy to domesticate or neutralize their approach without really confronting it, like the "co-opting" and "repressive tolerance" we heard about in the sixties. What they demand instead is that the formalist/humanist enemy engage them in a "struggle" or "contest for meaning" in the interpretation of literary works, a contest that they of course expect to win.[37]

Unfortunately, however, the cultural materialists never explain how they will win it. Unless they intend to force us into submission (poetics comes out of the barrel of a gun?), they will have to persuade us. But how can they persuade us that their interpretation of any work is superior to ours, when they insist that objective knowledge of the work is an illusion, and that all interpretations of it are "interventions" or "productions" determined by the interpreter's own ideology? For this would mean that they cannot appeal to any neutral or agreed-upon evidence within the work in a contest with non-Marxists, and consequently it is difficult to see how non-

Marxists could ever be persuaded by a Marxist interpretation. There would not even be any reason for them to read it through, once they realized that its only claim to attention (and to superiority) was based upon its relationship, not to the work being interpreted, but to an ideology that they opposed. Presumably they would first have to be converted to the Marxist ideology, on political rather than aesthetic grounds, which is what Eagleton seems to be saying at one point where he asserts that the disagreement between two readings generated by different critical approaches is really "a distinction between different forms of politics. . . . There is no way of settling the question of which politics is preferable in literary critical terms. You simply have to argue about politics."[38]

The same kind of question also arises in feminist criticism, if we can turn now to what I said was the second major ideological approach of our day. And here I can speak from personal experience, for a recent letter in the *PMLA* Forum, signed by Janet Adelman and twenty-three others, objected to an article I had written criticizing some feminist readings of Shakespearean tragedy because, among other things, I "fail[ed] to understand the serious concerns about inequality and injustice that have engendered feminist analyses of literature."[39] What they were saying, in other words, is that my negative judgment of those feminist readings showed that I did not accept the feminist ideology. I replied that I did accept this ideology and considered myself a feminist (it should be clear by now that I do not consider myself a Marxist), but that this had no effect on my judgment of the readings, because a just cause cannot justify interpretive errors. But suppose I did not accept feminist ideology—would that disqualify me from judging feminist readings? Are we to say that only feminists can criticize feminist readings, and only Marxists can criticize Marxist readings? If so, it would follow that only liberal humanists can criticize liberal humanist readings, which would put a number of feminist and Marxist critics out of business.

I think this points to the most basic problem posed by the role of political ideologies in criticism, the problem of whether it is possible to reach a correct judgment, or even a correct understanding, of interpretations generated by one of these ideological approaches without accepting the ideology itself. If it is not possible, then we are in the dilemma just described, where each of these approaches would be confined to its own hermeneutically sealed-off discursive space, and adherents of different approaches would not be able to discourse with each other about the interpretation of texts or even about critical theory, but only about the political validity of their respective ideologies, which is what Eagleton asserts ("You simply have to argue about politics"). I think there is a way out of this dilemma, however, that has already been indicated—namely, by rejecting the cultural materialists' rejection of objectivism and pluralism. If we believe, as I do, that one can attain objective knowledge of a literary text, it will then be possible to judge another critic's interpretation of the text even though her or his approach differs from ours; for instance, we can fault the interpretation for distorting the text (which was the main thrust of my critique of those feminist readings of Shakespearean tragedy). And if we believe, as I do, that there are a number of valid critical approaches, it will then be possible to judge interpretations produced by another approach in its own terms; for instance, we can fault the interpretation for being inconsistent with the postulates of that approach (which was the main thrust of my critique of the cultural materialists here). Moreover, the belief in these two "fallacies" enables not only negative judgments of interpretations derived from other approaches but also positive ones, since such judgments also depend on objectivism and pluralism. We can, for instance, praise the interpretation of a text based on an approach different from our own because through it we have learned something significant about the text that we were not aware of before. I think most of us have had this experience; but it is only possible, again, when we believe that something is objectively "there" in the text to be learned, and that our own approach is not the only valid method of gaining access to it. If I am wrong, however, if objectivism and pluralism really are fallacious, and interpretations and the judgment of interpretations really are determined by political ideology,[40] then it would follow that our professional journals and conferences such as this should stop discussing literary texts or critical theories and should concentrate instead on debates about the politics of the ideologies themselves—about the relative merits, for example, of "bourgeois democracy" versus true socialism. Then, when enough people have been converted to the one right ideology, critical pluralism can be suppressed in favor of monism, which is the only alternative I can think of, and all of us, whether we want to or not, will have to join the attack on artistic unity.

A Handy (But Incomplete) Check-Off List of Formalist/Humanist Fallacies, in the Order of Their Appearance:

1. Literary works have "organic unity."
2. Literary works are produced by "autonomous individuals," i.e., "authors."

3. The meaning of literary works is "transparent" and "self-evident."
4. We can attain "objective" knowledge of literary works ("objectivism").
5. We can attain knowledge of "eternal" or "universal" truths.
6. People and things have some "essential" attributes ("essentialism").
7. There are a number of valid approaches to literature ("pluralism").

Notes

1. "Ideological approach" can also be used in a third sense to designate the object of inquiry, and would then include not only the feminists and Marxists but also the New Historicists, who are often accused of not having an ideology (sense 1) of their own but are certainly concerned with the ideology (sense 2) of the works they examine.

2. For the reader's convenience I have added at the end a list of the fallacies referred to in this paper. A shorter version of the following section has already appeared in "Leaking Relativism," *Essays in Criticism* 38 (1988): 267–77.

3. Terry Eagleton, *Literary Theory: An Introduction* (Minneapolis: University of Minnesota Press, 1983), 80–81.

4. Francis Barker and Peter Hulme, "Nymphs and Reapers Heavily Vanish: The Discursive Con-texts of *The Tempest*," in *Alternative Shakespeares,* ed. John Drakakis (London: Methuen, 1985), 196–98.

5. Peter Stallybrass, "Rethinking Text and History," *Journal of Literature Teaching Politics* 2 (1983): 100–101.

6. Malcolm Evans, *Signifying Nothing: Truth's True Contents in Shakespeare's Text* (Athens: University of Georgia Press, 1986), 249, 254.

7. Graham Holderness, *Shakespeare's History* (New York: St. Martin's, 1985), 159.

8. Jean Howard, "The New Historicism in Renaissance Studies," *English Literary Renaissance* 16 (1986): 30.

9. Catherine Belsey, *Critical Practice* (London: Methuen, 1980), 109.

10. Jonathan Dollimore, *Radical Tragedy: Religion, Ideology and Power in the Drama of Shakespeare and His Contemporaries* (Chicago: University of Chicago Press, 1984), 60, 67–68.

11. Jean Howard, "Renaissance Antitheatricality and the Politics of Gender and Rank in *Much Ado About Nothing,*" in *Shakespeare Reproduced,* ed. Jean Howard and Marion O'Connor (London: Methuen, 1987), 180.

12. Belsey, *Critical Practice,* 128 (see note 9).

13. Toril Moi, "Sexual/Textual Politics," in *The Politics of Theory,* ed. Francis Barker et al. (Colchester: University of Essex, 1983), 3.

14. Pierre Macherey and Etienne Balibar, "Literature as an Ideological Form: Some Marxist Propositions" (1974), trans. James Kavanagh, *Praxis* 5 (1981): 49–50, 58.

15. Evans, *Signifying Nothing,* 85, 100, 137 (see note 6). He is of course referring to the definition of criticism formulated by that arch-humanist, Matthew Arnold.

16. Holderness, *Shakespeare's History,* 147–48 (see note 7).

17. Jean Howard, "Recent Studies in Elizabethan and Jacobean Drama," *Studies in English Literature* 27 (1987): 340.

18. Jonathan Dollimore and Alan Sinfield, *Political Shakespeare: New Essays in Cultural Materialism* (Ithaca: Cornell University Press, 1985), viii.

19. Belsey, *Critical Practice,* 138 (see note 9).

20. Kathleen McLuskie, "The Patriarchal Bard: Feminist Criticism and Shakespeare: *King Lear* and *Measure for Measure*," in *Political Shakespeare*, ed. Dollimore and Sinfield, 91–92.

21. Francis Barker, *The Tremulous Private Body: Essays on Subjection* (London: Methuen, 1984), 15.

22. I examine those expedients, which are most typical of thematic formalism, in *New Readings vs. Old Plays: Recent Trends in the Reinterpretation of English Renaissance Drama* (Chicago: University of Chicago Press, 1979), chap. 2. For examples of their criticism of disunified works, see the discussions of Poe's "Ulalume," Kilmer's "Trees," and Lanier's "My Springs" in Cleanth Brooks and Robert Penn Warren's *Understanding Poetry* (New York: Holt, 1938), 358–62, 387–91, 442–45.

23. Moi, "Sexual/Textual Politics," 3 (see note 13). Many of the others make the same point: Pierre Macherey tells us to find the "silences" of the text, "what it does not say," in *A Theory of Literary Production* (1966), trans. Geoffrey Wall (London: Routledge, 1978), 85, 155; Howard wants to "focus precisely on the silences" in it ("Renaissance Antitheatricality," 164, see note 11); Belsey looks for its "omissions" and "absences" and "what it is unable to say" (*Critical Practice*, 107, 109, 135, see note 9); Holderness for "its suppressions and absences" (*Shakespeare's History*, 159, see note 7); Evans for what it "endeavours to keep silent" (*Signifying Nothing*, 48, see note 6); and Dollimore for what it "does not represent" and "never speaks," although he has some reservations about this strategy ("Transgression and Surveillance in *Measure for Measure*," in *Political Shakespeare*, 73, 85).

24. When they do recognize it, they usually subordinate it to the more important thematic unity; see, for example, Robert Heilman, *Magic in the Web: Action and Language in "Othello"* (Lexington: University of Kentucky Press, 1956), 2–16.

25. Aristotle, *Poetics*, trans. W. Hamilton Fyfe, Loeb Classical Library 199 (Cambridge: Harvard University Press, 1973), 8.1451a32–35.

26. We will not be surprised to learn there is a thematic reading that claims the Clown's scenes are "integral parts of the structure" of *Othello* because they "serve an important function in the overall thematic scheme"; see Robert Watts, "The Comic Scenes in *Othello*," *Shakespeare Quarterly* 19 (1968): 349.

27. Aristotle, *Poetics*, 23.1459a19–21 (see note 25).

28. Aristotle, *Nicomachean Ethics*, trans. H. Rackman (Cambridge: Harvard University Press, 1975), 1.2.1094a25.

29. I collect a number of these statements in "Performance Critics vs. Close Readers in the Study of English Renaissance Drama," *Modern Language Review* 81 (1986): 550–53.

30. Of course we behave in a similar way if we are only seeing a collection of unrelated skits, since we still want to "get our money's worth"; but we are usually much more concerned if we are seeing a single work, when what we miss might be what Hamlet calls "some necessary question of the play."

31. For a good example of this older Marxist approach to the play, see Paul Delany's "*King Lear* and the Decline of Feudalism," *PMLA* 92 (1977): 429–40. Evans, in the new mode, finds that both worldviews are guilty of "essentialism" (another formalist/humanist fallacy) and are undercut by a third one embodied in the Fool, that is not intended or integrated into the play (*Signifying Nothing*, 224–32, see note 6).

32. See Catherine Belsey's account of how materialist critics can exploit the fact that the plot of *Macbeth* or any fictional work "depends on impediments" and "obstacles to be overcome" and "on the establishment within the story of . . . norms and the repudiation of norms" in "Literature, History, Politics," *Literature and History* 9 (1983):

23–24; cf. Belsey's *The Subject of Tragedy: Identity and Difference in Renaissance Drama* (London: Methuen, 1985), 9, 100, 111.

33. The cultural materialists of course can claim that Freudianism itself is part of bourgeois ideology and so is contradictory, while Freudians would have no trouble finding that an unconscious Oedipal conflict is the real cause of the cultural materialists' hostility to the bourgeoisie.

34. See, e.g., Moi, "Sexual/Textual Politics," 4 (see note 13) and Belsey, *Critical Practice,* 3 (see note 9).

35. Cultural materialists have trouble with aesthetic pleasure. Many simply ignore it. Belsey calls it "mysterious" (*Subject of Tragedy,* 10, see note 32), and one can see why, for she shows no sign of ever having experienced it. And still others admit its existence only to warn us against it, since it involves our empathic engagement in the action and so makes us "complicit" with the play's ideology. Thus McLuskie asks us "to deny" it ("Patriarchal Bard," 98, see note 20), and Margot Heinemann, in explaining Brecht's opposition to "the politics of empathy," connects it to fascism; see "How Brecht Read Shakespeare," in *Political Shakespeare,* ed. Dollimore and Sinfield, 214 (see note 18).

36. See Drakakis, *Alternative Shakespeares,* 17, 25 (see note 4) and his review of *Shakespeare Left and Right* in *Renaissance Quarterly* 46 (1993): 407; Evans, *Signifying Nothing,* 98, 198, 245 (see note 6); Barker, *Tremulous Private Body,* 48 (see note 21); Barker and Hulme, "Nymphs and Reapers," 193 (see note 4); Holderness, *Shakespeare's History,* 160 (see note 7); Michael Bristol, *Shakespeare's America, America's Shakespeare* (London: Routledge, 1990), 169; Eagleton, *Literary Theory,* 50, 198–99 (see note 3). Eagleton thinks that pluralism combines parts of different approaches, but this is usually called eclecticism. Critics can be committed to a single approach and still be pluralists if they recognize other valid approaches, and an English department can be pluralistic even though each of its members practices only one approach.

37. Belsey, "Literature," 19, 21 (see note 32); Barker and Hulme, "Nymphs and Reapers," 193, 205 (see note 4); Holderness, *Shakespeare's History,* 149 (see note 7); McLuskie, "Patriarchal Bard," 95 (see note 20).

38. Eagleton, *Literary Theory,* 209 (see note 3). He is referring to the difference between a formalist and a feminist reading, but presumably this would also apply to a "contest for meaning" between a formalist and a Marxist.

39. Janet Adelman et al., Letter to the Editor (Forum), *PMLA* 104 (1989): 77.

40. I would also want to question whether there is any necessary connection between the "politics" of these ideologies and the interpretations they generate, and as evidence I could note that only a few years ago both Marxists and feminists were turning out formalist readings (see note 31), even though formalism is now supposed to be the accomplice of capitalism and patriarchy (Moi, for instance, says it is an "inherently reactionary literary theory" ["Sexual/Textual Politics," 10], see note 13). But that is another argument.

Relevant Publications by Richard Levin

New Readings vs. Old Plays: Recent Trends in the Reinterpretation of English Renaissance Drama. Chicago: University of Chicago Press, 1979.

"*King Lear* Defamiliarised." In "*Lear*" *from Study to Stage,* edited by James Ogden and Arthur Scouten. Lewiston, N.Y.: Edwin Mellen Press, forthcoming.

"The Current Polarization of Literary Studies." In *The Emperor Redressed: Critiquing Critical Theory,* edited by Dwight Eddins. Tuscaloosa: University of Alabama Press, 1995.

"The New Interdisciplinarity in Literary Criticism." In *After Poststructuralism: Interdisciplinarity and Literary Theory,* edited by Nancy Easterlin and Barbara Riebling. Evanston: Northwestern University Press, 1995.

"On Defending Shakespeare, 'Liberal Humanism,' Transcendent Love, and Other 'Sacred Cows' and Lost Causes." *Textual Practice* 7 (spring 1993): 50–55.

"The Politicized Language of Literary Criticism." *Centennial Review* 37 (spring 1993): 281–304.

"Son of Bashing the Bourgeois Subject." *Textual Practice* 6 (summer 1992): 264–70.

"The Cultural Materialist Attack on Artistic Unity and the Problem of Ideological Criticism." In *Ideological Approaches to Shakespeare: The Practice of Theory,* edited by Robert Merrix and Nicholas Ranson. Lewiston, N.Y.: Edwin Mellen Press, 1992.

"Ideological Criticism and Pluralism." In *Shakespeare Left and Right,* edited by Ivo Kamps. London: Routledge, 1991.

"The Poetics and Politics of Bardicide." *PMLA* 105 (May 1990): 491–504.

"Unthinkable Thoughts in the New Historicizing of English Renaissance Drama." *New Literary History* 21 (spring 1990): 433–47.

"Bashing the Bourgeois Subject." *Textual Practice* 3 (spring 1989): 76–86.

"Feminist Thematics and Shakespearean Tragedy." *PMLA* 103 (March 1988): 125–38.

"Leaking Relativism." *Essays in Criticism* 38 (October 1988): 267–77.

"The New Refutation of Shakespeare." *Modern Philology* 83 (November 1985): 123–41.

8

An End to Hypocriticism

Robert Scholes

Robert Scholes, Andrew W. Mellon Professor of Humanities at Brown University, is well known as an interpreter of and commentator on the continually changing frontiers of literary theory. His Structuralism in Literature *(1974) was widely heralded as an essential introduction for those puzzled by the rise of the structuralist movement;* Semiotics and Interpretation *performed something of the same function as "semiotics" became a term to be reckoned with in the 1980s; and* Textual Power *(1985) was one of the earliest books raising questions about the role of the classroom teacher amidst the rising tide of literary theorizing. The contributions to the field of literary study made by his twenty-some books and many articles is yet much broader than these three books suggest (for instance, he has written extensively on science fiction and the kind of fiction he calls "fabulation").*

Scholes's interest in the teaching of English is not limited to the university level: he chairs the Pace Setter Task Force charged with designing a new model for twelfth-grade English courses and is on the board of the Standards Project for English Language Arts. This breadth and his strong ethical interest in what the class in literature can and should do for the student are reasons that his critiques of the field of literary study have a special interest. The following essay is both a critique of debilitating errors into which literary study has fallen and a suggestion for substantive rather than merely palliative changes.

The English curriculum as we have known it emerged from the ruins of rhetoric and classical studies a little over a century ago. Since that time it has persisted, with changes of emphasis and modifications of coverage, but without any radical displacement up to the present. What I mean by the ruins of rhetoric and classical studies can be embodied in a couple of brief examples:

> English and Rhetoric: The first mention of English Literature as a subject in the catalogues of Brown University came in 1851 when a Professor of Rhetoric and English Literature was listed. Rhetoric itself had been established as a field of study half a century earlier, when a Professorship of "Oratory and Belles Letters" was endowed in 1804. By 1891 Brown had a Department of Rhetoric and Oratory and another Department of English Language and Literature. In 1894 the English Department had two faculty members and the Rhetoric Department had five faculty members in rhetoric and elocution along with six "Assistants in Rhetoric." Even so, by 1900 the English Department had swallowed the Rhetoric Department whole—and instantly started grumbling about having to teach composition.

> English and Classics: In 1907—the last year in which Greek was required at Yale—98 percent of the students entering Yale College had prior knowledge of Greek and 60 percent of them elected to study Greek in their first year. In 1914 less than half of the entering students claimed Greek and only 29 percent of them elected it in their first year. By 1921 only 8 percent of Yale freshmen elected Greek. Just a bit over a decade later, in 1933, more than half of Yale's seniors were majoring in English Literature. The rise of English was accomplished at the expense of classics as well as rhetoric.

Without any attempt at proof, I shall offer an explanation for these phenomena that is the best I have found. We know that, during the years in which the study of English literature came to prominence, American universities also fell under the spell of Germany as a model for research and graduate instruction. In Germany the humanistic curriculum, from the universities down through the secondary schools, was based on the classics and on Greek above all; this remained the case up to the Second World War. Greek was central in the German curriculum because in Greek philosophy, art, and literature German scholars from Winckelman to Heidegger found the pure source of culture and, above all, of Spirit, or *Geist*. Many German thinkers, up to and most emphatically including Heidegger, felt also that there was some special affinity between the German Spirit and the Greek Spirit, that gave the study of Greek an almost mystical appeal in German schools and universities. This also meant, however, that this mystical appeal could be transferred from Greek to modern German literature and, finally, to the other modern literatures.

Under the influence of romantic thinkers, in Germany and in England, the locus of Spirit was extended from Greek to the modern languages, with Dante and Shakespeare as the supreme examples of modern literature. Enshrined by the aesthetic philosophy of Kant, Schelling, and Hegel, literature itself came to be defined as the embodiment in textual form of truths superior to those of empirical science. From Schiller to Schopenhauer, from Coleridge to Shelley, Carlyle, and Mathew Arnold, literature was presented as the antidote to science, the place where Genius embodied the fruits of pure intuitions in textual form. Even within the modernism of Eliot and Pound, this romantic emphasis on the spiritual powers of literature persisted. And it was precisely this glorification of literature that underwrote the drier procedures of the American New Critics. Only the supreme value of the poetical text justified such careful teasing out of its ironic and paradoxical chains of meaning—and that value was based on the poem's function as the repository of Spirit. This set of beliefs, which was powerfully operative when I attended Yale as an undergraduate just after World War II, has become harder and harder to maintain in the ensuing years.

The decline of these beliefs is no doubt due to many factors, but one of them is certainly our growing perception of them not as timeless truth but as an ideological construction thoroughly impregnated with the values of a particular social and historical culture. This perception has grown along with—or as a part of—our clearer understanding of our own cultural situation as different from that upon which these aesthetic assumptions were based. Let me try to make this process more concrete by an excursion into my personal history, as an aspect of the recent history of American education.

What we used to call the American dream involved a vision of upward social and economic mobility—for everybody, regardless of logic and economic realities. That is, the dream required, with the logic of dreams but not of reason, that everyone should move upward and no one downward. I do not mean to sneer at this vision, because, like many of you, I am sure, I have lived it myself. My mother was one of five daughters of a young Italian couple who came to Brooklyn and died there in their youth. With the help of their priest and their community these five girls raised themselves, and four of them moved into the professional class by getting certified as schoolteachers. My father, of an Anglo-Irish family in Philadelphia, worked his way out of the Pennsylvania steel mills and into the life of a middle-class business man. These parents sent me to better schools than they had attended themselves and made me the embodiment of their dream. Ultimately they sent me to Yale University, that bastion of capitalism and Protestantism (where I made up part of the ten percent quota of Roman Catholics admitted in 1946.) In that school, however, I did not become a Protestant, nor did I stubbornly persist in my native Catholicism. I learned instead, like many others, to find in literature a substitute for my church. Thus, in the last years of the 1940s, I was thoroughly indoctrinated into the religion of literature. That is, I came to believe, with others of my generation, that reading literature and criticizing it were the best things a human being could do with life (with the possible exception of producing literature that might lend itself profitably to such exacting critical scrutiny).

I present myself as an example here (only partly horrible, I hope) by way of acknowledging that I am implicated in the system of assumptions that I am about to criticize as, to say the least, no longer viable for English teachers. It is, at any rate, a faith in which I no longer can believe. I grew up in this system, I benefited from it, but I am deeply troubled by its inadequacies for our present situation. And when I speak of inadequacies, I am not just talking about some methodological problems that we can rectify by tinkering with our curriculum. I am talking about a set of assumptions about teaching that are so out of touch with our real situation as to be both ludicrous and dangerous. As Richard Ohmann began to tell us two decades ago (in *English in America*)[1] the education that such young people as he and I received in college—and which was transmitted to the secondary schools via entrance requirements and such devices as the SATs and the Advanced Placement Tests in English—was an education that presupposed a life of moneyed leisure on the one hand, and an acceptance of the social status quo on the other: not a life for the idle rich alone, to be sure, but a life that assumed the financial ease, the free time, and the excess energy required for serious aesthetic pursuits. Literature, under this regime of instruction, consisted of a set of verbal icons, the reverent study of which (something very close to "worship") could save, or at least sustain, the souls of individuals otherwise buffeted or soiled by the hubbub of daily life. These assumptions scarcely allowed for the lawyer or manager who brings so much work home that serious reading or study is out of the question, not to mention anyone whose work is more physically demanding and whose need for entertainment more insistent.

What I suggest here (and in doing so I may only be reviving or developing the insights of Ohmann's important and perceptive book), is that the centrality of literature in our English curriculum was dependent upon two cultural assumptions that were not in themselves literary. One was the Arnoldian assumption that literature had become the scripture of modern civilization. And the other was the even less defensible assumption that the graduates of our literary curriculum would live sufficiently gracious lives for "great" (and therefore difficult) works of literature to remain intellectually and spiritually important in those lives. Though I have somewhat more sympathy for the first of these two assumptions than for the second, I believe that they are both sadly mistaken. It is the disparity between these assumptions and the actualities of our lives—and our students' lives—that have turned our practice into what I shall be calling *hypocriticism*.

In trying to articulate this disparity, I am taking the liberty of using my personal experience as a case study, hoping that the gain in specificity will compensate for the loss of objectivity in this instance. In my parents' house there was some elegant furniture: the sort of objects that proved we had indeed attained the level of culture appropriate to the moneyed middle class. And, on one elegant table in particular, I remember, there were always two decorative bookends, with four or five books bound in soft leather resting permanently between them. In the days when, like a giant locust, I was reading my way through everything in the house (imagine me as a sort of Gregor Samsa with a voracious appetite for books) I finally reached the point where there was nothing left but these precious objects. I sensed obscurely that they were meant to be seen and not read, but it was clear that they were books, and I was hungry. So I pounced upon them. What were they? I remember only two titles: Sir Walter Scott's *Ivanhoe* and Dickens's *Pickwick Papers*—by no means the least readable books in the world. But these were on the thinnest of India paper and printed in the most elegant fine print. Furthermore, the culture out of which these texts had emerged was so foreign to me that I could not position myself as their receptive reader. I made some headway with *Ivanhoe,* I believe, but Dickens's facetious description of the Pickwick Club was as alien to me as the Egyptian Book of the Dead. Hungry as I was I could scarcely sink my teeth into these texts. Like the piano in the bourgeois household of Jean Renoir's film about the tramp Boudu, these books were meant to be possessed and displayed, not to be used.

In college, of course, I learned that Scott and Dickens were not especially serious authors—not nearly so serious, for instance, as Henry James or T. S. Eliot—but the image of those sacred books, pathetically representing a culture that my parents did not really possess, still haunts me. And I am grateful to that cultural ghost for rising now to help me make concrete the problem of the assumptions that lay behind the teaching of literature in my school days. For I believe that the gift of literature, which my teachers tried to give me, was much like those books in my parents' house, and like the furniture in that house as well. That is, this gift of literature assumed a level of gracious living that had little or nothing to do with the actual condition of my life as it was likely to be—so that this gift was all too likely to become an ironic symbol of pathetically unrealizable aspirations, like those leather-bound books upon their pretentious table. As it happened, I became an English teacher, and, with that, the gift of literature turned out to have a practical and vocational function in my life that I had never anticipated. But we do not all become English teachers, and those of us who do cannot afford to forget this fact.

It is a scandal in our profession that most university professors would rather teach graduate students than undergraduates, and many reasons are advanced for this situation. But the most telling reason is seldom even considered—perhaps because it exposes too deeply the futility of our enterprise. I believe that most professors are comfortable teaching graduate students because graduate students are expected to lead lives in which the reading of literary texts will continue to play a vital role. That is, at the supposed summit of our profession the ideal to be attained is the teaching of English literature to people who are themselves in the process of becoming teachers of English literature. Such people will not lead lives of moneyed leisure to be sure, but their profession will provide both the time and the motivation for the continued serious reading of complex literary texts. Teaching such people allows the professor to avoid or repress the fact that these graduate students are almost the only people in the world who will in fact be able to give *Ulysses* or *Paradise Lost* such a central place in their lives.

Most English teachers, however, spend most of their time teaching young people who are not destined to become English teachers themselves. At this point we must return and remember all those students who enrolled in Greek courses at Yale a century ago. They were, presumably, expected to continue reading their classics after graduation. We have all probably encountered the image (or the myth) of the plantation owner who in the evening read his Xenophon or Plato. But what actually happened in our academic institutions was that the reading of whole texts in Latin or Greek was largely replaced by the reading of excerpts and the memorization of quotations that could be dropped into legal briefs or political debates as signs of the superior culture of the person doing the dropping. I suggest that precisely this process is now occurring in the classics of English literature. They are being broken up, commodified, and packaged for handy consumption and recirculation. The infamous list of cultural nuggets proposed recently by E. D. Hirsch is nothing more than just such an attempt at packaging. Such texts as *Cliffs Notes* are another. As our romantic faith in the spiritual value of literary texts has waned, we have found ourselves more and more requiring knowledge *about* texts instead of encouraging the direct experience *of* these texts. This is one dimension of hypocriticism.

Another aspect of our situation has to do with the English curriculum itself and the internal dynamic of the professional study of English literature. The English curriculum that came into being around the turn of the last century is still the English curriculum. There have been adjustments in emphasis, to be sure, and many additions. Modern English and American literature have grown. Gender and ethnic considerations have resulted in additions to the canon. Colonial and postcolonial literatures in English have been acknowledged. And the discipline has to some extent theorized itself and built such theorizing into the curriculum. But courses in Chaucer, Shakespeare, Milton, the Romantics, and so on are still the "backbone" of the English curriculum. Though much has been added, not so much has been taken away. In addition to this, a century of professionalism in literary studies has resulted in a huge body of secondary writing in the form of bibliographies, biographies, and interpretations. Even someone dedicated to the study of a single major writer such as Joyce or Woolf can scarcely keep up with all the secondary literature in so narrow a field, let alone read everything the author wrote and much of what he or she read, and otherwise master the milieu in which this writer was formed. There is now so much written material associated with English and American literature that an enormous gap has become apparent between the ideal knowledge of the field and the actual knowledge attained by English majors, by graduate students, and even by faculty. Under the weight of all this "scholarship" it has become more and more difficult to pretend that literary study is a progressive discipline. We are forgetting as fast as we learn, and the processes of scholarship are now more clearly visible not as stages toward a more perfect knowledge but as fashions motivated by the need for change itself. One result of all this has been to turn us into professional *hypocritics.*

Hypocriticism is a word whose time has come. It acknowledges more fully than is usual the roots of the word *hypocrite* in the Greek words *hypo* and *krinein*—the first of which refers to things lower, weaker, or deficient, and the second to judging or deciding. I propose this word, then, to refer to a weak and deficient kind of criticism (and also, of course, as in the normal usage of the word *hypocrisy,* to refer to what *Webster's Collegiate* calls the "act or practice of feigning to be what one is not or to feel what one does not feel; esp. the false assumption of an appearance of virtue or religion"). Hypocriticism is simply the critical practice of people who, in order to function at all, need to pretend to more learning and critical rigor than they have. It is also the practice of people who claim to worship great literature but in their own private lives read little or no poetry, attend few plays, and read more "popular" than "serious" fiction. The professor of literature in our time pretends to be devoted to "high" literature and urges students to share this love—but privately practices the secret vices of watching films or videos and reading detective stories or Harlequin romances. Those of us who engage in traditional literary criticism at the present time are all in the same hypocritical boat—and the boat is adrift.

A boat adrift, however, is still a boat, and no one is going to climb out of it to follow some swimmer who claims that land is just over the horizon. The prudent castaway will hang on to that boat. For English teachers the boat is our belief in what we may usefully think of as the "Story of English"—a narrative that begins with Beowulf and now concludes perhaps with Geoffrey Wolfe or Tobias Wolfe. The Story of English is divided into chapters we call "periods." Each period must be "covered" for the story of English to be complete. And, since we are professionals, each period must be covered by an "expert," a person who, in addition to knowing the whole story, is especially knowledgeable about his or her own chapter or period. This means that every English department can be measured by its ability to personify the whole story with expertise if not eminence in each period. English departments live by this Story. It is the Story we tell to deans when we want to hire a new faculty member or replace an old one. We are a chain that cannot afford a single weak link, whether it be in the later Middle Ages or in the early romantic poets. As the primary and secondary canons swell, the links get smaller and smaller. A serious department with a graduate program must have someone "in" Shakespeare, of course, but also someone (usually someone else) "in" non-Shakespearean Elizabethan and Jacobean drama, and another someone in nondramatic literature of the English Renaissance, which field can now be divided into Henrician, Elizabethan, Jacobean, and Caroline specialists.

With every additional subdivision—each of which makes sense within the logic of professionalization—we are driven deeper and deeper into hypocriticism, for every move toward greater specialization leads us away from the needs of the majority of our students and drives a larger wedge between our professional lives and our own private needs and concerns. Even the New Historicism, which is one of the bravest flowers in the garden (or is it a jungle?) of poststructuralism, seems wedded to a historical period in which the lines of power organize themselves around a visible monarch—which makes all its learning and cleverness of questionable usefulness for our attempts to understand the confused dynamics of power in our own world. If the New Historicism is a very sophisticated way of clinging to the Story of English, just as the New Criticism was a very sophisticated way of clinging to a romantic notion of the poem as Spirit's dwelling place, we can see in their shared adjective of temporality a way of concealing the fact that neither of them could be so "New" as they both wished to be.

Nor have all the sophisticated moves of the still newer modes of critical theory saved us from hypocriticism. They have, in fact, contributed mightily to it in their own ways, which, though they are different from and even opposed to the older modes of thought, often put us as teachers in a position equally false. I must speak crudely and hastily, here, but the charge I am about to make could be developed at greater length. Many modes of poststructuralist thought privilege the unconscious, the irrational, the anarchical, the primitive, the illogical, the ungrammatical, the antisocial, the strange, the mad, the destructive, the outlawed. Without denying in myself some sympathy for aspects of these views, I observe that most of the people expressing them have made their own accommodations with society, with order, with institutions upon which they depend in order to function as they do. To the extent that these radical critiques made from safe and tenured positions may lead students to take chances that can damage their lives, those of us who make them are practicing hypocriticism of the poststructuralist sort, which is no prettier than any other form of hypocritical behavior.

What our students need is, first of all, some guidance in learning how to understand their world and survive in it, and secondarily some grounds for criticizing and trying to improve it. Excessive radicalism may be better than excessive traditionalism—but it is not much better. We have proved unwilling to give up our claims to special status as interpreters of quasi-sacred texts and unable to replace our pragmatic need to justify departmental structures founded on the historical narrative of The Story of English. And we are also unwilling to relinquish the comparable claims based upon the magical powers of literary theory, which now functions in many cases simply as a new way of claiming the old status. It is the disparities between our professional needs and our personal desires, as well as the gap between our pedagogical practices and the needs of our students that turn us into hypocritics. The remedy, I want to suggest, is to rethink our practice by starting with the needs of our students rather than with our inherited professionalism or our personal preferences. To understand the needs of our students we shall have to face more squarely than we usually do our present cultural situation.

And what is our present cultural situation? Without pretending to full command of such complexity (which would be hypocriticism with a vengance) I expect you to agree with me that we—teachers as well as students—live in a society that is more fully and insistently textualized than anything people have experienced in the past. Human beings have, since prehistoric times, existed as cultural animals, of course, in social contexts that were mediated by symbolic structures. But it is impossible to deny that languages and other semiotic systems and their associated media of communication have in the course of history multiplied and penetrated more and more deeply into our daily lives. We are at present—like it or not—the most mediated human beings ever to exist on this earth. It is abundantly clear, moreover, that to function as a citizen of these United States one needs to be able to read, interpret, and criticize texts in a wide range of modes, genres, and media. What our students need, then, to function in such a world, is an education for a society still struggling to balance its promises of freedom and equality, still hoping to achieve greater measures of social justice, still trying not to homogenize its people but to allow for social mobility and to make the lower levels of its economic structure tolerable and humane. This is a political program of sorts—but it is not a program for another revolution. Its goal is to make some contribution toward making good on the still unfulfilled promises of the first American Revolution—or, at the very least, helping to prevent the erosion of what has been already achieved.

This is, of course, not strictly the burden of teachers of language and literature, but the highly textualized and mediated nature of our society has constructed for such teachers a position of great importance as educators—if we are willing to change our discipline so as to occupy this position. This means, I should say, letting go of the Story of English as our main preoccupation, and giving up our role as exegetes of quasi-religious texts. It also means giving up any claim to be revolutionary opponents of "the system." We are in it and of it, and we had better admit this to ourselves and others, just to clear the air. The glamor that has attended the notion of "literature" itself for the last two centuries is just one of the things we must renounce. The glamor of "theory" is another. Which doesn't mean we must forget what we have learned—but we must put our learning to use, for instance, by beginning to deconstruct the opposition between the "English" courses and the "service" courses taught by English departments. "Service" courses, like the service entrances of mansions, are for those benighted folk who are not permitted to use the front door. In our case that means we distinguish sharply, and on a basis very close to social class, between those who seek to become like us (our English majors) and those with whom we must deal as lesser breeds whom we agree, for a price, to "sivilize" (which makes us the Aunt Pollies of American education). At present we deal with this situation in English departments mainly by consigning such courses to a lower class of teachers—adjuncts and graduate students—replicating with our departments the class structure that we impose upon our students. This is bad enough, but what we do in our "nonservice" courses is even worse. There, we assume that what is good for those intent on becoming English teachers is also good for everybody else. The traditional English major is designed for young people entering the loop of English teaching, in which English teachers teach future English teachers of future English teachers. This is the system that I believe we must end.

Putting an end to hypocriticism cannot be a simple or easy process, nor do I have any formula for achieving it. I shall try, nonetheless, to conclude this discussion by making some concrete proposals about how we can make a start on ending our hypocritical practices. As a first step, I propose that we undo the entire opposition between "service" and "major" courses and put our energies into a set of courses that will serve all the students of higher education—including that minority who may adopt teaching as a profession. The courses I shall propose can best be seen as a modern revision of the medieval Trivium—or perhaps as a Sophist's rethinking of a Platonic model of education. To the extent that this is a "trivial" proposal, it is a trivium in which one element, rhetoric, must be seen to pervade all the others. But let me get down to cases. Specifically, I suggest that we think of offering a new core curriculum in general education, based on four courses, each of which takes up a particular aspect of the field of textuality—and by textuality I mean the reception and production of texts in the full range of media that constitute our culture.

Each of these courses is based not on a canon of sacred texts but on certain crucial concepts that must be understood not simply in a theoretical way but in their application to the analysis of specific cultural or textual situations. This means that the specific texts selected could have considerable variety from course to course and place to place, though it may well be that certain texts should prove so useful that they would be widely adopted for use in textual curricula. In some cases, even, "classic" texts from philosophy and literature will present themselves as the most useful things available—which may tell us something about why they have become "classics" in the first place. At any rate, the specific titles given in the following descriptions are meant to be illustrative rather than prescriptive.

One of these four courses should take up the topic of *Language and Human Subjectivity.* The basis of this course would be the way that their mother tongue presents human beings with a set of words and grammatical rules in which they may attain subjectivity at the cost of being subjected. The very heart of such a course would be the grammar of the pronouns, beginning with "I" and "you," as opposed to "he," "she," and "it." But this grammar must be connected to the philosophical questions of subject and object and the ethical relationship of "I" and "Thou." The virtual loss of "Thou" in English, except in certain religious contexts would make one point of discussion. In designing such a course I would be careful to use a mixture of theoretical texts and illustrative embodiments of the problems of subjectivity. For instance, the necessary theory is conveniently embodied in such discussions as those of the linguist Emile Benveniste on "The Nature of Pronouns" and "Subjectivity in Language" (*Problems in General*

Linguistics, 1971);[2] in Hegel's dialectic Master and Servant in the *Phenomenology of Spirit;*[3] in Freud's *Das Ich und das Es,*[4] which is usually translated as "The Ego and the Id," but which is just as properly translated as "The I and the It"; and in other works by Piaget, Vygotsky, and Lacan, for example.

Some of this is not easy reading, I will grant you, but basic college work in the sciences is not easy either. There is no reason why we should not ask students to make an effort in the study of human textuality that is comparable to what they would make in economics, biology or any other discipline. On the other hand, we have the opportunity—and the necessity, I would say—of also presenting our topic through texts that embody the charms of specificity and narrativity. In the present instance, my colleagues and I have found that the cases of "wild" children—such as the boy found in Aveyron in the eighteenth century, whose case is available in print and in François Truffaut's excellent film on the subject—make these issues concrete and emotionally engaging. (See Lucien Malson, *Wolf Children and the Problem of Human Nature,* 1972, which includes a full translation of Itard's *The Wild Boy of Aveyron;* and Roger Shattuck, *The Forbidden Experiment: The Story of the Wild Boy of Aveyron.*)[5] Another extremely useful narrative approach to these matters is embodied in Samuel Delany's *Babel-17,* a work of science fiction focused on a language that is dehumanizing precisely because it lacks the pronouns "I" and "you."

Other matters that properly belong to a course on language and human subjectivity would include the problem of human alienation (Hegel and Marx) and the very specific problems of feminine subjectivity in language, especially those relating to the loss of women's family names in history through the adoption of husband's names by wives, and the use of the male pronoun as the general pronoun for males and females. This topic is clearly presented in Dale Spender's *Man Made Language* (1980)[6] and many other works. The whole question of style and personal voice in writing can also be properly deployed under this rubric, along with the study of the essay and the lyric poem as literary forms that have for several centuries enacted the problems of attaining subjectivity in language. Here, also, is the place for students to experiment as writers with the subjective modes of textuality. Many traditional dimensions of the English curriculum can find their places in such a course as this, and they will be engaged in the process by their functioning in a course with the specific conceptual goal of developing students' awareness of the relationship between language and human subjectivity.

Another of the four courses I am proposing would treat the topic of

Representation and Objectivity. Representation is an activity in which a textual subject positions someone or something else as a textual object. The growth of the sciences in modern Europe and America is a process elaborately connected to the development of "objective" discourses. One could almost define science as an objective discourse about a certain body of material. Because of the importance and power of such discourses it is essential for students to learn how they work and what their strengths, costs, and limitations may be. The problems of representation and objectification become especially important in those disciplines involving objects of study that have a strong claim to a subjectivity that may be suppressed (even violently) in order to represent them as objects. It is in the human or social sciences, then, that we will find the most suitable textual material for a course such as this one: sociology, anthropology, and history will offer us topics that are at least accessible to our competences if not within them.

A course in Representation and Objectivity should share some theory with the study of subjectivity in language, but it should also have a theoretical base of its own in theories of representation and narrativity, whether semiotic or New Historicist. It should also draw upon the self-reflective metadiscourse of whatever field is selected for emphasis in a particular version of the course. That is, if the course takes anthropological writing as its focus, it should include both samples of unreflective anthropologizing and works that stand in a metadiscursive relation to such unreflective work, such as selections from Lévi-Strauss's *Tristes Tropiques* and writing on the problems of anthropological discourse by Clifford Geertz and James Clifford.[7] If a historical topic is to be the center of the course, metahistorical work by Charles Collingwood, E. H. Carr, and, of course, Hayden White, might compose part of the theoretical basis of the investigation. It is also easy to imagine a course focused on European representations of its Oriental Other, which takes Edward Said's *Orientalism*[8] as a point of departure. No metatext should take a position of unquestioned validity, of course, but should be used to open up the questions of objectivity and representation so that students can enter them as writers. I think the best results will come in courses with a clear focus, such as the anthropologizing of native Americans, or the historicizing of a specific event in American life, or the sociologizing of a specific American class or culture. In studying such a topic, a range of objective, frankly subjective, and metadiscourses would function as ways of learning both about the specific topic and about the larger processes of representation and objectification that enable scientific discourses to function.

Another possible course in a core curriculum in textuality might be called *System and Dialetic.* Such a course would have as its object of study discourses that work at a high level of abstraction and systematization, in which texts are constructed not so much by representing objects as by abstracting from them their essential qualities or their principles of composition. This is preeminently the domain of philosophy itself, and especially of the tradition of Continental philosophy from the pre-Socratics to Derrida. It may well be that English departments would need help from our friends in philosophy to mount courses that approach this topic effectively, but several decades of literary theory ought to have made us readier to undertake such a project ourselves than we were some years ago.

The point of such study would be not only to make available to students the tradition of clear and systematic thinking that has been so crucial to "Western Civilization" (as it is called), so that they are able to employ the resources of logic and dialectic in their own thinking and writing, but also to give an important place to those countertrends, arising mainly within philosophy itself, that seek to criticize or even undo that very tradition. Put more specifically, absolutely essential philosophers such as Plato, Aristotle, Kant, and Hegel might be read and discussed in speech and writing, along with such antithetical writers as Nietzsche, Wittgenstein, Derrida, Rorty, and Davidson. Such a course might have a particular theme, such as philosophies of science (which would bring Aristotle, Bacon, Locke, Kuhn, and Feyerabend into prominence), or government (which would make Plato, Machiavelli, Hobbes, Montesquieu, and others important)—or education, or language, or justice, or freedom. The point would be for students to learn both how to use and how to criticize discourse that takes reason, system, and logical coherence as its principles of articulation.

The fourth course I shall mention, might well be thought of as the one that should come first if the four courses were to constitute a sequence taken over the first two years of college, for instance, but I have deliberately tried not to imply any particular sequential order in these descriptions. I do suggest, however, that four courses such as these, if they were to constitute a core curriculum for education, would constitute a coherent and reasonably complete modern elaboration of the medieval Trivium of grammar, rhetoric, and dialectic. Seen in this manner, the topics treated in the first three courses I have mentioned are grammar (in the large sense of subjectivity and objectivity) and dialectic. What remains is rhetoric in the narrow sense, which I shall call *Persuasion and Mediation.* In the medieval curriculum, I take the liberty of reminding you, the Trivium was the preliminary core of study that preceded advanced work in the Quadrivium made up of arithmetic, geometry, astronomy, and music. The core courses I have been suggesting here would function in a similar fashion for our enormously more varied body of further studies. They are not meant to be the whole curriculum, but only a useful preliminary to that curriculum.

The title of the fourth course I am proposing, *Persuasion and Mediation,* obviously includes the traditional arts of manipulation of audiences but also points toward the capacities and limits of the newer media, especially those that mix verbal and visual textuality to generate effects of unprecedented power. Such courses are well enough known and widely enough taught already in many schools, so that I can spare you any elaboration of them on this occasion. I will only insist that such courses should reverse the traditional priority of rhetorical training, concentrating on the critical defenses against persuasion and manipulation rather than on the practice of those skills. The best way to comprehend this level of rhetoric is to see it from both sides, producing manipulative texts and critiques of such texts—which, of course, can hardly escape the play of rhetoric themselves.

At this point, having tried to explore the nature of our hypocritical situation and to suggest the first steps toward undoing it, I must stop my own trivial textualizing and ask for your response. It's your turn now.

Notes

1. Richard Ohmann, *English in America: A Radical View of the Teaching Profession,* with a chapter by Wallace Douglas (New York: Oxford University Press, 1976).
2. Emile Benveniste, *Problems in General Linguistics,* trans. Mary Elizabeth Meek (Coral Gables, Fla.: University of Miami Press, 1971).
3. Georg Wilhelm Friedrich Hegel, *The Phenomenology of Spirit,* trans. A. V. Miller, foreword by J. N. Findlay (Oxford: Oxford University Press, 1979).
4. Sigmund Freud, *The Ego and the Id,* trans, Joan Riviere, rev. and newly ed. James Strachey (New York: Norton, 1962).
5. Lucien Malson, *Wolf Children and the Problem of Human Nature,* trans. Edmund Fawcett, Peter Ayrton, and Joan White (New York: Monthly Review Press, 1972); Roger Shattuck, *The Forbidden Experiment: The Story of the Wild Boy of Aveyron* (New York: Farrar, Straus and Giroux, 1980).
6. Dale Spender, *Man Made Language,* 2d ed. (London: Routledge and Kegan Paul, 1985).
7. Claude Lévi-Strauss, *Tristes Tropiques,* trans. John and Doreen Weightman (New York: Atheneum, 1974); Clifford Geertz, *Works and Lives: The Anthropologist as Author* (Stanford: Stanford University Press, 1988) and *The Interpretation of Cultures, Selected Essays* (New York: Basic Books, 1973); James Clifford, *The Predicament of*

Culture: Twentieth-Century Ethnography, Literature, and Art (Cambridge: Harvard University Press, 1988; James Clifford and George E. Marcus, editors, *Writing Culture: the Poetics and Politics of Ethnography* (Berkeley: University of California Press, 1986).

8. Edward W. Said, *Orientalism* (New York: Pantheon Books, 1978.)

Relevant Publications by Robert Scholes

Protocols of Reading. New Haven: Yale University Press, 1989.

Text Book: An Introduction to Literary Language (with Gregory Ulmer and Nancy Comley). New York: St. Martin's Press, 1988, 1995.

Textual Power. New Haven: Yale University Press, 1985.

Semiotics and Interpretation. New Haven: Yale University Press, 1982.

"Canonicity and Textuality." In *Introduction to Scholarship in Modern Languages and Literatures,* edited by Joseph Gibaldi, Modern Language Association, 1992.

"A Flock of Cultures—A Trivial Proposal." *College English* 53 (November 1991): 759–72.

"An End to Hypocriticism." *South Central Review* 8 (spring 1991): 1–13.

"Aiming a Canon at the Curriculum." *Salmagundi* 72 (fall 1986): 101–63.

"Contemporary Critical Theory and the Humanistic Interpretation of Texts." *Michigan Quarterly Review* 20 (spring 1981): 101–14.

Part II

Recapturing the Values of Reading Literature

9

Authors and Books: The Return of the Dead from the Graveyard of Theory

James Battersby

James Battersby is professor of literature at Ohio State University. His 1991 Paradigms Regained, *subtitled "Pluralism and the Practice of Criticism," is devoted as much to defining a specific kind of philosophical and literary/critical pluralism as to defending such a pluralism. His many-sided argument is too complex for summary here, but the following paragraph from his introduction well suggests the position he seeks to establish:*

> *For the pluralist, there are many true, right, and good (as well as, of course, many false, wrong, and bad) worlds, versions of texts and, thus, many true, right, and good reference relations, foundations, and correspondences. What there is not, of course, for the pluralist, is* one true *foundation, one reference relation which just is* the *reference relation, or one order of* truth. *In this view, a text is already a version, already an interpretation and a system of justification when we meet it.*

The present essay draws on the argument of Paradigms Regained *while perhaps more succinctly summing up, with special reference to the work of the philosopher Donald Davidson, the necessity of accepting such currently unfashionable concepts as objectivity, authorial intention, determinate meaning, stability of reference, and a nonlinguistic reality—if we are to think about and discuss literary (or other) experience. Of course, Battersby insists, each of these concepts must be understood in relation to a system of human thought, but human thought cannot (and does not, even in the most skeptical theoretical arguments) get along without them.*

Common theoretical wisdom has it that authors have given up the ghost and literary works have deferred pride of place to language or been resolved into ideology or politics, especially the politics of race, class, and gender. Given the prevailing assumptions in critical studies today, to express an interest in the literary text as a unique product of artistic making and an eagerness to focus attention on works within the system of their interests would be to express what many would undoubtedly take to be an antediluvian quaintness or perverse stubbornness. At any rate, it is glaringly clear that professing (or teaching) literature is what a good many modern critics are *not* doing, and not doing with a vengeance. By and large, literary critics today produce not literary criticism or literary studies, but theory and metacriticism and talk not about literary works or artistic products (i.e., unique products of art, verbal structures reflecting the representational and expressive interests of rational agents), but about writing, semiotics, the play of codes and conventions or, speaking even more broadly, about texts as instantiations, signs, exemplifications, or consequences of the more basic linguistic or social (political, ideological, gender, etc.) forces that serve as the conditions of possibility for the speaker, speaking, and spoken.

Interestingly enough, the language that is seen to the bottom of—or the bottomless abyss of—is one that gives special prominence to what we would old-fashionedly call syntax, as distinct from semantics or pragmatics, to, that is, that branch of semiotics which studies the relations of signs to one another apart from their contentful relations to the "world." Semantic relations, after all, are those that are concerned with truth, reference, and meaning, with that to which the signs point or direct attention. And modern theorists also tend to neglect pragmatics, the study of the relations between speakers and interpreters and, more broadly, of the ways we *use* signs. The current theoretical neglect of authors and individual purposes undoubtedly derives much of its impetus from its Saussurean heritage, with its emphasis on language, not as a representational system, but as a formal system of sign relations. In a fairly recent article on current trends in criticism, for example, Catherine Gallagher observes that not one of the well-known critics participating in a lecture series at Berkeley said anything at all about literature, though much was said about signs and the prisonhouses of language.[1]

Moreover, in *On Deconstruction: Theory and Criticism,* Jonathan Culler positively exults in the liberation of criticism from a concern with works of literature, since the view of theory as the handmaiden to literature has tended perniciously to cripple and debase critical thought or, more properly, Theory, a rigorous independent discipline. To Culler, it is a totally discredited and thoroughly outmoded view which insists that "the test of critical writing is its success in enhancing our appreciation of literary works, and [that] the test of theoretical discussions is its success in providing instruments to help the critic provide better interpretations."[2] In the Pantheon of those doing Theory, those in the line of succession from Carlyle, Emerson, Nietzsche, et al., Culler includes such writers as Saussure, Marx, Freud, Gadamer, and Derrida, all of whom, along with Lacan, Bakhtin, Althusser, and many others, make problematic what had hitherto been treated as given, by bringing to reflection what had before only been used.

Much of what Culler says dovetails nicely, of course, with the widespread, if not quite pervasive concern, not with the book, but with the *text,* and, not with the text as a discrete, distinguishable or isolable locus of meaning and value, but the text as complex of intertexts, or, in Julia Kristeva's terms, as a "mosaic of quotations."[3] The text, as another critic would have it, "emerges as interpretive discourse caught up in a network of other interpretive discourses."[4] Once everything goes textual (and signs are seen principally in terms of their relations to other signs), it is easy to show that no center or stable locus of meaning will hold. In short, once what *is* becomes only *semes,* once the sign of the thing becomes the "thing" of attention, it is difficult not to conclude that everything is intertextual, since interimplication is inevitable in a world where marks or inscriptions are, as Derrida insists, iterable in illimitable contexts and always and already other than themselves. Books, unlike texts, aspire to tell the truth about things, whereas texts are and can be nothing more than comments on other texts:

> The idea of the book is the idea of a totality, finite or infinite, of the signifier; this totality of the signifer cannot be a totality, unless a totality constituted by the signified preexists it, supervises its inscriptions and its signs, and is independent of it in its ideality [i.e., the totality of the signified is the ultimate center or ground of meaning that authorizes and makes valid what is said or done, but since

> neither signifier nor signified is stable—everything is relational, and stability is always deferred—there can be no fixed meaning; other meanings and uses are always and necessarily implicated in current meanings and uses]. The idea of the book, which always refers to a natural totality, is profoundly alien to the sense of writing.[5]

The idea of the book has gone, of course, with the loss of the Transcendental Signified, the sure grounding of the fixed relation between word and thing, leaving us only with relations among signs. At best, with the loss of real correspondences between words, thoughts, and things, we are left with various systems of thought, each legitimate and none privileged. As Hilary Putnam observes, "For deconstructionists, metaphysics was the *basis* of our entire culture, the pedestal on which it all rested; if the pedestal has broken, the entire culture must have collapsed—indeed, our whole language must lie in ruins."[6] (It is perhaps worth noting, for the sake of my subsequent argument, that Putnam goes on immediately to say that "but of course we can and do make sense of the idea of a reality we did not make, even though we cannot make sense of the idea of a reality that is 'present' in the metaphysical sense of dictating its own unique description.") Just because "reality" or the "world"—or, more appropriately, "worlds," since, with Putnam and many others, I assume that there are innumerable correct or right "realities" or descriptions of the world—cannot be seen or understood independently of our descriptions, we should not be led to suppose that there are only descriptions. From Putnam's antirelativist, "internal realist" viewpoint—which runs counter to the relativism and nihilism of most literary theorists—"some facts are there to be discovered . . . but this is something to be said [only] when one has adopted a way of speaking, a language, a 'conceptual scheme.' "[7] But if we have lost the possibility of providing a single, unique description of the way things just are, we have not lost our ability to make and live in real worlds of fact and value, nor our ability to produce artifacts, including poems, with determinate references and meaning, with internal interests and effects that are knowable, as we shall see. And it is worth remembering at the outset that for our purposes and for purposes of literary study we, if not Derrida and others, can separate the issue of realism, an ontological matter, from the issues of truth and meaning, semantic matters.

Nevertheless, despite their many differences, modern theorists by and large share the view that there is no mind- or discourse-independent world of things that authorizes or validates our claims and against which our assertions must be squared. If this view amounts to no more than saying that it makes no sense to talk about references, objects, or facts except in relation to some conceptual scheme or that content-bearing mental states depend on some particular use of language, then there can be no disagreement with the theorists, but it does not follow from this view, as the theorists seem to think, that as the world of unique descriptions (as the Transcendental Signified) goes, so goes the text as a bearer of stable, determinate meanings to which our interpretive statement can be adjusted and against which our opinions must be tested for accuracy and appropriateness. Still, the prevailing view is that once meaning goes immanent (once things and thoughts and all the rest go inside conceptual schemes, inside the language by which they are constituted what they are) and "reality" presumptively stands aloof in noumenal hauteur or is willing, for its own high ironic purposes, to wear any outfit supplied by any logodaedalic coutourier, while steadfastly refusing to endorse or approve of any one conceptual suit, then such things as determinate meaning, truth, justification, and so on disappear from the scene, along with authors, stable texts, and standards of value, which are nothing but precipitates of always-already-in-place categories and systems of meaning that shift from interpretive community to interpretive community and from period to period.

Many, if not all, modern relativists-poststructuralists apparently believe that if there is no gold standard (no Transcendental Signified, no one independently existing maker good and true of our assertions), if there is no solid gold (mind-independent real things) in some (metaphysical) Fort Knox to back up our paper (linguistic or merely verbal) negotiations, then no scrip(t) is better, more valuable, or more negotiable than any other scrip(t), and we can print as much of any kind of scrip(t) as we want and exchange one kind for another at will and ad infinitum. An impatient citizen, outside the loop of Theory, might protest at this point that a scheme which enabled her to form true beliefs, to satisfy desires and meet needs would certainly be preferable to one that made possible none of these or that was self-refuting or otherwise incoherent, but she would be speaking out of turn. To continue, though no scheme has any privilege over any other scheme, some schemes, it is affirmed, have greater authority and, hence, legitimacy than others do. This authority derives not from the adequacy of the scheme to some needs or values or from its truth, but from its power. Authority reduces to persuasion, which reduces to power. In a world of immanent meaning, emphasis is regularly placed on the constitutive energy of various more and less powerful paradigms, social formations, ideologies, or interpretive communities. Emphasis is placed, in short, on the determination of facts, things, values, and so on by the conceptual categories of one or another entrenched or influential community, archive, habitus, or power elite and, usually, on the "incommensurability" of the various schemes: the impossibility, that is, of speaking or understanding outside the historical-ideological framework through which not only "reality" but also the speaker is spoken.

Of course, the issues that occupy today's literary theorists and to which they subordinate artistic works are nothing other than locally differentiated avatars of more general and pervasive concerns of modern philosophy, both Continental and Anglo-American. The Continental side is preoccupied *either* with the endless deferral of meaning, the loss of stability in signifier and signified, and the emergence of the other to undermine or subvert what is affirmed on the surface (what is logocentrically asserted) *or* with the determination of the speaking and the spoken, the writing and the written, by social, political, cultural, and ideological conditions. The Anglo-American side concentrates *either* on the *incommensurability of languages* (theories, conceptual schemes), the view that each language is unique and, thus, not translatable into any other language, *or* on the *indeterminacy of meaning,* the view that too many statements (theories, meanings) are compatible with the data. In the philosophical debates, as in those strictly focused on literary theory, the chief disesteemed antagonists are objectivity, intentionality, determinate meaning, stability of reference, the authority of the author to structure meanings and determine effects—in short, all those terms and categories upon which the discussion and analysis of the discrete products of the creative, artistic imagination depend or rely.

In the space available in this essay, it would be impossible, of course, to put into question all that the theorists have put into question; impossible, but also unwise, since there are obviously many attractive neonates in the bathwater of modern theory. Still, to the extent that some of the prevailing principles and assumptions make impossible (or seem to make impossible) what we would most earnestly be about—namely, a brief discussion of some of what is involved and entailed in an approach to literature based on a conception of language in *use*—it is necessary to do a little ground-clearing and to reclaim some territory for tillage that has been deemed (at best) infertile. Elsewhere (in other writings) I have attempted to provide full-scale arguments in support of what I must here lay claim to by force of enthymeme and authoritative fiat (a kind of pointing in the right direction, directing the attention to the critics and philosophers with big shoulders and muscular arguments).

The philosophical literature on *incommensurability* (the impossibility of talking across paradigms or interpretive communities, or of translating from one discourse to another) and *indeterminacy of meaning or translation* (the inability of terms to describe uniquely the ways things are or to remain fixed in reference) is vast, but no one should assume that these issues have been settled once and for all in favor of the theorists. Quite the contrary, the accumulating evidence and argument lean the other way. Against the notion of incommensurability, which finds its strongest advocates in literary theorists influenced by Thomas Kuhn's *The Structure of Scientific Revolutions,* such as Stanley Fish (and many others), the strongest case has undoubtedly been made by Donald Davidson in "On the Very Idea of a Conceptual Scheme," in which, in addition to showing how field linguists regularly overcome the difficulties of translating languages radically different from their own (languages grounded in and informed by values and assumptions they do not share), Davidson forcefully argues that the notion of a scheme beyond our capacity to understand is incoherent, since to know that it is an alternative scheme is already to be well into the process of translation and understanding. In another compelling essay, Davidson argues that "we really do not understand the *idea* of such a foreign scheme," because

> We know what states of mind are like, and how they are correctly identified; they are just those states whose contents can be discovered in well-known ways. If other people or creatures are in states not discoverable by these methods, it can be, not because our methods fail us, but because those states are not correctly called states of mind—they are not beliefs, desires, wishes, or intentions. The meaninglessness of the idea of a conceptual scheme forever beyond our grasp is due not to our inability to understand such a scheme or to our other human limitations; it is due simply to what we mean by a system of concepts.[8]

Moreover, it is clear, I think, that we regularly discuss the conflicting claims of rival views; in doing so, we are representing both views from a position outside either view (managing in the process, it should be noted, to be fair to both but partial to neither), since no position can be *discussed* within the position itself. Within the position, we *use* the conditions of its expression; we do not *discuss* them. Even to say in Wittgensteinian fashion that something is "true" in such and such a "language game" is to speak a truth about the "language game," but not a "truth" within the game, or, as Putnam notes: "if we say that it is a *fact* that acceptance of a given statement of theory is 'justified relative to the standards of culture A' [as Rorty does, and as Fish says of "interpretive communities"], then we are treating 'being the standard of a culture' and 'according with the standard of a culture' as something *objective,* something itself *not* relative to the standards of this-or-that culture."[9] A similar point, with Kuhn's paradigm-locked view as the focus, is made by James Harris in *Against Relativism,* when he argues that

> to say that two paradigms are incommensurable requires one to assume an intellectual position such that one can "stand outside" the totality of any single paradigm. . . . Since rules and criteria for paradigm evaluation (including presumably even logical consistency) are clearly supposed to be internal to a paradigm, according to Kuhn, then "incommensurable" is a predicate which can only take on a meaning relative to a single paradigm. Obviously, however, incommensurability is a relationship between or amongst paradigms; so it must follow as a result of criteria or rules which are *not internal* to any given paradigm.[10]

Further, it is useful to remember that "rationality and justification are presupposed by the activity of criticizing and inventing paradigms and are not themselves defined by any single paradigm."[11] Although there is considerably more to say about our ability to understand and participate in structures of meaning and reference not of our own (or our interpretive community's, our episteme's, archive's, etc. own) making, we can conclude this discussion by noting that we can always talk *about* what we talk *with,* can always go "meta-" on any discourse or work and that without the sharing of content, the sharing of some references and meaning, there can be no agreement or disagreement.

Like incommensurability, *indeterminacy* is a vexed question, one not likely to be stripped of all vexation in a brief discussion; for our immediate purposes, however, we can say enough about it to justify and legitimize our concern with determinate art products. As Quine and others have shown us, there is a strong sense in which, since "nature" has no semantic preferences and has no point of view on "things" that determines which descriptions are uniquely true, and since every object of any kind is like Wittgenstein's rabbit/duck figure, in that logically it can be described in many ways and participate functionally in innumerable conceptual schemes, reference is fundamentally and inescapably indeterminate. And if we were metaphysicians of daily life, we might worry about our ability to negotiate our way through each day in a world without bounded entities (i.e., fixed objects) or a Foundation. But the fact that the contents of our experience have no fixed references doesn't mean, of course, that we can't bump into them or that they are not "real"; they are real enough for all our interests and purposes, since they are in large part the products of those interests and purposes. Although it is perhaps impossible to say where "things" would be *for us* without our interests in and descriptions of them, it is possible to say, I think, that what is true and right and fitting is not simply a matter of language. There is for us no way the world independently is, although there is an independent world (or, more properly, there are independent worlds), as Mark Sacks, echoing Putnam, suggests.[12] What is true, right, or fitting is not simply up to us, since we can distinguish between "conditions of reference," which we supply, from "reference," which we do not supply. As Michael Devitt observes, making the word "rose" refer in certain conditions (the conditions that we specify) "is not *making those conditions obtain,* and, hence, is not making roses"[13] (my emphasis). Nevertheless, with Quine and the theorists we recognize that reference is nonsense except "relative to a coordinate system," a frame of reference, a conceptual scheme.[14] Objects, facts, references, values, explanations, then, are context-sensitive, interest-relative, and purpose-conditional. On these matters most parties are largely in agreement. But if we can agree on this much—that meaning and reference are relative to conceptual scheme—then we should be able to agree on more (indeed, we have already agreed to considerably more in fact). We should agree, for example, *that* such schemes as have content are knowable (see the comments above on radical interpretation and on understanding systems not of our own making), *that* whatever has content has semantic properties (e.g., such semantic properties as meaning, reference, and truth conditions), and that there are only contents where there are systems of intentionality, since "aboutness" is the essential feature of intentionality and since only creatures with content-bearing mental states have intentionality and use language. Agents, authors, folks like you and me—not cultures, ideologies, epistemes, communities, and so on—are capable of marking things off from one another and having interests and systems of meaning.

The web of interlocking concepts is very tight here, but a few strands more will provide the conceptual strength we need to pursue our interests in literary works with a clear conscience in this flagitious era of theory (i.e., the prevailing theory that has made authors and works suspect, indeed, phantasmagorical notions). To be interested in something is to be able to think about it and refer to it (whatever it is); such directing of the attention to something is what we mean, in large measure, by intentionality (to have any world at all or anything at all to think about is to be caught up in intentionality). Now since all forms of intentionality (beliefs, desires, intentions, doubts, fears, thirsts, hungers, etc.) have conditions of satisfaction (e.g., truth is the satisfaction of belief, drinking the satisfaction of thirst, etc.), intentionality is inescapably normative; its conditions are satisfied *or not* (or satisfied more or less). Now, to take one instance of intentionality, for a belief to be satisfied is for it to be justified, to be true. And what something is depends on the conditions justifying it, as we learned above when with Quine and others we recognized that reference is relative to scheme. What is referred to in a sentence is determined and justified (or not) by its fittingness to a scheme. More simply, "there can be no meaning without some form of structure or pattern that establishes relationships."[15] It is only relative to justification or truth conditions, for example, that a "bill" belongs to a baseball cap rather than to a restaurant check. And for Michael Dummett, as Ernest Lepore and Barry Loewer remind us, "the justification [or truth] conditions of a sentence are its meaning, and since understanding a sentence is just knowing its meaning, it follows that anyone who understands a sentence knows its justification conditions, that is, the canonical conditions such that if they were satisfied the sentence would be true."[16] From all this, it is not a big leap to the understanding that a literary work (like a critical essay or an editorial) is a system of justification or rationality, a system of self-satisfaction, one that is knowable from within its interests and conditions of satisfaction. To have any world at all, including the world of specific conceptual and emotional entailments that make up a literary work, we must have standards of justification or, as Putnam regularly notes, standards of rational acceptability. Just as there are many ways of wrecking a ship in a storm and very few ways of bringing it home safe, as Aristotle observed, so there are many ways for a piece of literature to go wrong and very few ways for it to go right, to fit its internal conditions of satisfaction or justification. Since we, along with Davidson and others, are concerned with a psychological, semantic, truth-conditional view of truth and meaning, we acknowledge the wisdom of the notion that "the most basic law of psychology is a rationality constraint on an agent's belief, desires, and actions: No rationality, no agent";[17] indeed, no rationality, no content, no truth, meaning, or reference. Moreover, we tend to see things in literary and other works the way they are intended to be seen, because that is the way they are justified, that is the way the contents have justification, and once we start "seeing as," we tend to work within what "seeing as" makes possible. On this point, Wittgenstein, as elucidated by Eddy M. Zemach, is instructive:

> [As I initially see the content] it fits some things and not others. That is why Wittgenstein compares meaning in language to the meaning of a musical phrase; of course you can do anything at all with that motif [considered in isolation], but given the way we see it, having heard [or read] the work up to this point, some developments would look absolutely wrong to us. The phrase in that work has a meaning: it "asks" to be dealt with in certain ways and not others.[18]

In sum, then, meanings are determinate within systems, and such systems are, if not given to the understanding as immediately as the leaves are given to the tree, accessible to understanding, in just the ways that Donald Davidson has suggested.

The consequences of the foregoing remarks for critical practice are, I think, quite remarkable, if only because they enable us to reinvest with dignity and appropriateness many critical activities that have undergone the lash of excoriation and suffered the shame of excommunication in recent years, in the years dominated by what Culler calls Theory. From the heights of philosophical reflection, we can now descend to more mundane observations and concerns. In the interests of expedition, I shall be brief, presenting the case in truncated form (at least initially) as articles of commitment with only some of the implications spelled out.

1. Language in *use* is always centered, is always selective and restrictive. We cannot talk about what we cannot mention or distinguish, and we cannot talk about or imply all the attributes that what we talk about may have; as Quine has persistently reminded us, we cannot know what something is without knowing how it is differentiated from other things. (For Quine, of course, this means that identity is coextensive with ontol-

ogy.) More pointedly, as John Searle notes, "intentional states represent their conditions of satisfaction only under certain aspects, and those aspects must matter to the agent";[19] intentionality is aspectual or perspectival, a matter of seeing something "as," from some point of view, and "representation" is a matter of intentionality. In any given use of the word "chair," for example, I do not imply that it is my property or was made in North Carolina. Simon Blackburn has provided an interesting example of how "chair" satisfies conditions under one rather than another aspect (and, incidentally, of the interest-relativity of explanation): "the natural or best explanation of a physical thing having a physical property need not belong to physics. In most contexts, the best explanation of this chair being within three miles of Carfax may be that it belongs to me, and this is where I live."[20] Furthermore, once we have selected and, hence, restricted our terms, we can say no more, while those restrictions are in place, than what falls within the logical and semantic range of those terms as used. Among other things, we affirm here that no problem or situation can be completely formulated or represented, that any problem or representation is "relative to its formulation, and that any solution," to the extent that it is a solution to the problem or situation as formulated, "must also be relative to the formulation."[21]

2. The constraints on usage are not *always already,* as the popular theoretical phrase goes, in place; the constraints are not an automatic consequence of, for example, the nature of language, prior texts, ideologies, social formations, or gender. We are never locked into the prisonhouse of any language (any particular system of justification). Understanding depends on the sharing of many concepts, and the co-referentiality of terms is common (e.g., we can have many different views of *Hamlet,* the French Revolution, psoriasis, department chairmen, and so forth). And, as we have seen, we can always talk *about* what we talk *with,* always transcend our formalizations. Without such imaginative capacities of transcendence, mindless repetition would be our only expressive possibility. Now, as in the past, we all coexist more or less comfortably within a variety of professional and nonprofessional interpretive communities.

3. Our plenty makes us poor. That is, our various codes and conventions—whether derived from the analysis of language, culture, history, politics, or whatever—supply us with little more than a large stock of terms capable of entering into a multiplicity of substitutional, combinatorial, meaning, or referential relations, a stock of terms rich in meaning possibility or potentiality. But these codes and conventions, however refined and

elaborated, cannot determine the boundary conditions of their own operation, for, as we have seen, truth-, assertibility-, or justification-conditions are prior to reference (and meaning). They are rich in possibility, but poor in determination. Thus, just as the system of rules governing the relations in which chess pieces may enter does not and cannot determine the strategy of any particular game (as Michael Polanyi observes), so the conditions of language, considered as a relational system of possible substitutions and combinations, cannot determine the nature of any particular work.[22] The game cannot be played outside the rules, but the rules cannot organize a strategy. Even though it would be a mistake to assume that people are not played by systems—in the sense that we are all creatures of the terms available to or forced upon us and, as such, all limited to working out what falls within the logical and semantic range of those terms—it would be a greater mistake to fail to realize that, no matter how severe the constraints on expression may be, an unlimited number of purposes are realizable within them; or that the boundary conditions for the operation of the relational systems cannot be supplied by the systems themselves. Hence, it is the very *indeterminacy of language* that obliges us to locate the constraints on possibility in the textually embedded intentional acts of agents.

4. Codes and conventions make writing possible; writers make codes and conventions behave, answer to the bidding of their mental states, their various intentionalities. Since neither a sentence nor a work derives its specific meaning or emphasis from the words considered in themselves (indeed, they have no determinate reference considered in themselves) or in their possible relations (apart from justification conditions, which make them relations of something to something); since, in other words, no work can come into being or carry a determinate meaning (or have a particular expressive content of moral choice and emotional emphasis) unless its medium (i.e., its language) is deliberately arranged in some fashion for some reason or purpose, it is not possible in our engagement *with the work* to avoid the sorts of interpretive assumptions about agents and intentions that modern critical theory, in most of its branches and franchises, has denounced or proscribed. For example, in reading, say, *Othello,* we are most profitably rewarded by asking repeatedly of greater and less linguistic units, not "What do these words mean"? but, borrowing from Ralph Rader, "What significant creative intention must I assume to make these words intelligible?"[23] In posing the question this way, we are seeking to understand the justification conditions or, in slightly older, more "literary" terms, the principles of construction embedded in the text as products of

choice, only on the assumption of which can we account for all the particulars of the text. Making what is to me a companionable point, Putnam states that "what is *true* depends on what our terms *refer to,* and—on any picture—determining the reference of terms demands sensitivity to the referential intentions of actual speakers and an ability to make nuanced decisions as to the best reconstruction of those intentions."[24] Similarly, Martha Nussbaum views "literary texts as works whose representational and expressive content issues from human intentions and conceptions" and elucidates how Richard Wollheim, in *Painting as an Art* and in *Art and Its Objects,* shows that "the standard of correctness for the spectator's (or reader's) activity must be found by reference to the artist's intention; but that only those intentions are relevant that are causally involved in the production of the work."[25] Of course, in our reach for artistic intention, we may guess wrong, may misunderstand the creative intention, but the text, in its reluctance to accommodate itself to our constitutive hypothesis, has the capacity to force a revision of our assumptions; our guess is propensive, not tyrannical. Finally, it is useful to remember that in perhaps most of our dealings with most of our literature, we are concerned with language, not as organized into propositional networks or systems of truth claims, but as systems of moral perplexity, moral choice, and moral action; what most frequently needs to be grasped is not what the words mean, but what act by what sort of person in what sort of situation the words make possible. "Character," for example, must be inferred from its actualizations, and unless we make such inferences about "character" (the sort of person we are dealing with), the work has no significant moral or emotional effect.

5. The final commitment has several codicils attached to it, but basically it affirms a sharp division among interpretation, poetics, and criticism and sees them as hierarchically arranged in a regular order of dependence: criticism is dependent upon poetics, and poetics upon interpretation (the last, in turn, depending upon linguistics and, broadly considered, philology). Each of these divisions (along with ethics) will be quickly considered in turn in the conclusion to this essay, but here we can briefly chart the terrain. Once we have grasped the significant artistic intention that both implies and is implied by the details of this work and then that work and the next one (interpretation), we can begin to consider a variety of texts in terms of likenesses and differences (along several lines of differentiation). Since we can make relevant statements about essential aspects of two or more texts—aspects essential under distinct intentional conceptions (we are

not limited to particulars)—and since every work uses its medium in distinguishable ways, we can begin to outline the poetics of discrete artistic forms. Only when we have mastered these tasks (however casually or deliberately) are we in a position to see texts in their larger artistic, social, political relations; only then are we in a position to do criticism. For all our current talk about transcending works and authors and moving beyond interpretation, no one, it seems to me—not Derrida or Foucault or Greenblatt or whoever—can do any work with literature at all without first performing acts of interpretation (something must be understood as something before it can be talked *about*). Interpretation, however unimportant ultimately to the critic, is the necessary basis of larger speculation, to the extent that that speculation is concerned at all with *literature* and what it reveals about, say, history, mind, language, politics, or culture. We need not focus on interpretation, of course, but we cannot do literary criticism of any kind prior to or in the absence of interpretation. In literary criticism, then, we cannot profess anything else unless we also and first profess literature, if only in our studies before taking pen in hand.

In the following concluding section on the divisions among critical enterprises, the emphasis will be less on definition and theoretical defense of categories than on elaboration of the importance and value of the categories (given the analyses of meaning, reference, intentionality, and rationality presented above). Our task here, at the rudimentary or propaedeutic level, is merely to show that celebrations (or "funferals," as Joyce would say) on the occasion of the death of the author or of the work (at least as a determinate structure of intentionality) are premature or, as we might more modishly say, proleptic. Consequently, with our focus on agents (authors) and intentionality (as embedded in works), we will not be able to consider the difficulties involved in coming to a strong understanding of justification conditions (or, in an older terminology, principles of form) or in dealing with conflicting conceptions of those conditions (with rival or multiple interpretations).

Interpretation. Interpretation, in our view, involves coming to an understanding of the text's categories of intelligibility (its contents) in their functional relations within a system of rationality or justification. In the literature we have come most to value (in every culture), our understanding is enlarged with each renewed contact and perhaps never enlarged to fullness or completeness. In reading *Othello* for the fortieth time, we are struck by a new rightness or appropriateness that we had not noticed before. It is this understanding that is at the center of interpretation and is crucial to what Quine and Ullian call the training of taste: such training "proceeds by emphasizing skillfully selected elements of an object," and this "increased familiarity with the structure of the aesthetic object [with what we have been calling its conditions of satisfaction] can engender a liking, granted a suitable choice of object in the first place."[26] The skill part of such an understanding can be developed and refined and, to a large extent and in its main features, taught, principally by regularly asking questions about how these and those discernible elements *fit* or *satisfy* the intentional conditions of their possibility. Moreover, those to whom it is taught can develop and refine the skill on their own, largely because the questions it permits and encourages can be right *or* wrong, because the hypothesis (the controlling conception of "seeing as," in Wittgenstein's sense) from which we project meanings and possibilities is right and adequate to the (always already) justified structure, *or it is not;* our projections can be *disconfirmed* as well as confirmed.

And surely those of us who give days and nights to the study of literature can be forgiven for focusing at least some of our attention on what we ought not to be embarrassed to call the "internal goods"—the satisfied needs of the artistic structure—of texts; on the rather uncommon, wonderful, and remarkable fittingness and workingness of things in certain texts, once they are considered under this or that conception of justification. Perhaps we can even be forgiven for allowing ourselves to value more highly than other works those that not only manage to fit much of interest in but to make so much of what fits in contribute significantly to the working of the whole work. Surely we can be forgiven for continuing to admire and value *Paradise Lost*, the *Essay on Man, The Prelude,* and *King Lear* as "masterpieces," as monuments of unaging intellect, even though propositionally, as bodies of ideas or systems of thought, they are if not philosophically bankrupt, at least intellectually poor or suspect; and even though most of what is politically, ideologically, historically interesting in them can be found in many other earlier, contemporaneous, and later works (both serious and comic, both popular and elite, as well as in other cultural artifacts, like trade routes or jokes or whatever) and found perhaps in purer, starker, bolder form in them.

In addition to admiring these works for the largeness of their conception, the extent of their understanding, the importance of the matters they raise and deal with, we recognize as we applaud in each of them a superior kind of formal or artistic achievement; we discern in each rightnesses and appropriatenesses that are widely distributed and deeply embedded and that, by *enhancing the workingness of the whole,* make the realized work a rare and, hence, especially valuable achievement. Indeed, this formal richness is inseparable from the intellectual and moral achievement of the works; the structural echoings, entailments, and interlacings are the conditions of possibility, in a sense, of the conceptual reach, moral significance, and emotional power of the works.

In *Othello,* for example, every scene, virtually every word, not only contributes to the forwarding of the action and to our understanding of the bases of jealousy, but also enhances and enriches our sense of the internal integrity, of the architectonic cohesiveness of the work as a whole. One after another, each image, phrase, or scene finds itself involved with predecessors or successors in a complexly appropriate system of interimplication. If the making of such richly self-satisfied, formally and morally rich works (as, e.g., *Othello, Paradise Lost, The Essay on Man, The Prelude,* and so on, and so on) is a huge accomplishment (as it clearly is when measured against the standards established over the years by the accomplishments of other toilers in the same fields), then the participation, by means of understanding, in such achievements at the level of their interests and justifications is a huge pleasure, which many today, alas, do not experience but which, fortunately (in an odd sense of "fortunately," the sense in which ignorance is bliss), their theoretical principles and assumptions keep them from knowing they are not experiencing.

To talk of these pleasures and these accomplishments to the knowledgeably well-pleased is undoubtedly to talk unnecessarily; that is, it is to talk to the sailor of the sea, to talk to those who already know what one is talking about and who do not need to be convinced of the pleasure of pleasure. But something is surely awry when one is repeatedly invited to deny the pleasure, or to confess that it is second-rate, insignificant, illusory, or impossible, because language is such and such or because what really counts or what everything finally boils down to is ideology, undoing, colonialism, or whatever. Or if the pleasure is allowed, it is allowed only as a guilty pleasure, one inseparable from one's tolerance of or complicity with oppression, racism, sexism, or whatever. In this essay, our aim, in part, has been to reclaim the pleasure (to establish at least its possibility) and to take the guilt out of it by showing that the text, as a product of a rich network of interested human and humanly interesting intentionality (and not as a mere consequence, sign, instance of something else, such as history, ideology, gender, class, etc.), is already an uncommonly rich system of justification and that the system it is is knowable as that system (though coming to know it is no easy or automatic task). It is a system made and recovered by the more or less strenuous exercise of practical reasoning upon conceptual materials within our grasp or available to our reach.

Ethics, in brief. Of course, any differentiable part, any isolable element of the work can become the focus of independent interest and inquiry, and anything so isolated for attention can be examined and discussed in connection with any number of things linguistic, social, political, philological, ideological, anthropological, patriotic, mechanical, biographical, or psychological. Nevertheless, high among our interests in those works not motivated or justified by a system of *ideas* or *themes* but focusing on morally differentiated individuals in humanly interesting situations is an interest in what speaking broadly we can call "ethical quality." Most of our novels, dramas, narrative poems, as well as the majority of our lyric poems, for example, invite us to note clearly and then to consider carefully and disinterestedly what it would be like to think and feel in such and such a frame of mind and live in such and such circumstances, allow us to see vividly and to participate imaginatively in moral perplexities, in situations of moral choice and moral action, to confront those perplexities, not as a system of ideas or as a corpus of theses or moral propositions, but as a complex of social, personal, emotional circumstances impinging on or otherwise affecting and affected by particular character. What we witness and are moved by are ethical possibilities of living, and we are interested in what it would be like to live in them and live them out (i.e., to know the consequences of their adoption and use). For many simple reasons within easy reach, all of which are undoubtedly connected in some way or another with our insatiable interest in ourselves, we are tirelessly interested in "new" exhibitions of moral perplexity and possibility. Such exhibitions enable us to add to the stock of our conceptual storehouse, to enlarge our understanding, and to fit ourselves for further and future understanding.

Life is short, and, like Bottom, we cannot be in all roles or know much about the roles available or possible. Literary works, however, provide us with "ethical samples" of ethical possibilities, and they are, in a very large and untrivial sense, the schools of our moral sensibilities, teaching us surreptitiously much about the nature and bases of right behavior. As we read these works, the line of our sustained interest is the line of moral entanglement, complication, and, usually, resolution. In other words, the line of *our* interest and satisfaction follows the line of the text's moral concerns, and these concerns supply the categories of rightness and the conditions of justification that make up the text's interest and make for artistic fulfillment. But as we move beyond the texts we carry from them conceptual resources serviceable in the making and understanding of many new situations and texts, and in the making of the good life. Reading literature at the level of its ethical concern (which is, for many works, the level of its justification) with empathetic understanding will not necessarily make us better people, of course, but it will *exercise our capacity for and improve our skill at moral discrimination,* provide us with concepts useful to the formation of a regulative image of the good life, and, thus, make us better equipped for right action.

Poetics. From examining works in terms of their internal systems of justification, at the level of their motivation, functioning, and effect (i.e., from meeting the responsibilities of interpretation in some rigorous fashion), we can move quite easily to *poetics,* to a consideration, that is, of formal lines of affiliation among works as *kinds,* in terms of similarities and differences in their principles of reasoning and conditions of justification. Once we have understood the principles of workingness in first this and then that and then again that other work, we can begin to establish categories of likeness/difference discrimination, aligning works, for example, that use similar *means* in similar *ways* to bring about comparable *effects* in similar *conditions of distress or perplexity.* Because, as we noted earlier, we can make relevant statements about similarities in the essential features of several texts (i.e., features essential to the functioning of the works), we can begin to outline the *poetics* of distinct forms of literature. And if we can do *poetics,* then we can perhaps undertake a history of forms, tracing changes and variations over time in the constructional conditions of forms and noting instances of refinement and innovation in the use of one or another kind of essential feature, as generations of writers respond to the achievements of their predecessors and the possibilities implicit in the functional features themselves.

At this point, discussion can move from a concern with internal, constructional causes within schemes and kinds of schemes and with the changes brought about by refining and "perfecting" the possibilities inherent in the discernible and defining features of the various forms to a concern with any number of "preconstructional" causes of literary change in social, political, agricultural, religious, gender, musical, or whatever conditions. (Of course, what is actually made of this preconstructional material, what emphases it will have, and what purposes it will serve at the "constructional" level, at which specific choices are made, cannot be determined by the material itself; with R. S. Crane, we affirm that though the constructional cause of elements and emphases within works "presupposes the [preconstructional causes] as their necessary substrate, the [constructional] cannot be deduced from or resolved into the [preconstructional]."[27] Here we would be especially interested, for example, in the various ways social formations of one kind or another impinge on textual interests, emphases, values, and purposes, on kinds of topics discussed, kinds of characters presented, kinds of situations depicted, kinds of dilemmas confronted, kinds of diction employed, and so on. We would be interested here in, among other things, how Hobbes or Locke or landscape gardening or the Glorious Revolution or early capitalism or shifts in the nature of audiences or in means of production or distribution impacted on this or that textual feature or kind of literature.

Criticism. These concerns with the preconstructional take us right to the territorial border of *poetics,* beyond which lies the vast wilderness of *criticism,* where works are seen in their larger artistic, social, political, ideological relations, or as subsumed by one or another domain of interest (the psychological, psychoanalytic, linguistic, anthropological, chemical, rhetorical, or whatever domain). Here ingenuity roams at large and can make literature relate to whatever it wants and can make literature (or anything else) whatever it wants, as long as in the making it does not shoot itself in the foot (i.e., refute itself). In the Big Sky Country of criticism there is room for—you name it: for source and influence studies (of the traditional and anxious kind), for biography (of various kinds), for new or old historicist studies (though, because they are peculiarly susceptible to question-begging and to always finding the same One in the Many, these are very difficult projects to manage well), for figural, image, and diction studies (at the ordinary, run-of-the-mill, garden-variety level and at the meta-, mega-, supra-, infra-level), for all this and, of course, much more.

Additionally, in identifying likenesses and differences among works, creating with each line of association a classification, we are not restricted, *in criticism,* to the deep or full classification required by *poetics,* which has genre identification and the elucidation of shared conditions of satisfaction among works as its objects. Any distinguishable feature, any projectible property can serve as the ground or condition of filiation. As Catherine Z. Elgin observes: "We [can] classify [works] by *subject,* as crucifixion pictures or medical bulletins [or domestic tragedies]; by *style,* as impressionist paintings or symbolist poems; [by, we might add, *manner of representation or disclosure,* as first-person or omniscient-author narration]. And we classify them by *medium,* as watercolors or news reports; by *author,* as

Monets or Flauberts; by *historical or cultural milieu,* as Renaissance or Victorian works" (my emphases).[28]

In the outback of criticism, then, there is space for an indefinite number of projects to situate themselves, including the following three, with which we will conclude our discussion. First, we can do something to refine our understanding of the peculiar features of *thought, emotion, and expression* that characterize the productions of a given writer. Something there is in various artistic works that enables us to recognize with remarkable sureness, for example, the characteristic Milton or Donne or Wordsworth quality or to determine whether a particular unidentified piece can be attributed to a particular author. Concerning such attributions, disputes rage and passions are inflamed, but there is scarcely any reader who has read much by one writer who does not feel qualified to judge the authenticity or spuriousness of a document of uncertain provenance but attributed to a writer of his concern. It is perhaps reasonable to hope that the bases of this tacit understanding can be made more explicit than they currently are. And this can be accomplished by attending to the differentiable qualities of thought, emotion, and expression in the works of various writers, specifically, by reasoning back, in good Longinian fashion, from achieved effects or from the justification conditions of many works by a single author to the textually embedded, material exemplifications of mind, feeling, and style.

Second, what can be done for the writer can also be done for this or that writer's "age" (with age discriminated in the way all our categories are discriminated, i.e., by habit, practice, and agreement, by our seeing a value in such discriminations for certain purposes). With uncanny regularity we are able to distinguish a given work as a production of a given era or period, undoubtedly by bringing our accumulated knowledge and skill to bear once again on peculiarities of *thought, emotion, and expression* that we have come to recognize as characteristic of the era. Without yielding to either zeitgeistism or historicism (old or new), we here simply acknowledge that from time to time across wide variations in a rich multiplicity of conceptual systems there are certain persistencies in questions entertained and in idioms and terms employed. For all the manifold diversity of theoretical production in the eighteenth century, for example, there is within this mass of variety and conflict a persistent interest in a certain range of topics and a persistent reliance on a rather stable critical vocabulary. Similarly, however various and different the literary productions of, say, the first thirty years of the nineteenth century are (in style, genre, topic, diction, ambition, range of concern, etc.), a considerable number of them are sufficiently distinct as a group not to be confused with the productions of an earlier or later period. Although intertextualists and other theorists have not been reluctant to drive their Land Rovers across this terrain, much remains to be done, employing categories of discrimination more generous and capacious than those currently in use, to illuminate the ground of our intuitive determinations, our tacit judgments.

Finally, for our purposes of illustration, where wilderness yields to jungle, there is room in criticism for commentary—largely suggestive and speculative but anchored as firmly as possible in the categories of understanding actually informing particular works—on the social, political, ethical, ideological, religious, or cultural values implicit in literary and other artistic works. The concern here is with what the works may have to contribute to our understanding of, say, ways of knowing or ways of living, of ethics, polity, epistemology, and so on. Intellectual roving in this territory is always difficult and always full of danger, because we are always working from restricted evidence to large conclusions and because we are trying to give clarity and precision to the conceptions of the good, the true, and the beautiful that are implicit in works primarily interested in more local and mundane matters. Underlying our artistic versions (as well as all our other versions) are visions or conceptions of what we can know or do or what would be good for beings such as we to know or do. If such things are difficult to discover and express, their value to and interest for us is proportionate to the difficulty of their attainment, for when we get right down to it, what we most want to know something about is what's to know and how to live.

That these and many other projects are possible and worth undertaking only a preoccupation with signs and their relations, on the one hand, and individuals as fully constructed by the ideological conditions of their existence, on the other, could have obscured from our notice. But the key to a revival of interest in works (as distinct from "texts," sign systems, and the instability of reference and meaning in a world without transcendental signifieds or a Foundation) begins perhaps in the recognition that we are making and understanding creatures. We make what others can understand, and we understand what others can make (otherwise, what would be the point of all our making and efforts of understanding?). Among the many things that literature is (like anything else, it can be seen or represented under many descriptions), it is a form of behavior or action, and as such it is "rational," that is, its structure is intelligible only by reference to mental states (e.g., beliefs, wishes, desires, aims, purposes, intentions). Literature has content (i.e., semantic properties, such as meaning, reference, and truth conditions), and where there is content, there is rationality (assertibility or justification conditions), and our only access to the content is by means of a grasp of the rationality. Interpretation succeeds or not depending on whether the rationality is apprehended, and all the other operations that we perform with and upon literature depend on a grasp of the informing rationality, depend on interpretation, on reading texts within the system of their interests. These points are given admirable concision by Simon Evnine, in his assessment of Davidson: "Davidson has placed in centre stage the crucial insight that rationality, consistency, coherence, and logic are not 'optional extras' for creatures that have content-bearing mental states and use language. . . . [His] insight that without reason there is no thought is so valuable that I believe it should be bought at almost any price."[29] In the end, it is necessary to remember that this essay has sought, not to overthrow Theory, but to reclaim much senselessly abandoned critical territory by showing that there is nothing in Theory's insights into language or culture that has rendered obsolete, meaningless, second-rate, or illusory our interests in works and authors. Indeed, it seems that practicing literary criticism without focusing on works (initially or at some level) is, finally, not possible, if desirable, and not desirable, if possible. And with this recognition our hopes for a renewal of interest in books (and authors) among the Theorists are rejuvenated (or are not quite surfeited to death).

Notes

1. Catherine Gallagher, "Recovering the Social in Recent Literary Theory," *Diacritics* 12 (1982): 40.
2. Jonathan Culler, *On Deconstruction: Theory and Criticism after Structuralism* (Ithaca: Cornell University Press, 1982), 7.
3. Julia Kristeva, *Desire in Language: A Semiotic Approach to Literature and Art*, ed. Leon S. Roudiez, trans. Thomas Gora, Alice Jardine, and Leon S. Roudiez (New York: Columbia University Press, 1980), 66.
4. Vincent B. Leitch, *Deconstructive Criticism: An Advanced Introduction* (New York: Columbia University Press, 1983), 3.
5. Jacques Derrida, *Of Grammatology*, trans. Gayatri Spivak (Baltimore: Johns Hopkins University Press, 1976), 18.
6. Hilary Putnam, *Renewing Philosophy* (Cambridge: Harvard University Press, 1992), 124.
7. Hilary Putnam, *The Many Faces of Realism* (LaSalle, Ill.: Open Court, 1987), 36.
8. Donald Davidson, "The Myth of the Subjective" in *Relativism: Interpretation*

and Confrontation, ed. Michael Krausz (Notre Dame: University of Notre Dame Press, 1989), 160.

9. Hilary Putnam, *Realism with a Human Face,* ed. James Conant (Cambridge: Harvard University Press, 1990), 139.

10. James F. Harris, *Against Relativism: A Philosophical Defense of Method* (LaSalle, Ill.: Open Court, 1992), 84–85.

11. Hilary Putnam, *Realism with a Human Face,* 125.

12. Mark Sacks, *The World We Found: The Limits of Ontological Talk* (London: Duckworth, 1989), 81.

13. Michael Devitt, *Realism and Truth,* 2d ed. (Oxford: Blackwell, 1991), 244.

14. W. V. Quine, *Ontological Relativity and Other Essays* (New York: Columbia University Press, 1969), 50.

15. Mark Johnson, *The Body in the Mind: The Bodily Basis of Meaning, Imagination, and Reason* (Chicago: University of Chicago Press, 1987), 75.

16. Ernest Lepore and Barry Loewer, "A Putnam's Progress," in *Realism and Antirealism,* ed. Peter A. French, Theodore E. Uehling Jr., and Howard K. Wettstein (Midwest Studies in Philosophy 12 [Minneapolis: University of Minnesota Press, 1988]), 468.

17. Christopher Cherniak, *Minimal Rationality* (Cambridge: MIT Press, 1986), 3.

18. Eddy M. Zemach, "On Meaning and Reality," in *Relativism: Interpretation and Confrontation,* ed. Michael Krausz (Notre Dame: University of Notre Dame Press, 1989), 69.

19. John Searle, *The Rediscovery of the Mind* (Cambridge: MIT Press, 1992), 155.

20. Simon Blackburn, "Losing Your Mind: Physics, Identity, and Folk Burglar Protection," in *The Future of Folk Psychology,* ed. John D. Greenwood (Cambridge: Cambridge University Press, 1991), 20.

21. Elder Olson, "The Dialectical Foundations of Critical Pluralism," *Texas Quarterly* 9 (1966): 207.

22. Michael Polyani, *The Tacit Dimension* (Garden City, N.Y.: Doubleday, 1967), 34.

23. Ralph Rader, "The Concept of Genre in Eighteenth-Century Studies," in *New Approaches to Eighteenth-Century Literature,* ed. Philip Harth (New York: Columbia University Press, 1974), 86.

24. Hilary Putnam, *Realism with a Human Face,* 116.

25. Martha C. Nussbaum, *Love's Knowledge: Essays on Philosophy and Literature* (Oxford: Oxford University Press, 1990), 8, 9.

26. W. V. Quine and J. S. Ullian, *The Web of Belief* (New York: Random House, 1970), 135.

27. R. S. Crane, "Critical and Historical Principles of Literary History," in *The Idea of the Humanities and Other Essays Critical and Historical,* 2 vols. (Chicago: University of Chicago Press, 1967), 2:105.

28. Catherine Z. Elgin, "Confronting Novelty" in *Reconceptions in Philosophy and Other Arts and Sciences,* Catherine Z. Elgin and Nelson Goodman, joint authors (Indianapolis: Hackett, 1988), 118–19.

29. Simon Evnine, *Donald Davidson* (Stanford: Stanford University Press, 1991), 179.

Relevant Publications by James Battersby

Paradigms Regained: Pluralism and the Practice of Criticism. Philadelphia: University of Pennsylvania Press, 1991.

Rational Praise and Natural Lamentation: Johnson, Lycidas and Principles of Criticism. Rutherford, N.J.: Fairleigh Dickinson Press, 1980.

"Professionalism, Relativism, and Rationality." *PMLA* 107 (1992): 51–64.
"The Inevitability of Professing Literature." *Bucknell Review* 31 (1988): 61–76.
"Meaning as Concept and Extension: Some Problems." *Critical Inquiry* 12 (spring 1986): 605–16.

10

Literature and Theory

David Bromwich

David Bromwich, professor of English at Yale University, has written on a wide variety of topics: Wordsworth, Hazlitt, Burke, Hart Crane, Marianne Moore, and romantic conceptions of genius and of history. His most recent books, A Choice of Inheritance *(1989) and* Politics by Other Means: Higher Education and Group Thinking *(1992), address questions around which debate is swirling; he approaches them from an ethical point of view associated with democratic individuality and political liberalism rather than from a particular theoretical system. This may make his style of commentary appear surprising or anomalous to readers committed to relativism; others will find it not only refreshing but inspiriting. What literature can do, not as a demonstration of a theory or an example in an argument, but for those who read it as an expression of insight into experience, is what is important for Bromwich. The following is from the last paragraph of the first essay in* A Choice of Inheritance:

> *Concerning a poem which has survived a generation or more, we cannot say whose view it may have opened on fresh tasks, maybe for the first time, or again when the way seemed closed. . . . A vision of reality is usually saying that it is a vision. At the same time it obliges us to wonder how we can wish for more than that. It means*

> *to give an image of life, with the permanence proper to such an image, for the benefit of those with imagination.*

The following essay, which constitutes the final chapter in the same book, considers what an adequate relationship might be between criticism and literature so understood.

I thought of calling this essay "Recent Work in Literary Criticism." But the title felt wrong, and the reasons were easy to assign. The book that interprets the works of an author, the study in practical criticism that is widely read by nonspecialists, has ceased to be a kind of success that commands attention. Such books go on being written and published; but only the specialists know their names. What has replaced them, as the genre that represents the common interests of the discipline, is books on theory. I dislike this tendency, for what seem to me the faults of the intellectual temperament it has fostered: on the one hand, the pretension to social importance of much contemporary literary theory; on the other, its lack of social and historical information or even curiosity. Theory exists now in a protected condition, in comparison with which the situation of literature as well as criticism in the past may look admirably unprotected. Still, it would be pointless to ignore the drift of things. The objects of study are gradually being redefined, both for advanced students of literature and for the students whom they instruct in turn. To isolate a single effect: someone informed by theory, and aiming to write on a certain author or a group of texts, will read more widely than he would have done a decade ago, but also more thinly. If, for example, the result is an article on *Frankenstein,* then Rousseau and Nietzsche may be brought in, together with several current theorists. In the economy of the argument, they displace other works by Mary Shelley and her contemporaries; as, in the thinking and reading that helped to construct the argument, a similar displacement is likely to have occurred. The visible result is a change in the look of interpretations—or interrogations, to use the up-to-date word. A larger and less obvious change has to do with the traits that are looked on as useful in a critic.

Tact was an available name to sum up these traits, but what did it mean? A competence, supported by an instinct. A critic who expected to persuade readers of the sense of an interpretation would show some feeling for the language in which the work was written, for the period in which its author wrote, and for the particular inflections that its style gave to the idiom it inherited and revised. A false hope on which this idea of criticism was premised, but a hope inextricable from the acceptance of literature as an academic subject, was that something as elusive as tact could somehow be taught. It could not be, any more than insight into personal lives can be taught to a psychologist. It ought to be taken to imply, therefore, nothing but a form of practical wisdom, which most critics wished to encourage. By contrast, few critics since the Englightenment have believed that their efforts converged on a single right interpretation of a text. Their consensus was modeled rather on other sorts of common sense: in the reading of a literary work, there was such a thing as *getting things right.* This was linked with the conventions of making sense that governed more ordinary social practices as well. In literature, however, it related specifically to the practice of honoring the complex over the simple, the worth-rereading over the not-worth-rereading. A clue to what has happened in criticism over the past several years is that every key word in this paragraph would now be challenged by many theorists: "sense," "competence," "instinct," "complexity," "practical wisdom." All these are constructed, the theorist can say, for purposes that theory exists to expose. It might be replied that one such purpose is the creation of works of art. A powerful interpretation like the Orwell–Empson reading of *King Lear*—which says, "If a great man decides to give up everything, he really gives up everything, and that is terrifying"—leads to a powerful work like Kurosawa's *Ran.* Yet the idea of the work of art is not far from becoming just one more of the constructions that theory exists to expose.

People in other academic disciplines often assume that making sense of a literary work and valuing it are activities on approximately the same level. In criticism, they think, it is all a matter of opinion anyway. To forestall this reaction and limit the truth I want to assert, it will help to give an example of what "a competence, supported by an instinct" may mean. In *Day of the Leopards: Essays in Defense of Poems,* W. K. Wimsatt relates the following anecdote:

> There was a student once who wrote a paper saying that a couplet by Alexander Pope,". . . no Prelate's Lawn with Hair-shirt lined, / Is half so incoherent as my mind" (Epistle I.i. 165–66) ought to be read in the light of a couplet in another poem by Pope: "Whose ample Lawns are not asham'd to feed / The milky heifer and

> deserving steed" (*Moral Essays* IV.185–86). Since I believe in the force of puns and all sorts of other verbal resemblances in poetry, I do not know quite how to formulate the rule of context by which I confidently reject that connection. But I seek first ineluctable confrontations, only later, if at all, rules.[1]

To Wimsatt, lawn (the fabric) simply was not answerable to lawn (the plot of land), notwithstanding their identity as sounds and their possible relationship as signifiers.

A sense of where such confrontations did occur was on this view the only guide one needed to point out the improbability of their occurrence somewhere else. But the sense in question did not apply to verbal resemblances alone. The social judgments which a text presumed, and to which it might allude subtly or openly, also ruled in certain critical statements as interesting, while it ruled out others as spurious. To keep for a moment with Pope: in the line "Or stain her honor, or her new brocade," the rhetorical scheme is zeugma, with abstract and concrete nouns sharing a verb. Now, a remark that Pope's uses of this scheme were concentrated disproportionately in his satires on women would be interesting if true; while a remark that, just when he wrote the line, brocade-sellers were flourishing in England as never before would be spurious even if true. Whatever the latter might add to the reader's veiw of the economic arrangements of the time, it would say nothing about what made Pope worth studying as a writer. In the two decades since Wimsatt wrote, however, the criteria he evoked for the pertinence of a statement have partly dropped away from criticism. The questions How could that matter? (said of an unjustified turn in an argument) and But where is it? (said of a piece of evidence conspicuously overlooked) are asked less often. In their absence a thesis may be advanced with elementary errors that defeat its credibility but do not stop its publication. The interest is taken to lie elsewhere.

Thus a recent article in a respected critical journal proposed that *Jane Eyre* was an imperialist text.[2] The novel, that is, aimed to gain sympathy for a heroine whose passions were in complicity with the dominant prejudices of the age. It is not a startling general argument, and *Jane Eyre* is not the last place one would look for it to be tried. To make the case, Gayatri Spivak recalls the colonial origins of Mr. Rochester's mad wife, Bertha. Jane first sees Bertha Rochester's face reflected in a mirror, and the scene involves a repressed self-recognition. So far, the details and emphasis are familiar. The new element in this reading is the discovery that such a recognition could never be genuine since Jane Eyre herself is among the colonial oppressors. Her attitudes are established in part by an inquiry into her attachment to St. John Rivers, who is taken to represent the worst both of a male-dominated society and of an imperial ethic abroad. But here the *But where is it?* ought to stop one short. For the novel identifies Rivers as belonging to an evangelical sect that fought hard for the abolition of slavery: his parentage, though at a distance, includes men like Zachary Macaulay. If described as imperialist, it ought to be described carefully. Of all this the article says nothing. It is not treated as an irony, or as a complicating fact. Nor is it plain that late notice of the error would be received with much embarrassment by the critic. The standard defense for such an occasion will have been anticipated by people disposed to accept the reading. The aim, after all, was to reproblematize the text, and this meant that the details prized by a historian would yield to the details required by a particular anticolonialist metanarrative.

At what point in arguing against procedures like these does one have to appeal to some version of reality or of objectivity in interpretation? There has been a long line of critics—at least beginning with Hume's essay "Of the Standard of Taste" and Johnson's *Lives* of Swift and Milton—who say that without ever arriving at such a point at all, one may coherently judge interpretations as well as literary works themselves. Emphatically included in their idea of judgment was a belief in the worth of correcting errors. The roots of academic criticism, however, were always in a different tradition, with its beginnings in Coleridge and German idealism. The modern concern with the single right interpretation and the unified text to be right about may be traced largely to Coleridge's belief in the perfect work as a mediatory object between man and God. It was a misfortune, it seems to me, of the theoretical debates of the 1970s that critics who made similar emotional demands of truth were supposed to represent the common wisdom about interpretation; so that if one rejected them, one took oneself to be rejecting something like Hume's conception of taste or Johnson's of original invention, neither of which is committed to an epistemological way of truth. These writers, with Burke, Leigh Hunt, Shaw, and many others after them, are so far from supposing their judgments will lack validity without a diffuse but substantial something called reality to anchor them that they suppose their judgments to be founded on merely the common habits of reading and the long duration of certain opinions that acquire the force of custom. Such critics were not "essentialists" about meaning, and they would not have seen essentialism versus relativism as a choice that confronted anyone. Yet in the debates I mentioned above, one side, particularly in the writing of E. D. Hirsch and Gerald Graff, chose to make the stability of critical judgments depend on the stability of their objects.[3]

The theorist wants, and Hirsch tells him he is right to want, all or nothing: if interpretations do not tend toward truth, then there is no such thing as getting things right. The developments I sketched at the start of this review are symptoms of a very quick passage from all to nothing. The dilemma was taken seriously, I think, because both sides agreed that criticism gave the method for tracing the discoveries of literature itself. The idea of method was the first mistake; the picture of someone following up clues was the second. It would have made better sense to think of criticism as a language for discussing representations of the way people live and think and feel. The language is secondary in that it comes later. But it aims to give fresh interest to a narrative that owes everything to life, as life owes everything to the narratives that put it within our grasp. The idea of criticism as a language, rather than a map to a special province of truth, might well have gained acceptance while the New Critics were still active, had they chosen Wittgenstein rather than Coleridge as their guide. His questions in the *Philosophical Investigations,* on the difficulties of a private language, fall in very well with arguments more familiar to critics, and written about the same time, on the difficulties of reckoning intention as part of meaning: "And how do you know what you are to give yourself an exhibition of before you do it? This *private* exhibition is an illusion." Again, the best aphorisms there are on interpretation itself as a perspective come from the *Investigations:* "What I can see something *as,* is what it can be a picture of." Criticism resembles the making of a picture by seeing something as something else; and the work is the sum of the things that the picture can be of. Wittgenstein defines the interpreted character of a figure, which one may take to stand for a work, by talking of its possible aspects: "The aspects in a change of aspects are those ones which the figure might sometimes have *permanently* in a picture."[4] A critic can say, in short, certain things the picture will *not* be, so long as sight, cognition, the passions and interests of the lookers-on, stay even roughly as they appear to be at present. But this does not limit the ways in which one can see a thing *as*.

Further, Wittgenstein, as much as Hume, urges his readers to think of meaning as intelligible only in the light of habits or a more-than-private history of practices. He remarks in *Zettel* that it is a mistake "to say that there is anything that meaning something consists in." Saying a thing is a way of seeing what you mean; but meaning a thing is not seeing something that you do not say. "Only in the stream of thought and life do words have meaning."[5] In sentences like this and in the promptings, second guesses, and illustrations that enlarge them, Wittgenstein is the theorist who feels closest to the great, nonreligious and nonepistemological, critics from the eighteenth century to the present. Academic critics tend in practice to share their bias, and yet with rare exceptions for a critic like Empson or Wimsatt they are not close arguers, or conscious of the beliefs that their arguments presuppose. Faced by a question like "Do you believe in determinacy of meaning?" they sometimes fall back on memories of epistemological arguments, themselves modeled on religious beliefs, which have nothing at all to do with their practices. This may entail at first a ready assent to the sentence "If we know, we must be knowing something"—from which it may falsely be shown to follow that we know things as they are in themselves. I said the New Criticism need not have explicated its leading doctrines with the help of Coleridge; and its emphasis on the unity of texts may be traced to the accident of its early success with short poems. But an older idealism might have been noticed in the deference accorded to "the poem" in certain titles of the period. Its presence was confirmed by the reception of the New Critics themselves, together with modern Coleridgean scholars like M. H. Abrams, as the ground note in most of the standard recent histories of criticism.

The influential attacks on the text-in-itself came not, where they might have been looked for, from social or intellectual historians, but from a tendency within theory, for which the best name anyone yet has offered is "textualism."[6] When Derrida said there was nothing outside the text, he meant there was nothing apparently discrete from the text that its words would assist in keeping so. It took only implication, the play of the rhetoric, the return of repressed opposites, to bring it inside. The chapters on Rousseau in *Of Grammatology* and on Plato in *Dissemination* proceed by translating such distinctions as that between voice and writing, or cure and poison, into the undistinguishable doubles they become when the concepts of philosophy are read with the ambivalences language can never exclude.[7] The opponent in these inquiries is every hierarchy of knowledge, whether it is figured as a progress from writing to speech, or from a rhetoric that conceals the forms of justice to a dialectic that reveals it. Because modern philosophy habitually abstracts arguments from the words that make them, and words themselves from the history they were conditioned by, Derrida's writing had a plainer moral for philosophers than for literary critics. His deconstructions came to this: a showing that epistemology only asserts what the language of its asserting must call into question. A recognition of the way that happens might be expected to provoke a close historical study of the languages by which the problems of philosophy are generated from age to age. It has had that effect, in a small degree. But the ambition of Derrida's writing was not confined to a discipline in any case. It suggested that what is called philosophy and what is called literature are not different in kind. When philosophy begins to be read as writing, literature may be read as thinking. The signs of such a response have begun to appear in a few studies of novels as moral philosophy—studies that take their motive from a belief that literature gives a density to examples that argument alone cannot supply.[8] Yet it needs to be added that the use of literary texts as a sort of primary materials for philosophy was not what Derrida had in mind at all: as if novelists wrote to pose a problem ("the acknowledgment of others," for example) that had already been framed by philosophers. Within literature, Derrida's work has encouraged a reading of fictional and nonfictional, literary and philosophical, narrative and argumentative writings under their common aspect as texts. As a result, students of literature are perhaps freer now than at any time since the mid-nineteenth century to read books of several kinds—religious tract, political pamphlet, satire against mankind, essay in aesthetics—without a ranking of kinds and with the hope of attaining a competence for all rather than each.

In a review of Jonathan Culler's *On Deconstruction,* in the course of some extremely sensible comments on the all-or-nothing propensities of literary theorists, John Searle summarized an aim of deconstruction as the removal of metaphor from a marginal to a central position in language.[9] This was a good example of the all-or-nothing propensities of philosophers; and it brought out the persistence of the habits of mind that Derrida opposes. The point of his dealings with metaphor is that *any* rule separating the metaphorical from the literal will dissolve under scrutiny. Neither is central because neither can be prior; as the following illustration may attest: "The eminence was really an eminence when I saw him on the podium." Nobody ought to try to find the metaphor in the last sentence. And yet Shelley's "Defence of Poetry" is rich in suggestions like this concerning metaphor, as are many essays of romantic and modern criticism. What now appears strange in the reception of Derrida's work is that it has been taken generally as saying something shocking about how criticism is done. One strong definition of literary power has always held that it impresses the reader with a specific gravity at every point while leaving its final emphasis unsettled. Doubtless Cleanth Brooks's discussions of irony and Allen Tate's use of the word "tension" were not in this sense deconstructive. But Empson's discussions of complex words certainly were. Among the priorities that deconstruction set out to overturn, the only one that academic criticism had retained was the privilege of the single text to be examined as a unity, together with an unreflecting and incantatory style of speech concerning "the reconciliation of opposites." The former was chiefly a pedagogical convenience, though it may have looked like something larger. The latter was a rhetoric formed by the meeting of two unpleasant scholar's traits, the will-to-tidiness and an affectation of moral concern. Neither of these has vanished but for the moment deconstruction has forced them to seek new disguises.

About the status of Derrida's procedures there was always a puzzle. Was deconstruction a technique proper to the commentator, and necessary as a tactic against the naive constructionism of the author? Or was it something the author's writing practiced for itself, in which case the commentator's only role would be to tease out the language it had been speaking all its life? Derrida's interests did not require him to choose between these descriptions. But his mode of analysis became current in America, and later in Britain, largely through a long essay devoted to his reading of Rousseau, in Paul de Man's *Blindness and Insight.* There de Man appeared to choose the second description. Recounting Derrida's own argument on the metaphysics of presence, which had tracked the privilege of speech (as presence) against writing (as deception) from its prominent use in Lévi-Strauss back to its invention in the anthropology of Rousseau, "Jacques Derrida's Reading of Rousseau" pointed out that this and kindred oppositions were called into doubt in Rousseau's texts themselves. Rather than expose a self-deception, therefore, which literature shared with metaphysics, de Man vindicated literature as a place of self-suspicion that was exemplary for language in general. The same work was carried into de Man's later essays in *Allegories of Reading* and *The Rhetoric of Romanticism;* in the introductory chapter of the former book, on "Semiology and Rhetoric," de Man propounded his thesis unambiguously:

> A literary text simultaneously asserts and denies the authority of its own rhetorical mode, and by reading the text as we did we were only trying to come closer to being as rigorous a reader as the author

> had to be in order to write the sentence in the first place. Poetic writing is the most advanced and refined mode of deconstruction; it may differ from critical or discursive writing in the economy of its articulation, but not in kind.[10]

It is worth noting that the main points of this assertion—its leveling of text with commentary and its ranking of poetry, in degree, above criticism by virtue of its "rigor" and "economy"—were made with a slightly different emphasis in the opening chapter of Empson's *Seven Types of Ambiguity.* Of ambiguities Empson wrote: "Meanings of this kind, indeed, are conveyed, but they are conveyed much more by poets than by analysts; that is what poets are for, and why they are important"; of the implicit statements of speech and writing he also remarked: "printed commonly differ from spoken ones in being intended for a greater variety of people, and poetical from prose ones in imposing the system of habits they imply more firmly or more quickly."[11] In the same way, Derrida's comments on the assimilability of all language to rhetoric may seem to recall Kenneth Burke's inquiries in the *Grammar* and *Rhetoric* he published in 1945 and 1950. Empson and Burke are the critics of the last generation who wrote with genius and not just a refined competence, and if their limited, but real, affinities with later rhetoricians have been noticed without ever prompting a revival of their work, a reason may be the unchallenged anti–Anglo-Saxon bias that modern theory professes sometimes ironically and sometimes sarcastically.

De Man's most impressive essay for me is "The Rhetoric of Temporality," which has been reprinted in a second edition of *Blindness and Insight.*[12] It argues that two dogmas have shaped critical thought about the literary object since the early decades of the nineteenth century: the conception of irony as a fixed perspective, and of the symbol as a fusion of image and idea that cannot be found in allegory. Hazlitt, Shelley, Lionel Johnson, Edward Thomas, and a good many others might be cited as critics outside the consensus that de Man writes against, but the people he really has in view are recent and synoptic literary historians: M. H. Abrams, for example, in his discussions of the symbol, and Wayne Booth in his treatment of narrative irony. After one has read this essay, one's sense of the uses of irony can never be quite the same, and there seems to be very little point in ever talking of the symbol again, except for the historical purpose of exhibiting the preoccupations of a school. The essays on romantic authors which de Man wrote soon after, particularly those on Rousseau, Shelley, and "Autobiography as De-Facement," add up to a denial of the consolations of writing. It is always pertinent, Iris Murdoch observed in *The Sovereignty of Good,* to ask of a philosopher, What is he afraid of? De Man in these essays asks the same question of writers, as the makers of inscriptions that are meant at once to outlast and to represent them. "Autobiography as De-Facement" starts from the Proustian datum that a life cannot speak to us as a life until it is inscribed on a monument; and yet the speaking monument is the author who, in order to address us, must imagine himself as already dead. Nor is this stance merely figurative. In writing his life, the author changes it from pure face to defacement, as all monuments are defaced or scarred by their inscriptions. Any testimony from a writer, then, which we receive concerning the writer's life, is a testimony from the point of view of death. Accordingly, the very words that mean to reflect a life must deform it in order to make its story come into existence at all. Once, however, we concede that "autobiography is a defacement of the mind of which it is itself the cause," it follows that "death is a displaced name for a linguistic predicament," for the discovery that autobiography hoped to gain through writing "deprives and disfigures to the precise extent that it restores."[13] Here again, though de Man's text is Wordsworth's *Essays on Epitaphs,* his recognition is familiar above all to readers of Proust. Phrased as a truism, it may be supposed to mean: every book leaves something out. Beneath this nevertheless one may discern the starker claim that there are no true stories.

Thus de Man asks the reader to give up, as the writer's work itself has done, any curriculum by which one could move from allegories of reading to intimations of experience. This is not one of the things that literature does, and to fancy that it can is only to seek a "shelter" (a favorite term of reproach). Two concerns are perhaps separable here. In some of his later essays, de Man wrote of literature as dramatizing fears about the instability of knowledge, which other linguistic practices simply repressed. A possible explanation of the difference, though one not entertained by de Man, was that useless writing can do some things that use-bound writing cannot do. The distinction in any case passed out of sight in other essays, where "an aporia" was asserted "between performative and constative language," and the illustrations were drawn from literary and nonliterary sources indifferently. De Man gave as examples Archie Bunker's sentence "What's the difference?" in reply to a question about two ways of tying his shoes ("Who cares!" but also "Please describe the ways"); and Yeats's line "How can we know the dancer from the dance?" at the end of a great poem ("The dancer and the dance seem almost one" but also "Can we be sure?").

Neither of the examples is convincing to my ear; but any reader can think of his own. This line of argument brought a strong reply to de Man from Stanley Cavell, who recalled that it was precisely to defeat "the idea that constative and performative utterances differ in their responsibilities, or responsiveness, to facts and to distinguish among the ways in which words may have 'effects' or 'forces' " that J. L. Austin wrote in the first place about both sorts of statement. Cavell then offered a counterillustration: "Someone says that the difference between knives and forks is that you cut with a knife and spear with a fork; a second objects that you can also cut with a fork and spear with a knife; whereupon a third concludes that there is an aporia between knives and forks, that there is no stable distinction we can draw between them."[14] While the applications of this response are local, it shares Wittgenstein's approach to thinking, speaking, and action, the adaptiveness of the needs that one learns and the choices that language makes to the situations they fit. Indeed, the response brings out by contrast one of the intractable elements in de Man's criticism, which one may read for a long time before giving the problem a conscious formulation. He believed, what some philosophers but few critics have believed: that language and, a fortiori, literature are games that cannot be played.

An implication of most deconstructionist criticism is that an end of self-deception requires an end of the self. Writing and the self are said, in short, to confirm each other in the illusion that they can transcend the death that is another name for a linguistic predicament—the existence of what is called literature being the chief source of their positive reinforcement. From a critic who works pretty steadily within this train of speculations, Neil Hertz, have come some of the best essays of the past several years on romantic and modern authors; and in the summary chapter of his collection, *The End of the Line,* Hertz affirms his interest in a plot that is common to both the self-portraits of romantic autobiography and the sublime moments of poetry or fiction.[15] Tocqueville's account of the 1848 Paris uprising, Wordsworth's lines on his encounter with the blind beggar in London, Freud's reconstruction of the case history of Dora—all show the self's return to the knowledge it has promised itself, at the sacrifice of the others whose portrayal had justified the making of a narrative. The result, says Hertz (summarizing de Man but also, apparently, himself), is to "leave the field littered with the remains of acts of mutilation," so that the questions that concern an interpreter are At the end of the line, who pays? And why? The end of the line here signifies both a climactic turn in the narrative and a recovery of the affects, powers, and laws of the self that writing threatened first only to sanction later. It is a suggestion of Hertz's criticism, never fully stated, that these self-recognitions coincide with a form of social loss; and it is a suggestion of the sentence quoted above, again not fully stated, that the cost after all may be too high.

What conclusions follow from investigations like these? Sometimes, Hertz believes, political judgments of a sort will materialize in the direction that criticism seems to point, and his juxtaposition of the motifs of political and sexual hysteria in Tocqueville is ingenious but baffling unless such judgments do follow. He sees this difficulty, and goes the length of reprinting, after his essay on 1848, two very acute replies from critics who take him at his word and prod him to say just what the politics of his essay come to. Hertz's defense is curious: "Can political questions be boiled down to a dilemma?" The moments, he goes on to say, "that strike me as most suggestive" in the political writings of Foucault and Derrida

> are precisely those that work to elude symmetrical formulations of this sort. In Foucault these moments are often marked by long lists of plural nouns, which produce the exhilarating sense of just how many factors one must take into account in a particular issue; in Derrida, by the mullings and backings-and-fillings with which he works his way into a problem, his remarkable ability to both fish *and* cut bait.[16]

Note that these exhilarations bring us no closer than we were at the start to politics, either as a dilemma or as something less simple. Instead we are invited to share the "sense of just how many factors" one theorist asks us to consider, the ambidextrous finesse with which another shows that he is able "to both fish *and* cut bait." The deference to Foucault and Derrida—names brought into the discussion by Hertz's critics, but to which he adds no others—is also curious in the light of the consistent prejudice against psychology in both writers. But I think their authority does in fact have a bearing on the insufficient account of its motives to which criticism in this mode feels bound in principle to stay confined.

The effect is as follows. A promise of social analysis is made, tacitly by the tone itself of the criticism, more overtly by the choice of objects for analysis, yet the argument is foreshortened just at the point where what was promised might be performed. I have only a hunch about why this occurs, and since others have even less I will give it briefly. Deconstruction was a way to upset, from within, a system controlled by certain hierarchies of knowledge, which related in turn to hierarchies of power. Critics aware of what it could do to conventional linguistic arrangements saw how easily it might do something similar to conventional social arrangements. And yet here Foucault, whose *Discipline and Punish* has had a wide vogue in literary studies, proves to be as unrewarding a guide as Derrida. Talking about social arrangements, after all, means talking about the sorts of persons who live in them, and who suffer or profit by them. Talking about persons, however, is prohibited in advance by the exclusion that Foucault and Derrida alike enforce against comparable entities. It is almost like talking about character, almost like talking about the self. Foucault in this respect is all the more discouraging in that he writes from the perspective of a reformer. For the successions of *epistemes,* by which he denotes historical periods, have so total a control of the discourse of any thinker within them that they appear to preclude an account of change. If one reads several consecutive chapters of *The Order of Things,* one gets the impression that an old episteme grows dull like an illegible photograph or, to adapt the book's concluding image, grows smooth like a shallow inscription on a soft tablet, until, since of course it cannot remember, language thinks in a new episteme. There is no trace of pathos in such an account, and no sympathy with the victims who are described at length, because there is no idea of agency. On premises like these the subtle moralism of the attack on the self in literary theory has consented to build the little that it can.

In an essay of 1971 entitled "Nietzsche, Genealogy, History," Foucault came closer than anywhere else to a lucid statement of a credo. "Nothing," he wrote, "in man—not even his body—is sufficiently stable to serve as the basis for self-recognition or for understanding other men. The traditional devices for constructing a comprehensive view of history and for retracing the past as a patient and continuous development must be systematically dismantled."[17] The other thing besides the body, to which his phrase "nothing in man" referred, was evidently the mind, but here one may recur to Wittgenstein's criticism of all such maps of the alternative: "One of the most dangerous of ideas for a philosopher is, oddly enough, that we think with our ideas in our heads: The idea of thinking as a process in the head, in a completely enclosed space, gives him something occult." This did not affect the usefulness of an idea of thinking or for that matter a history of thoughts. "Only God sees the most secret thoughts. But why should these be all that important? Some are important, not all. And need all human beings count them as important?"[18] Foucault, having replaced God with "Power/Knowledge," replies to the second question with a simple yes. The impossibility of forming a comprehensive view ought therefore to stop us from seeking a view at all. And the lack of a basis, in our heads or bodies, either for self-recognition or for understanding of others, itself decides the next of "the problems that have been posed for human knowledge" by terminating the cause of the last. "Where religions once demanded the sacrifice of bodies, knowledge now calls for experimentation on ourselves, calls us to the sacrifice of the subject of knowledge."[19] Among the many things the word "subject" covers is the self. For genealogy, as Foucault explains it—the suspicious tracing of a descent from the past that replaces history—aims to reveal "the heterogeneous systems which, masked by the self, inhibit the formation of any form of identity."[20] The title and procedure of this essay commit Foucault to nothing more than an exposition of Nietzsche. But it will be granted, I think, by most of his readers that he here attributes to Nietzsche both aims and analyses to which he himself assented.

Notwithstanding Foucault's skepticism about the worth of histories, a question remains whether the "subject of knowledge" need be identical with the self. A version of the self though not of the subject does join one's sense of texts when it is part of their claim to be uniquely interesting. At any rate, Foucault's reading of Nietzsche as his predecessor is a separate matter. A chapter on "Self and Subject in Nietzsche," in Stanley Corngold's *The Fate of the Self,* argues that, however Nietzsche's genealogies may subvert any defense of humanism, they do not end in a rejection of an idea of the self. Or rather, they can be made to do so only in an interpretation that stresses a few passages of *The Will to Power* while excluding all consideration of *Thus Spake Zarathustra.* Corngold regards as peculiarly non-Nietzschean

> the too easy assertion that the self is merely a metaphor, always but a metaphor, always transparent to its own constructedness, always a fiction. . . . This is a view that cannot be lived. To live it is to go mad, so it will come as no surprise that many a professional killing has recently been made by arguing its necessity. It may therefore be helpful to suggest the hold against this unraveling which the memory of other selves offers. It is for us, really, to decide how far we want to let go of the self—our own and others—and to persist in asking: where does the self unravel? In what place, at what time? . . . The madness of *literature* without a self no more exists than does the sanity of a *self* without literature.[21]

That sentences like these now should sound unaccustomed proves that they needed saying. And yet the diagnosis they give of the character of literary theory seems to me incomplete.

Without "living" a view, or going mad in the attempt to live it, one may criticize others for the more tolerable views that alone permit their life and work. The theorist who chooses this perspective comes to look on the author as merely symptomatic of the conditions that determined him—another naive believer in the sublimation of texts from the materials that produced them, whose irony about his own position is less developed than the theorist's. This explains not only the antihumanism of some recent criticism but also a new tone, at once authoritative and clinical, that oddly resembles the tone of the very social-scientific texts that Foucault wrote with the hope of discrediting. Read either as social history or as history of ideas, his writings have tremendous power as an estrangement device; they were not mean to license a project of intellectual surveillance directed, this time, upon the guilty self of the author. But the tendency I am describing, though its vocabulary is largely Foucault's, has another and earlier source in the writings of Althusser. Here in fact one arrives at a part of theory's own genealogy of which few of its practitioners are aware. In the French Communist Party in the 1950s, the antihumanism of Althusser was an instrument of discipline with a specific purpose. It was offered as a weapon against the socialist humanism of Eastern European political thinkers, and was found extremely serviceable in justifying the Soviet suppression of the 1956 Hungarian uprising. Beyond that, a vocabulary that incorporated persons only as the bearers of structures became a highly respected, plausible, Western constituent of an apology for the historical necessity of Stalinism.

This is a history that has been recounted in detail by E. P. Thompson in "The Poverty of Theory." Yet it may still be asked why such a theory should find its appeal just now, among advanced students of the humanities in America, who are seldom political enough to be either Stalinist or anti-Stalinist. A short answer is the erosion of secular individualism in general, perhaps the worst intellectual disaster of the 1970s and 1980s. The result owes much to the isolation of radical impulses in the teaching of advocacy subjects like "cultural studies," and much to the connection of individualist rhetoric now with the public-relations genius of the big corporations. Thompson himself sees an additional reason, however, for the appeal of antihumanism in theory: it seems to afford an understanding that is prior and, in consequence, superior to any historical agency. Further, it does so at a time when the distance between intellectuals (who can help to understand the world) and the working classes (for whom, in a pre-Althusserian Marxism, the tasks of understanding it and changing it coincided) has widened to such a point that if it were not a cause of pride it would be a cause of shame. Thompson observes:

> What is so obvious is that this new *elitism* stands as direct successor in the old lineage: Benthamism, Coleridgean "clerisy," Fabianism, and Leavisism of the more arrogant variety. Once again, the intellectuals—a chosen band of these—have been given the task of enlightening the people. Whether Frankfurt School or Althusser, they are marked by their very heavy emphasis upon the ineluctable weight of ideological modes of domination—domination which destroys every space for the initiative or creativity of the mass of people—a domination from which only the enlightened minority of intellectuals can struggle free. . . . It is a sad premise from which Socialist theory should start (all men and women, except for us, are originally stupid) and one which is bound to lead on to pessimistic or authoritarian conclusions. Moreover, it is likely to reinforce the intellectual's disinclination to extend himself in practical political activity. To be sure, the (ideal) proletariat may, in this or that critical conjuncture, suddenly shift itself, like a geological fault, into a revolutionary posture, when it will be ready to receive the ministrations of Theory. Meanwhile, why bother to try to communicate—to educate, agitate, and organize—since the reason is powerless to penetrate the mists of "ideology"?[22]

In this respect the shift from Althusser to Foucault involves only a change of degree: a still further dimension of pessimism, with a still more attenuated emphasis on class. Together, these combine to make accounts of the domination by a mesh of power and knowledge over authors, readers, books, and the things a book can or cannot represent.

The emergent style has led to some remarkable examples of the interdisciplinary cross-sterilization of ideas. If I set out tomorrow to connect the Victorian decline of satire with the rise of sentimental comedy, the repression of women's sexuality, and the dietary practices that, with many other practices, controlled the arbitrary differences of a social order, I would need perhaps the following bits of evidence: an essay of eighteenth-century criticism that identified the satirical genres with the "acid" style; a textbook of etiquette for young ladies, published between 1830 and 1880, asserting that acidulous foods were particularly improper for persons of the female gender; and a letter from a standard Victorian author (Thackeray, say), with a comment in passing that satires tended to exacerbate rather than comfort people's resentments about their condition, and besides his wife had never enjoyed reading them. Whether these wire-drawn and empirical-looking hints carried conviction or failed to, the article in which I published them would not be attacked on the ground that connections like these could not possibly add up to anything cogent. They are the stuff the practice of theory is made of. Indeed, one's interest or lack of interest in the results is a master clue to the recent adoption, in discussions of the politics of interpretation, of the wholly misleading political terms of art "left" and "right." To want to make, as Benjamin did in his *Arcades* study, a direct inference from the duty on wine to Baudelaire's "L'Ame du Vin," without adducing any intermediate chain of evidence, is a *left* position. To say of such a procedure what Adorno said of an early draft of the study, that it is "located at the crossroads of magic and positivism," is a *right* position.

Adorno's responses to Benjamin remain instructive for another reason. Of the few critical essays that have been read by many people and are still felt to define a period, Benjamin's "The Work of Art in the Age of Mechanical Reproduction" is the most influential, and its conscious and unconscious ambivalences have been repeated again and again by recent critics. Since this has happened, I believe, because its motives are not commonly understood, a short summary of the way they affect the argument may be useful. The essay is divided logically into two parts, even if these do not quite correspond to the sequence of presentation. In part 1, Benjamin establishes his conception of the "aura," but relates it to some special orders of circumstance: first, an archaic mode of experience, no longer available after the Enlightenment; second, a mysterious valuation of the work of art, which high capitalism in turn is rendering precarious. It is plain that Benjamin cherishes the aura of the work of art as something distinct both from its text and its reputation. But he sees that the aura is being withdrawn above all by the mass culture of reproduction, in photography and the cinema for example, with the powers of which the masses themselves are in thorough complicity. In part 2, Benjamin escapes from the alternative he has pictured as hopeless on both sides by recasting the argument in a gnostic form. He resigns himself to the end of the work of art under the assault of mass reproduction; but he treats the work as an element of created life that must be destroyed for the sake of a blind assertion of freedom. Fortunately, the agents of destruction are the proletariat. So photography and the cinema, which had been his antagonists at the start of the essay, return as his heroes at the finish. They represent the forward striving of the masses (even if not created by the masses), and the change they effect will shatter the powers that have wrecked art (though only by "politicizing" the wreckage). Part 1 of this argument comes mostly from a reading of Baudelaire, part 2 mostly from conversations with Brecht; and Adorno denied that in combination they become Marxist when he wrote to Benjamin: "You have swept art out of the corners of its taboos—but it is as though you feared a consequent inrush of barbarism (who could share your fear more than I?) and protected yourself by raising what you fear to a kind of reverse taboo."[23] What Adorno did not foresee was that the same negative taboo—the things-forbidden redefined as things-welcome, for the sake of a revolution outside art—would eventually be cultivated as an aesthetic in itself. The trick is carried off with none of Benjamin's savage irony or regret.

A pertinent and much-discussed example of this tendency is Fredric Jameson's 1984 *New Left Review* essay, "Postmodernism, or the Cultural Logic of Late Capitalism." In an earlier work, *The Political Unconscious*, Jameson had proposed an analysis of the utopian moment in the capitalist work of art—a category that itself was indebted to Benjamin's use of the "dialectical image," the figure that yields a coalescence of the archaic into the modern. When, in objecting to such terms, Adorno wrote of the dialectical image as regression, he meant that the only form of classlessness it uncovered was "a phantasmagoria of Hell." But the phantasmagoria of late capitalism that Jameson wants to explore for its utopian possibilities is not a moment but the imaginary space of a whole culture. Its lineaments, says Jameson, may be traced in "a new depthlessness, which finds its prolongation both in contemporary 'theory' and in a whole new culture of the image or the simulacrum; a consequent weakening of historicity, both in our relationship to public History and in the new forms of our private temporality."[24] Thus, scanning the contributions of video, television, the urban sprawl of shopping centers and the megalithic hotels that have squatted among the remnants of uprooted neighborhoods, Jameson composes an appreciative montage of what he calls "a new kind of superficiality in the most literal sense [*sic*]." As a defining trait of postmodernism, this has its avatar in Warhol's Campbell's Soup cans, which, Jameson says with emphasis, "*ought* to be powerful and critical statements." If they are not yet, it is the fault of the critics who have not made them so. Packages, simulacra, or works of commerce like Warhol's adequately represent the feelings of people now—feelings that, Jameson reflects, "it may be better and more accurate to call 'intensities' " since they "are now free-floating and impersonal, and tend to be dominated by a peculiar kind of euphoria."[25] Other features of the postmodernist look are a flat and affectless style of pastiche and "an omnipresent, omnivorous and well-nigh libinidal historicism." To give force to these impressions, Jameson then typifies postmodernism by an amalgam of objects and persons. "Cage, Ashbery, Sollers, Robert Wilson, Ishmael Reed, Michael Snow, Warhol or even Beckett himself" are all on this account postmodernist; so too are De Palma's *Blowout,* Polanski's *Chinatown,* Michael Herr's *Dispatches,* and all of the novels of E. L. Doctorow.

The list betrays a general tastelessness that is in harmony with the essay's ambition to read a culture as a seamless general text. Jameson draws his main exhibit not from literature or the arts but from the economic rescoring of a large city through the building of a gigantic architectural complex, John Portman's Bonaventure Hotel in Los Angeles. There, as in any postmodernist text, the structure induces in the reader a "feeling that emptiness is here absolutely packed, that it is an element within which you yourself are immersed, without any of that distance that formerly enabled the perception of perspective or volume. You are in this hyperspace up to your eyes and your body." Also, for the postmodern *flâneur,* there are escalators: "Here the narrative stroll has been underscored, symbolized, reified, and replaced by a transportation machine which becomes the allegorical signifier of that older promenade we are no longer to conduct on our own." But is not all of this irrelevant to the habits of the crowd in an older narrative, since their successors are excluded in advance by the very placement of the hotel? Instead of allowing such objections to halt the inquiry, Jameson deduces from this "new collective space" as such "a new collective practice, a new mode in which individuals move and congregate, something like the practice of a new and historically original kind of hyper-crowd." His is the sort of analysis that follows from a resolution to "think this development positively *and* negatively all at once; to achieve, in other words, a type of thinking that would be capable of grasping the demonstrably baleful features of capitalism along with its extraordinary and liberating dynamism simultaneously, within a single thought."[26] Jameson associates his strategy here with that of Marx. What Marx did not do, however, was advise his readers to think the negative features of a system positively. At this crossroads of magic and positivism, Marxism has grown indistinguishable from what it contemplates. To judge by the above description of being "immersed . . . up to your eyes and your body" in a space that is "absolutely packed," its aesthetic has likewise come to share certain traits with an aesthetic of fascism. As for the excited account of the vistas, escalators, and other attractions of the place, it is done in a style not far removed from advertising—a special variety of it, for which the French reserve the phrase *pour tromper les clercs.*

Faced with the necessity of immersing oneself in the antihuman junk of capitalist culture, in order to think its destruction in a properly antihuman light, it may seem that a shorter way out lies in simply abolishing the profession of criticism. Leave the reading of old books to evasive or elitist types in the other professions: for those who have seen through them, the best employment of critical skills will be in the making of revolutionary ideology. This is actually the position of Terry Eagleton in *Literary Theory,* a book that in any other period would have found difficulty getting published because of its wholesale inaccuracies. But it has sold well and deserves to be considered here. An anomaly of Eagleton's design is the moralistic, unpragmatic, and academic compulsion to prove that, before the study of literature can be decently terminated, it ought to be shown to have *earned* its death warrant. The story of why it has done so is what interests me in the book—the rest being cribs of other theorists—and it occupies a first chapter on "The Rise of English" as well as a last on "Political Criticism." Eagleton believes that from Arnold on, literary study has been consciously expounded as a tactic, and a most important one, in the ideological defense of the capitalist state. This, and not something more oblique, was Arnold's point in saying that literature could take the place of religion. Eagleton describes the New Critics as disciples of Arnold (which they were not) and imputes to them the view that "the Decline of the West was felt to be avertable by close reading" (which they would have denied). He asserts very frequently that modern critics have deceived their audience by promising that "reading literature did make you a better person." It is questionable whether a single modern critic of any authority has ever held this view, apart perhaps from I. A. Richards in his more waywardly inspirational moments; but Empson, a closer student of his opinions than Eagleton, reports that he thought the only good of reading literature was to teach you how other people lived. Many critics would want to add, if they talked much about these things, that it could also help you to think about life. But they would not claim that it, more than other pursuits, had any marked capacity for prompting the right choices.

If criticism helps to strengthen the apparatus of the state, its practitioners must be conscious of the necessity to promote conservative authors. This Eagleton believes was true of Leavis in particular, of whom he reports that "almost all of [the authors in his canon] were conservatives." Now, among those whom Eagleton names are Blake, Keats, George Eliot, Lawrence, and Bunyan, none of whom could be called conservative on any definition of the word. Yet errors or careless falsehoods of this sort do not matter until they are repeated by others; and what is edifying about Eagleton's perspective is that it shows how extremes meet. The believer in the all-sufficing good of an ideological exposure of the text reaches a tacit accord with the believer in the substantial existence of a meaning of the text in itself. The only difference is that for the former the fixed meaning is political. "Let us imagine," Eagleton invites his readers, "that by dint of some deft archaeological research we discovered a great deal more about what ancient Greek tragedy actually meant to its original audiences, recognized that these concerns were utterly remote from our own, and began to read the plays again in the light of this deepened knowledge. One result might be that we stopped enjoying them."[27] But a first premise of hermeneutics suggests that the result would be less decisive. Situations like this confront us all the time, and we meet them with the principle of charity in translation.[28] We read the work differently, selectively, emphasizing some of its features rather than others—we even, as it may appear to later scholars, misread the work in order to preserve something of it that does interest us. But Eagleton's sole criterion of literary worth does not have to do with reading. It is simply a criterion of political membership and, further back, of political loyalty construed from an inspection of biographical facts. If an author's life shows him to have been radical, then we will learn to read him radically.

By the end of *Literary Theory*, all Eagleton lacked was a utopian moment of his own in literary history, an age of egalitarian discourse to show what literature ever since had fallen away from. In his next book, *The Function of Criticism*, he picked the moment almost at random. It was the 1710s, in the coffeehouses of London, where Addison and Steele wrote their papers: "What is said [in those coffeehouses] derives its legitimacy neither from itself as message nor from the social title of the utterer, but from its conformity as a statement with a certain paradigm of reason inscribed in the very event of saying."[29] Thus an ingratiating blend of Habermas with high common-room speculation is offered as a theory of the lost public sphere. Though answerable for none of the details, Eagleton wants to make his story as suggestive as possible, and this requires of course a dating of the fall. To serve the function he summons—the next critic most people can remember after Addison—Johnson. With Johnson, "we are evolving towards just that rift between literary intellectual and social formation out of which a fully specialist criticism will finally emerge." Johnson, as Eagleton argues or, rather, as he wonders if he might not half commit himself to arguing some day (theory needs a new grammatical *mood* to describe this sort of thought experiment): Johnson is "isolated and abstracted in contrast to the busily empirical Addison." The choice, by the way, of Addison over Steele is merely conventional, since, to anyone who has read them both, it is Steele who seems to have seen or heard or felt the life of the streets and taverns, while Addison kept to his closet and worked out his dicta with an agreeable pedantry. Still, let us take the contrast as it stands. Johnson (the "isolated and abstracted"), who equipped his rooms with a small chemical laboratory, spoke of having talked away his life in company, and once carried a prostitute who had collapsed of fatigue a very long walk up Fleet Street on his back. And Addison (the "busily empirical"), who supped and was snug with the great and almost great, never wrote a word without an eye on the Whig ascendancy, and codified the taste of his day without altering it one particle. Which of these looks like the hero of legitimate sociable public reason?

A moral of the foregoing pages may be that bad theory makes bad history. Yet it is the contempt for history among theorists as a rule that has led to the hatching of stories like Eagleton's on a regular basis. His books are forgotten two at a time, almost as fast as he writes them. Meanwhile, they are treated respectfully, since the presence of a Marxist whose iconoclasm about literature goes all the way is felt to round out the company at any theory colloquium with pretensions to tolerance. Earlier, I alluded to Wittgenstein as a counterweight to the philosophers most influential in recent theory, and I have to quote here a final passage from *Zettel:*

> What does it mean to say: "But that's no longer the same game!" How do I use this sentence? As information? Well, perhaps to introduce some information in which differences are enumerated and their consequences explained. But also to express that just for

> that reason I don't join in here, or at any rate take up a different attitude to the game.[30]

I have tried to point out how by gradual adjustments theory has been turning criticism into a game that is no longer recognizably the same. And I have tried to enumerate some of the differences, and to explain some of the consequences. If the description was adequate, my reasons will be plain for concluding, "Here is where I don't join in." A survey like this, however, would seem to me incomplete without some account of a proposition I believe is worth refuting, which many theorists either assert or do not want to be seen to challenge. It is, that once we give up the unity or complete intelligibility of the text as an attainable ideal, it makes less difference what texts we choose for analysis; so that the mass-cultural object has an equal claim with the work of art, all other considerations being favorable; and perhaps a better claim, if what interests us is the habits or projectable responses of the largest sheer mass of readers. I want to end by saying how this attitude came about and what may be wrong with it; and, finally, by defending the interpretation of great writing on nonaesthetic grounds.

At first glance, the rhetoric of theory sounds as if it wanted to look at texts the way a physicist looks at elementary particles. If the aim is to account for their behavior, one sample is as good as another. To discriminate at all ("Sorry, this kind isn't worth my trouble") seems therefore not so much retrograde as pointless: if your theory concedes in advance a prejudice against certain objects without yielding a rule to help identify them, it ceases to be a theory and becomes just a disguise for personal judgments, "value judgments." And yet, since judgments come into play however we try to neutralize them—a point that theorists admit without exception—the embarrassment about what to do with them suggests an ambivalence in the theoretical attitude. An ambivalence, rather than a contradiction, because theorists only act as if a concern with judgments would betray the very nature of their work. They do not in fact hold views that would make it a betrayal. Thus a reader-response critic might say consistently with his theory: "Melville's reader is more interesting than G. P. R. James's or even Stowe's: I will show that the responses are options taken at a higher level." A deconstructionist might make a similar move with respect to linguistic figuration, and so on. But this move is not made now, while the opposite one ("And this applies to any text you can think of—defining text as broadly as you like") is made all the time. A reason for the emphasis will appear if we realize that the physicist was only a rough-

and-ready analogy. The scientist from whom literary theory has consciously borrowed both a self-image and a rhetoric is the anthropologist. This influence is traceable to Foucault's method as well as his titles; and, in English, to Clifford Geertz, Mary Douglas, and a few others. What does the anthropologist's stance tell us? Above all, that, in seeking to understand a culture, we had better exempt none of its elements from consideration. The most familiar help as much as the least in reconstructing a cultural code. Nor is the case altered when the culture is our own. Our descriptions, if careful, will represent relations and not objects; but we cannot know what texts may end up serving our purpose until the interpretation itself is complete; and it is never complete. Besides, to a modern academic researcher, mass-cultural texts come at once under the headings of the most and the least familiar.

The theoretical geniality toward mass culture is also part of a larger history: it is the last chapter in the convergence of the avant-garde with the academy. The time lag between the advent of the new and its assimilation has grown shorter with every movement since the first appearance of an avant-garde around 1800. For Wordsworth, the period was forty years or so: almost the length of a career. For the younger American painters honored by museum retrospectives in the 1970s, it had shrunk to a little over a decade. What has always been known about high art throughout this period is its equivocal indebtedness to popular culture and mass culture. It draws on these without being subservient to them. Now, by joining, in the name of "intertextuality," the work of art with the product of mass culture, critics level themselves with artists as exponents of the new. The practice has occasionally been employed against the valuations of any possible canon; the canon, it is said, acts in the service of mere ideology. Such arguments carry a persistent appeal even though they risk confusing mass consumption with democratic expression. But I believe that Adorno was right to maintain very steadily that a radical practice of criticism could not retreat from the defense of the work of art. He gave his own justification of "immanent criticism" in an essay entitled "Cultural Criticism and Society":

> Where [such criticism] finds inadequacies it does not ascribe them hastily to the individual and his psychology, which are merely the facade of the failure, but instead seeks to derive them from the irreconcilability of the object's moments. It pursues the logic of its aporias, the insolubility of the task itself. In such antinomies criti-

> cism perceives those of society. A successful work, according to immanent criticism, is not one which resolves objective contradictions in a spurious harmony, but one which expresses the idea of harmony negatively by embodying the contradictions, pure and uncompromised, in its innermost structure. Confronted with this kind of work, the verdict "mere ideology" loses its meaning.[31]

Adorno wrote from the perspective of modernism, and other recent defenses of the modernist work of art, by Harold Rosenberg and Thomas Crow for example, have followed a similar pattern and rejected the interpretation of the mass-cultural object as a text like any other.[32]

In defining the interest and originality of modernist works, all of these critics notice a relation between such qualities and the accepted styles of mass culture. But the relation is not taken to be one of identity or resemblance. In short, they reject the anthropologist's idea of a seamless general text of culture. Their procedure seems to follow from reflection on a part of the critic's work for which the anthropologist cannot serve as a guide. This may be described broadly as the problem of allusion, or the ascription of self-consciousness in reading the motives of representation. Consider the use that art makes of clichés. It is a salient practice of modernist works in particular, and the tact with which a cliché is managed often serves as one index of an artist's temperament. Yet the anthropologist has no interest in this, and no equipment to measure it: from the point of view of the seamless general text the commonplace, the daily banality, the cliché, and the cliché quoted ironically (let alone the cliché quoted with an unsuccessful attempted irony, as in "Hugh Selwyn Mauberley"), all have the same status. It has lately been claimed that, by interpreting early folk versions of the story of Little Red Ridinghood, we can reconstruct Frenchness.[33] It would be odd to make a similar claim about a modernist work—say, that by interpreting Flaubert's *Dictionary of Received Ideas,* we could reconstruct even a piece of Frenchness, late romantic bourgeois philistine Frenchness. Partly, the trouble is that the work does too much of the reconstruction itself; partly, that it yields information in excess of the attitudes it records. Perhaps this is another way of saying that reading a modernist text is something different from reading a text. Grant that modernism owes its identity to a conscious relation with mass culture, and it follows that a modernist text knows a mass-cultural text as the latter does not know itself. Even the perspectivism of theory is logical and teachable, almost to the point of transparency, by comparison with the perspectivism of modern painting or poetry.

What is sometimes described as the resistance to theory is nothing but the usual tremors of passage as one professionalist vocabulary displaces another. New textualist methods of reading are pedagogically apt in much the same way that New Critical methods were, and the widening emphasis on theory belongs to a political action confined to the academy and its outworks. This verdict contradicts that of theory on itself, which may be summed up: "Literature dreams; theory knows." That what it knows may be dangerous to the order of things is a surmise undertaken and destined to stay in the register of as-if. States have no objection to theorists until they propose the undoing of existing structures by more than textual means. But to do so means also to step outside theory once and for all. At the same time, literature itself remains manifestly dangerous. Ignored by theory, the works of a Kundera, a Konrad, a Milosz evoke keen interest from the customs agents at any number of borders, and are interdicted as the works of a Derrida or a Jameson are not. This still happens because there was always a volatile element in the very texture of romantic and modernist works that their appropriation by the academy has caused to pass from view but that is still recognized outside it. By asserting an unstable but strangely renewable connection with the past, they called into question the self-images of the present. And they did so at a time when the latter, either through censorship or the opinion-making efficacy of the media, were beginning to be rationalized under a new political authority.

"Who controls the past controls the future," goes the party slogan of Orwell's *1984,* but it has a corollary: "Who controls the present controls the past." The modern statist wants to control the understanding of the present. Literature and, when it chose to be active, criticism have been among the forces that stood in the way. Like the other slogans of the party, this one was drawn, as Orwell made clear, not only from the standard procedures of totalitarian states but also from emerging tendencies in America and Europe. What Orwell observed both in his novels and in many of his critical essays was that commercial democracies were starting to share certain aims with revolutionary dictatorships. They might see the aims as temporary, while the dictatorships saw them as final, but year by year anyway the damage was being done. The modern state wanted not merely to govern but to control; to control the present it was necessary to control the past; and if that meant obliterating the past, it would not shrink from doing so. Orwell's predecessor as a critic was Edmund Burke, who wrote: "People will not look forward to posterity, who never look backward to their ancestors." But the state has a gaze more flatly purposeful than the writer's. When an Eastern leader cites Tolstoy approvingly, or a Western leader cites Lincoln approvingly, the same thing is happening, and to capture it one needs another phrase of Burke's: "They unplumb the dead for bullets to assassinate the living."

The first mistake of theory has been to suppose that criticism can have a direct relationship with the political control of the present. A second mistake has been to suppose that its main rival is literature. Orwell and Burke together suggest a different idea of what criticism ought to do. It cannot itself attain, or even supply others with tools for attaining, control of the present. But it can insert itself between those who control the present and their wish to control the past. It can, that is, weaken the state's inertia and qualify its authority, by affording a few of its citizens a backward glance that is not the same as the look sanctioned by the state. To the degree that it teaches the differentness of the past, criticism acts on behalf of a future.

I am proposing that for criticism today a consciousness of the past as such performs a critical function. To believe this does not require a faith in the objectivity of interpretation or a prior belief that history is the sum total of positive facts. It presumes only that other times hold other persons in other situations which we may think of as alternative to ours: in some respects better, in some respects worse, in all respects different. And that these materials are not altogether tractable: they will not do everything we want them to. This last is what the modern state most needs to forget. How much so we Americans were shown memorably when a president, on a foreign visit, recalled, and almost succeeded in making us recall, the Second World War as a contest against the Soviet Union in which Americans and Germans fought side by side. I give this last illustration for the same reason that I offered Orwell and Burke as representative critics, because it seems to me that literary criticism, when it matters, is not easily separated from cultural or social criticism. In the past few years, academic critics have seen all at once that they too are engaged in unclassifiable activities, and the recognition has led them to talk vaguely but ominously about power. Much of the talk conceives of power as a synonym for habits, customs, usages, practices of any kind, as if commentaries on texts could help people to live eventually without these things. The idea that they could is nonsense, with a short future in practice. Nevertheless, critics still do make a usable record of the ways people have thought and felt, or might think and feel, outside the mastery of the present. By translating, from a distant or otherwise hidden time, the testamentary parable or the unforeseen inheritance, they interpret for readers the hidden powers of living men and women.

Notes

1. W. K. Wimsatt, *Day of the Leopards: Essays in Defense of Poems* (New Haven: Yale University Press, 1976), 196–97.

2. Gayatri Chakravorti Spivak, "Three Women's Texts and a Critique of Imperialism," *Critical Inquiry* 12 (autumn 1985): 243–61.

3. See E. D. Hirsch Jr., *Validity in Interpretation* (New Haven: Yale University Press, 1967), and Gerald Graff, *Literature against itself: Literary Ideas in Modern Society* (Chicago: University of Chicago Press, 1979). A good exposition of Hirsch's views, with a polemic against them, may be found in David Couzens Hoy, *The Critical Circle: Literature, History, and Philosophical Hermeneutics* (Berkeley and Los Angeles: University of California Press, 1977), chap. 1.

4. Ludwig Wittgenstein, *Philosophical Investigations,* trans. G. E. M. Anscombe, 3d ed. (New York: Doubleday, 1968), 103, 201.

5. Wittgenstein, *Zettel* (Berkeley and Los Angeles: University of California Press, 1970), 31.

6. See Richard Rorty, *Consequences of Pragmatism: Essays, 1972–1980* (Minneapolis: University of Minnesota Press, 1982), chap. 8. I have profited from the remarks on Derrida in chapter 6 as well, and in the same author's "Deconstruction and Circumvention," *Critical Inquiry* 11 (autumn 1984): 1–23. My reservations about the idea of a "general text" appear later in this chapter.

7. The afterword to William James's essay "On Some Hegelisms," in *The Will to Believe* (New York: Longmans, Green, 1897) includes some notations on the circumstances of his temporary conversion to the Hegelian philosophy, under the effects of nitrous oxide gas: "Strife presupposes something to be striven about; and in this common topic, the same for both parties, the differences merge. . . . *Yes* and *no* agree at least in being assertions," and so on. The leading vehicle for his conversion, as James describes it, was *puns,* and he gives as a specimen "What's mistake but a kind of take?" (295).

8. See, for example, Martha Nussbaum, "Flawed Crystals: James's *The Golden Bowl* and Literature as Moral Philosophy," *New Literary History* 15 (autumn 1983): 25–50, a study of the novel's characters as responsible moral thinkers. One would not quite guess from this account that they are interested in money and power.

9. John Searle, "The Word Turned Upside Down," *New York Review of Books* (27 October 1983): pp 74–79. A more accurate skeptical estimate of the claims by theorists to do without an idea of making sense is Hilary Putnam, "The Craving for Objectivity," *New Literary History* 15 (winter 1984): 229–39. I have borrowed in this essay something of Putnam's emphasis on the worth of trying to "get things right."

10. Paul de Man, *Allegories of Reading: Figural Language in Rousseau, Nietzsche, Rilke, and Proust* (New Haven: Yale University Press, 1979), 17.

11. William Empson, *Seven Types of Ambiguity,* 2d ed. (London: Chatto and Windus, 1947), 4.

12. Paul de Man, *Blindness and Insight: Essays in the Rhetoric of Contemporary Criticism,* 2d ed. (Minneapolis: University of Minnesota Press, 1983).

13. De Man, *The Rhetoric of Romanticism* (New York: Columbia University Press, 1984), 81.

14. Stanley Cavell, *Themes Out of School* (San Francisco: North Point Press, 1984), 42.

15. Neil Hertz, *The End of the Line: Essays on Psychoanalysis and the Sublime* (New York: Columbia University Press, 1985).

16. Ibid., 208.

17. Michel Foucault, *Language, Counter-Memory, Practice,* ed. Donald F. Bouchard (Ithaca: Cornell University Press, 1977), 153.

18. Wittgenstein, *Zettel,* 98.

19. Foucault, *Language,* 163.

20. Ibid., 162.

21. Stanley Corngold, *The Fate of the Self: German Writers and the French Theory* (New York: Columbia University Press, 1985), 12; on Nietzsche, see chaps. 3 and 4, passim. Richard Poirier gives a related account of an ambivalence between the Nietzsche–Foucault hostility to the self and the status they share as authors with signature and styles, in "Writing Off the Self," *Raritan* 1 (summer 1981): 106–33.

22. E. P. Thompson, *The Poverty of Theory and Other Essays* (New York: Monthly Review Press, 1978), 185–86.

23. "Letters to Walter Benjamin," in Ernst Bloch et al., *Aesthetics and Politics* (London: NLB, 1977), 123.

24. Fredric Jameson, "Postmodernism," *New Left Review* (July–August 1984): 58.

25. Ibid., 64.

26. Ibid., 86.

27. Terry Eagleton, *Literary Theory: An Introduction* (Minneapolis: University of Minnesota Press, 1983), 12.

28. On the principle of charity, see Davidson, "On the Very Idea of a Conceptual Scheme"; and W. V. Quine, *Word and Object* (Cambridge: MIT Press, 1964), chap. 2. Roughly, the principle holds that in moving from one language to another, we accommodate as many of its unfamiliar properties as we can to our familiar ways of undertstanding. Given, therefore, a choice between treating a piece of language as utterly opaque and treating it as intelligible, we make the necessary adjustments of our general view to bring about the latter outcome. Interpretation has a comparable principle of charity, in keeping with which a reader, when shown a difficult passage or work by a great author, tries before losing patience to work out how the author may have been making an unexpected sort of sense.

29. Eagleton, *The Function of Criticism: From The Spectator to Post-Structuralism* (London: Verso, 1984), 15.

30. Wittgenstein, *Zettel,* 60.

31. Theodor W. Adorno, *Prisms,* trans. Samuel and Sherry Weber (Cambridge: MIT Press, 1981), 32. The letters to Benjamin cited above also contain a defense of the work of art: "The reification of a great work of art is not just loss, any more than the reification of the cinema is all loss. It would be bourgeois reaction to negate the reification of the cinema in the name of the ego, and it would border on anarchism to revoke the reification of a great work of art in the spirit of immediate use-values" (123). On Adorno's "logic of aporias," see his *Aesthetic Theory,* trans. G. Lenhardt (London: Routledge and Kegan Paul, 1983), chap. 12.

32. Harold Rosenberg, "Art and Its Double," in *Artworks and Packages* (New York: Horizon, 1971), describes the mutual influences of the arts and the media as continuous throughout the modern period, but with the arts now on the brink of vanishing into the

media. Thomas Crow, "Modernism and Mass Culture in the Visual Arts," in *Modernism and Modernity,* ed. Benjamin H. D. Buchloh, Serge Guilbaut, and David Solkin (Nova Scotia: Press of the Nova Scotia College of Art and Design, 1983), 215–64, sees the exchange as repeating a single pattern: "the appropriation of oppositional practices upward, the return of evacuated cultural goods downward."

33. See Robert Darnton, "Peasants Tell Tales: The Meaning of Mother Goose," in *The Great Cat Massacre and Other Episodes in French Cultural History* (New York: Basic Books, 1984).

Relevant Publications by David Bromwich

Politics by Other Means: Higher Education and Group Thinking. New Haven: Yale University Press, 1992.

A Choice of Inheritance: Self and Community from Edmund Burke to Robert Frost. Cambridge: Harvard University Press, 1989.

Hazlitt: The Mind of a Critic. Oxford: Oxford University Press, 1983.

"How Moral is Taste?" *Yale Review* 82 (January 1994): 1–23.

"Why Authors Don't Give Us Their Own Worlds." *Salmagundi* (fall 1988): 126–43.

"Reflections on the Word Genius." *New Literary History* 17 (autumn 1985): 141–64.

"The Uses of Biography." *Yale Review* 73 (winter 1984): 161–76.

"The Genealogy of Disinterestedness." *Raritan* 1 (spring 1982): 62–92.

11

Toward a Critical Re-Renewal: At the Corner of Camus and Bloom Streets

Quentin Kraft

Quentin Kraft, professor of English at Denison University, is engaged at present in completing a series of essays called "Episodes in the Emergence of the Novel." His interest in the novel is evident in the essay here reprinted, but the issue it addresses is not a matter of genre but of the ways of conceiving of individuals as "present" in a world even though pure "presence" may be impossible and as acting in that world even though the world itself may be finally unknowable. Indeed, Kraft argues that it is from the constraining conditions of such a world that theory itself takes its start "as an attempt to give a plausible account or explanation of what we do not know for sure and what, without a theory, we would never know at all."

In speaking about novels I tend to claim for authors and their works a little more than has, as a rule, been allowed in recent years. This essay seeks to make the case for doing so, that is, for claiming more than is readily granted. Originally I called it a "preface" because that is just what it started out to be, a short piece with which to begin another essay. Even though it has outgrown itself, and become too big for its original purpose and place. I continue to think of it as a preface because it is still meant to precede something, and to lead up to it, namely a certain way of working with literature. But I have changed the title in order to give emphasis to what, it seems to me, we need to move toward, and that is a renewal of criticism as a whole. This is not, of course, the first time that criticism has ever seemed in need of renovation—hence the redoubling of "renewal." Specifically, what we need is to correct an imbalance, and then to form a new balance between theory and practice. At the very least we need to find some way to reassert the value of individual texts, and we need to do so without ignoring or dismissing all we have come to understand over the last thirty years, most notably about the "ubiquity of language" and therefore about the ubiquity of texts and textuality. Today, that is, at the beginning of the 1990s, almost any talk of the "integrity" of a text may be sufficient in some quarters to convict one of critical simplicity or maybe just plain anachronism. But talk of the integrity of a text is not, I think, as naive as one can get; it is, I believe, even more naive and unsophisticated to think that in speaking of "integrity" one must mean some absolute state or quality, something like a condition of hermetic self-enclosure. At best, the integrity of texts—as opposed to the integrity of persons—is a relative matter, and probably always was, though if so its relativity was on many an occasion hidden in a very unrelative rhetoric. At any rate, texts do have a relative integrity, and that relative integrity is enough to distinguish them from the whole textual web to which they respond and of which they nevertheless remain a part. Our way of dealing with them—even when, as in Roland Barthes's *S/Z*, the aim is to disprove integrity—is proof enough. This essay does not in an explicit way pursue much further the case for a degree of integrity in texts, but it does try to establish grounds for once again noting differences and making distinctions between things. The new distinctions must be understood as radically qualified. Still, they should help to make a difference in how we conceive of many things, including texts. They might even enable us to speak of "works" again.

I

The relation of the individual wit or intelligence to an overall cultural intelligence is in this essay a key issue. It is stressed here mainly because it has been so little an issue in what may be considered the powerline of contemporary theorizing, the line that negates the old New Criticism and then runs through structuralism to deconstruction. It has been so little an issue because in that line the individual has all but disappeared. Indeed, there has been a strange and self-defeating irony in much of this theorizing. On the one hand, it has challenged and "deconstructed" everything monolithic: orthodox views, official words, dogmas of all kinds, indeed any voice of authority and thus any and all claims to certainty. In this way it has affirmed difference and liberated the individual. On the other hand, it has been quick to deconstruct and disable what it has affirmed and liberated. It has allowed to the individual very little, if any, power to construct or reconstruct or even, for that matter, to deconstruct, though it tends to remain rather silent on the negation of its own activities. Indeed, the mainline of this theorizing has been so wholly bent on antihumanism as to seem suicidal.

According to the tenor of its thinking, if there is anything we can still call an intelligence, it is not ours; we are its, merely its "bits" and nothing more. As Stanley Fish put it, "since the thoughts an individual can think . . . have their source in some . . . interpretive community, he is as much a product of that community (acting as an extension of it) as the meanings it enables him to produce."[1] We are post "human" and post everything else. Not only do we "come after" Auschwitz and the Holocaust and a host of other horrors, as George Steiner urged us to acknowledge,[2] but also after the death of gods and of heroes and even of characters, which means as well that we come after the death of authors, persons, subjects, and selves. According to Vincent Leitch, first structuralism proclaimed "the death of the subject" and then deconstruction "declared the end of man and humanism."[3] Thus it has been written that "what can no longer be written is the Proper Name."[4] Much the same line of thought has placed us at the end of nature and of history and literature and philosophy and therefore of knowledge itself. It would seem at last that we might have come to the end of all our ends.

And, indeed, if "after" is anywhere, it is in a place of no discernible beginnings or endings, a labyrinth filled with abysses and *aporias*. And if that labyrinth in which we are lost is to be found anywhere, it is to be found in language. We are, it seems, the denizens of Borges's story, "Tlön, Uqbar, Orbis Tertius." In language we cease to be and, worse yet, we cease to be able. Some say we do not speak language but language speaks us. We are merely its utterances. And others, according to Terry Eagleton, say:

> [I]t is an illusion for me to believe that I can ever be fully present to you in what I say or write . . . my meaning is always somehow dispersed, divided and never quite at one with itself. Not only my

> meaning, indeed, but *me:* since language is something I am made out of . . . the whole idea that I am a stable, unified entity must also be a fiction. . . . I can never have a pure, unblemished meaning or experience at all.[5]

Thus the deepest wisdom, and perhaps the most fashionable, seems to be that we see no evil, we hear no evil, we speak no evil but only because we know nothing at all and, indeed, we are nothing at all, at least nothing worth mentioning. We do not even have, it seems, a "clean well-lighted place" in which to drink our brandy and say our prayer: "Our *nada* who art in *nada* . . ."

Perhaps the worst thing about this whole line of thought is its tendency to be self-fulfilling. If we tell ourselves often enough, we are bound to convince ourselves that there is nothing we can do, at least nothing of importance. Then we will have made ourselves into full-fledged "philistines," according to the definition Georg Lukács stresses, all those people who remain "resigned" and therefore passive in the presence of "degrading circumstances."[6] The important question is therefore: where does this line of thinking get its start? Among others, one sure starting place is, I think, the whole business about "presence." Like most everything else in Derrida, "presence" is a concept I probably do not understand fully. And no doubt the Derrida I invoke is not the "real" one, the Derrida of full complexity, but only a condensed version, the simplified figure of widest influence; but it is, after all, the wide influence that I am primarily concerned with. In any case, I would not touch on the matter of presence now if I did not believe it to be a key issue, one that affects most everything else in a theory including the slant one takes on authors, texts, readers, and characters. Fortunately my concern is not with the metaphysical argument itself. Thus, I do not have to contend with anything like the "Nietzschean critique of metaphysics" or the "Freudian critique of presence" or the "Heideggerian destruction of metaphysics"—all projects about which Derrida writes.[7] My concern is only with what comes after the critique, that is, with the position we take in response to it. As I understand it, beneath all that is baffling or dazzling in Derrida's uses of the term, "presence" means something fairly simple, to wit, the idea of an unmediated relationship between consciousness and an object, a relationship that is pure because it is prior to and, therefore, uncontaminated by language. Derrida sees such a relationship, pure presence, as underlying all Western metaphysics—hence the phrase "metaphysics of presence." That means in his view a *fiction* underlies all Western metaphysics. Presence is for him a fiction because, as he puts it, "From the moment that there is meaning there are nothing but signs."[8] If there are signs, there is mediation and adulteration, and if there is mediation and adulteration, there can be nothing like the pure relationship he calls "presence." So far, so good, but once we reach this point, the crucial question is: what follows from it? The question is crucial because this point is one of the major ones from which consequences start, perhaps *the* major point. Must we—should we?—conclude that if there is no pure presence, there is in effect no presence at all? More to the point, should we write as if there were nothing but writing to write about?

That has been the conclusion of some so-called poststructuralists. Indeed it may be what makes them poststructuralists. At any rate, it is what distinguishes two traditions of philosophy as defined by Richard Rorty in his essay on Derrida, "Philosophy as a Kind of Writing." The first tradition, Philosophy with a capital P, linked primarily with the names of Plato and Kant, is the more traditional tradition. As its major question it asks "how representations are related to nonrepresentations."[9] That means it concerns itself with presence, which is to say, with things other than signs, things conceived as outside the text, things ranging from the otherworldly and eternal to the worldly and temporal (xv). This tradition "thinks of truth as a vertical relationship between representations and what is represented" (92). The second tradition, lower-case philosophy, in which Rorty includes himself and Derrida, the pragmatists and the deconstructors, is much less traditional. Its major question is quite different: it asks only "how representations can be seen as hanging together" (92). Though as philosophy it is nontraditional, it depends for its very existence on tradition because it "thinks of truth horizontally—as the culminating reinterpretation of our predecessors' reinterpretation of their predecessors' reinterpretation." According to this tradition, philosophy is "seen as a kind of writing," and writing is seen as something that does not lead anywhere outside of itself (92). For Derrida, the "dialectical" (93) as opposed to metaphysical philosopher, "writing always leads to more writing, and more, and still more" (94). Thus we have two images: (1) the "Philosopher" who conceives of himself as functioning in relation to the world and perhaps to an otherworld as well and (2) the "philosopher," coming after the critique of presence, who conceives of himself as functioning only in relation to writing and to texts. In Rorty's words, "Consider Derrida as trying . . . to create a new thing for writing to be about—not the world, but texts" (95).

Among literary critics, Fish is a good example of one who practices in the tradition of lower-case philosophy. In mapping the course of his own thinking, he says he reached the point at which reader and text "fall together" and thus cease to be separate and distinguishable.[10] As something prior, and therefore external, the text simply disappears along with any traces of the author as its maker. For Fish, there is no literary presence because there is nothing present to be present to. "Interpretation is not," he declares, "the art of construing but the art of constructing. Interpreters do not decode poems; they make them" (327). Not only do reader and text "fall together" but both together fall into an "interpretive community" in which they all but vanish. Strangely—or not so strangely—the notion that the reader produces the text goes along with the notion that there is nothing outside texts. Both notions depend on the more fundamental notion that presence is a fiction, merely an illusion, and that, as we are enclosed in language, so we are closed off from everything else. Summarizing what is "common" in the theories of language "propounded by the deconstructors," Leitch writes: "Assigned a powerful foundational role, language determined man more than he determined or directed it. In a sense, language constituted a (prison)house of being. It engendered man and his reality. Nothing stood behind: there were neither origins nor foundations outside language. Irreducibly, the world was text. Extralinguistic reality was an illusion."[11]

II

All of this is, it seems, the consequence not so much of the critique of presence as of the denial of all possibility of presence. If we go the way of the deconstructors, we gain a sense of the "ubiquity" or omnipresence of language but we lose rather more. Not only does the world vanish into textuality but so do any and all distinctions between one kind of text and another. All kinds of writing dissolve into the one great, all-embracing text of textuality. So we lose not just the world, but every different thing in it, and that includes authors, characters, "works," indeed any distinction between the literary and the nonliterary. There is no literature; there is only writing. Moreover, defined by this way of thinking, we, who are made and used by language, are worse off than the cave prisoners who are said to see only the shadows of things. Prisoners we are, but we see nothing so real as shadows. We see only what our culture or our interpretive community happens to project onto our screens, which is to say, onto our prison walls. And so defined, we are not likely to break down any screens or walls, whether linguistic or T.V. or Berlin. We are allowed no such capacity; we can only sit and acquiesce. Perhaps we might wonder whether this is the image of ourselves that should emerge from a theory and method promising to undermine authority, to displace the totalitarian and to put in its place a principle of play and difference.

Indeed, in the face of the current tendency to negate positions of the past in order to be post-positional and after everything, we may want to stop and wonder for a moment whether we are better off now following a poststructuralist line of thought than we were before, a long time ago now, following Camus's attempt to think through the notion of the absurd. No doubt for many today the absurd is already an antiquated notion, but the issue is not whether it is antiquated but whether it works as well or better than what seems more up-to-date. Viewed with hindsight, the absurd as defined by Camus has, we can see, a strange duality about it: it is at one and the same time an extreme version of presence and also, in effect, a critique of presence. It is a version of presence because it is, in Camus's definition, "born" of an encounter of human and world, more specifically a "confrontation between the human need [for reason and meaning] and the unreasonable silence of the world."[12] At the same time it is, in effect, a critique of presence because it is not inconsistent with the Derridean proposition. "From the moment that there is meaning there are nothing but signs." To seem true, this last statement needs some explanation. Certainly the world for Camus was not nothing, and it does remain after the inception of meaning; it is never replaced by a text; it is, in fact, something always and inevitably outside the text. But Camus saves only enough of pure presence, and no more, to affirm the existence of himself and the world. As he states it, "This heart within me I can feel, and I judge that it exists. This world I can touch, and I likewise judge that it exists" (14). That, he says, "ends all my knowledge"; it ends therefore before any characterization with only the bare assertion that the world exists. All the rest, he says, is "construction" (14). Construction, we may note, is more or less the equivalent of signs or, rather, of a text—that is, of something to be deconstructed. As Rorty notes, "No constructors, no deconstructors" (108). At any rate, this being so, Camus comes very close to Derrida because he is saying that signs, or rather writing—what he calls construction—informs and takes priority over all but the most rudimentary experience of presence. And perhaps it informs the rudimentary experience too, since absurdity itself as a three-term affair (consisting of self, world, and their encounter) is obviously a formulation or construction. And if that is true, then it seems likely that "construction" determined the experience of absurdity. He did not first experience the absurd and then define it. Rather he defined it and experienced it in the process. Thus Camus could alter Derrida's proposition to say: "From the moment that there is meaninglessness, 'there are nothing but signs.' "

Such an account leaves moot the question of how the notion of absurdity got started in the first place, but one could easily make a case for its starting from other texts, other writing. So on this point Camus and Derrida may be not just close; they may be in the same position—except for one thing. Derrida claims there is nothing outside the construction: "*Il n'y a pas de hors-texte*."[13] This claim opens a different distance between the two. And since the quoted assertion has become, as Derrida notes in a much later piece, "a sort of slogan . . . of deconstruction" and since "in general" it has been, as he also notes, "badly misunderstood,"[14] it behooves us to listen carefully to what he has to say about its meaning. He has explained it, he says, a "thousand times" without being heard, and that makes him wonder: "why this resistance?" The text is "not the book, it is not confined in a volume itself confined to the library. It does not suspend reference—to history, to the world, to reality, to being . . ."[15] This is, it appears, the key point in Derrida's explanation: though there is nothing outside the text, there is still a world with a history; there is still reality and being. But the only way these statements can make sense together is for the "outside" (the world and its history) to be on the "inside" and for the text to be self-referential. And that is just what Derrida does claim. The outside (the world) is on the inside (the text) because, as he explains, history, the world, and reality "always appear in experience, hence in a movement of interpretation" (137). In other words, "one cannot refer to this 'real' [whether world or history or being] except in an interpretive experience" (148). And interpretation, indeed all experience, is on the inside, a process of the text. So what appears to be on the outside is actually on the inside: the world takes shape and place within the text.

As Derrida explains, he allows for a change or two in the terms of his statement. The "badly misunderstood" slogan means nothing else, he says, than "there is nothing outside context" (136). That change enables him to speak of "truth" and "objectivity" even though he "does not believe that any neutrality is possible in this area." He writes:

> What is called "objectivity," scientific for instance (in which I firmly believe, in a given situation), imposes itself only within a context which is extremely vast, old, powerfully established, stabilized or rooted in a network of conventions (for instance, those of language) and yet which still remains a context. . . . We can call "context" the entire "real-history-of-the-world," if you like, in which this value of objectivity and, even more broadly, that of truth (etc.) have taken on meaning and imposed themselves. That does not in the slightest discredit them ["objectivity" and "truth"]. . . . One of the definitions of what is called deconstruction would be the effort to take this limitless context into account. (136)

Finally, on the basis of this passage, it appears that "nothing outside the text" means not only "nothing outside context" but also "nothing outside history" and "nothing outside the world" as well. In Derrida's words, "What I call 'text' implies all the structures called 'real,' 'economic,' 'historical,' socioinstitutional, in short: all possible referents" (148).

Nevertheless, when all is said and done, we are right back at the point from which the explanation began. Though Derrida has explained how he can "refer" to the "world," he has left his original statement standing unaltered: still, there is nothing outside the text. And that statement still makes a major difference between Derrida and Camus. In the process it also makes a major difference not just between two views of the "text" or two views of the "world" but also between two views of experience and of knowledge and ultimately between two views of human life. Certainly it makes a consequential difference whether or not one conceives of other people as merely entities of the text or as also beings in a world outside the text. And it makes an even more consequential difference whether or not one conceives of "degrading circumstances" such as poverty, racism, oppression, and disease as merely formulations of the text or as also, and mainly, actual conditions in a world external to the text. Obviously, in either case "the text"—our particular text—is crucial: it determines what we understand and how we understand it. But the argument is not with the importance of the text or even with the proposition that "the text" or texts are all we actually *know*. The argument is with the claim that there is nothing outside the text and thus nothing to be known beyond the text. Since this is the claim Derrida makes, for him there can be no "presence" simply because there is nothing external to the text to be present to. But it should be noted—and emphasized—that if, in fact, "the text" is all we know, then there is no more evidence that there is *nothing* outside the text than that there is *something* outside the text. In short, one must choose one's view (one's text) on the basis of the same lack of convincing evidence. Camus claims there is something else, a world beyond any construction or textuality. Thus for him there can be "presence," though obviously it is mediated and adulterated and therefore very different from the original idea of presence as a pure and unmixed relationship.

But what is gained by salvaging this contaminated, residual presence? Nothing on which to found a metaphysics, no doubt, but still a little something of importance, to wit, a world for fiction and the novel. More than that, it enables us to think we are thinking about a world and its things and not just another text. And that sense of ability is, as I have just tried to suggest, the minimal precondition for the avoidance of "philistinism." One of the aims—or rather ends—of Camus's project is to keep the absurd presence in place. In fact, he comes to define living as "keeping the absurd alive."[16] Thus he urges us to a kind of dualism, a conception of things as including both a world and a consciousness of it. Only on the basis of such a dualism, this difference between human and world, do we have the basic ingredients of story, that is to say, both characters and a situation in the world. And only in the space cleared by that difference do we have a place of action, room for the events that mark time and make up narratives. In effect, Camus aims to maintain a principle of *difference in the world,* no matter how qualified those differences may have to be. He writes: "Any thought that abandons unity glorifies diversity. And diversity is the home of art" (*Myth,* 86). By contrast the deconstructor's sense of things tends to be monistic and, indeed, absolutistic. Without presence, with the collapse of the world into a text, there are no ingredients for story and no time-space for narrative events. At best there can be only metafiction, and not even that insofar as metafiction depends for its existence on fiction proper with its characters and world and their interaction. Everything becomes just one thing, just a text or textuality. If there is anything else, it is only a reader, but even the reader so conceived is not a separate thing, only a textual offshoot, whether product or producer of the text does not make much difference. In short, for all of Derrida's emphasis on the play of differences in writing, the tendency of the overall project of deconstruction would seem to be toward likeness or rather *indifference in the world.*

In Camus's view, "to negate one of the terms of the opposition" (*Myth*, 40)—in other words, to cancel difference, presence, absurdity—is to commit philosophical suicide. Seen from this position, the deconstructors appear to be postsuicidal. Not only do they come after everything else; they also come after life itself. Their concern is with reading texts rather than living life. Thus for them the question of life is not likely to come up. But for Camus it is central, the very motive for his reading and writing. Hence the opening sentences of *The Myth of Sisyphus:* "There is but one truly serious philosophical problem, and that is suicide. Judging whether life is or is not worth living amounts to answering the fundamental question of philosophy" (3). While the deconstructors seem to move toward indifference, Camus starts from it. Indeed he starts from the predicament defined by Ivan in Dostoevsky's *The Brothers Karamazov.* "Awareness of the absurd," Camus writes, "makes murder seem a matter of indifference. . . . If we believe in nothing . . . if we can affirm no values whatsoever, then everything is possible. . . . the murderer is neither right nor wrong. We are free to stoke the crematory fires or to devote ourselves to the care of lepers."[17] But he moves through and from this indifference portrayed in *The Stranger,* to its opposite portrayed in *The Plague*—call it *difference* for the lack of a better term: "For having proved that the act of murder is at least a matter of indifference, the absurdist analysis, in its most important deduction, finally condemns murder. The final conclusion of absurdist reason is, in fact, the repudiation of suicide and the acceptance of the desperate encounter between human inquiry and the silence of the universe" (6). In accepting this encounter, Camus accepts presence and, in accepting presence, he accepts the duality of world and conscious living agents—the primary elements of story and narrative. And in accepting those opposed entities, he accepts what he calls the "fundamental question of philosophy," which is the question of the value of life itself. Finally, in taking that on, he takes on as well the basic issue of narrative fiction, the issue of difference or, rather, of what makes a difference.

III

Ultimately, it seems as if we need to respond simultaneously to at least two sets of metaphors for language. One set we need for its limiting qualities. By means of language we see something, but not everything, and we see that something in a certain way, not in all ways, and certainly not as it is in itself, whatever that may mean. Thus it is as if we see a sign rather than the thing. Consequently language seems to enclose us, to close us in on ourselves as it closes things out and away from us. Hence the first set of metaphors, the ones most frequently associated with deconstruction and the whole linguistic turn of our time: language as a web, a labyrinth, a screen, a prisonhouse. But another set is needed for its enabling qualities. Only by means of language are we enabled to see "things" at all, to have vision rather than mere sensations. In other words, language is what we have, probably all we have, to make sense with. Rather than just limiting and confining us, as it often seems to, it also liberates us. It is our primary means of egress, our way out of ourselves, our means of directing ourselves to others and to the world. Hence a second set of metaphors, much more traditional than the first set: language as a glass, however dark and distorted, a window, a door, a pathway. But these last metaphors are not only traditional; they are also associated with the outmoded ideas of language as simply transparent and referential and of art as simply mimetic. So no doubt we need still another conception of language, if possible one that will acknowledge at once both its limiting and its liberating features. But first, before we can consider that need, we need to consider in more general terms what, given the limiting circumstances of our thinking and knowing, we could possibly arrive at in the way of a conception.

We may start by placing Camus and Derrida side by side, instead of one after the other, and noting that as Camus is to the world, so Derrida and the deconstructors are to words and texts. Something very like absurdity separates each of them from the thing they aim to know, whether world or word or text. Thus Camus's "construction" is inevitably misconstruction—and, by the same token, the deconstructor's reading is misreading, and interpretation is misinterpretation. So it might seem there is nothing we can say that has much value or validity, for, according to this line of thought, what we might take as true is actually mis-take. Indeed this and related circumstances have led to the view that theorizing is futile or inconsequential. This view, developed most notably in the essay "Against Theory" by Steven Knapp and Walter Benn Michaels, defines theory as an attempt "to govern interpretations of particular texts by appealing to an account of interpretation in general."[18] In other words, a theorist is one who attempts "to stand outside practice in order to govern practice from without" (30). Such an attempt is bound to fail because no one can ever get to the outside—the outside being external to the patterns of one's thought and practice. This inability to get outside and to define a "foundation" or standpoint external to practice makes theory, in the words of Fish, who joins Knapp and Michaels in their opposition to theory, "an impossible project which will never succeed."[19] ("Consequences," 110). It cannot succeed because "it cannot . . . but borrow its terms and its content from that which it claims to transcend, the mutable world of practice" (111). There are, it seems, no alternatives. The one possibility Fish acknowledges is so-called antifoundationalism. But its strategy is always, he states, "to demonstrate that the norms and standards and rules that foundationalist theory would oppose to history, convention, and local practice are in every instance a function or extension of history, convention, and local practice" (112). Thus in Fish's view, "anti-foundationalism really isn't a theory at all; it is an argument against the possibility of theory" (112). Accordingly Fish ends his essay in an elegiac vein: "theory's day is dying; the hour is late; and the only thing left for a theorist to do is to say so, which is what I have been saying here, and, I think, not a moment too soon" (128).

So once again we have reached the point of disability around which we have by now, it seems, developed a whole tradition, the tradition of no-can-do. Since practice precedes and determines theory, theory, it is said, never can touch practice in any consequential way. In your practices—indeed in all your actions—you are more-or-less stuck, that is to say, you can never alter or correct them, because "it is belief and not theory that underwrites action" (Fish, "Consequences," 118) and because beliefs "are not what you think *about* but what you think *with*" and, most important of all, because you do not have beliefs but "beliefs have *you*" (116). It is not that your beliefs will never change or that your actions will always be the same. It is only that, in this view, *you* will never do the changing, something else will, presumably the culture or "interpretive community" in which you dwell and which dwells in you.

Fish and Knapp and Michaels are, it seems, as absolutist as the theorists whose theories they critique. In effect, they say, if theorizing cannot be done perfectly, then it cannot or should not be done at all. In other words, if theorists cannot do the impossible and get outside their thinking and think about it from a vantage point or foundation external to it, in short, if they cannot do some thinking that is other than and independent of their thinking, then their whole project—thinking about thinking or thinking about practice—is bound to fail and thus be inconsequential. This line of argument makes clear why it is that one more specific thing must be included in the list of those things to which we are denied "presence"—

namely, the self, or rather the patterns of thought and action that make up the self. Just as the project of knowing the world has been said to have come to an ignominious end, so Fish and others say the project of knowing the self and its functions must come to a similar end. Accordingly we could amend Rorty's comment on Derrida, quoted earlier, to read that we have a new thing for writing to be about—not the world, to be sure, *and certainly not the self and its functions,* but just texts. But if we have followed the argument through, we know that texts are only misconstructions. All that our writing can be, therefore, is a misreading and thus a misinterpretation of a misconstruction. That is, it seems, the extent of the possible in our postmodern era, in these latter days "after philosophy" and "against theory." We might like to "make music that will melt the stars," but the best we can do is bang out "crude rhythms" on a "cracked kettle."

But that is just one way of assessing our situation. Another is possible. It becomes possible as soon as we choose to note and remember something that is at once noted and strangely ignored in the argument against theory. That something is the all but self-evident fact that we can do only what limited beings can do. Remembering that truism changes the emphasis. It transforms "limitation" into mere "condition." That is to say, in the light of this changed perspective, our limitations cease to be negations marking what we cannot do and become instead the conditions in which, and from which, we must work if we are to work at all. And theory becomes something we can define in a more possible way, a way that is still consistent with our ordinary uses of the term. We say "I do not know exactly what happened, or what this is, but I theorize that . . ." and we go on from there. Conceived according to this common usage, theory is not a matter of doing the impossible; rather it begins just where possibility begins and that is *in uncertainty and doubt.* Indeed, theory in this sense is a response to uncertainty and doubt, an attempt to give a plausible account or explanation of what we don't know for sure and what, without a theory, we would never know at all. Such a notion of theorizing does not involve standing on a foundation outside one's thought; it involves only doing the best one can from the inside, and doing it in full recognition that one's theory is vulnerable and thus open to challenge and change. In short, it involves, in the words of Alasdair MacIntyre, a "form of falliblism" because the "possibility has always to be left open that . . . some new challenge to the established best theory so far will appear and will displace it."[20]

In theorizing, so conceived, what takes the place of absolute truth and certainty—that is, what takes the place of all those statements whose aim it is to be the end of all statements—is an openness to dialogue and discussion. For such a notion of theory we can imagine a mythical beginning. It begins at the same moment the novel is said to begin and for much the same reasons. Lukács wrote, "The novel is the epic of a world that has been abandoned by God."[21] A world abandoned by God is a world from which the voice of the absolute has departed. In such a world no single voice dominates except through intimidation and arbitrary power: in the absence of these, there are many voices, all of them limited, making at worst a horrendous noise and at best a complex of ongoing dialogues (something like Bakhtin's *polyglossia*).[22] Conceived in these terms, theory begins with the beginning of argument, difference, and dialogue. Rorty writes, "To accept the contingency of starting-points is to accept our inheritance from, and our conversation with, our fellow human beings as our only source of guidance."[23] And Barbara Herrnstein Smith writes: "If, as I believe, there can be no . . . eradication of disparity . . . also neither perfect knowledge nor pure charity, then the general optimum might well be that set of conditions that . . . encourages . . . *evaluation,*" in short, a "continuous process" involving "the local figuring/working out, as well as we, heterogeneously, can, of what seems to work better rather than worse."[24] This working-out process is not, I think, totally separate from the concrete. Rather it is, at the first level, a matter of "making sense" of concrete things and only then, at a second level, a matter of making sense of our ways of making sense. In any case, any sense we do make is made from a certain perspective and is thus subject to response from another perspective.

IV

Frank Kermode began his seminal "studies" in the theory of fiction, *The Sense of an Ending,* with a crucial distinction: "It is not expected of critics," he said, "as it is of poets that they should help us to make sense of our lives; they are bound only to attempt the lesser feat of making sense of the ways we try to make sense of our lives."[25] In other words, the poet is located in life but not the critic—the critic is off somewhere else, in a library or study or some other academic setting in which the primary reality is not "our lives" or the world but rather poems and fictions, in short, texts. Fish speaks in the same vein when he challenges the long-held assumption of the "relevance of philosophy to every aspect of human culture," an assumption that depends, he says, on the "debatable proposition that almost everything we do is a disguised and probably confused version of philosophy." He tells us, "That proposition will begin to seem less plausible if we remember that philosophy is not the name of a natural kind but of an academic discipline."[26] What exactly he might mean by "natural" is not clear, but by "academic" he seems clearly to mean: separate from and largely irrelevant to "almost everything we do" and thus to much of what is included under the phrase "every aspect of human culture." Implicit in Fish's discussion are not two but three agents: not just poet and critic but poet, critic, and theorist or philosopher, theory being, he says, "another name for philosophy" (123). And consequently there are several levels of abstraction, or perhaps we should call them several gradations of the "merely academic." The poet may indeed be located in life and therefore in the world, as Kermode suggests, but in the minimal Derridean view he or she is once removed. Accordingly, then, the practicing critic is at least once and maybe twice removed, while the theorist or philosopher is at least twice and probably thrice removed—and thus out of sight. In all this there may be a moral. It is that if philosophy—to say nothing of criticism and literature itself—seems academic, and often merely academic, it may be in part because of the way we think of it, or it thinks of itself, as having a simple either/or choice. As Rorty notes, in a passage already quoted, it can be Philosophy with a capital P or it can be philosophy with a lower-case p. That means it has a simple choice of trying to function either in *unmediated* relation to the world or *only* in relation to writing and to texts.

It makes sense, and works much better, I think, to reject this choice. Such a rejection might help to make philosophy seem less academic; indeed it might help to make the academic seem less a matter of being either utterly naive or totally irrelevant. In any case, it would be to stipulate that we are never, nor should we ever be, only in relation to writing and texts. It would also be to stipulate that we are never in an *unmediated* relation to the world. In short, to be located in life and the world is, we know now, to be located at an intersection or corner, a place where two metaphorical roads meet and cross. One road, as old as history, we may call Anxiety or Influence, whichever, after the work of Harold Bloom, specifically the Harold Bloom of *The Anxiety of Influence,* who argues that "poems rise not so much in response to a present time" as "in response to other poems" and that true "poetic history is the story of how poets as poets have suffered other poets."[27] Perhaps we should just call this road Bloom Street. The other, perhaps even more ancient, though its age is a matter of debate, we may call Absurdity, or just Camus Street, after the work of Albert Camus. Absurdity is the name of our perpetually repeated encounter with what we call the world, the place where we live and move and carry on our lives together with countless others. Anxiety or Influence is the name of the endless attempts that have been made to construe that world and to turn the absurd into the "familiar." In other words, it is the long and complex series of texts that lead up to, and define, the present. The attempts are endless because none ever succeeds for more than a moment or two, for as noted, all our constructions are but misconstructions.

Whether poet, critic, philosopher, or something else altogether, we can be said to be at this corner because we are always in relation to the world but never in an unmediated relation to it. We see it and we hear it through eyes and ears predisposed by the seeings and hearings that have preceded our own. In other words, we hear through the "buzz and hum" of our culture; we see through its lens; and we think in its idiom. But even though the already written and recorded takes priority in the register of our experiences, our experiences themselves do not always fit neatly into the prescribed patterns. Indeed, typically, experiences take place for us between two texts, a pre-story and a post-story. The first is a story of good intentions, a projected narrative in which we tell ourselves what we are going to do or what is going to happen. As a rule, this narrative tends to follow a wish-fulfillment pattern, the pattern of daydreams and fairy tales. Then comes experience itself in the form of actions and events that are resistant to our dreams and intentions. Almost always it requires of us a radical revision. So we have a new story to construct, a rather more sophisticated narrative in which we look back, rather than forward, and try to come to terms with the difference between our original intentions and the actual events or actions. Characteristically it is a tale told in some degree of bad faith, though perhaps not always. Conrad's *Lord Jim* may well be the best single example. But many of the master fictions of the traditional canon, from *Oedipus Rex* to *Waiting for Godot,* are in one way or another about just such a discord between preconception or pre-text and experience. Among others they include such works as *Don Quixote, Tristram Shandy, Pride and Prejudice, Great Expectations, Moby-Dick, Middlemarch, The Brothers Karamazov, The Death of Ivan Ilych, The Ambassadors, The Metamorphosis,* and *Nausea,* to mention some obvious examples. And, almost inevitably, strong works in the nontraditional or revised canon give even more emphasis to the antagonism between prescription and experience and thus to the antagonism between one text and another. The point is, nonconforming experiences of this sort lead to changes on Bloom Street, that is on the path of influence. In other words, because we so often experience contradiction and disconfirmation, our fictions change, as Kermode has argued; they grow more ironic and more subtle and more devious; narrative patterns become more complicated, developing detours and peripeteias on the way to their conclusions, sometimes even arriving at unanticipated and unpredictable ends.[28] Thus are paradigms altered and occasionally destroyed. And with each change, the whole corner moves on, up the road, not *toward* something but *away* from what came before, from the way things were as we recorded them then.

This conception of ourselves as located at a moving intersection has some advantages. By means of it we can avoid the too-simple either/or choice. We can acknowledge that we live in a world and, at the same time, we can acknowledge as well that we see and know that world—indeed, that it takes shape for us and becomes a world—only through the mediation of language and texts. Moreover, it suggests how we can gain some knowledge of ourselves. Granted, we cannot step outside of our thoughts and know ourselves clearly and distinctly and objectively and therefore absolutely and finally. But if it is true that our intelligence is informed by the texts that meet us on the path of influence, we can learn a good deal just by plotting the location of our corner in reference to its past locations. According to MacIntyre, "the present is intelligible only as a commentary upon and response to the past."[29] But that means we can indeed gain some knowledge of ourselves, of our thought patterns and the determinants of our mentality, by confronting ourselves in the cross-section of texts that lead up to and help to characterize our cultural moment. In them we can see our likenesses and, more than that, in them we can discover our differences.

Of course, any knowledge we gain in this way will be as provisional as any other. MacIntyre writes that in the "commentary upon and response to the past" that makes the present intelligible, the past may be, in a sense, "corrected and transcended," but, if so, it is corrected and transcended only "in a way that leaves the present open to being in turn corrected and transcended by some yet more adequate future point of view" (146). Any adequacy is thus a contingent and therefore temporary matter; our knowledge is always just the best we have to work with for the time being. But that limitation may be less a defect than a virtue. For the danger is not in knowing that our knowledge is impermanent; it is instead, I think, in mistaking it for something absolute and final—wishing it were what it isn't and what it can never be. In that wish and that mistake we tend to confuse nature and the world with our conceptions of them. And if we do that, if we think that nature and the world are in fact just as we conceive of them, we are easily led, as we almost always have been, to assume a right of dominance over them; we can easily convince ourselves, as we have so often convinced ourselves, that we can do with them whatever we want to do just so long as it is consistent with our conceptions. In that confusion we are never likely to be persuaded to think of them—the world and nature—as things we should keep inviolable. Skepticism alone will not solve the whole problem. Nevertheless, only by understanding that all our conceptions are mediations and that "reality," whatever it is, resides at least one remove beyond anything we think we know about it, are we likely to respect and preserve the "world's body" to say nothing of all the other, lesser bodies that go into the makeup of its body. Hence the importance of the corner and of the two streets, Camus Street as well as Bloom Street.

V

If we do establish ourselves at this intersection, we are, I think, prepared to understand a third conception of language, this time language as mediation but with "mediation" meaning something a little different from most uses of the term. It is not a conception of language as letting us through to the other side—to what lies beyond language. There is no window or door, nothing altogether transparent, and no mirror of nature. But it is not, on the other hand, a conception of language as enclosing us in on ourselves. There is no wall, much less a prison—at least there is none by necessity. Rather mediation is something that goes on in the middle; it is a medium, a means, something that intervenes between consciousness and an object. In that sense, it separates and makes a difference by maintaining a middle distance. But it also connects; it is what makes interaction possible; indeed it is an *interaction* and not a thing. Thus, as used here, mediation is more verb than noun, not anything just statically situated between a person and the world, not a screen, but instead an activity or interaction going on in the space between, as often an attempt to do something as an attempt to know something.

In short, what is meant here by "mediation" is presence, not the mythical pure presence but the actual adulterated presence, the only kind ever available to us. And by "presence" is meant the whole range of possible interactions between a consciousness and the world. Language is the primary mediator; science and literature are two extreme forms in the range of mediation. They are separated not as truth from fiction but only by a difference in aim. Science is interested in leaping over its mediation to know what lies on the other side. It never quite gets there; still its mediation is distinctive and highly successful. Literature is also interested in the other side (as in, for instance, Sartre's *Nausea*), but its primary interest is in what can take place in the space and time of mediation itself. Hence the claim that the work of art is "not a simple description of the present but a judgment of this present in the name of the future."[30] Thus literary mediation is also distinctive, and it too can be highly successful, though its success may be harder to measure. The point is, mediation should not be considered the end or the negator of presence but rather its beginning or initiator. Not until we have language—a whole system of symbols and signs and therefore a whole system of mediation—are we able to encounter the world as a world in any way sustained enough and complex enough to be meaningful. That means that what makes our knowledge suspect, in other words, what contaminates it, is also what makes it possible in the first place. And that means as well that what contaminates presence, and mixes it with absence, is what makes presence possible in the first place.

Such a view allows for differences. Texts of whatever nature are acts performed. And the acts implicit in texts give evidence of actors and, more than that, of a world. But these differences do not cancel the possibility of interconnections. It still makes sense to conceive of the reader's "I"—or, for that matter, any "I," whether reader, writer, or other—as "already itself a plurality of other texts" and not just an "innocent subject, anterior to the text."[31] And thus it still makes sense to urge as Foucault has urged: "the subject (and its substitutes) must be stripped of its creative role and analyzed as a complex and variable function of discourse."[32] But that does not exhaust the possibilities for sense-making. We may value the subject in Foucault's words; that is, we may value the speaker or writer who in this case hides himself in the passive voice. That means we may value the actor, the one who makes the value judgment and urges us to do one thing rather than another. And, if we do, it makes sense for us to reverse his statement and say: we must strip the subject of its role as mere function of discourse, however complex and variable, and analyze it as at least the co-creator of its discourse. In short, the "I" may not be an innocent subject, but also it is not just a plurality of texts.

No doubt at most other times this would seem an altogether unremarkable point to make, the claim that the individual subject is something more than a mere product of its pre-texts. If it seems at all remarkable now, it is only because, as noted at the beginning of this essay, it has so often been summarily dismissed in the criticism of the last thirty years and more. More often than not the dismissal has been effected neatly, if deceptively, by something very like guilt by association. The idea of the individual has been identified with humanism and dismissed with it when it has been discredited. Or, more consequentially, it has been identified with capitalism and dismissed with it when it has been discredited. Despite its historical connections with these two isms, the identifications are fallacious, and the idea is needed elsewhere—anywhere where criticism retains its radical edge. That is to say, whenever and wherever criticism is more than just another rubber stamp, it has need of the idea of the individual for things as well as for persons. Thus, in reference to a tendency in some Marxist criticism, Christopher Butler asks: "If individuals don't have any status for the theory, what sense does it make to speak of them as 'dominated' by social structures or of 'liberating' them from them?"[33] Clearly, the very existence of feminist criticism and African-American criticism and any other criticism coming from a minority or oppositional standpoint depends on the capacity of the critic to be something other than just a "plurality" of the given texts; it depends, as well, on that critic's capacity to give a description of individuals and a definition of groups that differ radically from those engrained in the dominating texts of the social establishment. But defining an oppositional standpoint is easier to prescribe than to do at this point. In the words of Elaine Showalter, "Black and Third World critics haunted by the messages of poststructuralism are now facing the same dilemma [as feminist critics]. Is there a critic-position as well as a subject-position?"[34] Edward Said identifies his "secular" critic with the "individual consciousness" and describes the individual consciousness as "an isolated voice out of place but very much *of* that place, standing consciously against the prevailing orthodoxy and very much for a . . . humane set of values."[35] That locates the individual subject nicely, very much *of* a place, to be sure, but also, and at the same time, inevitably out of place—in short, right at the metaphorical intersection defined in this essay.

But in and out, all at once, is not just the precise location of the individual subject; it is as well the very place to which the idea of the individual tends to move the subject—that is, from within outward. For the idea of the individual is, after all, an attempt to conceive of a thing inconceivable, to ideate something irreducible to idea, to make the abstraction that will move the subject closest to the concrete itself. If we take it seriously, and value it, and if we also value what it attempts to conceptualize, it is what most urgently tells us to move on, out of ourselves, out of our conceivings and out of our consciousness; in short, by its very inadequacy, any conception of the individual tells us of the need to move "outside of the text." It is, therefore, not only the motive for metaphor, but also a motive for theorizing. Because we do try with some success, however limited, to theorize about the outside and, even more, because the outside so often contradicts and disconfirms our attempts to conceive of it, each of us as a subject is more than just a plurality of preexisting texts. At the very least, each is also a history of its experiences, an historical register of the impact of the outside on the inside. Indeed, such experiences may even dislodge an "I" from its pre-texts and make it the initiator as well as the product of texts. Thus, on occasion, an individual "I" may help to move our corner on up the street a bit—and thus it may be said to help change the location of the place where Bloom Street runs into Camus Street.

Notes

1. Stanley Fish, *Is There a Text in This Class?* (Cambridge: Harvard University Press, 1980), 14.
2. George Steiner, *Language and Silence* (New York: Atheneum, 1967), ix, 4.
3. Vincent Leitch, *American Literary Criticism: From the 30's to the 80's* (New York: Columbia University Press, 1988), 276.
4. Roland Barthes, *S/Z*, trans. Richard Miller (New York: Hill and Wang, 1974), 95.
5. Terry Eagleton, *Literary Theory: An Introduction* (Minneapolis: University of Minnesota Press, 1983), 129–30.
6. Georg Lukács, *Writer and Critic,* trans. Arthur D. Kahn (New York: Grosset, 1971), 15.
7. Jacques Derrida, "Structure, Sign and Play in the Discourse of the Human Sciences," in *The Structuralist Controversy,* ed. Richard Macksey and Eugenio Donato (Baltimore: Johns Hopkins University Press, 1972), 250.
8. Jacques Derrida, *Of Grammatology,* trans. Gayatri Chakravorty Spivak (Baltimore: Johns Hopkins University Press, 1976), 50.
9. Richard Rorty, "Philosophy as a Kind of Writing," in *The Consequences of Pragmatism* (Minneapolis: University of Minnesota Press, 1982), 92.
10. Fish, *Is There a Text in the Class?* 12.
11. Leitch, *American Literary Criticism,* 275–76.
12. Albert Camus, *The Myth of Sisyphus,* trans. Justin O'Brien (New York: Vintage, 1959), 21.
13. Derrida, *Of Grammatology,* 158.

14. Jacques Derrida, "Afterword: Toward an Ethic of Discussion," in *Limited Inc.* (Evanston: Northwestern University Press, 1988), 111–60.
15. Derrida, *Of Grammatology,* 137.
16. Camus, *The Myth of Sisyphus,* 40.
17. Albert Camus, *The Rebel,* trans. Anthony Brower (New York: Vintage, 1956), 5.
18. Steven Knapp and Walter Benn Michaels, "Against Theory," in *Against Theory: Literary Studies and the New Pragmatism,* ed. W. J. T. Mitchell (Chicago: University of Press, 1985), 11. Originally published in *Critical Inquiry* 8 (summer 1982): 723–42.
19. Stanley Fish, "Consequences," in *Against Theory,* 110 (see note 18).
20. Alasdair MacIntyre, *After Virtue: A Study in Moral Theory,* 2d ed. (Notre Dame: University of Notre Dame Press, 1984), 270.
21. Georg Lukács, *The Theory of the Novel* (Cambridge: MIT Press, 1971), 88.
22. See M. M. Bakhtin, *The Dialogic Imagination,* ed. Michael Holquist (Austin: University of Texas Press, 1981), esp. 11–12, 60–61.
23. Rorty, *The Consequences of Pragmatism,* 166.
24. Barbara Herrnstein Smith, *Contingencies of Value: Alternative Perspectives for Critical Theory* (Cambridge: Harvard University Press, 1988), 179.
25. Frank Kermode, *The Sense of an Ending: Studies in the Theory of Fiction* (New York: Oxford University Press, 1967).
26. Fish, "Consequences," 122.
27. Harold Bloom, *The Anxiety of Influence: A Theory of Poetry* (New York: Oxford University Press, 1973), 99, 94.
28. Kermode, *The Sense of an Ending,* 23–24.
29. MacIntyre, *After Virtue,* 146.
30. Jean-Paul Sartre, *What Is Literature?* trans. Bernard Frechtman (New York: Harper, 1975), 153.
31. Barthes, *S/Z,* 10.
32. Michel Foucault, "What Is an Author?" in *Language, Counter-Memory, Practice: Selected Essays and Interviews,* ed. Donald F. Bouchard (Ithaca: Cornell University Press, 1977), 138.
33. Christopher Butler, "The Future of Theory: Saving the Reader," in *The Future of Literary Theory,* ed. Ralph Cohen (New York: Routledge, 1989), 232.
34. Elaine Showalter, "A Criticism of Our Own: Autonomy and Assimilation in Afro-American and Feminist Literary Theory," in *The Future of Literary Theory,* ed. Ralph Cohen (New York: Routledge, 1989), 368 (see note 33).
35. Edward Said, "Introduction: Secular Criticism," in *The World, the Text, and Critic* (Cambridge: Harvard University Press, 1983), 15.

Relevant Publications by Quentin Kraft

"Toward a Critical Re-Renewal: At the Corner of Camus and Bloom Streets." *College English* 54 (January 1992): 46–63.

"On Character in the Novel: William Beatty Warner versus Samuel Richardson and the Humanists." *College English* 50 (January 1988): 32–47.

"Narrative Transformation in *Tom Jones:* An Episode in the Emergence of the Novel." *Eighteenth-Century: Theory and Interpretation* 26 (winter 1985): 23–45.

"*Robinson Crusoe* and the Story of the Novel." *College English* 41 (January 1980): 535–48.

"Science and Poetics, Old and New." *College English* 37 (October 1975): 167–75.

12

Deconstruction and the Redemption of Difference

Michael Fischer

Michael Fischer, professor of English and department chair at the University of New Mexico, has combined his knowledge of and interests in romanticism, contemporary literary theory, and philosophy in essays such as "William Blake's Quarrel with Indeterminacy" and a collection of essays jointly edited with Morris Eaves, Romanticism and Contemporary Criticism *(1986). His most direct consideration of the general field of contemporary theory is* Does Deconstruction Make Any Difference? Poststructuralism and the Defense of Poetry in Modern Criticism. *In that volume he seeks a balanced assessment of deconstructive and similar critical theories. "In my view," he writes, "many readers have unfairly maligned deconstruction as an airy theoretical nothing, indifferent to the many practical difficulties that plague the academic profession, among them the 'uncomfortably hermetic quality' of contemporary literary scholarship . . . the waning of literacy, and the misplaced priorities of American society" (xii). On the other hand, Fischer finds that: "The weapon that, in deconstruction, frees literature—the 'undecidability' of meaning—ends up further accommodating literature to the academic establishment that deconstructionists resent" (xiii). The present essay pursues, from a somewhat different perspective, the same sort of careful, evenhanded assessment of the political value of deconstruction.*

Virtually everyone who comments on contemporary theory at some point questions its political value. Current theory appears politically suspect because of its esoteric language (*différance,* heteroglossia, etc.), its association with elite academic settings (conferences, graduate seminars, and highly rated English departments), and its gnomic, counterintuitive pronouncements (there is nothing outside the text, the self is a construction, and so on). Although every kind of theory is susceptible to political attack, deconstruction is especially vulnerable. For friends and foes alike, deconstruction often epitomizes theory, maybe even *is* theory, and Jacques Derrida's writings in particular exemplify everything theory stands for, from outlandish jargon to subversive-sounding talk about disrupting Western metaphysics. At least in America, critics have always faulted deconstruction for failing to make any difference, for distracting professors from urgent political problems while claiming to be doing something about them.

I argue here that this dismissal of deconstruction is too sweeping. I agree that what I will be calling the ethos of deconstruction encourages ineffective hand wringing in critics like Geoffrey Hartman and J. Hillis Miller when these critics take up political questions. By "critics like Geoffrey Hartman and J. Hiller Miller," I mean critics who lack any overriding political agenda for deconstruction to complicate. When these critics address a political issue, they are paralyzed by their deconstructionism (as Hartman's commentary on the Paul de Man affair will show).[1] But the debilitating influence of deconstruction on these critics should not obscure the benefits it can provide other kinds of critics—activist critics who see literary study as a political weapon in the class struggle, for example, or the fight for racial and gender equality. Worried about getting bogged down in self-questioning, these critics are susceptible to oversimplifying things and settling for rigid good guys/bad guys dualisms. They accordingly need the heightened awareness of complexity that deconstruction can foster.

The activist critics I focus on here align themselves with what Cornel West has called the new cultural politics of difference[2] and what other commentators refer to as identity politics. These critics insist on the difference made by ethnicity, gender, sexual orientation, class, age, and other variables. They often advocate opening the canon to previously excluded works by women, gays and lesbians, working-class writers, African Americans, Native Americans, Hispanics, and others. Canon expansion in turn gets intertwined with such larger political goals as decentering Eurocentric white male authority and taking affirmative action in admissions and hiring.

For recent neoconservative critics of contemporary literary study like Dinesh

D'Souza, deconstruction plays into the hands of African Americans and other advocates of the politics of difference by undermining the standards that these groups do not meet.[3] D'Souza is especially hard on Stanley Fish and other Duke University English professors: "By maintaining the arbitrariness of all standards, the Duke critics make it more respectable within the university for minority-group members to be admitted or hired without reference to the reactionary notion of academic merit" (76). In the scenario described by D'Souza, deconstruction claims that there is no such thing as knowledge. This (mistaken) claim meets with the approval of black students, for instance, who have trouble satisfying conventional tests of knowledge: who get low SAT scores and poor grades, for example, and who drop out of school. Unable to win, blacks challenge the rules, encouraged by white professors armed with the skeptical tools of deconstruction. In the absence of knowledge, ignorance loses its sting. Students can now see themselves as victimized by criteria shown (by deconstruction) to be arbitrary.

D'Souza thus sees a cynical marriage of convenience between politically correct white professors misled by deconstruction and opportunistic black students and junior faculty eager to capitalize on the opportunities opened up by the assault on knowledge and competence. Many African-American critics, however, are much more ambivalent about the deconstructionism that supposedly benefits them. Their uneasy reception of deconstruction will be my focus here in part because it echoes the dissatisfaction deconstruction has always excited. In my view, these critics have good reason to be leery of deconstruction. Nevertheless, I think deconstruction can help them; not because it repudiates standards that these critics cannot meet (as D'Souza charges) but because it interrogates the very identity terms (such as "blackness") that these critics uphold.

I

We can better understand African-American critics' mixed feelings about deconstruction by first examining how other politically engaged groups—Marxist and feminist critics in particular—have struggled with it. Despite attempts by Michael Ryan and others to work out some rapprochement between Marxism and deconstruction, Marxist responses to deconstruction have been cool. Barbara Foley's "The Politics of Deconstruction" expresses the antagonism many Marxist critics have felt.[4] Foley begins by rehearsing the accusations against deconstruction other leftist critics have made. According to these accusations, deconstruction, despite its heated oppositional rhetoric, is finally ineffectual and thus readily co-opted by the status quo it pretends to challenge. Foley takes this critique one step further by arguing that deconstruction sponsors positions that are "distinctly anti-working class, anti-communist, and even racist" (118). Although she acknowledges some differences between Derrida and his American acolytes, even Derrida's project is for her "fundamentally anti-progressive" (125). Deconstruction breeds discomfort with all authority, even the authority of the working class; contests all cognitive claims, even the presumably scientific claims of Marxism itself; and distrusts all teleological thinking, even an inspiring vision of history that foresees in communism an end to class conflict. Foley concludes that we get from deconstruction "a polemic against any *praxis* that would attempt to transform social relations by means of a plan on the one hand and power on the other" (129).

I will be returning to Foley's own plan in a moment but first note that she is especially severe on what she sees as deconstruction's lack of attention to class, for Foley the principal category of Marxist thought. In writers who align Marxism with deconstruction—she mentions Ryan, Gayatri Spivak, and Stanley Aronowitz—concentration on class gives way to concern about women, non-Westerners, and other disadvantaged groups. According to Foley, would-be deconstructionist-Marxists like Spivak remain "notably silent about how these groups' rebellious practices could relate to the agenda of proletariat revolution—or, indeed whether such an agenda is in order at all" (131). In the absence of any master plan, we end up with what Foley contemptuously refers to as coalition politics, a loose aggregate of disparate groups pursuing their own local, provisional goals and resenting any incursion on their autonomy. For Foley, coalition politics meshes with deconstruction's "antipathy to centralism of all kinds" (132). The energies of revolt get dispersed in the absence of any authority to coordinate and direct them to some common goal. Advancing in many different directions at once, disconnected acts of rebellion go nowhere—or so Foley fears.

Deconstruction has always been accused of fostering anarchy, but by "anarchy" critics of deconstruction like E. D. Hirsch have usually meant a chaotic free-for-all of interpretations cut loose from any determinate meaning that these interpretations are obligated to get right. Foley, by contrast, suggests that deconstruction foments anarchy not in the established order but in the radical political movement that would change it. In her frankly Leninist analysis, a working-class revolution is bringing about social change, only to be derailed by deconstruction. "Derailed" here means deprived of the presumably knowable historical mission (communism) that should focus its grievances, like a magnifying glass bringing together rays of sunlight to start a fire.

As Foley suggests, the threat posed by deconstruction derives from its distrust of ends and centers; or, what comes to the same thing, its emphasis on heterogeneity, dispersal, and dissemination. She correctly feels that deconstruction jeopardizes not only Marx's teleological picture of history but his sense that society is divided into two readily identified antagonistic camps, the bourgeoisie and proletariat. In *The Communist Manifesto,* Marx described this division in these words: "Our epoch, the epoch of the bourgeoisie, possesses, however, this distinctive feature: it has amplified the class antagonisms. Society as a whole is more and more splitting into two great hostile groups, into two great classes directly facing each other: Bourgeoisie and Proletariat."[5] Although other differences matter to Foley, she suggests that they finally should be subordinated to the overriding difference made by class.

I detect in Foley nostalgia for the good old days when working-class people knew what they were fighting for and what obstacles stood in their way. I would admit that there is a politically energizing clarity about this vision: we not only know who our friends and our enemies are, we know where we are headed. By complicating this picture, deconstruction may undermine the political anger and action the picture can inspire. But in my view, Foley's agenda ought to be challenged, and deconstruction deserves credit for questioning her ominous master plan. The coalition politics she loathes—different groups determining their own agendas and learning as they go rather than following any preordained script—sounds more democratic to me than the totalizing strategy Foley advocates.

It seems to me, in short, that Foley could use a little more distrust of centralism. Forced to choose between her lockstep march and Derrida's decentered free play, I would take Derrida. Still, there are political shortcomings to deconstruction as Foley suspects. These limitations surface more clearly when we turn from Marxists to another group often leery of deconstruction: feminist critics.

II

Initially, deconstruction met with the distrust of many feminist critics. In the same way that Foley faults deconstruction for circumventing class, these feminists accused deconstruction of slighting the importance of gender. The case against deconstruction in the early 1980s, made by Elaine Showalter, Nina Baym, and others, held that deconstruction attacked presence (just when women were beginning to make themselves present in the academic profession); questioned the privileging of speech (just when women were finally speaking up); blocked the appeal to experience (just when women were wanting to make their experience count); and subverted female identity (just when women were asserting the differences made by gender).

I put this antipathy to deconstruction in the past because many feminist critics today take a more appreciative, though still cautious, approach to deconstruction. Barbara Johnson is an especially interesting case here, not only because she tries to reconcile feminist politics and deconstruction but also because of her interest in African-American literature—an interest that will take me to the final group of critics I will be examining, African-American critics concerned about the effect of deconstruction on identity politics and writing about race.

The Critical Difference (1980) established Johnson as a major practitioner of deconstructionist literary criticism.[6] Reading canonical texts from French and American literature, Johnson showed how differences typically become hierarchical, binary oppositions: man/woman, literature/theory, and innocence/guilt are some of her examples, with the first term being privileged over the second one. Johnson deconstructed these dualisms by demonstrating that seemingly invidious differences between two terms in fact conceal differences within each one. "Literature," for example, defines itself against "theory" in order to repress its own theoretical dimensions. Internal differences are expelled rather than acknowledged because they threaten the identity or purity of the privileged term.

In *The Critical Difference* Johnson says very little about the political implications of her analyses but the results in my view are mixed. At first, deconstruction seems to provide leverage against the positive terms it undermines. Contesting the integrity of these terms would appear to strike a blow against their privilege. Johnson's readings, however, typically end with our being paralyzed, not moved to action, by the undecidability of meaning—stymied ("suspended" is her favorite term) by our inability to tell the difference between justice, say, and unfairness. Her deconstruction eats away at all distinctions and affirmations, even ones we might want to make. Her concluding remarks on *Billy Budd* capture the political perplexity that can result: "As a political allegory, Melville's *Billy Budd* is thus much more than a study of good and evil, justice and injustice. It is a dramatization of the twisted relations between knowing and doing, speaking and killing, reading and judging, which make political understanding and action so problematic" (108).

It is thus not surprising that when Johnson herself announces her own feminist political commitments, she expresses disappointment in deconstruction. As a feminist, she wants to make political understanding and action clear, not problematic. Johnson opens her feminist critique of deconstruction with "Gender Theory and the Yale School" (1985), which chastises the work of the Yale critics, among which work she counts her own previous writing. "The Yale School," she says memorably, "has always been a Male School."[7] Yet even in this essay she makes it clear that she wants not to get rid of deconstruction but to put it toward feminist ends. Her *World of Difference* (1987) takes an important step toward deconstructing feminism and politicizing deconstruction.[8]

Johnson concedes the political shortcomings of deconstruction. Deconstructing binary oppositions—showing, for example, that men define themselves against women by repressing their own feminine side, their own differences from themselves—seems to have little immediate practical effect. As Johnson puts it, "if you tell a member of the Klu Klux Klan that racism is a repression of self-difference, you are likely to learn a thing or two about repression" (*World,* 2–3). As a feminist, Johnson now wants to "re-referentialize" difference, to show that there is a world of difference between how men and women are treated, however theoretically vulnerable to deconstruction the man/woman opposition may be.

Yet, even as Johnson wants to advance beyond deconstruction, she still argues for its value to feminism. Deconstruction helps her as a feminist to pry open the established canon, "to question the claims to universality and the forces of exclusion" (*World,* 143) that have shaped it. In *A World of Difference* Johnson still links deconstruction to bringing out how an entity—whether the canon or an individual text—fails to coincide with itself. The "otherness" that seems to lie outside, forgotten and silenced, is rediscovered (by deconstruction) within the very structure that tries to eliminate it. In literary criticism, Johnson thinks that this return of the repressed licenses new attention to previously marginalized writers as well as to texts. Whereas *The Critical Difference,* like most Yale deconstructionist criticism, stuck to the established canon, *A World of Difference* thus deals with Zora Neale Hurston as well as Mallarmé.

Nevertheless, even though deconstruction now helps Johnson foreground otherwise suppressed texts, I still have questions about its political usefulness, questions that will help explain the lingering doubts many African-American women critics have about it. In my view, timing is everything in politics and what may be valuable in one context may be not so valuable in another. Commenting on her own legendary teacher, Paul de Man, Johnson asks

> why de Man's discourse of self-resistance and uncertainty has achieved such authority and visibility, while the self-resistance and uncertainty of *women* has been part of what has insured their lack of authority and their invisibility. It would seem that one has to be positioned in the place of power in order for one's self-resistance to be valued. Self-resistance, indeed, may be one of the few viable postures remaining for the white male establishment. (*World,* 45)

For the moment I want to use this suggestive comment to pose the question: What happens when deconstruction touches the marginalized texts it motivates Johnson to study? Does deconstructing Hurston pay the same political dividends as deconstructing Mallarmé? Or does the deconstruction of an African-American text, like a woman's self-resistance and uncertainty, only exacerbate the lack of authority and the invisibility that Johnson wants to overcome? These questions recall the fear of early feminist critics of deconstruction: that self-deconstruction, when practiced by the dominated, may amount to something like unilateral disarmament exactly when aggressive self-assertion is called for.

Johnson does with Hurston what she does with Mallarmé, which is to notice how internal inconsistencies beset the search for wholeness, oneness, and universality. In Johnson's deconstructionist reading of Hurston, differences proliferate, like rapidly subdividing cells: gender divides African Americans; race divides women; and national, regional, economic, and vocational differences add other distinctions to be reckoned with. At one point Johnson asks, "How can the human world be totalized, even as a field of divisions?"(*World,* 169). Her answer: it can't—and not because "the human world" is too large to be seen as a whole, but because it is an ever-shifting kaleidoscope of differences. In Johnson, the same deconstructionist reasoning splinters everything in its grasp: not just human nature but women, blacks, black women, even Hurston herself, whom Johnson imagines as "a voice that assumes and articulates its own, ever-differing self-difference" (*World,* 170).

Johnson's reading of Hurston's never-ending "self-difference" focuses on her response to the question "how it feels to be colored me." Instead of answering this question, Johnson says (with approval) that Hurston

> deconstructs the very grounds of an answer, replying, "Compared to what? As of when? Who is asking? In what context? For what purpose? With what interests, and presuppositions?" What Hurston rigorously shows is that questions of difference and identity are always a function of a specific interlocutionary situation—and the answers, matters of strategy rather than truth. (*World,* 178)

In a deconstructionist spirit, Johnson is suggesting (via Hurston) that there is no single right answer to the question "how does it feel to be colored me?"—no invariable essence of blackness or transcendental signified that cuts across all contexts and melds together all black people or, for that matter, any black individual at every moment of her life. De-essentializing blackness, or deconstructing it, brings out otherwise submerged differences among and within individuals.

In my view, although this heightened sensitivity to difference is valuable, we can here begin to see why some African-American critics are uneasy with it. Go back to the scene Johnson re-creates: Hurston, asked how it feels to be colored me, deconstructs the question instead of answering it. Hurston's freedom not to answer the question is significant here. The question is evidently not a command; at least the person asking it isn't in a position to demand an answer. Something gives Hurston the power to interrogate her questioner instead of answering right away. When Johnson goes on to say that whatever answers Hurston might provide are "matters of strategy rather than truth," Hurston's independence again appears. "Matters of strategy" suggests Hurston's picking and choosing among identity claims as if they were so many hats, selecting the option, the strategy, that best advances her interests. The freedom and power presupposed by this scenario are again striking. Earlier I asked whether deconstructing a marginalized text exacerbates its lack of authority. In this case, making Hurston out as a proto-deconstructionist exaggerates her autonomy, her freedom from constraint. Johnson concludes her discussion of Hurston by admitting, "If I initially approached Hurston out of a desire to re-referentialize difference, what Hurston gives me back seems to be difference as a suspension of reference. Yet the terms *black* and *white, inside* and *outside,* continue to matter" (*World,* 183). "Yet" suggests some puzzlement, some emotional or experiential distance from the ongoing, everyday importance of these distinctions. The very fact that "black" and "white" come to Johnson as terms, not stark realities, further indicates her detachment from them.

III

I can't imagine an African-American writer like Audre Lorde having to remind herself that "black" and "white" continue to matter. How could she forget? I say this not to dismiss Johnson but to suggest why many African-American women critics have felt as little kinship with deconstruction as they have with white middle-class feminism. Even as deconstruction began making critics like Johnson more responsive to racial and gender difference, Barbara Christian in "The Race for Theory" (1987) and Joyce A. Joyce in "The Black Canon: Reconstructing Black American Literary Criticism" (1987) were objecting to the obscurity and elitism of deconstructionist writing.[9] Christian and Joyce were so repelled by deconstruction that they branded as traitors black critics who impose it on African-American writing.

Joyce is especially hard on what she sees as Henry Louis Gates's deconstruction-inspired "rejection of race" and "denial of blackness" (337). According to Joyce, deconstruction moves Gates (like Barbara Johnson) to put "blackness" in suspicious quotation marks, thereby questioning its reality. With blackness thus deconstructed and black literature recast in fashionable theoretical jargon, Gates and his subject matter blend into the academy like chameleons. Via theory, Joyce concludes, Gates shores up his credentials as an academic critic and becomes an upwardly mobile professor. But as his vita expands, his ties to the black community and its literature snap. As Joyce puts it,

> It is insidious for the Black literary critic to adopt any kind of strategy that diminishes or in this case—through an allusion to binary oppositions—negates his blackness. . . . The Black creative writer has continuously struggled to assert his or her real self and to establish a connection between the self and the people outside that self. The Black creative writer understands that it is not yet time—and it might not ever be possible—for a people with hundreds of years of disenfranchisement and who since slavery have venerated

> the intellect and the written word to view language as merely a system of codes or as mere play. Language has been an essential medium for the evolution of Black pride and the dissolution of the double consciousness. (341)

Literature has meant too much to African Americans for them to deconstruct it. Seduced by theory and the endowed chairs it makes possible, Gates has turned his back on the embattled black community that needs him. Or so Joyce argues. Despite the criticism she has received, she still holds that "adopting poststructuralist ideology requires Black critics both to renounce the history of African-American literature and criticism and to estrange themselves from the political implications of their *black* skin."[10]

Much as some Marxists think that deconstructionists downplay class and some feminists think that deconstructionists annul gender, Joyce feels that Gates liquidates race. From Joyce's point of view, de-essentializing blackness ignores its everyday importance as a target of white hatred and as a source of black pride, a rallying point bringing together all black people. Joyce's critique exemplifies identity politics, which urges stigmatized groups—women, lesbians, gays, African Americans, and others—to assert their difference from the white male norm instead of concealing it. Asserting one's difference here means courageously identifying oneself as part of a collective that has been oppressed. Joyce thus wants a clear, defiant answer to the question "how it feels to be colored me"—an answer grounded in shared experience of oppression and resistance. She is accordingly upset with deconstruction for seeming to attenuate the reality of blackness and to dissolve the community held together by it.

I will be arguing that there is a place for deconstruction in the identity politics that it challenges. First, however, I emphasize that there is something in deconstruction, a characteristic stance or ethos, that critics like Foley and Joyce are correct in picking up. For me, that deconstructionist stance comes through most clearly in the several interviews Derrida has given.[11] These interviews feature Derrida responding to pointed, practical questions such as "Where should composition be taught in the university?" or "What do you think of Marxism and feminism?" I think Derrida's often evasive responses bring to light what Joyce and others associate with deconstruction and theory, namely,

- a reluctance to take sides, to be pinned down, or to say yes or no
- an interminably self-qualifying, self-complicating, ever-lengthening style

- a touchiness when criticized, springing from a willingness to accuse critics of misunderstanding deconstruction out of polemical impatience and political haste
- a highly individualized disavowal of any school or method associated with one's name
- a constant plea that we keep in mind the complexity of the issues and texts under consideration and that we proceed very slowly and cautiously, out of respect for the difficult, endlessly ramifying, overdetermined questions we are dealing with.

I can easily imagine Derrida criticizing Joyce for rushing to judgment and impatiently simplifying things. This is roughly how Gates and Houston Baker respond to her, and I think they have a point.[12] Still, I persist in feeling that deconstruction—again characterized as the stance described above—can lead to hand wringing and indecisiveness when directness is called for. Christopher Prendergast's devastating analysis of Geoffrey Hartman's response to de Man's wartime writings illustrates my point:

> Hartman's performance is nothing short of lamentable, as at once an account of deconstruction and a demonstration of it in action. Hartman's way with the undecidable is for the most part to avoid decisions, to hop first on one foot, then on the other. . . . Hartman condemns [de Man], initially in no uncertain terms ("all the marks"), yet retracts condemnation. . . . What on earth can we do with all these endless backtrackings and proliferating qualifiers, phrases, and sentences that take away with one hand what they give with the other?[13]

When political issues are at stake, complexity does not energize critics like Hartman but paralyzes them. Instead of facilitating judgment, close reading in this instance forestalls it. Prendergast's frustrated "What on earth can we do with all these endless backtrackings and proliferating qualifiers . . . ?" captures the exasperation Foley, Joyce, and feminist critics of deconstruction also feel.

IV

However, while I share Prendergast's impatience with Hartman, I am not so ready as Prendergast to give up on deconstruction. We need to consider its possible usefulness to other critics in other circumstances. As a step in this direction, I suggest that deconstruction does not so much stall Hartman's political writing as fail to get it moving. In Hartman and, for that matter, J. Hillis Miller, deconstruction lacks any activist ideology to work against. There is no polemical impatience for deconstruction to moderate in these critics, no headlong rush to action for it to slow down, no strident political commitment for it to temper. The injunction to proceed cautiously out of deference to the complicated issues at hand comes to critics already given to slow, meticulous reading and to second-guessing their own already highly qualified convictions. Instead of challenging these critics' authority, deconstruction thus reinforces their (deserved) reputation as sophisticated readers—which is perhaps one reason why Johnson noticed that far from undermining de Man's stature as a teacher, his self-resistance and uncertainty only gave his classroom authority even more weight.

But the same deconstructionist ethos that further slows a Hartman or Miller can spur on a critic stuck in a different way. I have in mind the potentially liberating impact of deconstruction on Marxism and academic feminism. I say potentially liberating because, as we have seen in Foley, some Marxists and feminists resist the opportunities for self-criticism that deconstruction offers. Others, however, benefit from the complexities it introduces. I have cited Prendergast irritably wondering what to do with the qualifications deconstruction spawns. I reply that if we are Marxists like Gayatri Spivak, we can complicate the much too simple bifuraction of society into two discrete antagonistic classes. If we are feminists like Johnson, we can counter monolithic tendencies in feminism by qualifying seemingly universal claims about women—by asking whether by "women" we really mean white women, heterosexual women, and so on.[14] In what once was mainstream feminism and hardcore Marxism—Foley's Leninism having fallen out of favor even at the time she was writing—deconstruction encountered rigid Manichaean dualisms (between working class and bourgeoisie, women and men) that needed refining and dogmatic self-assurance that needed dissolving. Seeing deconstruction as unsettling self-interrogation accordingly led Derrida to insist in a 1985 interview that "deconstruction is *certainly* not feminist." Instead, "deconstruction is a deconstruction of feminism, from the start," "a certain thinking of women [*pensée des femmes*] which does not however want to immobilize itself in feminism."[15] "Immobilize" here captures the fixity, the unyielding dogmatism, deconstruction can help loosen.

But what about African-American writers and others stigmatized by race? Given the urgent social problems faced by black Americans, I can see why Joyce is frustrated with the deconstructionist stance. Take the characteristic deconstructionist demand for close attention to complexity and patient, self-criticizing commentary. As Johnson asks in *A World of Difference,*

> how can the plea for slowness, for the suspension of decision, for the questioning of knowledge, ever function as anything other than a refusal to intervene? Nothing could be more convincing than the idea that political radicality requires decisiveness, not indecision; haste, not hesitation. . . . The privileging of ambiguity would always appear to be an avoidance of action. (30)

Rampant poverty among African Americans, crushing unemployment, abysmal housing and medical care—these are the realities on Joyce's mind. These hard facts are not problematic but all too painfully clear. They would seem to require urgent intervention, not fastidious self-questioning. When someone is bleeding to death, plain-and-simple help is called for, not erudite hemming and hawing. One doesn't tiptoe to an accident; one runs.

Joyce's sense of urgency motivates identity politics and its call for racial solidarity, self-assertion, and pride in difference. Nevertheless, even here deconstruction can make a contribution. As Gregory Jay has recently explained, faced with socially discredited terms like "gay," "woman," or "black,"

> deconstructive criticism is a strategy of affirmative action: it affirms the [stigmatized] other and solicits its value. This first and by no means simple stage of critical struggle is perceptible in the fashionable but no less necessary invocation of terms like "race," "class," and "gender" in so much contemporary theory. The empowerment of these terms cannot be abandoned in a rush to deconstruct the conceptual identities and abstractions informing them. Their affirmation, on the contrary, is required by a politico-discursive situation that everywhere exhibits the cost of their previous denigration or erasure. Here the return of a certain will to believe can be justified.[16]

I am disappointed in Jay's suggestion here that for the sake of affirming "blackness," "gay," and other denigrated terms, "the return of a certain will to believe can be justified"—presumably a certain will to believe in the reality of "blackness" and so on. This suggestion sounds smug to me. At any rate, believing in the referentiality of these terms may be a strain for a deconstructionist like Jay but, as we have seen, comes readily to an African-American woman like Joyce. For her, interrogating these terms needs to be justified, not standing by them. If Jay underrates the necessity of belief, Joyce slights the desirability of complexity. Nevertheless, for pragmatic, political reasons, Jay cautions, stick with terms like "black" and fight against their violent erasure. The empowerment of these terms cannot yet be abandoned—a warning Joyce would certainly endorse.[17]

But, Jay immediately adds, "at another level," we should rethink these apparently empirical terms, deconstruct them, hold them in skeptical suspension, even put them under erasure—in short, do everything with them that Gates does with "blackness." "At another level" keeps theory apart from practice but still in the same house, like rooms on different floors. Jay wants deconstruction to influence political practice—in this case identity politics—but at the right time or pace. Deconstruction resembles a drug dripping into a patient from an IV. Injecting deconstruction all at once would be premature and lethal: it would put an end to identity politics too soon by exploding "blackness" and other terms that, as Joyce reminds us, still matter in everyday life. Avoiding deconstruction, however, would keep identity politics vulnerable to dogmatism: to deterministic, stereotypical ideas of race and gender that deny individual differences and the multiple identities struggling for acknowledgment in each of us.

I share Jay's wish to engage in identity politics and to question them, but I acknowledge the difficulty of the tension that he and I favor. Along similar lines, Derrida has spoken of preserving tradition and interrogating it. "This double gesture," he admits, "is very difficult to sustain because it can lead to unavoidable situations of contradiction and 'double bind.' Personally, I live this double gesture as a sort of rapid alteration, doing both as fast as possible."[18] Combined with identity politics, deconstruction does lead to difficult, now-you-see-it, now-you-don't dilemmas, where "it" can be any one of several terms crucial to identity politics, such as "gay," "woman," "black," and so on. These dilemmas, however, help keep identity politics flexible, open to the differences that challenge its potentially prescriptive notions of race and gender.

I am suggesting that there is still a need both for deconstruction and the identity politics it leavens. "Leavens" is my way of saying that deconstruction in this context is an ingredient but not the whole recipe for change. I would make the same claim about identity politics. Both identity politics and deconstruction need one another, lest deconstruction degenerate into Polonius-like circumlocution and identity politics turn gender, race, and class into unyielding templates. The reactive, corrective role I am assigning deconstruction will disappoint critics like Foley who want to be done with it and disciples of deconstruction like Miller who think it is sufficient. But in my view the very patience and questioning that make deconstruction valuable as a component of a political program make it ineffectual when it stands on its own.

The place I am allotting deconstruction recalls Robert Penn Warren's defense of irony, paradox, and ambiguity in "Pure and Impure Poetry" (1943).[19] Warren praises writers who have tried to "remain faithful to the complexities of the problems with which they are dealing, because they refused to take the easy statement as solution" (992). Their scrupulousness, he admits, "will scarcely satisfy the mind which is hot for certainties; to that mind it will seem merely an index to lukewarmness, indecision, disunity, treason" (992). In response, Warren maintains that "the hand-me-down faith, the hand-me-down ideals, no matter what the professed content, is in the end not only meaningless but vicious. It is vicious because as parody, it is the enemy of all faith" (992). I am more ready than Warren to concede that the cultivation of ambiguity can be a pretext for lukewarmness and indecision. Nevertheless, I accept his point that literature (and, I have been claiming, deconstruction) are valuable exactly when they irritate the ideologue hot for certainties and quick answers.

As a response to social problems like racism and poverty, the study of literature, after all, is highly mediated and indirect—although in saying this we shouldn't lose sight of the political dimension of literary study or romanticize seemingly more direct responses like social work or health care (these, too, can feel like roundabout detours rather than immediate interventions).[20] By calling the study of literature "highly mediated and indirect," I mean in part that it takes place in classrooms, conferences, and libraries one or two removes from the social problems that concern us. In these relatively safe settings where no urgent decisions are at stake, we can take our time and not rush to any conclusions. Going slowly, moreover, is rewarded by the complex texts we usually deal with, which always seem to have new meanings to uncover, new ambiguities to think through. All of this is to say that patiently attending to complexity, suspending judgment, and questioning knowledge may be intrinsic to the academic study of literature: they do not just come on the scene with deconstruction. Again, the privileging of ambiguity can license indecisiveness—as I claim happens in Hartman—but I also believe it can make available a much-needed perspective on action. Instead of trying to collapse literary study into more direct political action, we therefore should value the tension between the two. Social change is too important to leave to activists—or to the literary theorists who question them.

Notes

1. See Geoffrey Hartman, "Paul de Man, Fascism, and Deconstruction: *Blindness and Insight,*" *New Republic* (7 March 1988): 26–31.

2. Cornel West, "The New Cultural Politics of Difference," *October* 53 (1990): 93–109.

3. Dinesh D'Souza, "Illiberal Education," *Atlantic Monthly* (March 1991): 51–79.

4. Barbara Foley, "The Politics of Deconstruction," in *Rhetoric and Form: Deconstruction at Yale,* ed. Robert Con Davis and Ronald Schleifer (Norman: University of Oklahoma Press, 1985).

5. Karl Marx and Friedrich Engels, *The Communist Manifesto,* trans. Samuel Moore (Baltimore: Penguin Books, 1967), 80.

6. Barbara Johnson, *The Critical Difference* (Baltimore: Johns Hopkins University Press, 1980).

7. Barbara Johnson, "Gender Theory and the Yale School," in *Rhetoric and Form: Deconstruction at Yale,* ed. Robert Con Davis and Ronald Schleifer (Norman: University of Oklahoma Press, 1985), 101.

8. Barbara Johnson, *A World of Difference* (Baltimore: Johns Hopkins University Press, 1987).

9. Barbara Christian, "The Race for Theory," in *Gender and Theory: Dialogues on Feminist Criticism,* ed. Linda Kauffman (London: Basil Blackwell, 1989); Joyce A. Joyce, "The Black Canon: Reconstructing Black American Literary Criticism," *New Literary History* 18 (winter 1987): 335–45.

10. See Joyce A. Joyce, "Black Woman Scholar, Critic, and Teacher: The Inextricable Relationship Among Race, Sex, and Class," in *(En)Gendering Knowledge,* ed. Joan E. Hartman and Ellen Messer-Davidow (Knoxville: University of Tennessee Press, 1991), 165. For an even harsher criticism of Gates's apparent theory-enabled careerism, see Harold Fromm, *Academic Capitalism and Literary Value* (Athens: University of Georgia Press, 1991).

11. I especially have in mind Derrida's wide-ranging interview with James Creech, Peggy Kamuf, and Jane Todd ("Deconstruction in America," *Critical Exchange* 17 [winter 1985]: 1–33); and his conversation with Gary A. Olson ("Jacques Derrida on Rhetoric and Composition: A Conversation" in *(Inter)views: Cross-Disciplinary Perspectives on Rhetoric and Literacy,* ed. Gary A. Olson and Irene Gale [Carbondale: Southern Illinois University Press, 1991]).

12. Houston Baker Jr., "In Dubious Battle," *New Literary History* 18 (winter 1987): 363–69, and, in this same issue, Henry Louis Gates Jr., " 'What's Love Got To Do With It?': Critical Theory, Integrity, and the Black Idiom" (345–62). In replying to Joyce, Baker in particular finds himself having to defend what he sees as a desirable "*complexity* in the Afro-American critical and theoretical arsenal" (363). He finds it "impossible to

believe that an essay as dreadfully flawed by factual mistakes as Professor Joyce's work on Afro-American criticism would have been accepted or printed by a major critical or theoretical journal" (366).

13. Christopher Prendergast, "Making the Difference: Paul de Man, Fascism, and Deconstruction," in *Intellectuals: Aesthetics, Politics, Academics,* ed. Bruce Robbins (Minneapolis: University of Minnesota Press, 1990), 334. Along similar lines Andrew J. McKenna argues that "Derrida repeatedly warns against oversimplifying . . . but the symmetrical danger of overcomplexifying is in danger of nuancing itself out of a job, at least an academic one, unless its role is to disenfranchise everyone else, absolutely everyone who lays claim to knowledge, whatever and wherever the claim. . . . It is no good having clean hands if the process renders them incapable of grasping anything." See McKenna, *Violence and Difference: Girard, Derrida, and Deconstruction* (Urbana: University of Illinois Press, 1992), 189.

14. Elizabeth Meese is another feminist-deconstructionist who maintains that deconstruction challenges feminists who characterize the essence of "woman" in their own image. See *(Ex)tensions: Re-Figuring Feminst Criticism* (Urbana: University of Illinois Press, 1990).

15. James Creech, Peggy Kamuf, and Jane Todd, "Deconstruction in America," *Critical Exchange* 17 (winter 1985): 30.

16. Gregory S. Jay, *America the Scrivener: Deconstruction and The Subject of Literary History* (Ithaca: Cornell University Press, 1990), 79–80.

17. So would Henry Louis Gates, who warns against the dangers of treating "homosexual," for example, as "only" a socially constructed term: "Now, if there's no such thing as a homosexual, then homophobia, at least as directed toward people rather than acts, loses its rationale. But you can't respond to the discrimination against gay people by saying 'I'm sorry, I don't exist; you've got the wrong guy.' " See Gates's *Loose Canons: Notes on the Culture Wars* (New York: Oxford University Press, 1992). Similarly, bell hooks, for all her interest in contemporary theory, also insists that "given a pervasive politic of white supremacy which seeks to prevent the formation of radical black subjectivity, we cannot cavalierly dismiss a concern with identity politics." See hooks's *Yearning: Race, Gender, and Cultural Politics* (Boston: South End Press, 1990), 26.

18. Creech, Kamuf, and Todd, "Deconstruction in America," 7–8 (see note 15).

19. Robert Penn Warren, "Pure and Impure Poetry," in *Critical Theory Since Plato,* ed. Hazard Adams (New York: Harcourt Brace Jovanovich, 1971). Originally published in the *Kenyon Review,* 5 (spring 1943): 228–54.

20. Gates makes a comparable point about the indirect (at best) political impact of literary study in *Loose Canons,* 19, 180–81 (see note 17).

Relevant Publications by Michael Fischer

Doing Things with Texts: Essays in Criticism and Critical Theory [essays by M. H. Abrams] (editor). New York: Norton, 1989.

Stanley Cavell and Literary Skepticism. Chicago: University of Chicago Press, 1989.

Romanticism and Contemporary Criticism (coeditor with Morris Eaves). Ithaca: Cornell University Press, 1986.

Does Deconstruction Make Any Difference? Poststructuralism and the Defense of Poetry in Modern Criticism. Bloomington: Indiana University Press, 1985.

"Perspectivism and Literary Theory Today." *American Literary History* 2 (fall 1990): 528–49.

"Stanley Cavell's Wittgenstein." In *Redrawing the Lines: Analytic Philosophy, Deconstruction, and Literary Theory*, edited by Reed Dasenbrock. Minneapolis: University of Minnesota Press, 1989.

"Accepting the Romantics as Philosophers." *Philosophy and Literature* 12 (October 1988): 179–89.

"William Blake's Quarrel with Indeterminacy." *New Orleans Review* 10 (winter 1983): 43–49.

13

The Purloined Profession; or, How to Reidealize Reading for the Text

Charles Altieri

Charles Altieri, professor of English at the University of California–Berkeley, is known for his sophisticated application of philosophically grounded modes of thought (as opposed to the importation of bits drawn from currently fashionable philosophers). His views of literature and culture have been especially influenced by Wittgenstein, the importance of whose work was intriguingly developed in Altieri's Act and Quality *(1981). Additionally, much of his theorizing has been stimulated by his critical work in postmodernism. Altieri's concern to state his arguments as accurately as possible, qualifying them wherever necessary, and to be fair in his judgments of different and opposing perspectives give a density to his prose that requires close attention from the reader. This careful buttressing at times makes the positions at which he arrives seem more cautious than, on reflection, they prove to be. Altieri's claims for the value of literature are in fact powerful ones: he writes for instance in the introduction to* Canons and Consequences:

> *a vital canon provides the richest imperatives to make ourselves new: in the works it preserves, we find alternatives to what the dominant culture imposes on us; and in the modes of questioning and comparing that we develop for adapting the canon, we find*

> *ways of organizing psychic energies capable of engaging and even extending our own age's most radical thinking about the psyche.*

The present essay is a reassertion of one of Altieri's constant contentions: that literature provides us with a repertory of possible ways of thinking and acting not otherwise available.

I

For much of the twentieth century literary criticism was dominated by an aesthetic humanism loosely woven out of strands from Kant, Schiller, Matthew Arnold, and their ostensibly more rigorous and ironic modernist heirs. Now of course those days are long gone, their dominant values reduced to the rubric of "aesthetic ideology" and their vision of the powers they might convey relegated to masks for a range of nefarious social interests. For me the most disturbing aspect of this shift is that much of it is justified, if only because of how these artists and critics went on to apply their own principles. Therefore any attempt to return to what was best in that ideology faces two serious problems: it must argue for what is largely already known, so that there is little room for images of oneself as breaking new ground; and it must confront an atmosphere where resistance to that aesthetic humanism seems by now so natural that it no longer depends on carefully mustered arguments. Arguing against aesthetic humanism seems as ridiculous as arguing against God; some fictions seem dead so long there is no point burying them again.

But aesthetic humanism has not yet had its resurrection, so perhaps it is worth one more hearing, if only in terms careful to focus on what it can offer as social powers clearly important to literary education. To secure this hearing I must begin by insisting that one can separate what is best in the traditions of aesthetic humanism from a problematic formalism. Formalism concentrates on the intricate syntactic organization of particular works of art. The aesthetic humanism I will argue for preserves this concern for particularity. But it attempts to use the close attention involved in order to place that particular in relation to a corollary question: How can the mental and affective energies we put into tracking this intricate organization be said to compose powers of mind and a responsiveness to values not readily available within more discursive and generalizing intellectual practices?

Accordingly, we read for structures of internal relations enabling an audience to watch itself exploring imaginative identifications that range from the actions of characters to the author's efforts to understand what might be at stake in the ways those actions are rendered. Such experiences then play significant social roles because they influence how agents represent their own capacities, project values correlated with those capacities, and develop a sense of community in terms of both how they imagine others engaging the work and how they imagine authors and characters responding to the values that the readers develop. Rather than treat individual works as instances illustrating the ways that theory can sustain general cognitive claims, this approach treats the theoretical claims as a background for appreciating and for testing the imaginative strategies by which the artists manage to take responsibility for their basic commitments. Theory then poses questions about how individual agents might take responsibility for what they develop in engaging those commitments.

II

As my way of testing those claims I will argue that they offer richer ways through which literature contributes to its audience's personal lives than do more overtly politicized ideals of reading that have currency in American academe. However, since there is a wide variety of possible political ideals (all I think indirectly addressed by what follows), I will confine my specific opposition to the conjunction of principles shaping the view that the basic aim of literary education is to develop powers of critical thinking enabling us to demystify the various masks employed by oppressive power to preserve its hegemony. Even this version of the political, of course, has a good deal of significant work to do: there is much in the social order to demystify, and there are many features of the imaginary identifications or forms of investment cultivated by such work from which we need distance ourselves. But we must also recognize that the capacity to demystify cannot be the ultimate goal of education or of political consciousness. We must be able to formulate directions worth taking for the positive values they afford, and we must therefore find ways not merely of resisting seduction but of representing and pursuing images worth being seduced by. If we cannot do that, we leave ourselves vacillating among three quite limited options, whose capacity to slide into one another manages to protect what we might call the dominant imaginary structures within "sophisticated" literary criticism. (1) In its purest form the cult of demystification preserves the subject position, and hence the imaginary satisfactions that accompanied the modernist ideal of a lucidity too fine for any commitments not pervaded by ironic distance (which we now call "free play"). (2) Such distance can be politicized if it is cast as resistance, since this at least opens other possible modes of investment, but there remains a constant danger that any positive alternative will itself have to be resisted, so that there remains the constant falling back into irony. (3) And finally there is the Lacanian means of idealizing demystification by locating the source of mystification not in any specific beliefs but in the phallocentric disposition to take beliefs as demands we then feel justified in imposing on others. Here the dream is that we can cultivate something like a masochistic suspension of imperious demands so that we forgo all tyranny and allow others to work out their own destinies. But when we take that step we also risk surrendering the very intelligence we want to cultivate, since all it can do is catch us at our imaginary self-projections. Therefore if we are to continue idealizing critical intelligence, we also need vital institutional means of complementing and supplementing that intelligence by developing positive dispositions for which we can take responsibility. Aesthetic humanism on the other hand, holds out the possibility that in our encounters with the arts we foster powers for trying out identifications with agents in various social and psychological situations, for exploring possible attitudes individuals might cultivate, for gaining better understanding of how other people live, and above all for experimenting with idealized versions of selves and social relations that clarify the positions from which we criticize and that have the capacity to show what we can build because of those criticisms.

But how do we realize such powers, or, more elementally, how can we idealize the pursuit of such powers without the pursuit itself becoming simply another attempt at seduction? A plausible answer to these questions requires two quite different lines of argument. The first is quite general. We must be able to provide an adequate reason for turning to the kind of indirect claims about powers and attitudes that literary experience sustains when there seem to be far more direct measures of the value of literature. Why not just ask if a text is true or politically useful (in the sense of either exposing interests or orienting action in accord with particular agendas)? What possible considerations could make us decide that something we do not take as true or directly useful still has significant values to offer us? Traditionally, aesthetic theory has located the necessary distinguishing qualities in specific properties of literary language or literary structure: in the work's ability to use language and structure to provide a density and complexity and affective development simply not available to other modes of discourse. But in the present political climate this reliance on aesthetic features in themselves seems a bit self-serving because it locates in the object what turns out to be the priorities of the subject, and it encourages an unecessarily sharp opposition between what is within the work and the political and historical frames involving how the work was produced and is consumed.

It does remain possible to insist upon distinctive features of literary experience so long as we locate them not in the object but in the ways that over time traditions develop and implicit contracts get formed between writers and readers calling for specific modes of attention that in other disciplines might not be equally foregrounded. But such appeals to tradition are not in themselves adequate to defend value claims. We can show that literary practices have emphasized distinctive attitudes, but we cannot show that we ought now to emphasize the same values, especially when we live in intersecting and competing traditions. Why do we or should we choose one tradition over another, or one level of one tradition in preference to another level of another tradition? Instead of relying directly on traditions we must try to develop functional or pragmatic accounts that can clarify the basic values at stake by bringing to bear questions about needs and possibilities by which we can hope to measure the different claims of these traditions. And we might even be able to force representatives of those traditions to meet the same basic demands for explanation and application.

To meet these challenges I turn to my second line of argument. I want to develop three specific claims which I hope can justify insisting that aesthetic attitudes toward literary experience nonetheless make available socially significant powers. Moreover each specific claim affords a point of possible comparison which we can use to decide whether competing approaches to criticism can provide alternative versions of the same powers or offer a more compelling account of what powers ought to be primary. First, an aesthetic perspective on texts enables us to shift from a concern for how texts provide cognitions (as means of knowledge or as objects of knowledge) to an emphasis on the specific dynamics by which wording the world proves inseparable from willing the world. Second, we can cast literary texts as engaged in processes of willing because it requires our not being satisfied with treating what we read simply as texts; these materials must also be approached as works, as performances that foreground the processes of wording and willing. The performance gives a body to actions whose specific qualities become possible justifications for the values asserted. Third, this stress on performance makes it possible to discuss the social force of literary texts in terms of how their singular modes of thinking and feeling become representative, so that the emphasis is less on how works might portray or even reveal certain truths than on the powers they make visible, the complex identifications they facilitate, and the attitudes or connections they invite us to pursue.[1] Performances place the singularity of the work in its means of taking responsibility for itself within its concrete unfolding; they then make it possible to take such actions themselves as the materials the mind uses as its means of making projections beyond the text. Performances provide examples that then become labels we can use in describing, comparing, and assessing further experiences that they help us identify.

III

Let me begin with the general claim about wording and willing; I will then provide an extended reading in order to show how the performance of such willing can be said to take on exemplary social force. One could argue that all discursive practices are concerned with connecting how we word the world to how we will the world. But most of these practices treat the words as instrumental: words provide building blocks for the concepts that we then judge in terms of the values they might help us realize. This model of value, however, is not very helpful in getting us to see why we have the modes of evaluation we do or how we might change our evaluative principles on grounds that are not reducible to seduction and mastery. To flesh out those topics we need to be able to shift from what makes assertions true to what makes us care about that truth, and this cannot be effectively done within a language devoted to truth. Treating the wording as central to the willing helps us make the necessary adjustment because it also invites reflection on how concepts and related images might be held and adapted to existential situations. When we concentrate on what is involved in the kind of speaking that calls attention to itself, we position ourselves to make judgments not only that something is the case but also that basic interests might be satisfied if we tried to identify with this particular way of putting the situation. And then a tradition of such efforts becomes not just a series of failed efforts to know the world; it becomes a set of resources of ways of imagining how approaches to interpreting the world might have consequences for the values we adopt.

It is difficult to treat this relation between wording and willing as directly political because it cannot be handled adequately by concepts. Its ways of being representative do not depend on discursive universals but on what I call the possibility of proleptic identifications, whereby agents use certain figures as means of exploring possible states they might enter, or as means of attributing qualities to states that they have already experienced. Yet it is precisely such representativeness that allows us to treat particular manifestations of this will in wording as elemental constituents that must be considered when we imagine how we might use social concepts or align ourselves with general social programs. For it is the specific examples that help us define what is at stake in how individuals represent that which binds them to other persons.

Lyric poetry provides the clearest examples of the ways wording and willing live one another's life and die one another's death. Like public rhetorical performances, lyric emphasizes eloquence as its ground for engaging its audience. But where the rhetorical performer cultivates ethos in order to win over an audience to concerns that subsume the individual, the lyric tends to make ethos an end in itself by emphasizing what goes into the mode of consciousness that the individual articulates. Both the public rhetorician and the lyric poet make the memorability of their phrases a basic index of the ways in which one might will or consent to what they have to say. But again the rhetorician tends to treat memory as a means of attaching us to what has been said, while for the lyric memory is a mode of identification inviting us to try who we become by virtue of internalizing whatever power the words might confer. Think of the moment in Dante's *Paradiso* where Piccarda describes heaven to the pilgrim as a state where "la sua voluntade è nostra pace." As Eliot realized in often quoting this passage, its significance is simply the possibility of its statement: the combination of simplicity and intimacy and total identification defines for any speaker what salvation must be.

One finds a range of powerful secular examples in Yeats's work. For him metaphor is not primarily a way of naming the world; instead, it becomes the condition for appreciating one's access to powers that resist all our established names. Thus a line like "the soul's a bride that cannot in this rag and tinsel hide," makes the depth and scope of the metaphors themselves the measure of how far beyond rag and tinsel the soul can reach. Something even more dramatically performative takes place through the puns in "nothing can be sole or whole that has not been rent," because here the eloquence at once opens the soul to victimage and self-division and literally wins its right to assert its powers to win powers of self-unification from such divisions. The force of the ideas depends on how the wording sustains the performing will. And for the audience the use value of such performances consists in how well and how long it provides a plausible way for our taking up the attitude exemplified by the poet. We can do that most obviously simply by taking on those specific words as our own, but we can also treat them as provocations demanding that we find our own way of engaging (Stanley Cavell would say "owning") the situation they address and the personal state they dramatize in terms of that address.

Because poetry so well represents complex examples of wording as willing, it is tempting to treat that mode as the exclusive model for literary value, and thus to repeat the blindnesses of the New Criticism. Yet there are ways to resist that temptation, since this emphasis also provides a way of locating a central cultural force for novels and plays without going directly to thematic readings or political appropriations. In lyrics the idealized wording usually appears as a timeless possibility for the imagination. In other genres more sensitive to changes through time, wording too is forced to submit to tests of duration and possible dissipation. Consequently we often engage somewhat different aspects of willing. Instead of a focus on directly wording general attitudes or specific moments of attention and connection, these genres ask us to dwell imaginatively on the conditions of possibility enabling, and often distorting, the ways that wills get worded. The focus is not on immediate intensity but on how characters might be capable of determining themselves by certain expressions, which in turn may also be the source of their blindness. Othello's "put down your swords for the dew will rust them," defines a state of personal being we can encounter fully only by granting both the possibility and the vulnerability of such imperious self-confidence. And Lear's closing words to Cordelia provide an emblem for the will at its most glorious and most pathetic, so fully caught in love that it can blind itself to the harshest of facts.

A full account of such wordings requires our bringing the author into the picture. So I propose treating the aesthetic organization of the work as the author's means of showing why his or her own investment in the wording offers us a candidate for shaping our own ways of willing. The author is not only the maker of formal patterns; he or she also stages the work as responding to certain cultural pressures against which one can measure the values they work out—whether these involve specific social agendas like Tolstoy's or seek to interpret why it matters to attempt maintaining a Flaubertian distance. From this perspective, Molly Bloom's repeated "yes" at the close of *Ulysses* constitutes a profound comment on the very idea of literary form. That "yes" establishes the text's own sense of what its exploration of Dublin allows the will, so long as it can cast its experiences in this way.

IV

If I had the necessary time and talent I would now argue that these examples can offer as much guidance in developing a theory of will as they do in our formulating the values at stake in different ways of reading.[2] But on this occasion the closest I can come to that is to shift to the second of my claims where I hope to distinguish the ways the concept of performance has become popular in gender and postcolonial theory from its force as a focus for aesthetic interests. When theorists like Judith Butler or Homi Bhabha invoke performative values, they in effect cross Austin with Derrida in order to explain how agency can become articulate and even define values without relying on preestablished criteria or submitting to what we might call the regime of knowledge. The qualities projected in a singular performance can define who a person or even a nation can be by virtue simply of how the action proves exemplary, without having to invoke some kind of deep foundational principle to which the agent appeals. And by bypassing such principles, the performance avoids any fixed notions of gender, just as subaltern performance manages to weave assertions of identity bound neither to colonial authority nor to some romantic, outdated notion of native authenticity.[3]

I cannot deny that the concept of performance can thus play significant roles in freeing oppressed groups from what have now become the second-order oppressions of identity politics. But the very need for such freedom tempts theorists to ignore other aspects of performance basic to the arts, and crucial to a full political understanding of both what performance depends on and how it can hope to engage audiences. From an aesthetic perspective, performances can only achieve significant individuality if they remain aware of how they depend on the very traditions they hope to modify. Correlatively, performances in all these domains will not accomplish much in the long run if they attend only to the specific urgencies of the performer, without worrying about how they might engage the judgments of others and through such engagements open possible lines of communication. Performance in other words does not make a very compelling ethical or psychological absolute. Performances only establish significant identities when they figure within the activity a sensitivity to how an audience might engage in and judge what is performed. Even Nietzsche, the archetypal performative artist thinking about performance, did not forget for a moment his complex dependency on those he could only despise even as he longed for their approval.

I cannot here work out a theoretical comparison of the two perspectives on performance. But I can turn to a particular example of how a lyric performance can mobilize that sense of audience expectations in order to develop concrete, singular relations between wording and willing that resist all sociological generalizations. (There is nonetheless no reason why these relations could not become the basis for complex sociological analyses of what agents might achieve within specific social contexts.) Poems self-consciously celebrating performative identity immediately spring to mind, like Yeats's "Prayer for my Daughter," or Shakespeare's sonnets punning on "Will." But my purposes are much better served by turning to an adamantly political poet, Adrienne Rich, who is paradoxically far more restrained than Yeats and Shakespeare as she tries to establish an identity based on acknowledging the social bonds that can be fostered by recognizing the limitations of one's power over words. Consider this simple moment from "Contradictions: Tracking Poems":

> You who think I find words for everything
> and you for whom I write this,
> how can I show you what I'm barely
> coming into possession of, invisible luggage
> of more than fifty years, looking at first
> glance like everyone else's turning up
> at the airport carousel
> and the waiting for it, knowing what nobody
> would steal must eventually come round—
> feeling obsessed, peculiar, longing?[4]

Here Rich takes on the challenge of affirming a sense of the limitations on the will. For the measure of her love is her capacity first to see that her old ways do not suffice, then to find in her relationship with the other person an alternative to the old confidence that one can find words for everything. In working out these terms, the poem manages to define a sense of subjective agency deeply responsive to that other person, or, more generally, to the demands on the self stemming from its awareness that it cannot control either the love that draws it to the other or the responses that the other makes. Thus in the very process of admitting limitations the poem also exceeds them in two marvelous ways, both also deepening the bonds between the "I" and the "you."

First we realize that despite the speaker's overt embarrassment about her verbal skills, this poem is deliberately only one sentence. Thus it makes its various syntactic turns a partial joke, a partial erotic display: the sentence displays a confidence and persistence within the relationship enabling the speaker to unify and to contain and to represent the density of bonding between the characters, even though no particular verbal formulation can describe it. But how do we reconcile this confidence and playful exuberance with the sense of limitations asserted by the final lines? Rich's second mode of excess provides one answer by inviting us to think of different kinds of knowledge, some of which allow personal ties to be forged in the very process of examining how little they can describe. Here even the poet's sense of self cannot depend on direct assertion but must be triangulated by coming to realize what she cannot do, and cannot be. Any effort to find descriptive terms for this self, and for this sense of the self's relation to the "you," would leave one in the position of examining the luggage coming around in the airport carousel. Whatever attributes I point to are likely also to belong to other persons, since very little differentiates us in the world of facts, or even of habits and beliefs. (In my allegory one might make the same claims about social and political framings of literary texts, since the understanding they seek is likely to subordinate the particularity of the text to some general condition it can be said to illuminate or illustrate. Therefore these framings risk surrendering the performative to a version of the faith that one can find words for everything.)

Rich's alternative is to invite us by these initial negations to focus on the specific qualities within the speech act that define the bonds between the two persons, especially the quality of the waiting. How the poem defines this waiting gives metaphoric resonance to the relation between wording and willing that the text elaborates. Consider the initial situation. This poem is so profoundly dependent on the speaker's openness to the other that it even risks its grammatical coherence to have the "you" hover syntactically and spiritually over the entire sentence. Beginning in direct address, the poem then lets the power of the addressee force the self into the interrogative mood. On the dramatic level it then seems that attending to the force of this "you" makes it impossible to rely on old habits of answering. Instead the questioning relocates the "I" so that it can only inhabit two locales: first, the condition of waiting, itself a mark of commitment: then the marvelous redeployment of the subject's affective energies defined by the complex syntactic situation of the last lines.

The movement of the sentence is driven by four participles: "looking," "waiting," "knowing" and "feeling." The first participle modifies only the luggage; then the next three expand the field of modifications to develop various features of the speaker's psyche. "Waiting" defines the overall condition where the speaker must throw herself beyond what she can control. From the point of view of "knowing," that waiting must be cast negatively: the most one can say about the sense of a distinctive self is that its place can only be in what cannot be observed or occupied by others. But then the "feeling" enters to transform the negative state of knowing by introducing a series of adjectives that make a new and complex emotional field. It seems as if the speaker's relation to her past opens into a present where the obsession and sense of peculiarity leads beyond the waiting to an awareness of the forces that frame it—forces deriving from aspects of the self that are now inseparable from a longing for the "you" to remain part of the dialogue that desire has generated.

"Longing" becomes the aspect of wording most deeply and complexly established as a condition of willing, in large part because it also carries the poem's most subtle verbal play. Syntactically "longing" is the last in a list of adjectives that characterize this feeling of waiting. But "longing" also carries participial functions, so that it takes on a force strangely parallel to the work done by the last actual participle; that is, the work of "feeling." So at the very core of describing her own sense of doubt and loss, the speaker discovers the active state of feeling that most tightly binds her to the "you." Pushed beyond assertion, she finds a mode of need that leads back into and completes the dialogical situation. "Longing" gives a direction and purpose to negation and ultimately makes self-conscious the emotional commitment that the speaking here offers the speaker.

V

Suppose now that readers agree entirely with my interpretation and assessment of this lyric performance. How can we go on to attribute any social significance to that reading, and to that way of reading? Why are the actual dynamics of this speaking more noteworthy than the specific social conditions affecting Rich's general sexual politics, and perhaps even shaping the way that she links desire with frustration and with longing? Even to begin answering such questions we must turn to my third claim: that an aesthetic orientation offers us a plausible account of how we might use such performances, and therefore of what there is in Rich's speech act that matters for her audience. On the simplest level, this poem becomes an emblem for the kind of intelligence, both abstract and emotional, that lyric poetry can carry, even within its simplest overt expressive modes. And intelligence like this is something worth respecting: it defines a condition of value and offers us an example of psychological intricacy that ought to remind us of what is involved in dealing with other persons. But on this level the specific intelligence is honored only as a fact, as something that comes around on the luggage carousel of high culture. The crucial question is whether each of us as individuals can use that specificity as part of our own repertoire for living our own lives. I think we can give a positive answer to this question by treating the text as exemplifying certain states of mind or attitudes that then become representative for us to the degree that we identify provisionally with them—either as direct articulations of emotions we experience vaguely or as possible emotions we can then bring to bear in thinking about or even projecting on our own relationships with other people.

We can restate these observations in general theoretical terms by claiming that the approach to language emphasized in Western high-culture lyric practices (as well as in other genres) need not be directly opposed to the practices that establish "knowledge." Instead we can show that these performances offer a mode of reflection that can help frame what counts as significant knowledge, and hence how words can carry possible forms of willing. Texts as performances have the semantic status of examples. We do not ask what they denote (which would involve asking who the "you" is in Rich's poem) but how they can serve as labels or models by which we locate aspects of experience they help us to name. Such examples take on value to the degree that they prove representative, that is, to the degree that we can put them to work as aspects of individual self-reflexive processes. That representativeness then has complex social uses because it allows us to interpret and to give words to our own experiences, or even to will attitudes toward our own experiences, which we know are triangulated within a culture and hence can become themselves part of a dialogue with other people. We can thus use the representative examples either to clarify positive aspects of our own experiences and commitments or to spell out contrasts by which we think we differ from the example. At the same time we can use the example both to make interpretations of experiences that others have and to create a space where we can negotiate what we cannot quite put into words. We can use such examples to understand and direct longing without assuming that we have or need the power to find words for everything.

I claim that relying on the power of example offers a more valuable way to approach literary texts than the sociological or political because this stance can mediate between knowing and willing and not-quite-knowing in ways that force us to recognize the density and the singularity of individual situations. And it requires us to pay very careful attention to how words build the frameworks within which that singularity takes on considerable expressive force. We do not need Rich to understand how this society creates problems for those who avow nonnormative sexuality. But we may need Rich to understand how certain emotional states are possible within that social situation, especially states where we learn to hear the "you" and to make frustration generate modes of longing that can be seen as possible bonds among people. And we may need poets like Rich to show us that there are complex psychological fields that open up as we imagine possible links between syntactic structures and mental dispositions. Those structures even make possible ideals of personal agency for which willing what we come to say is a fundamental ethical act: responsibility then lies in how we propose public expressions for aspects of subjective agency that cannot be located as entities; they are manifest only in what we make as we confront our limitations as knowers and speakers.

Such reading practices will not explain Rich's sexual choices or provide political agendas organized by the pains and projections that her poetry dramatizes. But they will enable us to honor what she makes of her situation. And honoring that in turn challenges our own sense of responsibility and can broaden our own capacity to respond to the singular relations between wording and willing that define most significant subjective agency. Aesthetics can be at least a protopolitics because it offers perhaps the only ethical models responsive to the individualities we all abstractly profess to honor.

VI

Although claims about the social value of the aesthetic depend ultimately on positive cases like the one I have just been making, I worry that we cannot be open to these positive cases so long as we remain tempted by what I consider the inadequate conceptual models underlying our most prestigious ideals of critical and pedagogical practice. Therefore as a coda, or perhaps as a grounding of my positive case, I shall develop an allegory to dramatize the limitations of what are now widely shared poststructural models for critical thinking. At stake ultimately is what we can attribute to performativity within works of art. So let us turn to the test case posed by the recent debate between Lacan and Derrida on Poe's "Purloined Letter."[5]

Lacan's reading of Poe's story is fundamentally structuralist. Because the queen tried to hide a letter expressing desires that could not be shown to the king, the narrative must find a path for restoring the letter within a stable symbolic order. And that journey of the letter in turn provides an allegory for the psychoanalytic process of restoring a patient's relationship to that same symbolic order. The analyst must bring agents to reject the imaginary impositions they put on the letters that circulate within society. For in the effort to own the letter we give our fictions about ourselves priority over the domain of social exchange, thereby losing any way of resisting the identifications we make in the order of the imaginary.

But how do we manage to restore the letter to its circulation, and in the process come to terms with our own demand structures? Poe's story offers three positions defining possible subject positions in relation to the letter:

> The first is a glance that sees nothing: the king and the police.
> The second, a glance which sees that the first sees nothing and deludes itself as to the secrecy of what it hides: the queen, the minister.
> The third sees that the first two glances leave what should be hidden exposed to whoever would seize it: the minister and finally Dupin. (32)

The first of these positions illustrates the blindness of authority, both in the form of the unruffled symbolic order that the king represents and in the form of the police inspector's mad empiricism, which obsessively repeats a narrow interpretive framework that is incapable of locating the kind of site a hidden letter is likely to occupy. Neither the king nor the police grant an unconscious. The queen and then the minister, on the other hand, are seduced by their awareness of the hidden letter into thinking that they can see without being seen, so they cultivate a version of imaginary life in which they think they can have the power that stems from being the one who possesses the letter. Only the third position, that of the analyst, realizes that there is no possessing the letter without being possessed by one's fantasies of possession. Only here is it possible to return the letter to its original owner, so that it no longer threatens the king's capacity to serve as representative of a secure public symbolic order.

It seems that Dupin provides a perfect example of the analyst's position. But Lacan cannot allow that conclusion because he is disturbed by Dupin's final gesture—disturbed for what I think are reasons that lead us back to the power of the performative and of limitations inherent in theory's tendency to idealize the analyst's position. Recall this final gesture. Dupin tells us that he not only returned the original letter to the queen, reaping a reward, but he also left his own message in the "blank interior" of the substitute letter he left in the minister's card rack. That message is the following quotation from Crébillon's *Atrée:*

> —Un dessin si funeste
> S'il n'est digne d'Atree, est digne de Thyeste.

Lacan cannot see any positive reason for this outburst, so he concludes that Dupin has also submitted to the imaginary, to fantasies that he cannot be seen and hence can enact unresolved feelings about his relation to the minister. But in imagining himself invulnerable he in fact makes visible his own symptoms. Dupin takes money for returning the letter, as if he could put a public form to private use. And, more important, his replacing the message cannot but be understood as constituting an "underhanded blow" against the minister, "whose insolent prestige . . . would seem to have been sufficiently deflated by the trick Dupin has just played on him" (49). It seems then that Dupin still fears and resents the minister, even after the letter has been returned. So Lacan suggests that the minister continues to represent for Dupin a fear of castration requiring that Dupin deny his own lack. The minister's own vulnerability to manipulation betrays the terror inherent in all attempts to possess the letter by transforming it into a version of the phallus. And that betrayal is accompanied by a challenge that Dupin is afraid he cannot meet because the minister can assume the dandy's role of playing with death, while Dupin has no such defense. Dupin can only take up a manifestly feminine, already castrated position (51), even as his panic generates a corresponding need for violence that undoes his claim to be the one who knows.

I am not the first to find Lacan's own imaginary busily at work in this effort to relegate Dupin's performance to the mere manifestation of symptoms, symptoms that then require our according only Lacan the position of truly disinterested analyst.[6] But I may be the first to use that criticism as a means of highlighting differences between the orientations of poststructural criticism and the modes of discourse emphasizing aesthetic performativity. My basic charge is an obvious one: Lacan reads Dupin's performance allegorically, and hence he cannot honor Poe's efforts to make Dupin a figure for the artist-mathematician that is true genius. But the charge becomes interesting because it allows aesthetic humanism its version of the analyst's position, from which I suggest three basic limitations forcing Lacan's reading to be so reductive about performance: (1) a tendency to treat literary actions as primarily examples within some larger class of phenomena that the theory has the power to explain; (2) a corresponding cavalier willingness to dismiss questions about specific authorial intentions; and (3) his own version of a jealous uneasiness fearful that the text's own powers of singular self-definition threaten his having the last interpretive word about how the letter returns to its place in the social order. Thus in his reading of Poe's story, Lacan simply cannot entertain the possibility that Dupin's final act is a creative response to his situation: namely, an assertion of his power to recast deadly designs and to refigure the interior of the minister's letters so that the minister cannot evade the fact of his defeat and of Dupin's resulting power to judge all the elements of the event. For Poe, Dupin assumes the role of author, capable both of naming the minister's act and of putting it within a history of literary gestures that now Dupin has earned the right to identify with.

Among critics of Lacan and Poe, Derrida proves the most useful for my purposes because he is very sensitive to the limitations of Lacan's truth claims and of his way of positioning the analyst. But keen as he is in the role of theoretical analyst, Derrida proves surprisingly, and revealingly, blind in his own dealing with the roles that Dupin's sense of the performative play in Poe's story. I cannot here recuperate the many facets of Derrida's brilliant arguments. It must suffice to rehearse his criticism of two basic Lacanian assertions: that the letter must return to its place, thereby illustrating that there can be a truth about what appears as lack; and that fiction can be the allegorical means for demonstrating that truth. Then I will try to show that Derrida nonetheless provides little help in elaborating the basic imaginative values at stake in the "Purloined Letter."

Psychoanalysis depends on the ultimate legibility of the hidden letter. That is Lacan's stake in claiming that the letter always returns to its destination. But for Derrida that claim is far too abstract. It ignores the phenomenological consequences of the very possibility that the letter might not arrive at its destination. Even the possibility of nonarrival will affect how we read any letter, since that possibility then belongs to the structure of the entire exchange situation. When the letter does arrive "its capacity not to arrive torments it with an internal drifting" (201). The addressee cannot be sure he or she has the letter intended by the addressor, and the addressor cannot be sure of how the letter sent becomes the letter read. This "internal drifting" then prevents us from relying on any firm distinction between truth and fiction, so it becomes impossible to secure the analyst's authority to make allegorical readings of any fictions, whether they be Poe stories or patient's dreams. In order to postulate an ultimately legible letter, Lacan must ignore the various frames that seem aspects of Poe's story. For the play among these frames requires us to treat all truth claims as positioned within fantasies, and perhaps all fantasies as capable of bearing significant truth statements (as in the case of paranoia). Lacan's own powerful teaching about the irreducible effects of the imaginary ironically make it impossible to make the distinctions about truth and fantasy necessary to stabilize the roles of analyst and patient. So Derrida suggests that only a deconstructive play among these possibilities can sufficiently evade the castration anxieties fundamental to the ideal of truth (184–85).

Now the ironies deepen. Derrida shows that Lacan makes psychoanalysis itself irreducibly performative, for both patient and analyst. It differs from art then only in the effort by both parties to subsume performance under fantasies of telling and receiving truths. But while Derrida's work is always excruciatingly aware of his own performative activity, and of the implications that activity has in undermining any reliance on a philosophical pursuit of proper sense or proper argument, it seems that in writing on Poe he cannot accord Poe the same privilege. In his "Facteur de Vérité"

Derrida concentrates on the circulation of the letter. He says nothing about the action Dupin performs on and within the letter. Instead Derrida relies on an oddly direct general claim about the fatal design to which all letters are prone because of the indeterminate interplay of the true and the fictive. But in Poe's story the fatal design is not one generalized for all letters; it is a specific reference to the minister's deed and to Dupin's power to play the role as judge of that deed. Dupin is not content to point to the fictionality basic to our play in and upon letters. He makes a specific gesture in a specific rivalry with a specific desired effect.

How can theory respond to that specificity? Or how can we expose the limitations of a Derridean model of performance that attributes all the power to the reader's play within the text, leaving the authorial performance only a fiction developed by the reader? First we need what none of the philosophical readings provide: a simple paraphrase of Dupin's final gesture. The quotation may apply both to the minister's deed and, indirectly, to the design of Dupin's own writerly performance. Applying it to the minister's deed is sufficient for recognizing how Dupin claims the power to characterize the society within which the minister really belongs. But if we also take Dupin's statement as suggesting that this letter itself is his deadly deed, we are invited to a more complex sense of what it is that Dupin wants the minister to see, and hence what it is that Poe offers the reader. In effect we are told that this entire story casts these two characters in the role of fraternal struggle. While Dupin cannot quite claim the injured dignity of Atreus, he can make himself a Thyestes to deal with the one who inaugurated the fatal events. And in assuming this allusiveness Dupin can also directly engage the minister's dandyism. Rather than submit to fears of feminization and castration, he can take on another dandy's role, wherein he stages himself as self-reflexively mastering all the threats presented by the minister, since he composes the interior of the letter that the minister must live with. Dupin insists on direct competition with the minister, and he offers a specific act as distinctively his, and hence as the one claim one can make to countering the fact of death. Dupin accepts fraternal strife, and he makes that acceptance the condition of producing something with which the self can fully identify. His is a response to monstrosity not afraid to engage in conflict, and not needing to moralize itself by invoking an authority that then has the power to castrate.

In other words, Dupin does not need theory to direct or justify his behavior. He performs an action that challenges our standard moralities, and that opens domains of artistic practice for which we may need theories. To understand that action, as drama and as metaphor, we need to contextualize it not only by notions of fictionality but also by fleshing out the full dynamics of fraternal strife, especially as a theater within which identity depends on conflict. On the metaphoric level, this sense of conflict takes the form of setting the artist's constructive activity against the powers and the limits of theoretical intelligence. The minister's grasp of psychology allows him an easy victory over the prefect's empiricist efforts to see on the basis only of established interpretive practices. But the minister's power depends on manipulating the needs of others, without fully reflecting on what shapes his own interests. And, in this story at least, that disposition marks the difference between the theorist who claims to know about not-knowing and the artist for whom the crucial act is making an object that can fully compose a distinctive singular position. The artist can revel in the "funeste," making himself monstrous in order to change the terms of fraternal struggle through his power within the letters as they circulate. Dupin can even dream of another way in which letters return, not as secure elements within the symbolic order, but as means of haunting another's memories, since the artist's power may affect even the blank interior of what constitutes our social exchanges.

If we make the reader, and his avatar the theorist, our basic figure for the performative, we risk losing most of what Poe has accomplished. That version of performance allows no deep sense of a strong other, no direct challenge to our own imaginary versions of possessing the letter, and, to return to Rich's poem, no help in redefining ourselves so that we might adapt to those aspects of other persons that call to us.

Notes

1. The only new claim I will be making is the one about wording and willing. I have made claims about performance and an ideal of representativeness on many occasions, perhaps most succinctly in the introduction to my *Canons and Consequences* (Evanston: Northwestern University Press, 1990). I am sorry to keep repeating myself, but I promise to stop if there is any evidence that people are listening, and hence might be bothered by the repetition. I should add that I do think the way my basic claims are combined here is new, at least new for me, as is the treatment of "The Purloined Letter" and its critics.

2. I make an effort in this direction in my "Contemporary Poetry as Philosophy: Subjective Agency in John Ashbery and C. K. Williams," *Contemporary Literature* 33 (1992): 214–42 and in my *Subjective Agency* (Oxford: Blackwell, 1994).

3. For Judith Butler, see *Gender Trouble: Feminism and the Subversion of Identity* (New York: Routledge, 1993); and for Bhabha, see "Postcolonial Authority and Post-

modern Guilt," in *Cultural Studies,* ed. Lawrence Grossberg, Cary Nelson, and Paula Treichler (New York: Routledge, 1992), 56–66. I should also note that my comments below are supported by the theory of performative actions I worked out in my *Act and Quality* (Amherst: University of Massachusetts Press, 1981).

4. Rich, *Your Native Land, Your Life* (New York: Norton, 1986), 97.

5. All the relevant materials, as well as substantial commentary on both thinkers is contained in John P. Muller and William P. Richardson, eds., *The Purloined Poe: Lacan, Derrida, and Psychoanalytic Reading* (Baltimore: Johns Hopkins University Press, 1988).

6. Two essays in particular must be cited for their treatment of Lacan's blindness (both reprinted in *The Purloined Poe*). Jane Gallop suggests that Lacan is ironizing his own authorial position in order to show how it is impossible to escape the imaginary and to occupy the position of pure analyst. And Barbara Johnson offers a less intentionalist analysis of how all the commentators on Poe's story display a dialectic of insight and blindness, or, perhaps better, of the relation between framing and indeterminacy:

> Not that the letter's meaning is subjective rather than objective, but that the letter is precisely that which subverts the polarity "subjective/objective," that which makes subjectivity into something whose position in a structure is situated by an object's passage through it. The letter's destination is thus wherever it is read: the place it assigns to the reader as his own partiality. Its destination is not a place decided a priori by the sender. (248)

But because both base their sense of motive on what we might call a logic of textuality, neither seems to me to place Poe sufficiently in the picture, or, correspondingly, to get at the forces at work within what textuality mediates. Gallop must ignore a basic difference between the specific mode of local self-mocking ironies often employed by Lacan and the usually un-ironized overall thrust of his arguments. It is hard to reconcile a claim to irony with Lacan's repeated insistence in other essays on the structures we must locate in order to describe the circulation of the letter. And Johnson's brilliant sense of contradiction must be content with abstract claims about reading effects that are never tested against efforts to produce agreement, at least insofar as we can also agree to occupy provisionally a single general frame. So long as one does not seek terms that might make such agreements possible, one cannot give literary works as works any significant social power, and claims about readerly differences prove ultimately tautological.

Relevant Publications by Charles Altieri

Subjective Agency: Towards an Expressivist Ethics. London: Blackwell, 1994.

Canons and Consequences: Reflections on the Ethical Force of Imaginative Ideals. Evanston: Northwestern University Press, 1990.

Painterly Abstraction in Modernist American Poetry. Cambridge: Cambridge University Press, 1989.

Act and Quality: A Theory of Literary Meaning and Humanistic Understanding. Amherst: University of Massachusetts Press, 1981.

"Frank Stella and Jacques Derrida: Toward a Postmodern Ethics of Singularity." In *Deconstruction and the Visual Acts,* ed. Peter Brunette and David Wills, Cambridge: Cambridge University Press, 1994.

"Contemporary Poetry as Philosophy: Subjective Agency in John Ashbery and C. K. Williams." *Contemporary Literature* 33 (1992): 214–42.
"Temporality and the Necessity for Dialectic: The Missing Dimension of Contemporary Theory." *New Literary History* 23 (winter 1992): 135–58.
"The Powers and Limits of Oppositional Postmodernism." *American Literary History* 2 (fall 1990): 443–81.
"Going On and Going Nowhere: Wittgenstein and the Question of Criteria in Literary Criticism." In *Philosophical Approaches to Literature: New Essays on Nineteenth- and Twentieth-Century Texts,* ed. William E. Cain, Lewisburg: Bucknell University Press, 1984.

14

"National Literatures" in English: Toward a New Paradigm

Christopher Clausen

That the research agendas of faculty and the classroom syllabi of English departments need not be conceived along national lines is not a radical suggestion; some very significant scholarship and criticism and a number of courses cross national boundaries. Nevertheless, classifications of writers by nationality seems even more ingrained than the division of literary history into periods. Christopher Clausen, professor of English at Pennsylvania State University, here presents the case that abandoning nationality as a primary category would be a major step toward a multiculturalism that is encompassing rather than divisive. For instance, rather than redefining American literature through a new emphasis on conflict rather than unity as many writers of literary history have recently been doing, it might well be more profitable to lay to rest the attempt to intertwine literary history and national characteristics. Largely as a result of a brief "Point of View" statement published in the Chronicle of Higher Education *in 1988 ("It Is Not Elitist to Place Major Literature at the Center of the English Curriculum"), Clausen has been regarded by certain controversialists as representing curricular conservatism, but, as this and other of his essays illustrate, what he opposes is not fresh approaches, but unnecessary polarizations.*

The concept of "national literatures" in English has outlived its usefulness and should be abandoned, both as a way of thinking about literary history and as a way of organizing curricula. Whatever evaluation one makes of them as political phenomena, the nationalisms that gave rise successively to the concept of a distinctly British literature, then an American literature, and now Australian, Canadian, and a host of what are often described equivocally as "new literatures," constitute a barrier to clear thinking about what has long since become an international enterprise carried on in many cultural settings. As the medium that defines the horizon of intelligibility, language is a more principled and useful (though not absolute) basis than nationality for distinguishing one literature from another. To define English literature as "literature in the English language, no matter where or by whom written" rejoins conceptually what has been artificially fragmented, makes possible a genuine multiculturalism in English literary studies, entitles writers who are neither British nor American to more widespread attention, and helps us think more fruitfully about literary relations among authors, literary movements, societies, and periods.

I

For nearly a hundred and fifty years a majority of the people who speak English as their native language have lived outside Europe. Not since the seventeenth century has English literature been only the literature of the British Isles. A powerful case can be made that during the twentieth century, literature produced in Britain has ceased to be the most important limb of what has often been called a tree of many branches, watered from a variety of sources. Cultural nationalists in former colonies have frequently objected to the tree metaphor, pointing out that a tree has only one trunk and arises from a single plot of ground. Let us therefore say that literature in English is now a thoroughly hybridized stock with roots in many soils. The idea that the literary world has a single center from which normative standards and judgments emanate looks not just outdated but quaint. In a postcolonial world, moreover, cultures rarely coincide with national borders. Overlooking the international character of a strain that has mutated so profusely merely disguises, in the name of nationalism, the new phenomenon of a worldwide literature that is the product of no single culture yet exhibits inescapable family resemblances, reciprocal borrowings and influences too intimate for the claim of separateness to be really plausible.

Two factors have made those mutually enriching borrowings and influences more pronounced in the twentieth century than ever before: improved communications and the phenomenon of the international writer, the T. S. Eliot, Malcolm Lowry, Salman Rushdie, or Janette Turner Hospital who can be fitted only imperfectly into a single nation's literary heritage. The decline of the imperial structures that originally spread the English language over so much of the earth's surface has increased the incidence of such national ambiguities, not reduced them. The fact that some writers are conscious nationalists has no bearing on the question of how the literature to which those writers belong should be conceived, or how the discipline that studies them should be organized. Looked at from a supranational point of view, the nationalism of some English-speaking writers is less striking for its own sake than for the extreme similarity of their ways of being nationalists. Literary nationalism in English is itself an international phenomenon that follows its own predictable laws.

To assert that literature in English is more profitably conceived as a variegated whole than subdivided along national lines is not to minimize the importance to a writer or reader of living in a specific place, a particular nation, a distinct culture. It is instead to say that such differences are fluid, ambiguous, and most fruitfully studied by comparison rather than exclusion. Despite the common practices of American literary study, for example, we might learn more about Emily Dickinson's poems by comparing them with those of Christina Rossetti, her British contemporary, than by measuring them against Walt Whitman's or wondering obsessively what relation they have to the Civil War. A persuasive case can be made for studying Mark Twain's *Huckleberry Finn* and Rudyard Kipling's *Kim* (published sixteen years apart) together rather than as the products of two presumably discrete traditions. Authorial nationality as a context is not so much wrong—its importance for some kinds of literary understanding is indisputable—as simply too narrow to justify making it a fundamental principle of division.

The claim that English literature is in a vital sense one need not deny that it is also various but proposes that the arbitrary convention of dividing it along national lines exaggerates a particular kind of difference, does violence to the ways in which literary influence works, and serves purposes that need to be scrutinized rather than accepted without reflection as obvious or worthy. With the arguable exception of countries with long non-English literary traditions, such as India, any "national literature" in English has a closer relation to any other than it has to any non-English literature. In the twentieth century even the most nationally specific historical material has become international literary property. Both the Australian Thomas Keneally and the Englishman Richard Adams have written novels about the American Civil War, while the American Thomas Flanagan has published three novels about the Irish struggle for independence. Another American, Stanley Wolpert, is the author of a novel about the assassination of Gandhi that became popular in many countries. These examples could be multiplied.

To define English literature as I do above may inspire a charge of "essentialism" on not one but two fronts: it may seem to claim that both *literature* and *English* are unvarying categories. No such claim is involved. For my purposes here, literature may be whatever forms of writing literature departments are concerned with—not only novels, poems, essays, plays, but whatever hybrid or completely new forms may result from the modification of originally British literary traditions by people in different cultures with differing tastes and needs. It goes without saying that those traditions, like the English language itself, have been changing throughout their existence, and internationalization has increased both the rate and the range of innovation. Influences reach the contemporary writer in English from many sources (and through many languages) that originate outside Europe. Few writers in any period, however, make sustained literary use of more than one language. Whether by choice or necessity, a writer in English is accessible to the international audience that reads English and not, except in translation, to any other. Moreover, there is little sign that the forms of written English employed in different countries are likely to become mutually unintelligible. Such a development would after all defeat the advantages of using English in the first place, which are commercial and political as well as literary. So long as writers in English continue to use what is recognizably the same language, local variations—whether in England, America, India, or Africa—enrich rather than obstruct the network of intelligibility that transmits such benefits (literary and otherwise) to them and to their readers.

II

In Britain as in other European countries, the concept of a "national literature" arose in the context of nineteenth-century nationalism. Fortuitously, the professional study of nonclassical literatures took shape in universities at about the same time. The result was nearly inevitable: literary curricula were delineated according to nationalistic assumptions that, when examined today, look philosophically dubious and thoroughly old-fashioned. From the start, the notion of a national literature was subject to the same ambiguities as the idea of the nation itself in its murky relation to a race or state, but they seem not to have reduced its power as a model.[1] The surprising thing is that scholars in subsequent ages of literary study, even one that boasts of its theoretical sophistication and denounces ethnocentrism at every opportunity, have largely taken the original nineteenth-century assumptions for granted by extending a new place within the old pattern (and sometimes within the curriculum) to each new nation as it came into existence. Seldom has the continuing intellectual power of nationalism been so well illustrated.

In 1873, Henry Morley's popular *A First Sketch of English Literature* described the relationship between English literature and English nationality in explicit terms: "The literature of this country has for its most distinctive mark the religious sense of duty. It represents a people striving through successive generations to find out the right and do it, to root out the wrong and labour ever onward for the love of God. If this be really the strong spirit of her people, to show that it is so is to tell how England won, and how alone she can expect to keep, her foremost place among the nations."[2] While the religious emphasis strikes a note that must have sounded archaic even to many contemporary readers, the sense that a nation's literature embodies its own distinct moral outlook in a unified way has often been echoed in other countries. In describing the relation of this idea to the rise of English literature as a field of study in English universities, Stefan Collini calls the result "the Whig interpretation of English literature" and declares:

> A constitutive feature of the Whig interpretation of English political history was the insistence on unbroken continuity, and it is noticeable how strongly this same claim was pressed for the nation's literary past. . . . A further important property of the type of narratives to which, generically, "Whig" interpretations belong is that they can order the relevant past in terms of currently prevailing values. Thus, the characterization of the informing spirit of the national literature was subject to constant adjustment depending upon the particular scale of moral values to which it had to be accommodated, and it should be no surprise that in the late nine-

> teenth century English literature was alleged to display . . . character, manliness, duty, and altruism. . . .
>
> Thereafter, it is clear that the very establishment of separate courses in *English* literature at the end of the century in part reflected an increased national self-consciousness.

The First World War, with its perceived threat to the nation itself, hardened this conception of the "national literature" by requiring "the expression of an aggressive nationalism (again overwhelmingly English rather than British or imperial), and the men of letters and the literary professoriat were not slow to make their contribution here. The canon of English literature was mobilized to serve the nation's cause."[3] The concept of literature as a weapon was not a British innovation; by reconceiving its literature in this nationalistic fashion before and during the war, Britain was simply following the lead of Germany and France.

Similar patterns have been repeated in other countries, both European and postcolonial, during the last hundred years. Once British literature came to be seen in nationalist terms, it became probable that the same paradigm would be applied every time another English-speaking country wished to free itself from British domination. The founding of American literature as a distinct field of study echoes the same notes in a similar idiom, perhaps because it occurred almost contemporaneously. Fred Lewis Pattee, the first officially titled professor of American literature, published a history of his subject in 1896 that went through many editions and helped popularize it in schools and universities. The first sentences of his introduction defined literature in terms that had already become conventional: "The literature of a nation is the entire body of literary productions that has emanated from the people of the nation during its history, preserved by the arts of writing and printing. It is the embodiment of the best thoughts and fancies of a people."[4]

After discussing the factors that influenced a nation's literature in a vocabulary based on Hippolyte Taine's famous trinity of *race, milieu,* and *moment,* Pattee went on to defend the existence of a distinct American literature:

> The term *a literature* may be defined as "all the literary productions in a given language."
>
> By this definition English literature would embrace all the writings that have emanated from the race [*sic*] speaking the English lan-

> guage. The writings of America would, therefore, be only a branch drawing life from the great trunk of English letters. But this is not so. It is now generally admitted that the literature of America has become an independent one. It is an exception, and the only exception, to the rule given above. In no other case in all history have there been two distinct literatures written in the same language.[5]

The half-conscious political assumptions here are worth emphasizing. American literature has become "independent" despite its use of the English language. What does independence mean when ascribed to a literature? Simply that the United States itself is a fully independent country. The only justification Pattee thinks necessary for asserting the separateness of American literature is that "we have been for more than a century an independent nation; and we are recognized abroad not as Englishmen in America, but as a distinct type with as marked an individuality as have the English themselves."[6]

Considerably more is being claimed here than that writers are affected by social and political factors. In flat contradiction to his original definition of literature as based on language, Pattee ends by implying that the possession of a separate literature is a necessary and inevitable badge of political independence. Cooper, Emerson, and Whitman had urged long ago that an independent America needed writers with some independence from European influences to establish its own literary traditions. What we have in Pattee is something different: the literary historian, the shaper of curricula, who defines American literature into existence as an entity, a field of study, a national possession like a flag or a navy. The relationship between nationalism and the possession of a "distinct literature" could hardly be clearer.

As in Britain, the First World War gave American cultural nationalism a sharper edge. But the continuing theoretical elaboration of American literature as something distinct took place primarily in opposition not to German but to English literature—necessarily so, because English was the only other literature under which it could plausibly be subsumed. In that respect the assertion of American literary separateness could be described as an act of secession, the first full-blown cultural rebellion against colonialism in the modern world. The nineteenth-century American literature that Pattee and more recent historians describe is a succession of attempts by writers to free themselves and their audience from dependence on English (and sometimes generically European) models, to render American experiences in innovative ways that expressed the national character and paralleled the distinctiveness of American political institutions. By the time Robert Spiller and his colleagues published the third edition of their magisterial *Literary History of the United States,* Pattee's general assumptions could be taken for granted rather than reargued: "American literature," they declared in the "Address to the Reader" that prefaced their three bulky volumes, "is not merely in a state of becoming. Our national history is already long enough to have had its periods of maturing and fruition."[7] The application to literature of a political model of national independence and development had in effect become a matter of common sense, undefended because unchallenged. Thirty years later, even so critical an Americanist as Lawrence Buell could complain about the "cisatlantic hermeticism" with which American literature is typically studied and plead for a greater sense of its postcolonial relationship to newer literatures without fundamentally questioning the national model itself.[8]

When Pattee implausibly described American literature as the only exception in all history to the rule that literature is defined by language, it seems not to have occurred to him that the nationalistic logic he had used to declare American literary "independence" involved abandoning the criterion of language altogether and could easily be adopted in other colonies as they became independent. By the time he published the first edition of his history Canada had been a self-governing dominion for nearly thirty years and Australia was about to become one; both countries were already producing literary works recognizably different from anything being written in the British Isles. For writers in such countries then and later, American literature represented simultaneously a model of independent status and a potential new threat to cultural independence, not only in Canada, where the dangers of exchanging one imperial influence for another were geographically obvious, but also in places as distant as Australia.

Bruce King has described the predictable twentieth-century consequences of the fact that there were now not one but two national models:

> The recent importance of various national English literatures is a reflection of such cultural and political developments as: the dissolution of the British Empire, the emergence of new nations, the weakening of Commonwealth ties, the increased awareness of independence in former colonies, the importance of the United States, and a general, if vaguely defined, feeling that the English cultural

> tradition is no longer relevant outside the British Isles or that it supports the dominance of a British-influenced elite. The break-up of our older concept of English literature, into national literatures, thus reflects the growing cultural fragmentation of the English-speaking world.[9]

As in Pattee and Spiller, political and cultural independence from the former colonial power implies axiomatically both the existence and the desirability of a "national literature." The model is so obvious that King seems not even to notice that his description depends on repeatedly shifting the meaning of *English*—using it sometimes to denote a language, sometimes to identify a country or a unitary "cultural tradition."

"It is difficult to separate nationalism from the search for a native tradition," John Pengwerne Matthews observes in *Tradition in Exile,* his evocatively titled study of nineteenth-century Canadian and Australian poetry.[10] The attempt to create new "national literatures" within the former British Empire has repeatedly led to such anomalies as Matthews describes in the case of the Australian nationalist poet Bernard O'Dowd: "The idea of Australia obsessed him as much as the idea of America had obsessed Whitman, and the American poet remains the largest single influence on his work."[11] Like writers and critics in many other countries before and since his time, O'Dowd equated writing about one's country from a native point of view with creating a separate literature that would symbolize the nation's new status in the world. The problem lies not in the worthiness of the first aim but in linking it with the second, particularly when one makes use of foreign models to assert one's own uniqueness. If a national literature is like a national flag, inevitably every former colony will insist on having one, whose collective unity and distinctness from every other literature must then be energetically defended. The significance of individual writers or literary works from any other point of view becomes a secondary question.

The contemporary novelist Robertson Davies was for many years more highly acclaimed in Britain and America than in his own country, largely because Canadian critics found him insufficiently committed to promoting what they saw as the national identity. At the same time Hugh MacLennan, who wrote about little else, was being hailed at home as the great Canadian novelist. Literary critics and historians in such circumstances become a cultural army protecting the territory and honor of the nation. As with American literature a century ago, the separateness that must be asserted at all costs is cultural independence of the former colonial power; in this paradigm any wavering about full literary independence would suggest limits to the nation's political independence and national character. Sometimes the priority could even be reversed: a defiantly nationalistic literature might help bring the nation back into existence as a political entity. The Ireland of Douglas Hyde and W. B. Yeats is an obvious example. Despite the fact that the notion of national character has been long discredited, the link that nineteenth-century cultural nationalism forged between the status of the nation to which it belongs and the status of the literature that expresses it has never been broken.

III

Below the level of the language that provides the fundamental rationale for their existence, the most important criteria by which American departments of English organize their literary curricula are nationality, period, and genre. Hence the familiarity of such course titles as Twentieth-Century British Drama, the Nineteenth-Century American Novel, Renaissance Poetry (written in a period before the specification of nationality becomes necessary), and lately New Literatures or Postcolonial Literatures, catchall terms that have largely replaced "Commonwealth Literature" as ways of referring to literature in English that is neither British nor American. Similar phrases tend to define the specialties of literary scholars and therefore the way histories of literature—and the discipline itself—are organized. Although the concept of period in particular has been much criticized, the structure as a whole has proved to be remarkably durable. The major recent exceptions to it have been courses dealing with writers who are women or members of ethnic minority groups. Even these courses are usually accommodated to the original three categories by giving them titles such as Twentieth-Century American Women Novelists or The Harlem Renaissance, in which genre is sometimes displaced by the race or sex of the authors but nationality and period remain intact.

Classification according to genre appeals to intrinsic formal qualities; classification by period appeals to the power of history. Although plenty of ambiguities arise on the borderlines between genres or periods (is Gerard Manley Hopkins a Victorian or a modern? what shall we do with closet dramas in verse?), both categories are principled in a way that nationality is not. Time in particular is a far less flexible variable than place, and the sovereignty of history over writers is correspondingly more significant than the fact of belonging to a particular nation, old or new. In the experiences that it permits and denies, the power of history seems more like the power of a language over those of its users who know no other. As we have seen, a nationalistic Australian poet in the late nineteenth century took Walt Whitman as his model. Moreover, it is one of the celebrated ironies of literary nationalism that Whitman was widely admired in England before American critics began to recognize him as a great poet. By the early twentieth century his influence was deeply felt throughout the English-speaking world and beyond it. One can say with absolute confidence, however, that whatever retrospective effects it may have on the ways critics read earlier poetry, *Leaves of Grass* exercised no influence on writers anywhere before the year 1855.

If any fact in literary study is absolute, it is the power of chronology. We take it for granted, and therefore underestimate its importance, because describing it seems to verge on tautology. Temporal borders may be as arbitrary as any others, but wherever we draw them they can be crossed in one direction only and at a single speed. No Victorian writer was influenced by an experience comparable in its concentration of traumatic effects to the First World War; no one still writing in the year 2000 will personally remember it. In comparison with the despotism of history and the scarcely less powerful exigencies of writing in a particular language, the literary significance of nationality, while sometimes considerable, is a thoroughly relative matter, exercised within borders that can be crossed in either direction by an infinity of influences and by writers themselves.

It is not my purpose here to argue for or against genre and period as principles for organizing our knowledge of literature. Nor am I concerned with larger theoretical questions about the most appropriate or "natural" unit of literary study—a single poem, an author, a form, a theme, an era, or the history of culture in a grand sense—except insofar as the nation is identified as such a unit. I want simply to make the case that accepting the principle of multiple "national literatures" in English hides more than it reveals. It elevates parochialism into an axiom of study for historical reasons that have rarely been challenged in recent criticism. Insofar as literary nationalism of the kind I am describing once served a useful purpose—making room first for literary works in English whose authors were not British, then at a later stage for works from cultures that were neither British nor American—that purpose has been achieved. Holding onto the model in which a national literature serves as a badge of independence now actually defeats the original purpose by excessively identifying each writer with his or her own local "tradition," whether that tradition has its headquarters in London or Nairobi, Sydney or New York.

In such a taxonomy, writers from large, powerful nations will inevitably be more widely read beyond (and sometimes within) their own borders than writers from nations that the world regards as less important. A surgeon does not save a limb by amputating it, and perhaps the greatest disadvantage of the existing academic paradigm is that writers who are neither British nor American remain segregated into the category most often referred to at the moment as postcolonial literatures, a label that singles out for emphasis their countries' past subjection to British imperial power. Despite frequent use of a Marxist vocabulary, critics who specialize in this field tend to approve of nationalism in present or former Commonwealth countries; as the Australian Simon During puts it, "nationalism in postcolonial nations has virtues that perhaps it lacks elsewhere."[12] Consequently the term "postcolonial literatures" has a transitional air, as though many of those who use it were awaiting the moment when full diplomatic recognition could be extended to a new cohort of national literatures. As the historical relationship that the term identifies recedes further into the past, the nationalist paradigm dictates another round of fragmentation in the way we think about literature in English.[13]

What would happen if we abandoned the assumption, so well stated by Pattee, that a necessary mark of success in achieving nationhood is the recognized possession of a distinct national literature, and therefore ceased to be quite so intimidated by the customs barriers dividing one country's literary accomplishments in English from another's? I can only hint briefly here at two important consequences. First, a less parochial kind of literary history would become dominant—literary history more on the model of David Perkins's *History of Modern Poetry* than on that of the forthcoming *Columbia History of American Poetry*—with far-reaching consequences for criticism. Abandoning the national paradigm would encourage the development of more flexible and comparative models of literary-cultural interaction. The historical study of literature in English would become more broadly based both geographically and intellectually, a direction in which a variety of New and Old Historicists have been fitfully moving.[14]

Second, English courses would look very different. Nearly everyone now agrees that "coverage" of the sort that English departments aspired to in the days when there was a smaller and more confidently fixed body of literature to be mastered has become impossible. That recognition strengthens the case for more inclusive courses. If, to take one example, effectively "covering" the twentieth-century British novel is impossible anyway, then the specialist rationale for excluding novels that are not British becomes much less persuasive. A course that reflected this discovery might enlarge the understanding of both teacher and students by finally allowing James Joyce and William Faulkner the curricular proximity that their writings demand; putting Toni Morrison in touch with Chinua Achebe; rescuing Patrick White, V. S. Naipaul, Robertson Davies, and Raja Rao from their long incarceration on the margins of a dead empire. Similarly, those of us whose field is nineteenth-century poetry might learn more and teach better if Emily Dickinson and Christina Rossetti were finally allowed to shed light on each other, along with Tennyson and Whitman and (perhaps) the latter's Australian disciple Bernard O'Dowd. The choices, permutations, and new perspectives opened up by this way of conceiving such a course would be nearly inexhaustible. Nothing would be lost except the illusion that by concentrating on a single nation, one can master a discrete quantum of literary tradition.

Despite the ambitions of nineteenth- and twentieth-century nationalism, the idea of the nation—whether defined as an existing state or in nineteenth-century quasi-metaphysical terms—represents no such quantum, particularly when many nations give their own inflections to the same literary language. There is no distinct national character or essence for literature to express, even if we disguise the obsoleteness of the concept by rechristening it "cultural practices." Instead there is something better: a nearly inexhaustible complex of changing cultures and polities that influence each other ceaselessly through a common medium of communication. Literary nationalism is a stage through which scholars and critics go, frequently by necessity, in order to establish the claim of their countries' writers to respectful attention and simultaneously protect them from cultural domination by the metropolis. It ought to be a transitional rather than a final position. Least of all should it be permitted to balkanize forever a collective literary achievement and field of study that offers such extraordinary rewards to exploration as a multiethnic, multicultural whole.[15]

Notes

1. See, for example, H. M. Posnett, *Comparative Literature* (London: Kegan Paul, 1886), in which a chapter entitled "What Is National Literature?" points out the

unsatisfactoriness of a concept *(nation)* that may be defined by language, government, or other factors but then asserts that "the true makers of national literature are the actions and thoughts of the nation itself" (345) and seems untroubled by any ambiguities. For a contemporary critique of nineteenth-century national ideas, see Lord Acton's "Nationality" (1862), in J. Rufus Fears, ed., *Selected Writings of Lord Acton,* vol. 1 (Indianapolis: Liberty Classics, 1986), esp. 418–23. Benedict Anderson, *Imagined Communities: Reflections on the Origin and Spread of Nationalism* (London: Verso, 1983) discusses the sources and ambiguities of "nationness," emphasizing the problems nationalism presents for Marxism.

2. Quoted in Stefan Collini, *Public Moralists: Political Thought and Intellectual Life in Britain, 1850–1930* (Oxford: Clarendon Press, 1991), 360. There is a large recent literature on the history of English as a discipline. Two influential examples that treat nationalism in a general way are D. J. Palmer, *The Rise of English Studies* (London: Oxford University Press, 1965); and Gerald Graff, *Professing Literature: An Institutional History* (Chicago: University of Chicago Press, 1987).

3. Collini, 359–64.

4. Fred Lewis Pattee, *A History of American Literature,* rev. ed. (New York: Silver Burdett, 1903), 1.

5. Pattee, 3–4.

6. Pattee, 4.

7. Robert Spiller et al., eds., *Literary History of the United States,* 3d ed. (New York: Macmillan, 1963), 1:xx.

8. Lawrence Buell, "American Literary Emergence as a Postcolonial Phenomenon," *American Literary History* 4 (1992): 413. "The pedagogy and criticism if not the personal conviction of literary Americanists still for the most part give the appearance of being driven, as Spengemann put it, by 'the idea that an appreciation of American writing depends upon our keeping it separate from the rest of the world' " (414). In attempting to internationalize our understanding of the "American Renaissance," however, Buell seems to take the naturalness of "national literatures" in English for granted.

9. Bruce King, ed., *Literatures of the World in English* (London: Routledge and Kegan Paul, 1974), 2. A few years earlier the Canadian poet-critic A. J. M. Smith saw matters tending in the opposite direction. As a result of "the technological revolution that is altering the whole world," he declared, "Canadian poetry in the fifties and sixties has become more like modern poetry in the United States, England, and France, and less like Canadian poetry in the nineteenth century. The distinction that was once valid between a native and a cosmopolitan tradition has grown rapidly less significant." See A. J. M. Smith, ed., *Modern Canadian Verse in English and French* (Toronto: Oxford University Press, 1967), xviii. More recently the German scholar Dieter Riemenschneider, perhaps reflecting his own country's history, finds danger in the nationalist position and seeks a rather marshy middle ground: "It is perhaps obligatory to steer clear of the Scylla of the 'New English Literatures' and the Charybdis of distinct national literatures in English"; see Dieter Riemenschneider, ed., *Critical Approaches to the New Literatures in English* (Essen: Blaue Eule, 1989), 10–11. His alternative model divides the world into five regions and seems conceptually indebted to the cold-war system of security alliances.

10. John Pengwerne Matthews, *Tradition in Exile: A Comparative Study of Social Influences on the Development of Australian and Canadian Poetry in the Nineteenth Century* (Toronto: University of Toronto Press, 1962), 49.

11. Matthews, 1984.

12. Simon During, "Literature—Nationalism's Other?" in Homi Bhabha, ed., *Nation and Narration* (London: Routledge, 1990), 151.

13. For a well-informed, up-to-date theoretical account of the whole "postcolonial" field, see Bill Ashcroft, Gareth Griffiths, and Helen Tiffin, *The Empire Writes Back* (London: Routledge, 1989).

14. See Robert D. Hume, "Texts Within Contexts: Notes Toward a Historical Method," *Philological Quarterly* 71 (1992): 69–100.

15. With the confessional mode so firmly established in contemporary criticism, probably I should point out that I write as an American who did his Ph.D. in Canada on an English Victorian poet whose chief subject was the religions of India. My director was an Australian specialist in what was then called Commonwealth literature; my committee included a South African, two Canadians, an Englishman, and an American.

Relevant Publications by Christopher Clausen

The Moral Imagination: Essays on Literature and Ethics. Iowa City: University of Iowa Press, 1986.

" 'National Literatures in English': Towards a New Paradigm." *New Literary History* 25 (winter 1994): 61–72.

" 'Canon,' Theme, and Code." In *The Hospitable Canon,* ed. Virgil Nemoianu and Robert Royal. Amsterdam and Philadelphia: Benjamins, 1991, 199–213.

"Moral Inversion and Critical Argument." *Georgia Review* 42 (spring 1988): 9–22.

15

Looking at History

Gayle Greene

The following essay by Gayle Greene, professor of English and women's studies at Scripps College, differs in two special ways from the others in the present collection: the voice adopted is much more personal, especially in the beginning, and it was originally put together as an introduction to the volume Changing Subjects, *edited by Greene and Coppélia Kahn, rather than as a separate essay in itself. In regard to the first difference, as Gayle Greene makes clear in the final paragraphs, an autobiographical mode of writing has become increasingly common among feminists. As she writes: "To say 'I,' to get personal, is a way of centering ourselves, grounding ourselves; to articulate the relation of that 'I' to the social and political forces that have shaped us is a way of making that 'I' more than personal, of reenvisioning the personal as the political—it is a way of saying 'I' while also saying 'we.'"*

The following essay's origin as an introduction to a collection of feminist essays published in 1993 gives it force as a summary of the particular problems now evident to those committed to the feminist movement as well as a call for ways of building on what has been learned and accomplished. The present version differs from the original primarily through the deletion of some of the references to essays included in Changing Subjects. *The concern that academic writers take greater social responsibility and her opposition to such aspects of our culture as "the planned obsolescence of consumerism" and the influence of television set forth in this essay are reflected in her move from literary to direct socioeconomic criticism in her present project, tentatively titled "Cancer Scam: What You Don't Know Can Kill You."*

Leaving Shakespeare

It's by no means clear how a girl like me, coming of age in the California suburbs in the 1950s, got hooked up with Shakespeare in the first place. When I think about high school—the homecoming games and proms, the local drag strip we cruised searching for action, the Mel's Drive-In where we hung out, boy-crazy, clothes-crazy, decked out in crinoline petticoats, charm bracelets, bobby sox, ponytails—it seems a bizarre and eccentric attraction. It was an affair of the heart, I know that: for me, anything interesting or worth doing, anything that makes me do real work—is about love. Not all my loves have been happy or productive, though—far from it: in fact some of the strongest have been tormented and destructive. This thing with Shakespeare—What was it?

I'd been intrigued by *Hamlet* in high school, but it wasn't until my freshman year at college that I was really bowled over by a Shakespeare play—*Richard II*. I was barely seventeen, at the University of Chicago, homesick and lost, and I read *Richard II* in a humanities course. Though this course had little to do with Shakespeare, or with much of anything else as far as one could tell, when I heard the language, really heard it, it was like a spell. I was hooked, caught, cathected, transfixed by that spectacle of ruined royalty, entranced by that sweet sound. I suppose there was something in Richard's adolescent self-pity that validated my own: I too was ready to sit upon the ground and tell sad stories of the death of kings, sure as I was that all was vanity, and certain, also, that I'd been deprived of a birthright. What else could explain my unsatisfactory existence? I was not so critical of Richard as I'd later be, though I was not completely uncritical of him either. I sensed even then affinities between his problems and my own. I had read other plays, but it was Richard, Richard, that ravished me, that struck a chord so deep that it drew me back again and again.

When I think about what else drew me to Shakespeare in those early years, I recall Lawrence Olivier, stunningly blond and anguished in black tights, James Mason, looking distant and Roman in a toga: all that tortured nobility, so tragic, so eloquent—so *male.* I thrilled to Mark Antony's pronouncement over the body of Brutus, "this was a man," and to Hamlet's words to Horatio, "give me that man / That is not passion's slave, and I will wear him / In my heart's core, ay, in my heart of heart, / As I do thee." It didn't occur to me that all this homosocial intensity was obliterating me: the men were grooving on the men and so was I, and it took me years to notice my own absence—such was my alienation from my experience. It was years before I thought about the women in the plays, riveted as I was on those dazzling men, and then it was only working on *The Woman's Part* that succeeded in focusing my attention on them. I suppose falling in love with those heroes was a version of falling in love with movie stars, which I did plenty of in those days—except that it was a more respectable passion, one that I sensed might get me further than a crush on Jimmy Dean. Doubtless that attraction to anguished and inaccessible masculinity was about my father, always a powerful and disturbing presence, or absence, in our so-called family, someone I hadn't a clue how to think about.

Our family went through what a lot of families in the suburbs in the 1950s were going through—that suburban loneliness you could die of, that sense of not being connected anywhere, to anything. But our loneliness was exacerbated by my parents' unconventional arrangements and their politics. We were not a happy family; my parents were always in the process of separating, and, when I was ten, they finally did, leaving my mother that most miserable of anomalies, a woman alone in the suburbs in the fifties, in her forties. My father was mainly away, even when he was around, and he was a womanizer, a philanderer, who was nevertheless oddly devoted to his children and in other ways a nice guy (it took some talent not to get rich as a doctor in those California boom years, but he was an old-style GP who didn't insist on collecting payment when his patients were poor, as they often were). He was Jewish, my mother was not, and when the marriage finally came apart and she changed our name, I was completely confused—I became aware of being Jewish at precisely the time it was denied that I was Jewish, whatever "Jewish" meant. Moreover, at the height of McCarthyism, my parents were lefties, the few friends they had living under shadows, some blacklisted; yet my parents didn't identify wholeheartedly with politics either, so we were lefties and not lefties. We were quite simply without the consolations of any kind of group identity, even oppositional. In those years when everyone was conforming and when, as an adolescent, I wanted nothing more than to belong, conforming was never an option, since I'd been taught so thoroughly that everything out there—the ideology of happy families, of a greater America—was fucked. We were rootless, headless, godless, adrift, and there seemed no way of conceiving of alternatives, no way to imagine any other way of being or living.[1]

I turned, for a sense of other possibilities, to reading. But what I found there was not very helpful: the "tiresome, hysterical pretentious Jewess" of Durrell's *Justine;* Caddie of Faulkner's *The Sound and the Fury,* "doomed and knew it"; Hedda Gabler, fatally fixated on the pistols of her father the general; doomed Brett; doomed Gudrun—all male-authored except for Scarlet O'Hara, whose spunkiness I found irresistible, but who also turned out to be doomed. I found myself, disastrously, in Madame Bovary and Anna Karenina. God knows why they were a comfort, these intense, fragile creatures living at the edge of experience—I suppose it was all that exquisitely expressed anguish: they did their despair so beautifully. I was also drawn to the women of Austen and Eliot, who had more interiority and were occasionally even allowed to survive, but I found their happy endings unlikely. I didn't mind the idea of marriage to Mr. Knightley, but it seemed implausible. By now we know about those death and marriage plots, where they get us, but at the time, in my teens and twenties, this was all there was.[2] The books I needed—the feminist fiction and theory that would help me make the connections between the confusions I was living through and something out there—were only then being written, and it was decades before I would find them (*Martha Quest* was published in 1952, *The Golden Notebook* in 1962, *The Second Sex* was translated into English in 1953: I did not read these until the late sixties).[3]

There was never any doubt that I would study literature: it was the only thing I'd ever really—wholeheartedly, unequivocally—loved. I muddled through two undergraduate majors, in English and Comparative Literature, fulfilling requirements that didn't make much sense (it never occurred to me that they should), living in terror that the computer would spew me out at the last minute and keep me from graduating. (I had transferred to Berkeley my sophomore year, on account of a boyfriend; by October we'd broken up; this ought to have taught me more than it did.) I never got to know a professor, I never had a woman professor in the five years it took to the M.A., and "woman writer" wasn't a category in the curriculum. But in spite of the Berkeley English Department I continued to love reading, and in spite of two dreadful Shakespeare lecture courses I elected to take a senior seminar in Shakespeare, where, turned loose on a play of my choice, I turned to Richard, Richard again, and sunk once more into that sweet despair.

To this day, I don't know whether the decision to go with Shakespeare rather than the novels I lived on was a bad or a good choice—whether it was a choice that reflected (as many of my choices did) alienation from my deepest needs, or whether it actually expressed those needs. It must have expressed something deep—Shakespeare seemed to be something I very badly needed to do, since, when I found myself at Columbia a few years later (a move which, I'm happy to say, was not precipitated by a man), where I was surrounded by exciting activity in the nineteenth century and a vacuum in the Renaissance, it would have made more sense to work on the novel than to persist in a Shakespeare dissertation, a project that turned out to be self-directed. (No one wanted to touch it. The resident Shakespearean said it was "too modern and psychological" and that I "couldn't possibly master all the scholarship" and the resident Miltonist was afraid of offending the resident Shakespearean—though he eventually did read and rubber-stamp it and set up a defense committee and smuggle me out the back door.) It now strikes me as stubborn and perverse to have persisted in doing Shakespeare with everyone advising against it. Perhaps it had to do with Steven Marcus scaring me off George Eliot by naming every German philosopher she'd ever read and assuring me that I'd have to master all of them to write on her. Mastering the Shakespeare scholarship seemed like a piece of cake by comparison (and from what they all said, the dissertation was about "mastery"). Or perhaps there was a lurking fear that working on a woman writer would make me second-rate. Or perhaps it was a deeper fear of those doomed, desperate women that drove me away from those novels I nonetheless devoured.

I now think that my determination to work on Shakespeare had to do with power. Not in any simple or obvious way—not in the way E. M. Forster's Leonard Bast, or Rita in the film *Educating Rita,* latch on to culture as upward mobility; more in the sense of identifying with the male, wanting to be my father. The thing is, our family was so marginal, and I was on the losing side even of it. I knew I didn't want to be my mother, an abandoned wife and mother, without resources, dependent on a man. Although she had stayed with us children, and although she was the more attractive of my parents, I felt complimented when people said I looked like my father: he was the doctor, he had the Yale degree, he had position, power, women, and freedom; she had us. So it was inevitable that I identify with him, and perhaps also inevitable that I work on Shakespeare. Mind you, my father was never even remotely impressed by my doing graduate study in literature—"In all that time you could have been a real doctor" was his comment when I finally got my Ph.D.—so working on Shakespeare wasn't in any obvious way about pleasing him. It was just that I felt that doing Shakespeare would in some way validate me, would prove I was an intelligent person, and I had a fierce need to prove myself an intelligent person. One of the sad ironies of my life is that I expend enormous energies trying to get the attention of people who turn out not to have been looking, over what turns out not to have been the point.

But there was power of another sort that Shakespeare seemed to offer: it had to do with order, with the edifices built by his language, structures I found shelter in—his works seemed a tower of male strength, what Mrs. Ramsay calls the "admirable fabric of the masculine intelligence."[4] I suppose it was understandable, given the shifting sands of my childhood, that I'd flee anything resembling postmodern uncertainties and seek a solid place. Oh, it was always already crumbling, this place, I knew that; that was part of its fascination: but it still seemed to represent something more certain, more clarifying, than anything around me, than the prospects of growing up female in the fifties, than the misery of my mother as she whittled herself down to the confines of her life. I've sometimes wondered how much my attraction to Shakespeare had to do with those wasteful tormented affairs that consumed large parts of my twenties, thirties, and yes, even forties, where I sought validation in brilliant, articulate, narcissistic men who turned out to be using *me* to validate *them,* for whom I functioned mainly as an admiring audience. Still, painful as much of that was, I did not make the usual mistakes: some sort of conditioning that was marching my friends—compulsively and often disastrously—through the steps of marriage, motherhood, divorce, seemed to have been left out of me. Though I thought I wanted to marry (someday, someone, never now), conventional domestic arrangements held a kind of horror for me—houses, entrapment, babies. I did feel an occasional twinge of envy for the matching dish-sets and stemware of my married friends (you could tell those of us who "lived together" from those who were married, in the middle classes in the sixties—by our mismatched dishware), but they didn't seem worth the price, those dishes.

One thing I knew, nothing was as it was claimed to be—and for this, I found corroboration in Shakespeare; for always in his plays, though I was drawn to the grandeur, the splendor, I was driven to ferret out the soft spots, to find the rifts and cracks in the structures. What fascinated me about Richard and Brutus and Othello was the way the fine language masked insecurity, the way those dazzling talkers used words to cheer themselves up, to shore up their realities, while in fact their self-delusions left them wide open to self-deceptions and the lies of others. The thing is, I always knew that people lied: the happy fifties masked insanity, a suicidal military stockpiling. The war in Vietnam came as no surprise, though what did surprise me was that people imagined their protests might halt it (this early cynicism combined with shyness to cut me off from sixties activism in a way I now regret). I always knew that my father lied, but, more important, I knew that my mother lied—in pretending to be all right when she was really coming apart, in telling us to love our father when she hated his guts, in trying to inculcate virtues of love and loyalty in us from a situation that travestied them. So I went for and found in Shakespeare's plays confirmation of my deepest sense of reality—that words were unreliable, that people could build facades and get trapped by them, could get confused and ensnared by their own stories. On this, in *Richard II,* in *Julius Caesar,* in *Othello,* in *Troilus and Cressida,* I wrote obsessively. I was struck by the pairings of worders against worders—Richard and Bolingbroke, Brutus and Antony, Othello and Iago—winners and losers differentiated by their ability to wield words. I eventually wrote my (self-directed) dissertation on *Julius Caesar* and discovered that Shakespeare had homed in on something very big, as he so often does, and was intuiting a cultural moment—no less than the revolution in attitudes toward language that was occurring from the medieval to the modern world, the transition from sixteenth-century belief in language and rhetoric to seventeenth-century skepticism, nominalism, and the plain style.

I guess, in an odd way, "mastering" the master was a way of incorporating his power, harnessing (if not exactly understanding) some of the forces that were driving me, demystifying some of that male mystique. I think what I really needed was time and a safe place from which I could take stock—of myself and possibilities—before I could see what I needed to do next. Shakespeare gave me this. I got tenure from him, developed skills of writing and editing, used him to explore certain questions. I learned from him the way language functions in constructing identity and how this process has social (if not political) implications; I learned about systems (value systems, social systems, philosophical, epistemological, and aesthetic systems) and how at times of stress these are prone to come apart; and I learned a lot about power from him—and long before new historicists or poststructuralists or deconstructionists were naming these issues. His plays corroborated my sense, gleaned from a life on the margins, of the contingency of systems and the arbitrariness of convention, of language as a code to be broken: all of which turned out to be fundamental to feminism. I learned what I needed for my next move, to feminist theory and fiction, and when I learned this I left him.[5]

I now work on Doris Lessing, Margaret Drabble, Margaret Laurence, Margaret Atwood, Toni Morrison, Alice Walker, Paule Marshall—contemporary writers whose novels include me and speak to me as no other literary works do, and whose protagonists survive, often alone, to tell their tales. The route I've taken, from a canonized male writer to women writers, has been traveled by other feminist scholars—in fact it describes the trajectory of feminist scholarship, which began with the study of the canon and shifted to the study of women writers. I think for me it was related to recognizing the influence and importance of my mother, accepting my mother in me, realizing that it was okay to be her. It took me years to figure out that though my mother never finished a degree, she was really the smart one, the strong one, in ways that counted. It took me years to understand that I could never be my father, and more, that I didn't want to. I think this was necessary before I could turn to women writers with a sense that I wasn't doing something second-rate—could approach them with the love and intensity that I'd first brought to Shakespeare.

But in a way, my relationship with Shakespeare has been the most lasting and stable one I've ever had with a man. It was a connection, a kind of wonder, a sort of faith—and faith was something sorely lacking in my life. Probably it was faith in some things I'd have been better off not believing in, but I wouldn't have traded it for a wilderness of critical theory: I wouldn't have wanted my Shakespeare parcelled out in little "isms"—poststructuralism, new historicism, cultural materialism, Marxism, no, not even feminism. It seemed to offer something beyond what was available to me as an adolescent going through a confused coming of age in a low, dishonest decade, and though I probably stayed with him too long, as I tend to do in relationships, it made certain things possible.

It may also, of course, have made other things impossible. Perhaps it did keep my lid on when it should have been blowing off—as the study of literature tended to (was intended to) produce political zombies in those days; perhaps if I'd written that George Eliot dissertation I'd have found a faster route to feminism. I know that it took Simone de Beauvoir, Doris Lessing, Sheila Rowbotham, Juliet Mitchell, Kate Millett, Shulamith Firestone, and Adrienne Rich to show me the connections between the roles my mother and father had played out and the social and political structures out there in the world; it took feminist theory and fiction to make me understand the sexual politics of my interactions with lovers, professors, advisers (yes, even with Shakespeare)—to make me see that the political was personal and was what hurt.

My mainstay writer now is Doris Lessing, and I know exactly why. What draws me to Lessing is her articulation of the problems of women and men in our time and her illumination of connections between those problems and the times; her ability to pierce the veil of hypocrisy, the veneer of official versions, and to deconstruct systems (colonialism, capitalism) and to demonstrate (my old theme) that "listening to the words people use is the longest way around to an understanding of what is going on."[6] Here were women—Martha Quest, Anna Wulf—who were not only facing the sorts of problems I was facing, struggling with their sense of themselves, with commitments to work and to men, but who corroborated my deepest sense of reality: that the most important conversation going on is not usually the one that is being verbalized, that the "small ironical grimace" is what signifies—"you have to deduce a person's real feelings about a thing by a smile she does not know is on her face, by the way bitterness tightens muscles at a mouth's corner."[7] Here was confirmation that if I was inhabiting "another room" (in Lessing's term), so too were others.

The above was written for a seminar on "Gender and Cultural Difference," chaired by Madelon Sprengnether at the International Shakespeare Conference in Tokyo, August 1991. The paper ended with a tribute to Shakespeare, as I supposed it had to, given the occasion. But this is the way I really want it to end—though it's less an end than a transition:

Here was confirmation of my sense that if I was inhabiting another room, hearing another conversation, so too were others. It was, of course, the women's room, where the women were—at least the women I knew, who had always been having another conversation, inhabiting another culture, and whose relation to the dominant culture was just then being articulated by feminist theory. I still turn to books for validation—I think most people who study literature do—but it is validation of another sort, that has less to do with the "male approval desire filter"[8] and more to do with—what? Something closer to, something more like, what I can only call a center. Something less mediated by the law of the father.

What I love about contemporary women's fiction is the way it can empower women, the way it empowered me. I came to feminism through reading and teaching feminist fiction and theory; it was this that showed me connections between my life and the world, connections that were a lifeline because they made me less isolated and meant that change was possible: my confusions weren't a personal affliction, a private calamity, but were "shared, unnecessary, and political" (in Adrienne Rich's term, "Translations"). It is connections like these that I try to teach my students.

Looking at History

Feminism happened when women learned to say "I"—when we learned what Adrienne Rich called the courage to say "I."[9] This required that we unlearn much of what we had been taught, that we de-condition ourselves as women socialized to subservience: being dutiful daughters, dancing attendance on men, putting the needs of husbands, lovers, children first. It necessitated personal and professional risks, often costing marriages, relationships, jobs, promotions. Once we got our Ph.D.s—which was for some of us no mean feat, since writing flew in the face of our own and others' expectations—then, becoming feminist scholars meant retooling and not only learning a new theoretical vocabulary but in many cases *inventing* that vocabulary. And—pardon my nostalgia, I'll keep it to a minimum—it was terrific. It is difficult to overstate that heady sense of possibilities as we set about re-creating our lives, as we felt ourselves becoming authors and directors of our stories.[10] We imagined that our writing was part of an ongoing collective effort, that it might make a difference. We imagined, naïvely, that our "I" was "we"; as DuPlessis writes, "we thought all women were us, and we were all women."[11]

Since then we've realized the limits of that "I" and "we"; contemporary theory has rendered suspect the view of personal experience as a site of authoritative discourse and exposed the essentialist, appropriative implications of saying "we." In some sense the questions Coppélia Kahn and I have asked our colleagues—What experiences made you a feminist scholar and how did your feminism affect the way you teach and write about literature?—flew in the face of current theoretical positions, in assuming that writing grows out of experience and expresses a self, since both "self" and "experience" are discredited categories. "Yet it remains true," as DuPlessis says, "that feminist criticism exists, that it came from the women's movement, . . . that some of the 'we' in or around these pages did some of this: invented and sustained a major intellectual renaissance—possibly even a 'paradigm shift'—in the past twenty-odd years."[12]

It also remains true (though narrative itself has been called into question) that stories, stories about the self, stories by women and about women's selves, had enormous power and continue to have power in the creation of feminist consciousness.[13]

At a time when feminism has lost much of its political edge and is undergoing assaults from all sides, it is important that we learn to say "I" and "we" again, though "I" and "we" are not so simple.[14] In recent years feminism has come to seem even more endangered, more cut off from a popular and a political base, more threatened by conservative tendencies from without and by divisions from within. "Better get it on record before it disappears," as Ann Jones quipped when I told her that Coppélia and I were working on an anthology, a remark that has haunted me. As Annette Kolodny urges, we need "to take responsibility for recovering our history," lest others write it for us.[15] Rich's injunction in 1979—that we "come together telling our stories"—has a new urgency.[16]

Feminism has already disappeared once in this century, and we are now living through the second backlash that's occurred within fifty years. The similarities between the first reaction, immediately after women won the vote, and what's going on today are chilling. In fact the word "postfeminist"—which sprang to the pages of the *New York Times* in Bolotin's notorious 1982 article that described young women as disaffected with feminism, as seeing feminists as man-hating, masculine, lesbian, militant, and hairy-legged—was actually first used in 1919, when (as Nancy Cott tells us) "a group of female literary radicals in Greenwich Village" founded a new journal declaring an interest "in people . . . not in men and women"; they called their stance "postfeminist."[17] Assuming that women's rights are all won, women forget; and worse than forgetting, they make "feminism" a dirty word, a "term of opprobrium," as Dorothy Dunbar Bromley said in 1927.[18] By the 1950s there were fewer women in higher education—fewer Ph.D.s, fewer women on faculties—than there had been in any decade since 1900.[19]

"Postfeminism" today is not just a media hype, though the media have gleefully pushed it: backlash is evident in the attitudes of the young, in the erosion of civil rights and gains made by women and minorities, in the virulent reactions against change both within the academy and without.[20] It is further evident in tendencies to blame feminism for everything from the breakdown of the family to the increase in violence against women—in the "prevailing wisdom" that "it must be all that equality that's causing all that pain."[21] What equality? one might well ask, when old inequalities continue and new ones exist for which new terms—"the feminization of poverty," "the glass ceiling"—have been invented. "We've managed to enter a postfeminist world," as Wendy Kaminer says, "without ever knowing a feminist one."[22]

In 1985, Betty Friedan described "the new generation" of women as "each thinking she is alone with her personal guilt and pressures, trying to 'have it all,'" women "almost as isolated, and as powerless in their isolation, as those suburban housewives afflicted by 'the problem that had no name' whom I interviewed for *The Feminine Mystique* over twenty years ago."[23] Anita Shreve's interviews with women in consciousness-raising groups, fifteen years later, demonstrate how women who have struggled to "have it all" find themselves burned out and alone, and how even those whose lives were transformed by the women's movement now dissociate themselves from feminism.[24] Ruth Sidel's *On Her Own: Growing up in the Shadow of the American Dream* analyzes the discrepancy between what young women expect of their futures—their fantasies that they will move into prestigious upper-middle-class jobs like those portrayed in the media—and the low-paying dead-end jobs that are actually awaiting them.[25] What such studies show is the dead end of career feminism, the bankruptcy of a feminism imagined as "having it all," and the increasing isolation and bewilderment of women who seem to lack even the terms to analyze their situations—though "the problem" is no longer without "a name," since feminism has been naming it for twenty years. They also confirm—what one senses working with students—that young people have bought into an ideology of individualism and materialism that incapacitates them from challenging the system or even from realizing that it is in need of change.

These are bad times for women—and for children and minorities and poor people and old people and working people and what's left of the left; and this larger problem, a system losing its grip and thrashing about in search of scapegoats for its failures, is probably not something feminist scholars can single-handedly change. But the difference between the first wave of feminism and this second wave is precisely in the existence of feminist scholarship, of a large and diverse and vital body of work that constitutes a significant oppositional force. It is here that we've presented fundamental challenges to the structures and institutions of society—marriage, the family, gender roles, the academic disciplines—and to the structure of knowledge itself. There was no equivalent to this in the first wave of feminism. In this, critical theory has been an invaluable tool, for it has provided means to dismantle epistemological categories and reveal systems as systems, as conventional rather than "natural." This means that feminist scholarship is extremely important; far from being irrelevant, as academics are too prone to feel, we have a real mission. Our task as teachers and scholars is to develop critical and political consciousness in those who are coming of age in a world dominated by Republicans and reaction and cynicism and fear.

Yet it's discouraging to see how little feminist awareness has filtered out beyond the walls of academia, how badly feminism is misrepresented and misunderstood. Out there in the so-called real world, most women go their ways, working in underpaid dead-end jobs, continuing in exploitative relationships, and generally living as though the women's movement had never happened. Most women—if my students and nonacademic friends are any indication—have no understanding of what the women's movement is about. Most have accepted the media smear of feminists as bra-burning, hairy-legged, man-hating fanatics and have no sense that feminism might have anything to do with the problems they face in their lives. I remember when Gilligan's new research on teenage girls, articulating the crisis of confidence that hits girls at age eleven—a crisis from which most never recover—made the *New York Times,*[26] a very intelligent doctor friend of mine reacted the way we used to with our conversion "clicks"; how she Xeroxed the article and took it around to the nurses in her hospital who similarly thought it was big news—these same nurses who would never in a million years identify with feminism. But Gilligan's work has been around for a long time, long enough to have drawn fire from feminists who have been blasting away at it for its essentialism, its class bias, etc. Of course her assertions don't apply equally well to all women (whose do?) but how is it that we haven't realized how useful her differentiation between the way women (some women) and men (some men) approach problems might be to the many women struggling in the professions, isolated in male-defined hierarchies and environments that convince them, when they approach a decision differently from their male colleagues, that they are crazy and alone, as women in the 1950s were convinced they were crazy and alone? Seems like we've failed to communicate. Or maybe we just haven't cared.

I remember talking to women at the women writers' conferences in Dubrovnik in 1986, 1988, and 1990. It's becoming more and more the case that what goes on between the talks is more interesting than what goes on in the talks; usually what I return with these days is a wry sense of the sociology of a conference. Anyway, I spent a lot of time during those weeks talking with women from Yugoslavia, Switzerland, Germany, Hungary, England, Italy—some of them graduate students, some of them lecturers, most living on shoestring budgets, developing their feminist scholarship and fledgling women's studies programs at considerable cost and risk. These women had taken great pains and expense to get themselves to this "international" (U.S.-dominated) conference, and many of those I talked with did not feel their efforts were well rewarded. Many were mystified by papers on the repositioning of female subjectivity, on subtle delineations between Professor X's and Professor Y's ideas of subjectivity, theories spun off other theories that seemed to touch down nowhere. I heard outrage at how rarely these papers addressed questions of social significance or social change. While these women were looking to feminist scholars in the United States, where the women's movement is still stronger than anywhere in the world, we were purifying our theoretical apparatus, refining our relation to Derrida and Lacan, fine-tuning our definitions. I'm not saying that such definitions are without point—only that they are not the whole point. I came away feeling that the sense of disappointment and betrayal that I heard from European women was justified, and that it pointed to a major failing of academic feminism in the United States.

Marianne Hirsch and Evelyn Fox Keller begin their anthology *Conflicts in Feminism* with the observation: "A decade ago, we thought of ourselves as part of—even in the vanguard of—a movement that then seemed capable of changing the world. We thought of feminist theory as an arm of that movement, as providing a radically new, and potentially revolutionary wedge for rethinking, and accordingly, for reshaping the social, political and economic world in which we lived."[27] They conclude with the admission that "however illuminating the essays here may be about the nature of the conflicts that currently engage feminists, what remains unexplained is why feminist theorists find themselves with so little forward momentum at this particular moment in time" (385). This is a real question: at a time when it's more urgent than ever that we make ourselves heard, we seem to have lost our voice. As bell hooks says, the feminist movement has not "had an ongoing radical focus which addresses many people . . . it is our task (and here when I say 'our' I mean any of us who are committed to revolutionary feminist movement) to work at challenging and changing the focus, the direction of future feminist movements."[28]

Following hooks' precedent, I use "we" in the following pages to refer to those of us who are committed to change. I'm assuming that despite the problematization of this pronoun, despite the rifts within feminism, there is this much agreement: that we who still call ourselves feminists still agree that we want change, and our notion of change is not fundamentally different from what it was.

Changing the Focus

We—feminists in academia—inhabit an environment that is unbelievably hostile to what we do. This has got to be remembered, and it can hardly be overstated. Feminist criticism grew up in and was shaped by institutions dominated by men and dedicated to a tradition that has never served our interests; and in many ways, it shows. What has happened with women in academia is a microcosm of what has happened with women in society—and it is what always happens, historically: a few women are let in so that there are a few women in visible positions who can be pointed to as evidence that women have made it; meanwhile the majority of women are left where they always were. This means that much of what has succeeded in academia has been allowed to succeed because it's the kind of feminism institutions can live with. A theoretical discourse that's preoccupied by increasingly subtle deconstructions of subjectivity and experience is unlikely to be much concerned with changing people or experience; it's no accident that this is the going thing.

Feminist scholarship provokes as much, if not more, rage and hysteria today than it did in the mid-seventies, when Carol Neely and Carolyn Ruth Swift Lenz and I began work on *The Woman's Part.* This is evident in that 1988 *PMLA* attack on feminist criticism of Shakespeare by Richard Levin, enthusiastically supported in letters in subsequent issues,[29] which demonstrated, among other things, that despite the fact that the male power-base of institutions remains substantially unchanged, and despite reactionary forces proliferating against us, the old boys really do believe that we have taken over. And this turned out to be the tip of the iceberg, for attacks on what is now termed "political correctness" have made it clear how much opposition there is to radicalism in the academy, how real and dangerous the backlash is.

Yet it would be simpler if the enemy were always this obvious, the guys who attack us in public forums: what's more insidious is the enemy who has outposts in your head, as Sally Kempton argued in that wonderfully sassy early feminist essay "Cutting Loose."[30] Rachel DuPlessis admits to anxieties "to 'prove' something (unknown) to someone (unknown)"; Carolyn Porter struggles with questions of "male identification"; Betsy Ermarth warns of the power of the patriarchal compliment that takes you aside and seduces with the promise, "you are not like other women."[31] Jane Tompkins describes her initial embarrassment encountering "women's studies" ("how pathetic, I thought. . . . And in such bad taste").[32] Miller describes the loss of status incurred when one turns from "real" scholarship to the study of women writers[33]—a loss I can vouch for in the change I felt in people's attitudes when I left Shakespeare for contemporary women's fiction, although this was the boldest move I'd ever made. "You are too good to need to do that, to jump on that bandwagon," I was warned by an eminent Shakespearean whom I'd long admired. (He was wrong, it wasn't a bandwagon but a backwater, in the sense that it bounced me off the gravy train of grants and goodies that come with a conventional slot; there would have been much more respectability in staying with Shakespeare than moving in with that dubious lot—contemporary writers, *women* writers, what's more.) The signals reach us, directly and indirectly, through cajolery, flattery, warning, implicit and explicit—if we heed them we are rewarded, if we resist, we are dropped; and they are so subtle and persuasive that we may bend to them without noticing, without noticing how they have bent us out of shape.

At a time when traditional gender roles and relations are being energetically reasserted, there are strong incentives for not identifying ourselves as feminists, or even as women. The "feminine" has always been viewed as unprofessional, and now, as women are actually moving into the professions, it is more than ever suspect. At a time when feminism is being declared the root of all evil from the right and being dismissed as passé from the left (what these wildly contradictory positions have in common is the erasure of feminism), at a time when feminism is the new "F-word" both within academia and without, even feminist scholars will find ways of avoiding it in book titles, course titles, program titles. Susan Bordo suggests that the "gender scepticism" implicit in the essentialism debate may be a way of allowing us to eradicate "gender" as an analytical category rather than admit to our own ambivalences;[34] Hester Eisenstein suggests that "having failed to create a feminism that captures the imagination of women, we question whether women exist."[35] While it has been important to interrogate the language of identity and be clear about the implications of saying "we," pronouns may not be the most burning issue of the day.[36] Given the virulence of antifeminist and racist backlash, this is no time to become transfixed by our own ingenuity.[37]

It is strange, as Bordo points out, that white feminism, "now critically scrutinizing (and often utterly discrediting) its conceptions of 'female' reality and morality and its 'gendered' readings of culture *barely more than a decade after they began to be produced*" is being so fiercely attacked as " 'resistant' to recognizing its own fictions of unity."[38] As Bordo suggests, "where once the prime objects of academic feminist critique were the phallocentric narratives of our male-dominated disciplines, now feminist criticism has turned to its own narratives, finding them reductionist, totalizing, inadequately nuanced, valorizing of gender difference, unconsciously racist, and elitist" (135). Being a feminist literary scholar seems more and more to be "a matter of keeping abreast of the current repudiations," as Molly Hite says.[39] But I sense a self-defeating tendency in much of this, a critical implosion that has the sound of a grinding halt. I wonder, also, if turning in on ourselves with this fierce self-scrutiny isn't a form of self-erasure, an analogue to our obsession with thinness, a way of assuring ourselves and others that we'll take up less space—a kind of professional/pedagogical anorexia.

I'm by no means advocating that feminist criticism divorce itself from theory or be "untheoretical," though I do think we need to think about theory more broadly and enlist it more judiciously. Actually, there is no such thing as an untheoretical position, though there are untheorized positions—feminists have long known this—but theory has a more general meaning than we in literary criticism have come to think. It means, or at least it used to mean and still does mean to people outside lit. crit., "a lifting of thought to a more abstract, often more systematic level in an effort to provide a framework or grounding for interpretation and/or explanation" (as Elizabeth Minnich defines it). In fact there are more kinds of theoretical positions than are dreamt of in our current philosophies, as Barbara Christian and bell hooks remind us.[40] The fact that "theory" has come to be so narrowly associated with the ideas of Lacan, Derrida, Barthes, says something about what's happened in literary studies, where (once again) a group of white male-authored canonical texts is at the center.

In 1985, in the introduction to *Making a Difference,* Coppélia and I urged that feminist scholarship ally itself with poststructuralism.[41] But now I wonder: in this argument for alliances, who's being allied with whom, and for what? I wonder if this wasn't (at least partly) a pitch for intellectual respectability, for legitimization—a pitch that was never even necessary, even within these terms, since American feminism has from the beginning cut its teeth on ideas from France: Ann Jones, Leslie Rabine, Jerry Ann Flieger, Molly Hite, Betsy Ermarth, Carolyn Porter, and others have described how crucial theory was in their development, how it opened up questions and categories and provided tools for reconceptualization: the usual categorization of French feminism as "theoretical" and American feminism as "pragmatic" collapses under such testimonies. It seems a great waste of time to expend further energies establishing our credentials, demonstrating how feminism fits in with or around Lacan, Derrida, Lyotard, or how we're superior to our benighted compatriots (Showalter and Gilbert and Gubar are the favorite targets).

I'm not the first to worry that theory has become the new standard-setter, the source and center of professional prestige,[42] or to wonder how it happened that "theory" got to be defined as something that takes precedence over feminist theory, when—as Miller asks—"isn't the discovery (Beauvoir's) that femininity is produced by a complex concatenation of discursive and nondiscursive events as exciting as the proposition (Foucault's) that sexuality (as it turns out, male) is inseparable from the effects and articulations of power?"[43] (Why, right here at Scripps, at a women's college dedicated to the education of women, any course in feminist theory was refused credit as "the senior seminar": the senior seminar is in "real" theory and is taught by a white male.) Nor am I the first to wonder how "cultural studies" got defined as something different from "feminist studies": what else has feminist scholarship ever been but the study of culture? I'm troubled that we may be consenting to this hierarchy when we urge alliances, or when we urge feminists to "get theory."[44]

Why do we not insist, rather, that these guys seek alliances with *us*, that they learn our language? Because this is not an option, because we are still second-class citizens; because (as Miller notes) "the perception of authority diminishes in direct proportion to the speaker's proximity to feminist discourse."[45]

So what it comes down to, again, is power, who's at the center, who's King of the Mountain. The issue is legitimization, validation—personal, intellectual, institutional power—with theory as the means, in a set of moves that reinscribes traditionally gendered relations. Since only those who do theory are invited to speak in prominent places, get offered glitzy jobs, high salaries and other perks, is it any wonder that everybody's doin' it, and that our students are spinning out imitations—often rote, formulaic, and mindless for all their ingenuity—as fast as they can? Who wouldn't want to be a star? The problem is not with "theory" per se or with theory at all, but with the enlistment of theory in this scramble for power and position.[46]

At a conference on Feminism and Representation (Providence, 1989), for example, the stars came late, left early, and collected large honoraria, while the rest of us talked for free. The two-tiered structure, with plenary sessions for the stars and lots of little seminars for the peons, was a statement about hierarchy; but what was more troubling was the high positive correlation between stardom and incomprehensibility and that there were so many aspiring starlets in the seminars who were doing such convincing imitations of stellar incomprehensibility. Since most of the stars left right after they had given their papers there was no opportunity for dialogue, though there was much discontented muttering of the sort I'm venting here—and perhaps the fact that such muttering is making its way into print suggests that the tide is turning.[47]

The question is, once we've "got theory," what do we do with it? What's it for? Who's it for? What Tey Diana Rebolledo says of Chicanos applies as well to feminists: there's a risk that in using theory to legitimize ourselves we may actually be "privileging the theoretical discourse" in a way that "de-privileges ourselves."[48] Theory serves us well as a tool of radical critique of the systems that subordinate us, but it does not serve us well as a tool for personal power and higher salaries (though what do I mean—"us"?). In the early days of feminism, I remember a lot of talk about the dangers of co-optation; I don't hear a lot of that kind of talk any more, now when the disconnection of theory from the political and its connection to the star system endangers us more than ever. As hooks suggests, "Living as we do in a culture that promotes narcissism, that encourages it because it deflects attention away from our capacity to form political commitments that address issues rather than identity," we often seem "more engaged by who was speaking/writing than by what they were saying"; such "cults of personality" have "severely limited feminist movement."[49] Stardom is about hierarchy, self, career, commodification; it is not about dialogue or action or collectivity or the political (except in the most strategic, self-serving sense).

I realize it's not always easy to distinguish between those uses of theory that have social and political value and those that do not, when everyone who uses theory claims to be radical ("subversive" and "oppositional" are fashionable words, but increasingly void of political content); and I realize also that this is a judgment that will vary according to where one is. There is always the risk of dismissing something as incomprehensible or inconsequential because you haven't worked it through sufficiently to see its implications—but I think it's important to take that risk, to try to differentiate between criticism that's useful and not useful, to ask (as Modleski says) "what's in these developments *for feminism* and for women?"[50] As Jouve says, "you are still in the same business as the artists themselves. The business of making sense of life"; "Unless criticism springs out of genuine analysis of the real world, and in its turn affects it . . . then it inhabits the realm of fantasy."[51]

I am a literary critic who is concerned with social change. The books I've found most valuable in my work on contemporary women's fiction in the past several years—Rachel Blau DuPlessis's *Writing Beyond the Ending,* Molly Hite's *The Other Side,* Rita Felski's *Beyond Feminist Aesthetics*[52]—enlist theory to illuminate the relation of literature to change. DuPlessis demonstrates ways that twentieth-century women writers challenge the gender ideology inscribed in narrative forms; Hite describes ways that these challenges are as radical as those of canonized "postmodern" male writers; and Felski examines the problems of defining a "feminist aesthetic." In *Changing the Story* I analyze feminist metafiction as emerging from a decade of rapid change for women and developing narrative strategies that allow readers to work through processes of change. Such approaches enlist theory, or theories, to interrogate cultural assumptions and categories, to explore interactions of literary conventions with social conventions, with an eye to feminist politics.[53]

I'm urging that feminist scholars write with a clearer sense of responsibility to a social movement, that we try to revitalize some important connections—between ourselves and our audience, our writing and its effects. That we think about reaching people outside academia who might actually read our books if they were more interesting. I'd urge that we ask, of our books, articles, and conference papers: Is this a necessary or useful idea? To whom is it necessary or useful? Am I saying this to clarify some idea or information or to insert myself into a critical discourse whose purpose I have not questioned, perhaps, even, to place myself beyond accountability by being so ingenious that no one can possibly understand me?[54] I'd urge that we stop dancing attendance on those who still have power to confer rewards and benefits (and there are endless versions of this insidious game), that we envision our audience not as that patriarch in our head who may finally confer approval on us, but think of ourselves, rather, as reaching people to whom *we* have a responsibility, whom *we* might empower, whether or not they can do us any good. I'm not saying that everyone needs to leave Shakespeare to work on women writers: it's important that feminists not abandon the canon and the study of premodern periods to those who have traditionally held them. But I do think that everyone needs to do some equivalent to "leaving Shakespeare" in terms of thinking through questions of purpose and audience—Who are we writing for and why?—and that we try to balance career-building with concern for collectivity.

I'd urge that the tyranny of trends, the new for its own sake, be resisted—and I can't help associating this with the planned obsolescence of consumerism, the three-minute attention spans of students educated by television, and the flash and trash of show-biz, which academia seems to resemble more each season.[55] We should exercise some independence of judgment and not let novelty and ingenuity be our standards. Nor do I think that practical criticism ought to be despised just because it isn't spinning out a new theory, a theory that often, as Christian suggests, rides roughshod over the complexities of the literature itself.[56]

I'd even argue that it's okay to love literature, to teach that reading can be a pleasure, rather than being hard, closed, and the possession of an elite. I'd go further and say that reading can serve radical ends—and in fact it will do so the more effectively, the more accessible it is.

Reinstating the Subject

In the years since Coppélia and I began our anthology, the autobiographical mode has become more prominent. Miller notes that though "the authority of experience" was basic to feminist inquiry from the start, most academic feminists have used a depersonalized, academic style, in order to pass, but that some also deployed experimental, autobiographical, and personal modes; this created "a contrapuntal effect, breaking into the monolithic and monologizing authorized discourse."[57] Miller cites DuPlessis's "For the Etruscans," Carolyn Heilbrun's *Reinventing Womanhood,* Carolyn Steedman's *Landscape for a Good Woman,* Patricia Williams's "On being the object of property," Ann Snitow's "A gender diary," bell hooks's *Talking Back,* Cherrie Moraga's *This Bridge Called My Back,* and others, as evidence of a "turning point in the history of critical practices" (x). She poses important questions (2–3): Why is this form of writing appearing now? Is this a gendered form? Is it trivial, self-centered? Oppositional or recuperative? Is it "antitheory" or "a new stage of theory"?

Miller speculates that the surfacing of such writing now has to do with "the waning of enthusiasm for a mode of Theory, whose authority . . . depended finally on the theoretical evacuation of the very social subjects producing it" (20); and everything I've said here indicates my agreement. But I'd emphasize—as she does—that personal criticism, rather than a practice pitted against theory and reinforcing the usual binarisms (personal against public, female against male, concrete against abstract), may be imbricated in theory in a way that broadens the notion of theory; and that, far from turning in on itself in a response that is trivial, self-indulgent, "merely personal," such writing is "engaged."[58] Saying "I" may provide the condition of a new kind of contract, "the chance for a vividly renegotiated sociality" and "an enlivening cultural criticism."[59] Personal criticism need not be soloistic, self-indulgent, or naive, "a search for that lost, pure, true, real, genuine, original, authentic self,"[60] but may demonstrate—as Biddy Martin and Chandra Talpade Mohanty describe the essays in *Yours in Struggle*—how "individual self-reflection and critical practice might translate into the building of political collectivity."[61]

To say "I," to "get personal," is a way of centering ourselves, grounding ourselves; to articulate the relation of that "I" to the social and political forces that have shaped us is a way of making that "I" more than personal, of reenvisioning the personal as political—it is a way of saying "I" while also saying "we." The essays in this book speculate about the collective implications of saying "I."

Reinstating the subject is important for reasons explained by Joan E. Hartman and Ellen Messer-Davidow, in a brilliant collection of essays, *(En)Gendering Knowledge,* that argues for the necessity of a "feminist social epistemology." The essays in this volume demonstrate why feminist inquiry needs to remain linked to an investigation of the ways reality is constructed—to a sense of "knowers as social agents, knowing as social practice . . . knowledge as productive of social consequences."[62] This entails acknowledging the knower as part of the process by which knowledge is produced, inscribing ourselves into our discourse, "activat[ing] our identities,"[63] and presenting our knowledge as "corrected by critical reflection and self-reflection."[64] To our own social locations, to reveal "the differences [our] own race or sexuality, class and gender, have made in the knowledge [we] produce," is to "generate new ways of seeing the world,"[65] whereas to disown ourselves and hide behind a fraudulent objectivity is to perpetuate the paradigms of knowledge we wish to challenge. Yet white feminists have been more willing to scrutinize other groups—working-class women, women of color—than to turn the same lens on ourselves: "Why have 'we,' individually and collectively, been so unwilling or unable to take a good look at ourselves?"[66] Hartman and Messer-Davidow demonstrate how crucial "looking at ourselves" is to the project of feminism, how important a feminist social epistemology is to restoring agency, to reinvigorating "our capacity as agents to act as well as to know" (6), in order that we may "rejoin what we put asunder in the early days of the Second Women's Movement: our intellectual inquiry and our social activism" (1).

Notes

1. Marge Piercy's "Through the Cracks" captures this "isolation and dead-endedness" of the 1950s: "what was lacking" was "a sense of possibilities": "there was little satisfaction for me in the forms offered, yet there seemed no space but death or madness outside the forms"; "nowhere could I find images of a life I considered good or useful or dignified"; "I could not make connections" (*Partisan Review* 41 [1974]: 208, 215, 207).

2. I did not realize it, but I was not alone in seeking in fiction for the meaning and connections missing from my life: Doris Lessing, Margaret Drabble, Gail Godwin, Marge Piercy, Erica Jong write of characters growing up in these years who turned to reading this way.

3. Doris Lessing, *Martha Quest* (New York: New American Library, 1964); Lessing, *The Golden Notebook* (New York: Ballantine, 1962); Simone de Beauvoir, *The Second Sex* (New York: Knopf, 1952).

4. Virginia Woolf, *To the Lighthouse* (New York: Harcourt, Brace and World, 1955), 159.

5. It wasn't this simple, of course. I am omitting a good deal, making it all sound much clearer and cleaner than it was. I am leaving out the pain and confusion and loneliness—what I was like plodding through a Ph.D. program with the certainty that what awaited me when I got out, in the mid-seventies, would be unemployment; what it was like to be buffeted about by those strong sexual attractions against which there seemed no defense, that combined with the coldness of Columbia to leave me feeling unfit for life, let alone able to imagine a future. Perhaps this is what narrative does, looks back from an end and selects the steps leading to that end; or perhaps that pain is the subject of another story. The truth is that both stories are true—that despite the anguish of those years, there was this thinking, writing being struggling to survive and make sense of it. I write therefore I am. Of course there was also a lot of luck (though there was a bit of back luck too), and a lot of white middle-class support to fall back on—both financial and emotional—from a family that, despite its fuck-ups, had a way of coming through.

6. Doris Lessing, *Ripple from the Storm* (New York: New American Library, 1966), 7.

7. Doris Lessing, *The Summer Before the Dark* (New York: Bantam, 1974), 62.

8. Which "instructs by quiet magic women to sing proper pliant tunes for father, lover, piper who says he has the secret." Honore Moore, quoted in Nancy K. Miller, *Getting Personal: Feminist Occasions and Other Autobiographical Acts* (New York: Routledge, 1991), 36.

9. Adrienne Rich, "When We Dead Awaken: Writing as a Re-Vision," in *On Lies, Secrets, and Silence: Selected Prose, 1966–1978* (New York: Norton, 1979), 45.

10. Nancy K. Miller, *Getting Personal,* 37–38 (see note 8).

11. DuPlessis, Rachel Blau, *Writing Beyond the Ending: Narrative Strategies of Twentieth-Century Women Writers* (Bloomington: University of Indiana Press, 1985), 101.

12. DuPlessis, 97 (see note 11).

13. Rita Felski argues that "the autobiographical novel continues to remain a major literary form for oppressed groups, as a medium for confronting problems of self and of cultural identity which fulfills important social needs" (*Beyond Feminist Aesthetics: Feminist Literature and Social Change* (Cambridge: Harvard University Press, 1989), 78, 169. In chapter 2 of *Changing the Story* (Bloomington: University of Indiana Press, 1991), I demonstrate the ways feminist writing, fictional and theoretical, helped shape the women's movement.

14. But as Nicole Ward Jouve suggests, it is precisely "because subjecthood has become so difficult, has been so deconstructed, that there is need to work towards it. This is particularly so for women"; *White Woman Speaks with Forked Tongue: Criticism as Autobiography* (London: Routledge, 1991), 11. Jouve speaks of "the need to speak as a subject, and as a subject bent on self-knowledge. We have lost ourselves in the endlessly diffracted light of Deconstruction. . . . For we [especially women] have been asked to go along with Deconstruction whilst we had not even got to the Construction stage. You must have a self before you can afford to deconstruct it" (7). Or, as Nancy K. Miller puts it, "only those who have it can play with not having it"; see "The Text's Heroine: A Feminist Critic and Her Fictions," *Diacritics* 12 (summer 1982): 52.

15. Annette Kolodny, "Dancing Between the Left and Right: Feminism and the Academic Minefield in the 1980s," *Feminist Studies* 14 (fall 1988): 464. At the conference "What Ever Happened to Women's Liberation?" (University of California, Los Angeles, 3–4 May 1991), historians expressed this concern. In her paper "Memory as Resistance," Paula Giddings suggested that we need to write our own history or history will be written for us; in "History as Politics," Alice Echols described the tendency of histories of the sixties to erase the women's movement; she cited Todd Gitlin, James Miller, Tom Hayden, Stuart Burns as "marginalizing us better than the movement did." Adrienne Rich refers to "the erasure of women's political and historic past" wherein the "history of women's struggle for self-determination has been muffled in silence over and over" ("When We Dead Awaken," 9, 11 (see note 9).

16. Adrienne Rich, Foreword to *On Lies,* 9.

17. Nancy Cott, *The Grounding of Modern Feminism* (New Haven: Yale University Press, 1987), cites *Judy* 1, no. 1 (June 1919); *Judy* 2, no. 3 (1919): 282, 365 n. 3. In the Arthur and Elizabeth Schlesinger Library on the History of Women in America, Radcliffe College, Cambridge, Mass.; Cott, *Grounding* 365 n. 23.

18. Dorothy Dunbar Bromley, "Feminist—New Style," *Harper's* 155 (October 1927): 152–60; repr. in William Chafe, *The American Woman: Her Changing Social, Economic, and Political Roles, 1920–1970* (London: Oxford University Press, 1972), 92. Lillian Hellman described "the emancipation of women" as "stale stuff" in *An Unfinished Woman: A Memoir* (Boston: Little, Brown, 1969), 35.

19. Cott, *Grounding,* 218. See also Elaine Showalter, "Women Writers Between the Wars," in Emory Eliot, ed., *Columbia Literary History* (New York: Columbia University Press, 1988), 822–41.

20. See Wendy Kaminer, *A Fearful Freedom: Women's Flight from Equality* (Reading, Mass.: Addison-Wesley, 1990), chap. 9; Deborah Rosenfelt and Judith Stacey, "Second Thoughts on the Second Wave," *Feminist Studies* 13 (summer 1987): 341–61; and Susan Faludi, *Backlash: The Undeclared War Against American Women* (New York: Crown, 1991).

21. Susan Faludi, *Backlash,* x; Wendy Kaminer also discusses tendencies to blame the women's movement for the problems of women (*Fearful Freedom,* passim) (see note 20).

22. Kaminer, *Fearful Freedom,* 1 (see note 20).

23. Betty Friedan, "How to Get the Women's Movement Moving Again," *New York Times Magazine* (3 November 1985): 89.

24. Anita Shreve, *Women Together, Women Alone: The Legacy of The Consciousness-Raising Movement* (New York: Viking, 1989), passim.

25. Ruth Sidel, *On Her Own: Growing Up in the Shadow of the American Dream* (New York: Viking, 1990), passim.

26. Francine Prose, "Confident at 11, Confused at 16," *New York Times* (7 January 1990): sect. VI, 23ff.

27. Marianne Hirsch and Evelyn Fox Keller, eds., *Conflicts in Feminism* (New York: Routledge, 1990), 1.

28. bell hooks, *Yearning, Race, Gender, and Cultural Politics* (Boston: South End, 1990), 1. Annette Kolodny refers to the erosion of "the originating revolutionary potential of feminism" and the "severing of the link between feminist literary inquiry and feminism as a political agenda" ("Dancing," 457, see note 15). Cora Kaplan describes feminism as "cut off . . . from what women are actually writing and from a political movement"; see "Feminist Criticism Twenty Years On," in *My Guy to Sci Fi: Genre and Women's Writing in the Postmodern World,* ed. Helen Carr (London: Pandora, 1989), 19, 21.

29. Richard Levin, "Feminist Thematics and Shakespearean Tragedy," *PMLA* 103 (1988): 125–38. See also vol. 103: 817–19 and vol. 104 (1989): 77–79. The articles and the letters, as well as my response to the essay and other responses, along with responses to those responses, are published in *Shakespeare Left and Right,* ed. Ivo Kamps (New York: Routledge, 1991). It was an attack that, given its stupidity, generated an inordinate amount of attention.

30. Sally Kempton, "Cutting Loose." *Esquire* 74 (July 1970): 53–57.

31. Rachel DuPlessis, "Reader, I Married Me: A Polygynous Memoir," 100; Carolyn Porter, "Getting Gendered"; Elizabeth Ermath, "On Having a Personal Voice," 233: all in Gayle Greene and Coppélia Kahn, eds., *The Making of Feminist Literary Criticism* (New York: Routledge, 1993).

32. Jane Tompkins, "Me and My Shadow," in *Gender and Theory: Dialogues on Feminist Criticism,* ed. Linda Kauffman (New York: Basil Blackwell, 1989), 121.

33. Nancy K. Miller, *Getting Personal,* 39 (see note 8).

34. Susan Bordo, "Feminism, Postmodernism, and Gender-Scepticism," in *Feminism/Postmodernism,* ed. Linda J. Nicholson (New York: Routledge, 1990), 148.

35. Hester Eisenstein, UCLA Conference, 4 May 1991.

36. Naomi Scheman suggests that the reason we need to be clear about saying "we" is "not out of a desire for theoretical sophistication but out of the need to overcome the white solipsism that has blocked alliances between white women and women of color. Such alliances—and theories of gender that facilitate them—needn't be grounded in

similarities. . . . Rather, they can be grounded in our interconnectedness, in how our very different ways of being constructed as women have implicated each other." "Who Wants to Know? The Epistemological Value of Values," in *(En)gendering Knowledge: Feminists in Academe,* ed. Joan E. Hartman and Ellen Messer-Davidow (Knoxville: University of Tennessee Press, 1991), 189. I find Scheman's distinction between assuming similarities and assuming interconnections useful in thinking about identity politics.

37. As Deborah McDowell says, "we have become much too comfortable with radical language," which can "sometimes be an act of substitution" for "radical action." Interview with Susan Fraiman, *Critical Texts: A Review of Theory and Criticism* 6, no. 3 (1989): 25. Hooks notes that the subject of race is being mystified by the "buzz words" "difference, the Other, hegemony, ethnography," which have replaced "more commonly known words deemed uncool or too simplistic, words like "oppression, exploitation, and domination," and which enable race to be "talked about, as though it were in no way linked to cultural practices"; *Yearning: Race, Gender, and Cultural Politics* (Boston: South End, 1990), 51, 54.

38. Susan Bordo, "Feminism," 141–42 (see note 34).

39. Molly Hite, *The Other Side of the Story: Structures and Strategies of Contemporary Feminist Narratives* (Ithaca: Cornell University Press, 1989), 125.

40. As hooks suggests, "Increasingly, only one type of theory is seen as valuable, that which is Euro-centric, linguistically convoluted." "Rather than expanding our notions of theory to include types of theory that can be produced in many different writing styles . . . the vision of what theory is becomes a narrow, constricting concept"; see *Talking Back: Thinking Feminist, Thinking Black* (Boston: South End, 1989), 36.

41. Gayle Greene and Coppélia Kahn, "Feminist Scholarship and the Social Construction of Woman," in Greene and Kahn, eds., *Making a Difference: Feminist Literary Criticism* (New York: Methuen, 1985), 1–36.

42. See Barbara Christian, "The Race for Theory," *Cultural Critique* (spring 1987): 51–52. Kolodny also describes the shift in prestige to institutes of critical theory and explains it in terms of "high-powered men . . . bent on fleeing not only an increasingly feminized professoriat but . . . an increasingly persuasive feminist practice . . . the male 'muscle' of the profession aimed at theory in order to distinguish itself from a feminism that had never been systematically theory-driven." But when feminists came on over to theory, this produced "a new move 'against theory' " ("Dancing," 455–56, see note 15).

43. Nancy K. Miller, *Getting Personal,* 65 (see note 8).

44. Jane Tompkins, "Me and My Shadow," 22 (see note 32).

45. Nancy K. Miller, *Getting Personal,* 66 (see note 8).

46. Although Paul Lauter notes that "literary theory has proven remarkably easy to assimilate to the structure of American university life; indeed, it had become a strong re-enforcement of existing academic norms. The practice of literary theory in no sense challenges the individualistic, production-oriented forms of the American academy, much less the marketplace ideology and the organizational structures into which the colleges largely guide their students"; "And it helps maintain a hierarchical relationship between the privileged discourse of the academy and practical criticism, mainly carried out in the classroom. In that regard, the obscurity of language that has come to characterize most theoretical writing is no unfortunate accident but rather an essential element." See "The Two Criticisms—or Structure, Lingo, and Power in the Discourse of the Academic Humanists," in *Canons and Contexts* (New York: Oxford University Press, 1991), 141. Scheman suggests that "incomprehensibility serves in fact to protect the structures of privilege we take ourselves to be so brilliantly skewering" ("Who Wants to Know," 194, see note 36).

47. Lauter describes how "at one of the most crowded sessions on criticism at the 1982 [MLA] convention three rather complex, not to say obscure, papers were presented. At the end, with an unusual amount of time left, the chair asked for comments or questions. A heavy silence spread through the room. No one spoke. People shifted disconsolately. The session finally ended." Speaking up, Lauter notes, "presents far too high a risk" ("Two Criticisms," 13, see note 46). Tey Diana Rebolledo describes "a typical talk" at "a recent Chicano Studies Conference": "the speaker begins, 'This paper will focus on the ideology of cultural practice and its modes of signifying.' S/he then spends twenty minutes discussing how the works of whatever theoretical greats s/he selects will define, inform and privilege the work s/he is doing. Such names as Jameson, Said, Williams, Hall, Burke and other contemporary *meros, meros* (mostly male) will be invoked over and over. The speaker is then sent a note by the chair of the panel that there is no time left. And whatever the Chicano/a writing or phenomenon that was to be discussed is quickly summarized in two minutes. The talk is over." "The Politics of Poetics: Or, What Am I, A Critic, Doing in This Text Anyhow?" in *Making Face, Making Soul: Creative and Critical Perspectives by Women of Color,* ed. Gloria Anzaldúa (San Francisco: An Aunt Lute Foundation Book, 1990), 347–48. Such virtuoso performances issue into nothing—not even talk.

48. Tey Diana Rebolledo, *Making Face,* 348 (see note 47).

49. bell hooks, *Talking Back,* 164 (see note 40).

50. Tania Modleski, *Feminism Without Women: Culture and Criticism in a "Postfeminist" Age* (New York: Routledge, 1991), 5.

51. Nicole Ward Jouve, *White Woman,* 9, 8 (see note 14).

52. DuPlessis, *Writing Beyond the Ending* (see note 11); Molly Hite, *The Other Side* (see note 39); and Rita Felski, *Beyond Feminist Aesthetics* (see note 13).

53. Gayle Greene, *Changing the Story: Feminist Fiction and the Tradition* (Bloomington: University of Indiana Press, 1991).

54. As Angelika Bammer suggests, "we should be particularly conscious of our acts of selection in relation to language." Are we using difficult language, she asks, "because it is appropriate to the complexity of our analysis? Can we make complexity accessible in order to permit communications?" Such questions, Bammer maintains, really come down to the question, "When is our language a means of exchange, and when is it a tool of domination?" "Mastery," in Hartman and Messer-Davidow, *(En)gendering Knowledge,* 253–54.

55. As Jouve notes, "the cult of the new, in the past twenty years, has been a sign of vitality: it has also done a great deal of harm. The pace of consumption has been too fast, generating panic, the constant need for more, the greed to be stimulated and to absorb and digest and move on" (*White Woman,* 8, see note 14).

56. Barbara Christian, "Race for Theory," 53, 59 (see note 42).

57. Nancy K. Miller, *Getting Personal,* 14–15 (see note 8).

58. Nancy K. Miller, *Getting Personal,* 24 (see note 8).

59. Nancy K. Miller, *Getting Personal,* xix, 25 (see note 8), 23. Elisabeth Young-Bruehl credits feminism with the fact that "I" has "made its way" into academic discourse and suggests that "those scholars, who, writing from multicultural or suppressed cultural perspectives, construct their work around the scrupulous observation of their 'I's' are creating the most compelling texts in academia today." "Pride and Prejudice: Feminist Scholars Reclaim the First Person," *Lingua Franca* (February 1991): 15, 18.

60. This is Trinh T. Minh-ha's term in "Not You/Like You: Post-Colonial Women and the Interlocking Questions of Identity and Difference," in *Making Face, Making*

Soul: Creative and Critical Perspectives by Women of Color, ed. Gloria Anzaldúa (San Francisco: An Aunt Lute Foundation Book, 1990), 371.

61. Biddy Martin and Chandra Talpade Mohanty, "Feminist Politics: What's Home Got to Do with It?" in *Feminist Studies/Critical Studies* (Bloomington: University of Indiana Press, 1986), 210.

62. Joan E. Hartman and Ellen Messer-Davidow, "Introduction: A Position Statement," in Hartman and Messer-Davidow, *(En)gendering Knowledge,* 1, 2 (see note 36).

63. Harding, "Who Knows? Identities and Feminist Epistemology," in Hartman and Messer-Davidow, *(En)gendering Knowledge,* 103 (see note 36).

64. Joan E. Hartman, "Telling Stories: The Construction of Women's Agency," in Hartman and Messer-Davidow, *(En)gendering Knowledge,* 22 (see note 36).

65. Harding, "Who Knows?" 113 (see note 36).

66. Bammer, "Mastery," 245 (see note 36).

Relevant Publications by Gayle Greene

Doris Lessing: The Poetics of Change. Ann Arbor: University of Michigan Press, 1994.

Changing Subjects: The Making of Feminist Literary Criticism (coeditor with Coppélia Kahn). London: Routledge, 1992.

Changing the Story: Feminist Fiction and the Tradition. Bloomington: University of Indiana Press, 1991.

Making a Difference: Feminist Literary Criticism (coeditor with Coppélia Kahn). London: Methuen, 1985. Includes the article, "Feminist Scholarship and the Social Construction of Women," coauthored with Kahn.

"The Empire Strikes Back." Review of Naomi Wolf's *The Beauty Myth* and Susan Faludi's *Backlash* in *The Nation* (February 1992).

"Daughters of the Revolution." Review of Lillian Rubin's *Erotic Wars, What Happened to the Sexual Revolution,* Anita Shreve's *Women Together, Women Alone: The Legacy of Consciousness Raising,* and Ruth Sidel's *On Her Own: Growing Up in the Shadow of the American Dream* in *The Nation* (29 April 1991).

"Feminist Fiction, Feminist Form." *Frontiers: A Journal of Women's Studies* 11 (1990): 82–88.

"Feminist Scholarship and the Social Construction of Woman" (with Coppélia Kahn). In *Making a Difference: Feminist Literary Criticism* (coeditor with Coppélia Kahn). London: Methuen, 1985.

Introduction (coauthor with Carol Neely) to *"The Woman's Part": Feminist Criticism of Shakespeare* (coeditor with Carol Neely). Urbana: University of Illinois Press, 1980.

16

On Daring to Teach Literature. Again.

André Lefevere

André Lefevere, professor of Germanic languages and comparative literature at the University of Texas, has written on translation and literary history as well as the possible functions of literary criticism. The study of literature should and can become more scientific, he argues in Literary Knowledge, *but only if it does not try to model itself on the physical sciences. The present essay assumes that whatever values literature may have, these depend upon successful communication, and that that communication can best be furthered, not by theory that sounds but fails to be scientific, but by the more traditional path of gaining familiarity with the conventions, genres, patterns, and prototypes of various sorts upon which literary construction depends.*

Communication within and about art and knowledge in a culture inscribes itself in a triangle. That triangle is transparent: those who work within it are often not even aware of its existence because they consider it "natural," or "given," and therefore not to be called into question. The three sides of the triangle connect three concepts: "power," arguably the basic one, used here in the sense attributed to it by Michel Foucault; "discourse," which deals with an aspect of art or knowledge; and "institution," which is one of the means through which power controls discourse.

The discourse known as "literature" is part of this triangle, as is the discourse variously known as "criticism" or "theory." Without cultural institutions, literature could be written, but not disseminated: it would remain without any socially noticeable reception, and therefore fail to make any impact on society at large. Without such institutions literature would probably be written about (although this is already somewhat more doubtful), but those writings would also not be disseminated. In particular, institutions of higher education keep both postmodernist and poststructuralist writings on literature (henceforth: "postmodstru") *and* a sizable list of classics alive simply by including them in syllabi as "required texts."

Since all interpretation is rewriting, the people who teach at these institutions find themselves incessantly rewriting the literature they teach, for pedagogical reasons, for ideological reasons, or most likely for a mixture of both. Rewriters of necessity also rewrite history, leaving out and weaving in, repressing and highlighting to suit their purposes. While making a work of literature more accessible to the reader, rewriters do so most emphatically on other than the reader's terms. Rather, they try to manipulate readers in such a way that they will agree with the rewriting proposed, often to the extent that they prefer the rewriting to the actual text. The fierce loyalties readers develop for a certain translation of a text, to the exclusion of all others, even if those others demonstrably avoid mistakes made in the preferred translation, serves to illustrate the power of rewriting in perhaps the most obvious way.

One type of rewriter tries to influence the production of literature, as when Pound produces *Cathay* to attack the model of what Victorian and Edwardian poets thought poetry should be. Another type of rewriter, who turns out to be much more influential, though much less known in the end, tries to control the reception of literature. A brilliant example of this kind of "symbolic violence"[1] would be the Brooks and Warren handbooks *Understanding Poetry* and *Understanding Literature* that imposed the New Critical way of reading on at least two generations of American students and their instructors.

Rewriters manipulate literature in ways accepted or rejected by both readers and writers. If writers make use of a given universe of discourse (the sum total of objects, ideas, persons available in a culture at the time a work of literature belonging to it is produced) to construct works of literature, rewriters make use of literature to construct images of works of literature, writers, or whole literatures. They do so by producing editions that emphasize or de-emphasize certain aspects of the work edited; anthologies that make their selections on unannounced criteria; literary histories, criticism, and theory produced against the background of an often hidden agenda; and translations that create a certain image of their originals. These manipulations turn out to be at least as influential in a society as the works themselves, affecting both writers and readers through its institutions, and thereby also affecting the development of literatures, which is why they should be studied on a par with the texts produced by writers. The very fact that they are not sufficiently studied in that way is perhaps the greatest compliment that can be paid to the rhetorical skills of a historically contingent group of rewriters generally known as the "Romantics," who managed to posit their own concept of the function of literature, and particularly its two leading notions of "genius" and "originality," in such a convincing manner that to question it almost two centuries later is still no simple matter. The Romantics, one might say, were sovereignly blind to their own historical contingency and that of literature generally.

Like all other rewriters, the Romantics have also been aided and abetted by the (still, or rather, once again current) confusion that would apply the label "literature" not only to texts produced with the intention of taking their place among the works recognized as "literary" in a certain culture at a certain time, but also to texts written about those texts. The differentiation between "literature" and "metaliterature" has been very slow to crystallize, as evidenced by the extremely gradual acceptance first of the distinction between "literature" and "criticism," and later of that between "criticism" and "theory." Paradoxically, "theory" in its postmodstru avatars, aspires to be "literature," once again. It needs to do so to survive in an era in which there is no longer a generally accepted reading of any given literary text. Now that the time of the single rewriting is over, rewriters are left with little option but to claim that they are actually producing "literature," albeit of a somewhat "different" kind, which allows them to inhabit the gray area of what they are alone in calling *creative* confusion.

Both literature and theory/criticism (henceforth "theocrit") operate within a discursive field delimited by power, whether in more (as in totalitarian societies) or less obvious ways. In the latter case power rarely intervenes directly in literary or theocrit discourses, preferring to control them by means of the more impersonal institutions, whose proverbial inertia is often sufficient for its purposes.

For most of its history theocrit has sided with power (in the case of literature, matters are more open to argument), either by actively espousing and propagating a worldview acceptable to the powers of its day, as most obviously illustrated in the fairly recent past by the theocrit produced on the basis of socialist realism, or at least by not actively going against that worldview. There has always been theocrit produced against the grain, taking up a critical, even subversive position, but historically the number of texts belonging to it are nowhere so great in number as those belonging in the opposite camp.

I contend that theocrit has changed camps at least since 1968, and definitely after it became dominated by postmodstru. The authors of theocrit/postmodstru produced since that year regard it as nothing if not subversive. Indeed, it is because recent theocrit/postmodstru so resolutely goes against power, that the power-knowledge-institution triangle stands revealed in our time, at least for those who want to see it: it has lost its transparent nature.

There are a number of reasons for this change. One is the increasing marginalization both of theocrit/postmodstru texts and of the people who produce them from the point of view of power. Arguably the most obvious symptom of this marginalization is the fact that, subversive as such writing sees itself as being, it is blithely taught in the institutions supported by the power it is supposedly trying to subvert. Instructors in institutions of higher education confidently declare that "all reading is misreading" and then proceed to scribble different grades on different kinds of misreadings.

But perhaps the most important reason is that most postmodstru has either never become, or has ceased to be theory. Most of it now occupies the gray area referred to above, in particular the borderland that stretches, at least since Nietzsche, between literature and philosophy. No longer analyzing literature, it uses individual works of literature to bolster the arguments it wants to make about the construction of the world, language, the human subject, and other postmodstru evergreens.

The kind of "theory" often referred to in postmodstru discourses about literature does not really deal with literature; rather, it *is* literature, and it needs to be literature. It desperately appeals to the fact that texts recognized as literature operate with what Siegfried J. Schmidt calls the "aesthetic convention," calling on the reader not to "subordinate his linguistic-cognitive actions primarily to categories like true/false."[2] How else could such "theorists" possibly get away with positing the primacy of writing over speech, for instance, or the "fact" that women's writing is less straightforward than men's because women are capable of multiple orgasms, as the starting points of their respective "theories"?

This "opportunist reversal," as Christopher Norris calls it,[3] further defining it as "a move to secure for criticism exactly the same value that has traditionally accrued to writing under its 'so-called' creative aspect," is widely evidenced in the pronouncements of "theorists" on the subject. "Literary commentary today," says Hartman, "is creating texts—a literature of its own."[4] Bloom contends that "all criticism is prose poetry," and Hillis Miller wonders whether a citation is "an alien parasite within the body of the main text, or is the interpretive text the parasite which surrounds and strangles the citation?"[5]

In our time as before, literature is produced for all who care to read it, and it can be read on various levels. Most of its readers are likely to be "nonprofessional," in the same sense as most people who tinker with their cars or potter in their gardens are not professional car-mechanics or gardeners. The most likely motivation for reading literature is curiosity. "Professional" readers are likely to have their curiosity aroused on the level of code (the background against which a work is produced) and selection (the elements of that background actually selected and combined by a given writer, and the variations to which that writer subjects what has been selected), whereas nonprofessional readers are likely to read on the level of story and character. There is no reason to suppose that nonprofessional readers are not likely to increase their understanding of the text if they are shown how it is put together, and why—and by professionals. Yet those professionals make statements about literature that are increasingly removed not just from reality, a description many of them would consider a compliment, but from the day-to-day experience of life, both professional (it gets harder and harder to teach postmodstru in its latest refinements) and personal (it gets harder and harder to keep up with said refinements).

Those who call postmodstru "removed from life" often feel vague guilt about "dropping out" of what is usually referred to as the "current theory debate." There is no need to feel this kind of guilt because most "theories" that are supposed to be debating each other are not theories that would be recognized as such in any philosophy of science. I feel justified in taking this as a yardstick, because the discourse we know as "science" is, after all, now dominant in the institutions of the society we live in—and it is the institutions, after all, that validate the discourse. Rather, the proliferation of postmodstru theories is indicative of a state of pre-science, characterized by "total disagreement and constant debate over fundamentals, so much so that it is impossible to get down to detailed work. There will be almost as many theories as there are workers in the field and each theoretician will be obliged to start afresh and justify his own particular approach."[6] In this pre-scientific state theories keep repeating the same move over and over again, whether they are looking for aporias, figurative vaginas, or alterities. Most of them therefore tend to amount to little more than fashions that usually stay around long enough only to help one academic generation achieve tenure, and then fade away.

It might therefore be advisable to try to develop a discourse about literature that approximates the discourse validated by society and its institutions if we want that society and those institutions to continue to take literature seriously (or to start taking literature seriously again). It is a pity, therefore, that so many people active in the humanities in general and in literature in particular—not, significantly, in what are commonly referred to as "the sciences" themselves—still insist on working under the "false assumption that there is a universal scientific method to which all forms of knowledge should conform."[7] This assumption "plays a detrimental role in our society here and now, especially in the light of the fact that the version of the scientific method usually appealed to is some crude empiricist or inductivist one" (141). The problem is then not just to convince those working in literature that they have little to lose by approximating the discourse used in science, but that the idea they have of science, which inspires reluctance to admit such discourse in their field, and sometimes inspires the construction of a scientific-looking facade is totally out of date. What is needed are theories "so structured as to contain within them fairly clear clues and prescriptions as to how they should be developed and extended" (79), not theories that keep repeating the same move until even those making the move lose interest. Truly useful theories, of literature or anything else, are "open-ended structures that offer a research *programme*" (79).

The growing irritation with postmodstru is also based on the mounting realization that its current variants may be undermining whatever academic respectability literary studies has left, because they simply use literature as a quarry for arguments and examples to make statements that are not necessary, or even primarily related to literature. They are what Niels Werber calls "supertheories" that "understand literature in each case as the medium of 'deeper' or 'more essential' processes, whether psychological, political, or whatever in nature."[8] It remains eminently true that "if the psychological or sociological analysis of a text is not judged worthy of belonging to psychology or to sociology, it is hard to see why it should be welcomed automatically as a constituent part of the 'science of literature.'"[9]

In what follows I contend, with Todorov, that "literature must be treated as literature" and I deplore with him that "this slogan, uttered in this very form for over fifty years, ought to have become a commonplace, thereby losing its polemical force. Yet it has not, and the appeal for a 'return to literature' in literary studies is as timely as ever"[10]—the more so, I might add, since the last attempt to "return to literature," which played an important role in the late seventies, was marginalized to a considerable extent by the advent of structuralism. The attempt did not fulfill its promise for two reasons.

The first reason is that all variants of structuralist poetics labored under the assumption that "science" meant something like "neopositivism" at a time when the sciences themselves, ironically, dismissed neopositivism as a viable ideal of science. At the time, linguistics, especially in its transformational grammar form, offered "an attractive methodological analogy";[11] it seemed to be the only one of the "human sciences" that could come close to what proponents of structuralist poetics thought was "science," but which, in practice, turned out to be just one ideal of science, the one that was already passé in the "sciences" at the very time when structuralist poetics turned to it.

The second reason is that any attempt at establishing a "structuralist" poetics was, by definition, doomed to be ahistorical. I fully agree with structuralist poetics that literature comments on life in its own particular way, that it is a communication system with its own code, and that "a set of conventions for reading literary texts"[12] not only exists but constitutes the proper object for the study of literature, over and against the production of rewritings (interpretations) of specific literary works with a certain agenda in mind. However, I contend that these conventions should be studied in their historical specificity and their historical evolution precisely because, understood in this way, these conventions constitute what is often searched for as literature's "specificity," its difference (with an *e,* not an *a*) from other discourses. In other words, the "literariness" the Russian Formalists (arguably the first to try to study literature as literature in this century) looked for in a certain use of language, is to be found instead in specific, historically changeable and changing codes. Again in Werber's words, and the concept can eventually be traced back to Niklas Luhmann: "the code specifies the communication."[13]

But the code, the conventions, should not be reduced to the vague and ahistorical. Culler lists as the conventions of the novel "significance" (115), "thematic unity" (115) and the fact that the novel "will produce a world"

(115), and as the conventions of the lyric "distance and impersonality" (164) as well as an "expectation of totality or coherence" (170). Todorov uses the categories "predicate, adjective, verb, mood" *(Poetics of Prose)* in his "Grammar of Narrative."[14] All these formulations pay a price for neglecting history. Culler appears to be aware of this when he states, somewhat wistfully: "but of course there are a great many possible metalanguages which have a certain logical coherence and could be used to describe any text" (207). What, we may well ask, compels us then to choose precisely the ones indicated above? The answer is nothing, precisely because these metalanguages are not in fact "largely interpersonal" to use Culler's words (128). Instead, they often become the mantras of selected and mutually exclusive, not to say warring groups.

And yet poetics, or rather, different sets of poetics for different literatures, do exist in all their historical variety and continuity, as the sets of conventions that make the production of meaning in literature—better, literatures—possible. They can be studied and they most definitely need to be taught. The study of poetics, of geographically, culturally, and historically different sets of poetics provides the "largely interpersonal" metalanguage for the study of literature. Though the structuralist study of poetics is passé, the study of poetics as such is not. It is not because poetics combines the opportunity to develop a discourse on literature that comes close to the discourse of post-neopositivist science (i.e., to construct an open-ended structure that offers a research *programme* with respect for the alterity of literature itself). Rather than produce interpretations that reduce literature to material for the construction of a "supertheory," poetics offers the possibility of understanding how a literature works, to grasp it in its specificity as it changes and develops over time. To study and teach these poetics, or codes, would serve the double purpose of making communication more meaningful and making artistry more obvious. Like any form of communication, literary communication is based on selection, and that selection plays on codes. Again in the tradition of thought that originates with Luhmann, Henk de Berg reminds us that "whatever has been selected is never something that is meaningful, or makes sense, by itself alone; rather, whatever has been selected only makes sense in relation to a background of other possibilities that have not been selected."[15] We therefore have to know not only what has been selected, but also what could have been selected. Only in this tension does literary artistry become visible and literary communication teachable. The *Duino Elegies,* for instance, can be best appreciated against the shared background of the evolution of the elegy as a genre and the universe of discourse of which Rilke was part at the time he wrote them. If we neglect this tension we reduce the specificity of literature. Needless to say, literatures that are furthest removed from us in time and space run the greatest danger of reduction. It is therefore counterproductive to lament, as Todorov does, that "we have forgotten" the "definitions of classical poetics" and that "we must produce new ones."[16] Rather, if we want to teach and learn the *Aeneid,* we have to know Homer and the generic conventions of the epic. If we want to teach and learn *Paradise Lost* we have to know the changes those generic conventions underwent between Homer and Milton. Categories like verb, predicate, mood, and adjective are but poor substitutes in this respect. Bakhtin had something similar in mind when he wrote that the "great heroes of literature and language turn out to be first and foremost genres."[17]

The study of various poetics across time and space can lead to the establishment of a body of knowledge that is not only both cumulative and teachable, but also constitutes a research program in itself. It tries to show how literature communicates, how it selects and combines elements from the universe of discourse in which it is written and why it selects precisely those elements; how it expresses these elements by means of selections from a code, or codes, how these codes evolve over time, and why.

A study of literature based on the study of a number of poetics also analyzes the historical succession of universes of discourse in which various literatures are produced because they, just as much as the codes, are the materials with which literature is constructed. The study of literature proposed here can empower readers who are willing to respect the alterity of literature to appreciate the selections a given author has made from a given poetics at a given time and, in so doing, to enjoy the artistry of the work they are reading. It can also show how readers who do not respect the alterity of literature can be manipulated to interpret texts in ways those who manipulate the codes wish. In exposing manipulation inside one system of communication and revealing the ways in which it works, the study of literature advocated here has something of value to offer to other systems of communication, as well as to the people who rely on them or even believe in them.

Individual works of literature are produced on the basis of selections from both a poetics and a universe of discourse available in a certain culture at a certain time. The recent return to a concern with the discourse of the historical moment is to be welcomed but too often the poetics of the time are ignored. Readings of the type advocated here cannot be produced on the basis of "general underlying structures," which usually pay for their "general" nature by coming perilously close to the trivial. Paul de Man was undoubtedly right in reacting against this example of " 'theory' in its more doctrinaire or reductive forms."[18] Unfortunately he thought he had to react against it only by producing readings that, in the end, rely mostly on his institutional status for their effect. It is highly doubtful whether a graduate student who would have written similar exegeses would have been taken seriously by the institution.

Readings of the type I have in mind can only be produced on the basis of a very historical study of *the* various (not *a* timeless) poetics of *different* literatures in their historical development. As stated in my *Translation, Rewriting, and the Manipulation of Literary Fame,*

> a poetics can be said to consist of two components: one is an inventory of literary devices, genres, motifs, prototypical characters and situations, and symbols; the other a concept of what the role of literature is, or should be, in the social system as a whole. The latter concept is influential in the selection of themes that must be relevant to the social system if the work of literature is to be noticed at all.[19]

Structuralist poetics eschewed the second component altogether, and was therefore at a loss to explain the appearance or resurgence of certain themes and genres in certain historical periods, and their virtual disappearance, or at least dormancy in others. When discussing Aristotle's *Poetics,* for instance, Todorov rightly states that it "gives no consideration to poetry (which certainly existed at the time)."[20] He does not venture to guess why that should be the case. Genette, writing at about the same time, explains why by referring to the second component of the definition given above: "For many centuries the Platonic-Aristotelian reduction of the poetic to the representative was to weigh on the theory of genres and to cause malaise and confusion."[21]

Furthermore, structuralist poetics tends to limit the first component of a poetics almost exclusively to genre, the concept of which is left vague. Culler "defines" it as "a conventional function of language," whereas Todorov tends, in practice, to equate genre more with type, which "does not present any reality outside of theoretical reflection," even though he defines a genre as "a type that has had concrete historical existence."[22] I would argue, with Jauss, that this concrete historical existence is all that is of importance, precisely because it constitutes a truly interpersonal metalanguage for the study of literature. "Literary genres should," therefore, "not be understood as *genera* (classes) in the logical sense, but as *groups* or *historical families*. As such they cannot be derived or defined, but only described, delimited, and identified from a historical point of view."[23]

Whatever else it may be, I contend that the type of study of literature advocated here is the only way of talking about literature that does not insult the reader's intelligence. If readers read, among other things, to make sense of the universe of discourse they move in, it is altogether likely that they will be the best judges of what they want to get out of texts, that they can be trusted, in Stuart Hall's phrase, to "negotiate" their own reading of the text. Whether they can be trusted to do so or not, they will proceed to do so anyway, unless they have to justify their reading for a grade, in which case they will read as their instructors want them to, not infrequently, and with natural ease, developing different, often totally contradictory reading strategies for different classes. Outside the classroom they will not need theocrit or postmodstru to interpret texts for them, and yet this kind of interpretation has usually been accepted as *the* raison d'être of literary studies. It made (and makes) perfect sense in a situation I would like to call doubly patriarchal, in the sense that all readers, not just women, are treated with the kind of paternalistic condescension that ultimately derives its strength not from the arguments it uses, but from the institutions that are behind it.

The crowning irony in all this is that a systematic description of the various poetics of various cultures in their historical evolution would empower readers to arrive at a more encompassing interpretation of the texts they are reading. The form of a work is part of its content, message, or whatever Greek word current theocrit may be inventing or resurrecting to refer to it. If you write a poem and give it the title "sonnet," you send a message to the reader which precedes and frames whatever you are going to say inside the sonnet itself. If you write a poem and give it the title "sonnet," and it turns out not to be a sonnet, you are sending a double message to the reader, suggesting a preliminary irony before the reader gets to the "body" of the text. Under present institutional conditions of (higher) learning it would probably be better, or rather, more accurate to say that you would be sending the kind of message just described if your readers knew what a sonnet was. If they read your poem and process it as a generic "poem" only, they are likely to miss part of your message or, again more accurately: they will be negotiating a reading for themselves without knowing, or even suspecting all that the text has to offer. But is this not always the case, especially in this age of multivalence? Of course it is, but with one main difference: the information needed here could very easily be supplied. Nor would this kind of information amount to patronizing the reader: all kinds of multivalent associations and inferences could be made with the same gay abandon as ever. They would merely fall outside the discourse used by the type of study of literature advocated here and could be most profitably engaged in at the dinner table, or in bars (or coffeehouses), where they historically originated. Many trees might be saved as a result and the effect on the ecology cannot but be beneficial.

What I am concerned with here is the fact that certain elements of a poetics act as a signal to the reader, whether that signal has been consciously intended by the writer or not. By agreeing to "play" by the same code, writers and readers establish a framework for communication, which is of course subject to the same misunderstandings as those that occur within the framework for communication known as "language," but that do not invalidate the existence of the framework as such, nor its use. The existence of this framework is of particular importance when we are dealing with literatures remote from us in time and space. It has become a "theoretical" truism that human beings learn to process all texts labeled "literary" in ways that are different from other texts. They do so mainly by observing the "aesthetic convention" referred to above, as well as the "polyvalence convention," which, in Schmidt's words, implies that readers "possess the freedom to treat texts regarded as literary in a way that is optimal for *their* needs, abilities, motivations, and intentions."[24] In other words, if there is such a thing as "literary competence," it is taught, not innate, though the facility for it may be. If it is taught, then why not, wonder of wonders, actually teach it? Why not tell students that the texts they process generically as poems, novels, or plays, are much more diverse and can be read as different "framing" messages of many different types?

No doubt students are indeed taught some of this when they read literature produced in relation to the poetics of their own culture, although even then it is doubtful whether English Literature majors, for instance, are really still initiated into the poetics of classical antiquity, without which the evolution of genres, forms, and motifs in English-language literature cannot be understood. Very often they are offered this knowledge in a very schematic and reductionistic way, one that singularly fails to do justice to Medvedev's requirement, for instance, that the notion of a form (whether transmitted in teaching or not) should "be adequate to the whole history of the evolution of the form."[25] When it comes to literature produced in a culture that is not their own, students are rarely offered this kind of knowledge; instead, the alterity that is respected in the case of the knowledge indigenous to their own culture is all too often reduced by analogy to the poetics of the literature of their own culture.

This kind of literary competence needs to be taught in its historical continuity and diversity, and I contend that it needs to be taught explicitly, that it should not be left to exposure, experience, or osmosis, or any of the other means teachers expect their students to avail themselves of in their "progress towards a general literary competence."[26] This is where the research program alluded to at various points in this text would come into its own: we need research on the actual evolution of genres, and not just in literatures distant from us in time and space, just as we need research on the actual meaning of symbols and motifs used in different poetics belonging to different cultures. We also need the pedagogical application of that research, which might most profitably and efficiently express itself in anthologies, not structured around the concepts of either historical periods or great authors, but precisely around the concepts of genre, symbol, and motif.

One has studied, one knows "literature" not if one is able to interpret texts produced inside of one's native culture only—even though that in itself is never a deterrent to subsequent gratuitous generalization—but if one has a knowledge of the different poetics of (at least a fair number of) the world's literatures, if one respects their alterity without reducing them to the measure of either one's own agenda or one's own poetics. Multiculturalism expresses itself in respect for the form, which reveals the different perception with which others regard their literatures and their universes of discourse, not in assimilating that perception to one's own and devaluing it in the process. The implications for the type of translations to be used in the anthologies sketched above are obvious: they should at least give an idea of the form of the original, not, as is frequently the case, silently reduce that form to its closest analogy within Western poetics.

Perhaps the most striking feature of Chinese Tang dynasty poetry is that it is written in two very tightly organized and circumscribed genres. It has been translated into English as either quatrains (because one of the genres has four lines only), or free verse, creating the impression that Tang dynasty poetry is either not different from what we know, or not generically structured at all. Yet if we do not have an idea of the generic code underlying that poetry, we shall never really "understand" it. The best we can do is to "assimilate" it, and we are likely to assimilate it on the basis of analogy: we shall interpret it through the grid of the nearest analogy available to us.

This type of assimilation, or acculturation by inaccurate analogy, amounts to a total lack of respect for the "otherness" of the text that is foreign, leading not only to misreadings, but to misreadings based on a totally transparent, unreflected and, ultimately, utterly arrogant privileging of a contemporary Western literature. This is, indeed, how, in Katherine Hayles's words, "a few European cultures have been identified with mankind."[27] It is also quite a blind spot indeed since much of theocrit self-professedly attempts to decenter dominance and produce insight that ought to lead to empowerment. Instead, understanding by means of the arrogance of analogy subjects all texts to its own center, even if that center actually advocates decentering.

Our knowledge of different sets of poetics will obviously never be "sure" or "pure" in any way. Just like our knowledge of various universes of discourse it will always be filtered through our own situation in time and space, but at least the researcher tries to filter it without the arrogance of analogy so as to respect its otherness. Nor is the inclusion of the study of the universe of discourse in which works of literature are produced a retreat from an attempt to teach literature in its own specificity. On the contrary: whereas recent "theory" has used literature as a quarry for its own arguments, literature may now (or rather, again) be seen as using the universe of discourse in which it is produced as a quarry from which those who produce it select the elements of its own construction. This last statement should also not be interpreted as a stealthy return to a position that somehow still tries to advocate the superiority of literature over other kinds of verbal discourse. Rather it merely states that the discourse known as "literature" is one of the discourses in existence in most cultures at most stages in their development, and that the study and analysis of it can produce some kind of insight, both in its own internal workings and, through it, in one of the ways members of a given culture reflected on it and represented it.

The study of literature as advocated here would reduce speculation and the use of jargon, both in its proliferation and its faddist cyclical rebirth in ever shorter cycles. It would build up a body of knowledge that is transferable, since it is based on underlying codes and their evolution, not on intellectual fashions outside literature. "Programs," as Gerhard Plumpe and Niels Werber put it, "change, codes remain stable"[28] in the Jaussian (which is ultimately the Wittgensteinian) sense that "family resemblances" remain discernible throughout the historical development—and the variations this entails—of texts taken to belong to the same historical families. This knowledge can be built upon and applied by all who apply themselves to it. It would be multicultural in the sense that no poetics or universe of discourse would be privileged above others, even though the influence of one on another would be acknowledged. It would reintroduce students to the mechanics of writing by showing them both how the text is constructed on the page and how the materials for that construction are taken from the universe of discourse and the poetics underlying that text. In doing so it could sensitize students to problems they encounter in their own writing. Finally, in studying gradual or abrupt manipulations of the codes of literary communications in history, it could easily establish its relevance in a society that is more subject to the construction and manipulation of images, from presidents to parochial school boards, than ever before. If changes in history have made it impossible to think of literature as a "school for life," as it was thought of in the past, the study of literature advocated here certainly makes it possible to think of it in terms of a strategy for survival.

Notes

1. Pierre Bourdieu and J. C. Passeron, *Reproduction in Education, Society and Culture* (London: Sage, 1977), 50.
2. Siegfried J. Schmidt, *Die Selbstorganisation des Sozialsystems Literatur im 18. Jahrhundert* (Frankfurt am Main: Suhrkamp, 1993), 431.
3. Christopher Norris, *Paul de Man* (London: Routledge, 1988), 75.
4. Geoffrey Hartman, *Criticism in the Wilderness* (New Haven: Yale University Press, 1980), 213.
5. Harold Bloom, *The Anxiety of Influence* (New York: Oxford University Press, 1973), 94. J. Hillis Miller, "The Critic as Host," in *Deconstruction and Criticism,* ed. Harold Bloom et al. (New York: Seabury, 1979), 217.
6. A. F. Chalmers, *What Is This Thing Called Science?* (Milton Keynes: Open University Press, 1992), 92.
7. A. F. Chalmers, 141.
8. Niels Werber, *Literatur als System* (Opladen: Westdeutscher Verlag, 1992), 13.
9. Tzvetan Todorov, *Introduction to Poetics* (Minneapolis: University of Minnesota Press, 1981), 8.
10. Tzvetan Todorov, *The Poetics of Prose* (Ithaca: Cornell University Press, 1992), 120.
11. Jonathan Culler, *Structuralist Poetics* (Ithaca: Cornell University Press, 1982), 123.
12. Jonathan Culler, 115.

13. Niels Werber, 17.
14. Tzvetan Todorov, *Poetics of Prose,* 108–19.
15. Henk de Berg, "Die Ereignishaftigkeit des Textes," in *Kommunkation und Differenz,* ed. Henk de Berg and Matthias Prangel (Opladen: Westdeuscher, 1993), 33.
16. Tzvetan Todorov, *Poetics of Prose,* 36.
17. Mikhail Bakhtin, "Epic and Novel," in *The Dialogic Imagination,* ed. Michael Holquist, trans. Caryl Emerson and Michael Holquist (Austin: University of Texas Press, 1981), 7.
18. Christopher Norris, 75.
19. André Lefevere, *Translation, Rewriting, and the Manipulation of Literary Fame* (London: Routledge, 1992), 26.
20. Tzvetan Todorov, *Introduction to Poetics,* xxiii.
21. Gerard Genette, " 'Genres,' 'types,' 'modes,' " *Poetique* 32 (1977): 399.
22. Jonathan Culler, 136; Tzvetan Todorov, *Introduction to Poetics,* 92.
23. Hans Robert Jauss, "Theorie der Gattungen und Literatur des Mittelalters," in *Grundriß der romanischen Literaturen des Mittelalters,* ed. Hans Robert Jauss and Erich Kohler (Heidelberg, 1972), 1:110.
24. Siegfried J. Schmidt, *Selbtsorganisation,* 431.
25. Pavel Medvedev, *Die formale Methode in der Literaturwissenschaft* (Stuttgart: Metzler, 1976), 40.
26. Jonathan Culler, 121.
27. Katharine N. Hayles, *Chaos Bound* (Ithaca: Cornell University Press, 1990), 213.
28. Gerhard Plumpe and Neils Werber, "Literatur ist codierbar," in *Literaturwissenschaft und Systemtheorie,* ed. Siegfried J. Schmidt (Opladen: Westdeutscher Verlag, 1993), 23.

Relevant Publications by André Lefevere

Translation, Rewriting, and the Manipulation of Literary Fame. London: Routledge, 1992.

Essays in Comparative Literature. Calcutta: Papyrus, 1989.

Literary Knowledge. Assen: Van Gorcum, 1977.

"The Dynamics of the System: Convention and Innovation in Literary History." In *Convention and Innovation in Literary History,* ed. Theo D'haen et al., Amsterdam: John Benjamins, 1990.

"Systems Thinking and Cultural Relativism." *Jadavpur Journal of Comparative Literature* 26–27 (1988): 55–68.

" 'Beyond Interpretation' or the Business of Rewriting." *Comparative Literature Studies* 24 (1987): 17–39.

"Why Waste Our Time on Rewrites? The Trouble with Interpretation and the Role of Rewriting in an Alternative Paradigm." In *The Manipulation of Literature: Studies in Literary Translation,* ed. Theo Hermans, New York: St. Martin's, 1985.

"Mother Courage's Cucumbers: Text, System, and Refraction in a Theory of Literature." *Modern Language Studies* 12 (1982): 3–20.

"The Growth of Literary Knowledge." *PTL* 2 (1977): 33–64.

17

Signing the Frame, Framing the Sign: Multiculturalism, Canonicity, Pluralism, and the Ethics of Reading *Heart of Darkness*

Daniel R. Schwarz

*Although Daniel R. Schwarz, professor of English at Cornell University, has written primarily on the novel and his most recent book is on the poetry of Wallace Stevens (*Narrative and Representation in the Poetry of Wallace Stevens, *1993), he has written two books on theory:* The Humanistic Heritage: Critical Theories of the English Novel from James to Hillis Miller *(1986) and* The Case for a Humanistic Poetics *(1991). In* The Case for a Humanistic Poetics, *he develops the argument for a perspective on literature that is humanistic in that it recognizes that literature derives its interest and value from the reader's recognition that it presents versions of human experience that encourage us to think about the meanings of experience. "Since humanistic criticism assumes that texts are by human authors for human readers about human subjects, a humanistic criticism is interested in how and why people think, write, act, and ultimately live," writes Schwarz in the final sentence of the opening chapter. However, the word "poetics" is as important as "humanistic" because it emphasizes that our responses to literature depend on techniques. Schwarz's paragraph that closes with the above statement opens: "I am calling for a revised humanis-*

This essay derived from the keynote address I gave at the 1993 Australian National University Conference in Canberra entitled "Renegotiating Ethics: Moral Inquiry and Literary and Cultural Discourses in the 1990s."

tic criticism that insists on the inseparability of such formal matters as rhetoric and narrative codes from the content, meaning, and significance of imaginative literature."

The essay printed here asks that we consider the necessity of an informed and ethical pluralism, or perhaps better, a pluralism and ethical commitment that constantly inform each other.

I

Elie Wiesel begins *Night,* his autobiographical novel of the Holocaust, with a description of Moshe the Beadle, an insignificant figure in a small town in Transylvania who taught the narrator about the cabala:

> They called him Moshe the Beadle, as though he had never had a surname in his life. He was a man of all work at a Hasidic synagogue. The Jews of Sighet—that little town in Transylvania where I spent my childhood—were very fond of him. He was very poor and lived humbly. . . . He was a past master in the art of making himself insignificant, of seeming invisible. . . . I loved his great, dreaming eyes, their gaze lost in the distance.[1]

But Moshe is expelled in early 1942 because he is a foreign Jew, and is not heard of for several months. He unexpectedly returns to tell of his miraculous escape from a Gestapo slaughter of Jews in the Polish forests. But no one believes him. Moshe cries: "Jews, listen to me. . . . Only listen to me" (5). But everyone assumes that he has gone mad. And the narrator—still a young boy—recalls asking him: "Why are you so anxious that people should believe what you say? In your place, I shouldn't care whether they believe me or not" (5).

Let us consider the significance of Moshe the Beadle. For one thing, Wiesel is using him as a metonymy for himself in his present role as narrator who is, as he writes, calling on us to listen to his words as he tells his relentless tale of his own miraculous escape from Nazi terror. Implicitly, he is urging us that it is our ethical responsibility not to turn away from the Witnessing Voice—Moshe himself, indeed all those who have seen, specifically, the Holocaust, and metonymically, for us, man's inhumanity to man—whether it occurs in Bosnia, Northern Ireland, or Somalia.

Why do I begin with *Night?* For one thing, it is a novel that depends upon and affirms the concept of individual agency; the speaker tells a wondrous and horrible tale of saving his life and shaping his role as Witness. We see dramatized the process of the narrator's developing into his role of Witness in the face of historical forces that would obliterate his humanity, his individuality, and his voice. Notwithstanding the efficiency of Nazi cultural production and technology of the death camps and gas chambers, the narrator re-creates himself through language. In the sense of the technological fulfillment of an ordered state that subordinated individual rights to the national purpose of the State, Nazi ideology has been thought of as a product of modernism. For those who have experienced, like Wiesel, the Holocaust firsthand—for whom Auschwitz is not a metaphor but a memory—language is more than the free play of signifiers. For these people and others on the political edge, their very telling—their very living—testifies to will, agency, and the desire to survive that resists and renders morally irrelevant simple positivistic explanations which argue that an author's language is completely culturally produced. In psychoanalytic linguistic terms, the narrator's telling is a *resistance* to the way in which the word "Jew" was culturally produced to mean inferior people who were progressively discounted, deprived of basic rights as citizens, labeled with a yellow Star of David, imprisoned, enslaved, and killed.

I select this spare, rough-hewn text because it is an eloquent testimony that depends on human agency and ethical commitment. *Night* reminds us, too, that the concept of author-function as a substitute for the creating intelligence does not do justice to the way in which language and art express the individual psyche. Readers will recall that the book's signification depends on its taut structure, the underpinning for an apparently primitive testimony, and depends, too, on its spare, even sparse, style. Its eloquence derives from its apparent ingenuousness. Yet *Night* speaks on behalf of meaning, on behalf of will—the will to survive, the will to witness—and on behalf of language's signification. *Night* eloquently reminds us of a grotesque historical irony, namely, that with its use of modern technology and Enlightenment rationally, Western man's progress led to the efficiency of the Nazi transport system, Nazi work camps, and Nazi gas chambers. *Night* is a text that resists irony and deconstruction, and cries out in its eloquence, pain, and anger as it enacts the *power of language.* The text traces the death of the narrator's mother, a sister, and, finally, father; it witnesses an encroaching horrible moral NIGHT, a night that includes the speaker's loss of religious belief in the face of historical events.

Assuming in its form—especially its prophetic voice—an ethical narratee, *Night* also demands an ethical response. By that I mean attention to issues that pertain to how life is lived within imagined worlds. Truth in novels takes place within the hypothesis "as if," which is another way of saying that as we think about our reading we are never completely unaware of the metaphoricity of literature. At one time, some critics may have naively ignored the metaphoricity of language and confused characterization with actual human character. But have not some theorists reached the other pole of willfully denying analogies to human life and naively repressing the possibilities of significance?

While I would be the first to acknowledge that the stakes are infinitely smaller, I think humanists and those interested in the ethical implications of writing, reading, and teaching have justifiably felt like Moshe the Beadle that their voices were for a while being ignored in the din of theoretical shouting. But in the wake of the de Man revelations and the insistence of many feminists, minorities, postcolonialists, and New Historicists that we look at what literature represents, the voice of those who all along believed in the ethical and aesthetic dimensions of literature and culture are once again being heard.

By beginning my discourse with Wiesel's *Night,* I am enacting my view that each of us belongs to different interpretive communities at the same time, and that these communities are in a dialogic relationship with one another. For example, I am an American academic, an English professor at Cornell, a divorced father who for several years has been the primary parent of two young adult sons, and, despite three or four generations of assimilation, still a Jew for whom the Holocaust has profound meaning. In my chapter on de Man's life and work in my book *The Case for a Humanistic Poetics,* as well as in my work on *Ulysses,* I write as a secular Jew who feels deep synchronic and diachronic ties to his heritage, and who tends to be drawn to the culturally marginalized—whether by nationality such as Conrad and Joyce, or by gender such as Woolf—and to those in economically straitened circumstances such as Lawrence. To situate ourselves and our interests is part of an ethics of reading.

A word more about Jewishness. Perhaps it is because the Jewish tradition—for me, at least, as a secular Jew who makes choices about how and what I believe—has always been open and exegetical that I resist theoretical dogma. When one looks at a page of the Talmud, one sees an unresolved dialogue among diverse commentators. In Judaism, there is no Nicene Creed, no attempt to resolve issues in a concluding statement. For example, in the Passover Haggadah, the various rabbis comment upon the meaning of the Exodus story and specifically the meaning of Passover customs, but again there is no attempt at resolution. Because historically Jews have lived on the margin—in ghettos and shtetls—never sure of what pogroms tomorrow will bring—they have tended to be skeptical of sweeping universals and to dwell in the particular. Moreover, Jews have been concerned with relations between man and God and man and man, not simply the hereafter—in part because the hereafter was often a luxury while they eked out a living and awaited what seemed like arbitrary changes in the political winds. And the Jewish tradition is ethically based—think of the Talmud as a debate about law and ethics—with an emphasis on living in what Aristotle called the "ineluctable modality of the visible" (and Joyce redefined into "What you damn well have to see").

Because each of us is a nodal point where multiple major influences as well as secondary influences meet, each of us encounters the texts we read on the seam of reading—and by "seam," I am playing with S-E-A-M, S-E-E-M, and S-E-M as in semiotics and dissemination. I stress how texts shape readers and readers shape texts. I am a pragmatic Aristotelian who stresses the relationship of the poem as a made object, the product of an author's conscious (and unconscious) art or craft designed to achieve foreknown ends that result from the psyche, values, and idiosyncrasies that differentiate her or him from others. Thus my version of cultural criticism would seek to create what Saul Rosensweig, speaking of his own "Freud, Jung and Hall the King-Maker," calls the "idioverse, the universe of events that constitutes the individual," as it is realized in the artist's works.[2] I am prone to pose the question "What is your evidence?" to myself and to my students, and expect my and their answer to consist of passages from primary texts. I am conscious of how plot enacts values, and how plot is a structure of effects. I try to balance the structure of tropes with a sense that the plot represents an anterior reality. (I do not believe the citation by one theorist of another theorist constitutes an argument. Indeed, if current theory is a production of knowledge, not the reproduction, how is it that current theory relies so much on the argument from authority?)

Narrative is both the representation of external events and the telling of those events. My interest in narrative derives from my belief that we make sense of our life by ordering it and giving it shape. The stories we tell ourselves provide the continuity among the concatenation of diverse episodes in our lives, even if our stories inevitably distort and falsify. Each of us is continually writing and rewriting the text of our lives, revising our memories and hopes, proposing plans, filtering disappointments through our defenses and rationalizations, making adjustments in the way we present ourselves to ourselves and to others. To the degree that we are self-conscious, we live in our narratives—our discourse—about our actions, thoughts, and feelings. While there is always a gulf between imagined worlds and real ones, does not the continuity between reading lives and reading texts depend on understanding reading as a means of sharpening our perception, cultivating discriminations, and deepening our insights about ourselves? For reading is a process of cognition that depends on actively organizing the phenomena of language both in the moment of perception *and* on the fuller understanding that develops as our reading continues, as well as in our retrospective view of our completed reading.

Reading is a dialogic activity in which multiple ways of looking at a text contend with one another; each perspective implicitly suggests interrogatives to other approaches. I suggest that as readers we can and should belong to multiple interpretive communities; rather than propose unitary stories of reading and choose between the either/or of possible readings, we can and should enjoy multiplicity and diversity in our readings. The kind of pluralistic criticism I imagine sees criticism as a series of hypotheses rather than as a final product. In its healthy and open pluralism, it is inclusive rather than exclusive. Even as we answer each question and pursue each line of inquiry, we become aware that each explanation is partial. It may be time to back off from the notion that the critic is *vates* and return to the more modest Socratic question-and-answer structure in order to leave rhetorical space for other explanations. Pluralism may at times define a position passionately but always in the mode of "This is true, or is it?" and always leaving space for a response. By contrast, dogmatism asserts its position without allowing for an alternative, while relativism accepts all positions as if they were equal.

The text itself, what it represents, what it signifies, and how it enacts a meaning should always be an important part of our pedagogy. Yet, as Stephen Greenblatt understands, all reading has an element of self-fashioning and we should be self-conscious about how self-fashioning creates angles of distortion. For example, how each of us responds to the narrative of Paul de Man's life and work depends on how we were personally situated, including the extent to which we invested in deconstruction. How we situate ourselves as individual readers and as members of interpretive communities is an important part of our reading and, as teachers, we need to make the students aware of how we and they might acknowledge *our differences.* We need to be careful about defining our own position because we do not always see ourselves as others see us. We can get lost in a welter of self-pity and can overestimate our own worth.

As I have argued elsewhere, finally, the largest interpretive community is one. Positioning oneself in relationship to a text is as important as positioning a text in relation to cultural contexts and our debates within the academic community about critical assumptions. Simply put, texts like Elie Wiesel's *Night* are different for those whose family disappeared in the concentration camps and different again for those fellow Jews who, like myself, by accident of place survived. Indeed, I believe that there is a place within literary studies for texts that reflect our own varied interests. Special interest has always been an engine that has driven literary studies—first as an offspring of classical study and philology, then of historicism and textual editing, later of New Criticism—and special interest has produced the wonderful revolution in feminist studies, postcolonial studies, and ethnic studies.

Where, let us ask, are theory, criticism, and the study of literature going? I have always doubted that theory was teleologically advancing in a kind of Manifest Destiny from the International Academic Datelines of Paris and New Haven. Why has theory evolved into theology and why do partisans of one or another approach become sects? Is it the power of theory's arguments or, for some acolytes, the importance of *belonging*—and excluding and scapegoating those who do not belong? Theories, including Marxism and deconstruction, are valuable as part of a pluralistic discourse but become oppressive and distorting when they become monolithic paradigms worshiped by monotheistic cults. At times literary studies have suffered from reductive rhetoric that has done intellectual violence to complex texts in the name of various monolithic theories.

I feel like someone who, with a small band of other surviving humanists, has created a little island outpost where we pursued our interests, and perhaps been grudgingly given a place in the General Assembly—certainly not the Security Council—of theory. While welcoming the destabilizing insights of much recent theory—including the idea that language does not signify absolutely and texts are historically and culturally produced—I am willing to be identified with such quaint ideas as humanism, pluralism, and canonicity, and use such terms as *ethics* and even *author.* I am for a pluralism of readings, a pluralism of texts, and a pluralism of cultures.

Because I assume human agency in writing and reading and believe that there is a space for a non-Marxist version of cultural studies, I am on occasion invited to play the role of Academic Dissenter (for some, read: Dinosaur) in journals and at conferences.

Within any theory of cultural production, whether of texts or readers, we need to leave space for the creative intelligence of authors and readers who make choices that have ethical implications. My focus, my concern, is the act of reading specific texts. I have always been wary of extravagant readings that use the text as point of departure for flights of fancy and/or to make a political point. Indeed, for me, extravagant reading is an oxymoron.

As a way of anticipating my approach to *Heart of Darkness,* I provocatively propose two columns:

ingenuous, or unsophisticated	**rigorous, urbane, or sophisticated**
essentialism	**materialism**
univocal, monistic	**dialogic**
positivistic logic and "A" causes "B"	**affinities, playfulness**
binary thinking	**free play of signifiers as revealed to an imaginative, interesting, and powerful reader**
conservative	**progressive**
traditional	**avant-garde**
close-minded	**open-minded**
simple, facile, deductively consistent	**complex, difficult, disruptive**
static	**destabilizing**
subjective	**objective**
rational, detached, restrained	**passionate, engaged, committed**
old-fashioned	**enlightened**
dogmatic insistence on monolithic truth	**belief that some readings are better and truer than others**

While the column on the left is usually used to describe humanistic criticism and the column on the right to describe various advanced theories—including deconstruction and Marxism—I suggest that the categories on the right, which are thought to belong to advanced theory, at times more aptly describe humanistic pluralist criticism, and I subversively invite a questioning—a **de-deconstruction**—of these binary distinctions as they are now applied. Moreover, I suggest that the best of all criticism understands these supposedly binary concepts in terms of "both/and" not "neither/nor," and that well before deconstruction Kenneth Burke, William Empson, R. P. Blackmur, Dorothy Van Ghent, and M. H. Abrams demonstrated in their works how these supposedly binary concepts cross-fertilize one another, invade each other's borders, and form a continuum.[3]

Gerald Graff calls literary theory "a discourse that treats literature as in some respects a problem and seeks to formulate that problem in general terms."[4] Some recent theory has claimed for itself a position as a master discourse rather than one of many discourses. Let us look for a moment at one of the most brilliant and influential theorists today, Fredric Jameson. When Jameson writes, "[O]nly Marxism can give us an adequate account of the essential *mystery* of the cultural past . . . by arguing its ultimate philosophical and methodological priority over more specialized interpretive codes whose insights are strategically limited as much by their own situational origins as by the narrow or local ways in which they construe or construct their objects of study,"[5] that is an ethical statement. It is also an example of how essentialism finds a home in the house of materialism. And his notion of history as an "absent cause," "inaccessible to us except in textual forms" is only paying homage to language's need to be understood—hypothetically and within its "as if" metaphoricity—as essential. Graff rightly urges us to "think of literary theory not as a set of systematic principles, necessarily, or a founding philosophy, but simply as an inquiry into assumptions, premises, and legitimate principles and concepts."[6] Yet, all too often the energy and unruliness of a text disappear in the hegemonic claims made by followers of Marx, Lacan, and Foucault.

Jameson believes that if we can locate the master narrative of a particular age, we can get at the political unconscious. For him, "only Marxism can give us an adequate account of the essential *mystery* of the cultural past." He disdains the notion of freedom from the "omnipresence of history and the implacable influence of the social."[7] Is Jameson's claim for Marxism an *ethical* approach toward texts and the variety of lived life? Or is such a reductive and extravagant approach unethical in its distortion of the specificities and differences of human experience? As an Aristotelian and pluralist, I ask why rewrite, resolve, and homogenize the whole rich and random multiple realities of concrete everyday experience into a monolithic story of the political unconscious?

II

Let me state my credo. I believe that the close reading of texts—both from an authorial and resistant perspective—enables us to perceive more clearly; I believe in a continuity between reading texts and reading lives. I believe that the activity of critical thinking—not merely literary criticism—can be taught by the analysis of language. I believe in the place of the aesthetic. I believe that we can enter into imagined worlds and learn from them. Following Aristotle, I believe that the aesthetic, ethical, and political are inextricably linked.

In considering ethical reading, I want to differentiate between an ethics *of* reading and an ethics *in* reading. For me, an ethics *of* reading includes acknowledging who we are and what are our biases and interests. An ethics of reading speaks of our reading as if, no matter how brilliant, it were proposing some possibilities rather than reporting God's Holy Word; it means reading from multiple perspectives, or at least empathically entering into the readings of those who are situated differently. For me, an ethics *in* reading would try to understand what the author was saying to her original imagined audience and why, as well as how, the actual polyauditory audience might have responded and for what reasons. An ethics in reading is different from but, in its attention to a value-oriented epistemology, related to an ethics of reading. An ethics in reading implies attention to moral issues generated by the events described within an imagined world. It asks what ethical questions are involved in the act of transforming life into art, and notices such issues as Pound's anti-Semitism and the patronizing racism of some American nineteenth- and early twentieth-century writers. What we choose to read and especially what to include on syllabi have an ethical dimension. Thus, I select other Conrad works for my undergraduate lecture course than the unfortunately titled *Nigger of the Narcissus.*

Why did ethics disappear from the universe of literary studies? Was it in part the disillusionment of the Vietnam War that seemed to give the lie to the view after the Second World War that we could cultivate our minds and control our lives after the defeat of the Nazis and the Japanese? As critics, we once addressed the ethics of reading and the ethics in reading; that in part is what Arnold meant by "high seriousness" and Leavis by such phrases as "tangible realism" and "bracing moralism" and Trilling by "the hum and buzz of implication." All theory is in part disguised autobiography and the current emphasis on the meaninglessness of language and on the overwhelming power of history to produce cultural effects without allowing room for explanations that stress creative intelligence, as well as the emphasis on the transformation of the author into author-function, reflect a kind of skepticism about human agency; such skepticism at times approaches a harsh, abrasive ahumanistic cynicism.

Let me continue my credo: literary meaning depends on a trialogue among (1) authorial intention and interest; (2) the formal text produced by the author for a specific historical audience; and (3) the responses of a particular reader in a specific time. Texts mediate and condense anterior worlds and authors' psyches. The condensation is presented by words, words that are a web of signs but that signify something beyond themselves; within a text, words signify differently. Some words and phrases almost summon a visible presence, others are elusive or even barely matter in the terms of representation—as in Joyce's encyclopedic catalogues in "Cyclops." The context of any discourse determines the meaning—or should we say the epistemological and semiological value—of the word or sentence. And once we use the word *value,* are we not saying that words have an ethical quotient? Human agency—on the part of author, reader, or characters within real or imagined worlds—derives in part from will, from the idiosyncrasies of human psyche and, in part, on cultural forces beyond the control of the individual. That is another way of saying that language is constituted and constituting, although it gives subjective human agency to the act of constituting. While we need to be alert to the implications of racist, sexist, and anti-Semitic nuances, we also need to stress reading the words on the page in terms of the demands made by the text's context and form—in particular, by its structure of effects, or what I have called the *doesness* of the text.

If self-awareness of oneself and one's relationship to family and community—including one's responsibilities, commitments, and values—is part of the ethical life, then reading contributes to greater self-understanding. Reading complements one's experience by enabling us to live lives beyond those we live and experience emotions that are not ours; it heightens one's perspicacity by enabling us to watch *figures*—tropes, that is, personifications of our fellow humans—who are not ourselves, but like ourselves. For me, books are written about humans by humans for humans, and elaborate "theories" that ignore narrative and representational aspects of literature in favor of rhetorical, deconstructive, or politically correct readings are unsatisfactory.

Let us welcome the turn to considering the relation between literature and theory but insist with Aristotle on the interrelationship between the political, aesthetic, and ethical. In prior academic generations our insulation from politics was mirrored in the supposedly objective and hermetic world of art, and New Criticism (and in more recent times deconstruction) often encouraged the binary opposition between art and life. For me, the intentional fallacy has always been to ignore how art is self-expressive and the affective fallacy has always been to ignore real readers reading. We need to worry about authors: *the failure to do so* was, for me, another version of the intentional or biographical fallacy (or how real readers read); *the failure to do so* was, for me, the affective fallacy. For New Criticism, the text existed in a Platonic world of ideas and was resolved in a unity that provided an aesthetic alternative to the political chaos—the Depression, the World War, the threat of nuclear war, the Vietnam War—that raged outside. Later, at the time of the totalizing vision of Reaganomics, accumulation of ostentatious wealth, and the patronizing bankruptcy of Bushery, texts were reexamined—sometimes by smug and patronizing deconstructive picaros—for their rhetorical subtext that undermined unity and order.

Humanists have also been attacked implicitly and explicitly for not opening up the canon or profession on their watch. Yet, notwithstanding resistance from others in their generation, in the 1960s and 1970s it was often liberal humanists espousing free speech, respect for others, the value of listening, tolerance to diversity of ideas, who opened the door to the theorists and pushed for inclusion of diverse perspectives, including feminism and Marxism, and who welcomed women and minorities. But we intellectuals differ from cannibals in that cannibals only eat their enemies while we eat our friends, particularly our elders, our predecessors, and our teachers. For some, committing intellectual matricide and patricide has become a ritual of our profession. At times the younger turn on us elders because we are not as zealous as they in pursuing imagined ancient enemies. Are not we like the Torajans of Sulawesi who celebrate funerals by killing a member of a village that contains, as tradition has it, the weakest members of their tribe because, according to oral history, centuries ago that village didn't join the rest of the Torajans in a war against their ancient enemy, the Bugis? Do we not need to remember that all of us literary intellectuals belong to that odd collection of freemasons whose secret rituals consist of reading books, speaking about them to colleagues and students, and writing articles and books about them?

Why have concepts like objective truth, essence, nature, identity, and teleology—once-progressive ideas that insisted on the separation of the aesthetic from the political—become labeled conservative and reactionary ideas? As Graff remarks: "If one wished, a plausible case could be made for the view that the interpretive *objectionists* are the real heirs of the radical tradition which has sought to secularize and demystify the concept of meaning, and that the deconstructionists are carrying on a rearguard attempt to preserve some element of linguistic mystery from secularization."[8]

How has the evidentiary test for testing our readings changed? Dominick La Capra has cautioned against overuse of "world-in-a-grain-of-sand anecdotes" as if these anecdotes imply universals; we should be as wary about finding the secret of a text in a few subversive lines. In the name of interesting or extravagant readings, have we strictly differentiated between logical argument and random association? Have we installed the critic/theorist as *vates* and substituted paralogic for logic? As La Capra writes, "Old historicism sometimes placed a premium on aimless exhaustiveness and contextualization. New historicism often opts for a rather precious play of analogies, ancedotes, and associations."[9]

Graff has commendably argued that those of us who use contemporary theory need to defend the truth claims of our readings. In the act of doing so, do we not need to consider in our arguments issues such as narrative cohesion, agency, aesthetic achievement, and authorial intention? Because on the whole, feminist and postcolonial readings that have drawn upon the texture—I use that word deliberately—of lived experience will find they have more frequently met that test than those extravagant readings that place being "interesting" before respect for what the text does say. The glory of the best of resistant readings—gay, New Historical, feminist—is that they often meet the truth test and provide logical, plausible readings based on evidence.

When we enter into an imagined world, we become involved with what Nadine Gordimer has called "the substance of living from which the artist draws his vision," and our criticism must speak to that "substance of living."[10] In Third World and postcolonial literature—and in politically engaged texts like *Night*—this involvement is much more intense. Thus the recent interest in the postcolonial and Third World literature—accelerated by Soyinka's and Wolcott's Nobel Prizes—challenges the tenets of deconstruction. Literature written at the political edge reminds us what literature has always been about: urgency, commitment, tension, and feeling. Indeed, at times have we not transferred those emotions to parochial critical debate rather than to our responses to literature? While it may not be completely irrelevant to talk about gaps, fissures, and enigmas and about the free play of signifiers in the poetry of Wally Serote ("Death Survey") and Don Mattera ("Singing Fools"), we must focus, too, on their status as persecuted blacks in South Africa and the pain and alienation they feel in the face of that persecution. Nadine Gordimer has written—and Joyce might have said the same thing about Ireland—"It is from the daily life of South Africa that there have come the conditions of profound alienation which prevail among South African artists."[11] When discussing politically engaged literature—be it Soyinka, Gordimer, or Wiesel—we need to recuperate historical circumstances and understand the writer's ordering of that history in his imagined world. We need to know not merely what patterns of provisional representation are created by language but the historical, political, and social ground of that representation. We need to be open to hearing the often unsophisticated and unironical voice of pain, angst, and fear.

When we read literature we journey into an imagined land, while at the same time remaining home. Reading is a kind of imaginative traveling; unlike real traveling, it allows us to transport ourselves immediately back "home." Travel is immersive; home is reflective. How we take our imaginative journeys depends on how we are trained to read: what we as readers do with the available data, how we sort it out and make sense of it. Although the text has a kind of stability because it cannot change, our ways of speaking about texts are always somewhat metaphoric.

Aristotle, we recall, inextricably linked the ethical and the aesthetic—seemingly opposites. As Aristotle puts it in *The Poetics,* "Poetry"—by which he means imaginative forms such as tragedy and epic—"tends to express the universal, history the particular. By the universal I mean how a person of a certain type will on occasion speak or act, according to the law of probability or necessity."[12] His very stipulations about what constitutes a good tragedy imply that the artist has an ethical responsibility to his audience to provide a certain kind of action within a set of conventions. What interests Aristotle is what actions reveal about character: "Character is that which reveals moral purpose, showing what kinds of things a man chooses or avoids. . . . Any speech or action that manifests moral purpose of any kind will be expressive of character."[13] And this includes, I propose, any narrative, including narrative about the history of the profession or about a particular theory.

III

With the welcome return to mimesis and representation, cultural criticism has opened the door once again to historicizing. Culture is dynamic, and at any given point culture is heteroglossic, a dialogue of diverse thoughts, feelings, goals, and values. According to Isaiah Berlin, "Cultures—the sense of what the world meant to societies, of men's and women's collective sense of themselves in relation to others and the environment, that which affects particular forms of thought, feeling, behavior, action— . . . cultures differ."[14] We need to honor cultural differences and respect the claims of cultural enclaves. Clifford Geertz has written, "The problem of integration of cultural life becomes one of making it possible for people inhabiting different worlds to have a genuine, and reciprocal, impact upon one another."[15] While I respect and welcome other views of culture and understand that civilization has many components, I have been arguing for a cultural criticism that takes seriously the notion of canons, periods, and culture as the best that was thought and created during a period of civilization.

Let us turn to the concept of canon. Canon, as I have argued, needs to be an evolving concept, a house with many windows and doors, rather than a mausoleum. Within my pluralistic concept of canon there is room for enclaves to establish their own subcanons. I still value the major Western texts—the plays of Shakespeare, the Homeric epics, *Paradise Lost,* the great metaphysical and romantic poems, the masterworks of the novel like *Emma, Wuthering Heights, Jane Eyre, Middlemarch, Bleak House, Lord Jim, Ulysses,* and *To the Lighthouse*—but can we not within a healthy pluralism teach some common texts and speak to each of our legitimate and multicultural interests in other texts? A curriculum, I suggest, can be something of a smorgasbord, and our courses (and maybe syllabi) need to have room for teachers and students to pursue their own interests.

The breakdown into enclaves and tribes—the effect, in part, of the end of the binary cold-war struggle between two superpowers—in the latter part of the twentieth century takes the form of curricula battles between people who once thought that they had more in common than they had differences. If we are not careful, the Balkanization of English departments means we will talk to only those in our ethnic neighborhood. Often in a spirit of intolerance, political enclaves seek to *cleanse* the syllabi of objectionable texts—whether it be objectionable works by dead white males or humanistic theorists. Canonical texts become—as Clifford wrote of what the West had become for Edward Said—"a play of projections, doublings, idealizations, and rejections of a complex, shifting otherness."[16] The debate about who owns the syllabi and who owns the curricula and canon parallels the debate about who owns the land, whether it be the land of Northern Ireland, Hawaii, Palestine, or Bosnia and Herzegovina. It is as if cultural stratification were akin to geological stratification. In nineteenth-century American studies, there is a black and female and Hispanic and Indian canon and cultural history that is at once part of and separate from the prevailing hegemonic cultural history. For while the same groups inhabited the same space at the same time, their cultural history is reflected and refracted, displaced, sublimated, and transposed in different texts.

IV

Let me suggest lines of inquiry to pursue in our reading and teaching of *Heart of Darkness*. Of course, we should regard the questions that follow as only instances of the multiple possibilities of a pluralistic approach. Let us think of these questions as concentric circles of inquiry, circles that vary in their relevance from reading to reading by one reader, from reader to reader, and from passage to passage. Let me point out, too, that my questions stress the inseparability of ethical, aesthetic, political, and contextual issues, and that the order of the questions is not meant to indicate the relative importance of each question or questions.[17]

1. **How is *Heart of Darkness* a personal story written out of moral urgency which reflects Conrad's Congo experience and his own epistemological and psychological inquiry at a time of personal crisis in 1898?** How can we use the Congo Diary and Conrad's letters to relate his life and work? How is Marlow a surrogate for Conrad? If we see Marlow as a fictional surrogate for Conrad, how does such an approach relate to the fiction-making and masques of the late 1890s and the first decade of the twentieth century, as instanced in Wilde's *The Decay of Lying,* Yeats's poems, and Joyce's use of Stephen Dedalus?
2. **How is *Heart of Darkness* a voyage of Marlow's self-discovery?** Do we need to stress how that self-discovery takes place in a political frame and is a political reawakening? Conrad's narrative enacts the

value that the Africans and Europeans share a common humanity: the English too were once natives conquered by the Romans and England too was once one of the dark places of the earth. Moreover, Europeans not only require laws and rules to restrain their atavistic impulses, but they become more monstrous than those they profess to civilize. Finally, terms like "savage" and "barbarian" are arbitrary designations by imperialists who in fact deserve these epithets more than the natives.

3. **How is *Heart of Darkness* a political novel concerned with the Belgian King Leopold's rapacious exploitation of the Congo? What attitudes do imperialists take to the natives and why?** How is it, as Marxists would contend, a story about the "commodity fetishism" of later capitalism? Is it, as Chinua Achebe has claimed, a racist drama whose images reinforce white stereotypes about the dichotomy of black and white?[18] Is *Heart of Darkness* an imperialistic romance about the conquest of Africa? Or is it more accurate to stress how it is an ironic inversion, a bathetic reification, of such a genre? Are black and white and light and dark always equated with the polarity of civilization and savagery, good and evil, corrupt and innocent, or is the dialectic of images more subtle than that?

   Conrad plays on the clichés and shibboleths of his era when Africa was the "dark continent"—the place of mystery and secrets—and the primitive continent where passions and emotions dominated reason and intellect. He asks us to consider whether we can cross cultural boundaries without transgressing them; we then need to ask: In situating himself in response to imperialistic exploitation, is Marlow able to separate himself from colonial domination? And can we as Westerners teach a story like *Heart of Darkness* in a non-Western setting without reinscribing ourselves as colonialists? When we teach *Heart of Darkness,* are we in the same position as Western museums displaying non-Western art; that is, are we invading a different culture with our texts about colonialism? *But not so fast.* For his time Conrad was avant-garde in acknowledging that at times Africans were more controlled and ethically advanced than Westerners; he, like Gauguin, knew that their cultural practices and their art—chants, dance, drumming—were alien to Western concepts of display, that their art was religious in function, linking daily experience to abstract beliefs, and that their art was used performatively in funerals, weddings, and initiation rites.

Heart of Darkness speaks with passion to the issues of colonialism and empire. Whether in Ireland, Malay, or Africa, Western colonialism in the name of civilization despoils the people and the land it touches. *Heart of Darkness* debunks the concept of the white man's burden and shows how the concept of empire is a sham. Conrad chooses to show Kurtz's "Exterminate the Brutes" as a stunning abandonment of the moral pretensions on which imperialism is based. Kurtz's radical transformation exposes his reductive perspective and that of Marlow, King Leopold of Belgium, other Europeans—indeed, all of us who would seek to adopt a stance where one culture views another from an iconoclastic stance.

4. **How is the disrupted narrative, the circumlocutious syntax, the alternation between impressionistic and graphic language indicative of modernism?** Should we also not think of *Heart of Darkness* as part of the awareness of modern artists that multiple perspectives are necessary? After all, in 1895, Conrad wrote, "Another man's truth is a dismal lie to me."[19] We need to stress how it takes issue with Victorian assumptions about univocal truth and a divinely ordered world. Conrad's use of the dramatized consciousness of Marlow reflects his awareness that "we live as we dream—alone," and the concomitant awareness (seen in the development of cubism and Joyce's ventriloquy in *Ulysses*) that one perspective is not enough.

   Picasso's and Braque's cubist experiments demonstrate how they, too, are trying to achieve multiple perspectives. Conrad, too, was freeing black and white from the traditional morphology of color, just as the fauvists and cubists were freeing traditional ideas of representation from the morphology of color. Conrad is also freeing his language from the morphology of representation—as in his use of adjectives for purely affective rather than descriptive reasons. Conrad's use of allegorized rather than nominalistic adjectives such as "subtle" and "unspeakable" invites the frame narrator and Conrad's readers to respond in terms of their own experiences and to validate in their responses that they, too, dream alone. When creating his Congo, Conrad knew Gauguin's 1893 Tahitian journal *Noa, Noa* and was influenced by that and perhaps Gauguin's paintings. Gauguin anticipated Picasso and other modernists in seeing the elemental and magical aspects of primitive lives as well as the passion, simplicity, and naturalness of primitive lives.

5. **How does *Heart of Darkness* relate to the intellectual history of modernism?** How is Kurtz indicative of the Nietzschean will-to-power that was a major strand of the intellectual fabric of imperialism and fascism? How does Conrad's text relate to his contemporary Freud's probing of the unconscious? How does *Heart of Darkness* speak to the breakdown of moral certainty, the sense that each of us lives in a closed circle, and the consequent fear of solipsism? Conrad feared that each of us is locked in his or her own perceptions and despaired in his letters that even language will not help us reach out to others. Thus, Marlow's fear that "we live, as we dream—alone" is also an idea that recurs throughout the period of early modernism, a period in which humans felt, to quote F. H. Bradley, that "my experience is a closed circle; a circle closed on the outside. . . . In brief . . . the whole world for each is peculiar and private to that soul."[20] That the frame narrator can tell the story shows that Marlow has communicated with someone and offers a partial antidote to the terrifying fear of isolation and silence that haunted Conrad.
6. **How is *Heart of Darkness* a comment on the idea of social Darwinism that mankind was evolving into something better and better?** *Heart of Darkness* refutes the position that history was evolving historically upward. Recall Conrad's famous letter about the world as a knitting machine, where the ironic trope of the world as a machine is a rebuttal to Christianity: "It knits us in and it knits us out. It has knitted time, space, pain, death, corruption, despair and all the illusions—and nothing matters. I'll admit however that to look at the remorseless process is sometimes amusing."[21] Conrad uses this elaborate ironic trope to speak to the late Victorian belief that the industrial revolution is part of an upwardly evolving teleology; this belief is really a kind of social Darwinism. According to Conrad, humanity would like to believe in a providentially ordered world vertically descending from a benevolent God; that is, to believe in an embroidered world. But, Conrad believed, we actually inhabit a temporally defined horizontal dimension within an amoral, indifferent universe—or what in the above passage Conrad calls "the remorseless process."
7. **How would a pluralistic approach address the meaning of "The horror! The horror!" as a part of an evolving agon that generates a structure of affects?** Let us look at "The horror! The horror!" in the context of what precedes. That Kurtz has achieved a "moral victory"

may very well be a necessary illusion for Marlow. But did Kurtz pronounce a verdict on his reversion to primitivism and achieve the "supreme moment of complete knowledge" (149)?[22] Or is this what Marlow desperately wants to believe? Coming from a man who "could get himself to believe anything," how credible is Marlow's interpretation that "The horror! The horror!" is "an affirmation, a moral victory paid for by innumerable defeats, by abominable terrors, by abominable satisfactions" (151)? When Kurtz had enigmatically muttered, "Live rightly, die, die . . . ," Marlow had wondered "Was he rehearsing some speech in his sleep, or was it a fragment of a phrase from some newspaper article?" (148). Marlow had just remarked that Kurtz's voice "survived his strength to hide in the magnificent folds of eloquence the barren darkness of his heart" (147). If Kurtz had kicked himself loose of the earth, how can Kurtz pronounce a verdict on his ignominious return to civilization or an exclamation elicited from a vision of his own imminent death? For the reader—the reader responding to the inextricable relationship between the ethical and the aesthetic in Conrad's text—Kurtz remains a symbol of how the human ego can expand infinitely to the point where it tries to will its own apotheosis.

8. **In what ways does *Heart of Darkness* reveal overt and covert sexist attitudes?** Is *Heart of Darkness* a sexist document? Brantlinger writes, "The voices that come from the heart of darkness are almost exclusively white and male, as usual in imperialist texts."[23] In a situation where opportunities for heterosexuality are limited, what does *Heart of Darkness* say about male bonding among the whites and about miscegenation? Are we offended that one of Kurtz's supposedly "abominable practices" is the taking of a savage mistress? If we understand Marlow's patronizing attitude toward women as naive and simple, can we not use the text to show the difference between authorial and resistant readings, between how texts are read when they are written and how they are read now? Does the lie to the Intended reveal Marlow's sexism? Is Conrad aware of Marlow's sexual stereotyping, even if he means the lie to the Intended to be a crucial moment of self-definition for Marlow? We need to examine the assumptions about women that dominate this final episode, and to align them with the passage when he tells us that the women are always "out of touch with truth." But, of course, the tale dramatizes

that all of us live in a world of our own, and none of us is in a position to patronize the other, be it natives, women, or others who go to the Congo armed with ideals.

9. **How is *Heart of Darkness* a heteroglossic text embodying diverse modes of discourse?** Marlow's recurring nightmare begins not only to compete with his effort to use language discursively and mimetically, but to establish a separate, more powerful telling. The narrative includes the semiotics of a primitive culture: gestures of the savage mistress and the Intended; the beating of the drums, the shrill cry of the sorrowing savages; and the development of Kurtz into Marlow's own symbol of moral darkness and atavistic reversion. This more inclusive tale, not so much told as performed by Marlow as he strains for the signs and symbols that will make his experience intelligible, transcends his more conventional discourse. Conrad shows that these instinctive and passionate outbursts, taking the form of gestures, chants, and litany, represent a tradition, a core of experience, that civilized man has debased.

V

Finally, why do we continue to teach and read Conrad? Does the concept of canon have value? Is it not the very kinds of urgent questions—and, yes, relevance to us and to our students' *minds*—that *Heart of Darkness* elicits that gives it value today? We need a criticism that, as Martha Nussbaum has put it, "talks of human lives and choices as if they matter to us all. . . . [Literature] . . . speaks about *us,* about our lives and choices and emotions, about our social existence and the totality of our connections. As Aristotle observed, it is deep and conducive to our inquiry about how to live, because it does not simply (as history does) record that this event happened; it searches for patterns of possibility—of choice, and circumstance, and the interaction between choice and circumstance—that turn up in human lives with such a persistence that they must be regarded as *our* possibilities."[24] A study of modernist culture and the colonial Congo, Conrad's *Heart of Darkness* also speaks to our culture and raises urgent issues for us. Is that not why we read it, even as we consign some former canonical texts to the margins? Because it is an urgent political drama, because it raises questions of racial and sexual identity, and because it is a wonderful story that probes our identity with our human antecedents, *Heart of Darkness* lives for us as surely as Kurtz lives for Marlow, and Marlow lives for the narrator.

What does Marlow's reading of Kurtz teach us about our reading of texts and lives? As an allegory of reading, *Heart of Darkness* resists easy simplifications and one-dimensional readings, resists attempts to explain in either/or terms. Even as *Heart of Darkness* remains a text that raises questions about the possibility of meaning, it suggests the plenitude of meaning. Just as Marlow gradually moves from seeing a drama of values to living a drama of character, so as readers do we. Like him, we make the journey from spectator to participant. Are we not trying to make sense of Marlow as he is trying to make sense of Kurtz? And are we not also trying to make sense of the frame narrator who is trying to make sense of Marlow making sense of Kurtz? Does not the tale's emphasis on choosing a sign for our systems of meaning call attention to the arbitrary nature of choosing a framing sign and make us aware of the need for multiple perspectives? Do we not learn how one invests with value something not seen or known in preference to the ugly reality that confronts us? Is not Conrad's ironic parable about belief itself, including the Christian belief in whose name much of imperialism was carried on? Thus, in essence, the tale urges us toward a pluralistic perspective. Finally, one-dimensional readings bend to the need for a pluralistic reading that takes account of Marlow's disillusionment and his magnetic attraction to Kurtz as the nightmare of his choice. For Conrad has turned a story about a present journey to Africa into a journey through Europe's past as well as into each human being's primitive psyche. Our students remind us that narrative, story, and response in human and ethical terms triumph over excessively ideological readings. Our students remind us, too, of the need to link hermeneutics and rhetoricity; for them, "bits of absurd sentences" of their reading (46)—to use Marlow's words to describe what he hears from the manager and the manager's uncle and tries to *read* in terms of his experience—need to be understood in terms of our most fundamental text: the story of our own lives.

VI

I conclude with a scene from the Book of Daniel when the Babylonian king Belshazzar is feasting and drinking from sacred vessels that his father

Nebuchadnezzar had plundered from the Holy Jewish Temple in Jerusalem; suddenly a hand unattached to a body appears and writes mysterious words on the wall: "Mene, Mene, Tekel, Upharsin." But neither Belshazzar nor his followers can understand the words, which seem to be written in an unknown tongue. So, desperate to know what has been written, Belshazzar summons Daniel, who has a reputation for wisdom. Daniel can read the words, which are in an early Semitic language, Aramaic, from which Hebrew is derived. Literally, Daniel explains, the words mean "numbered, numbered, weighed, and divided." But Daniel offers an ethical interpretation, foretelling the destruction of Belshazzar and his kingdom. Daniel's story of reading is a prophecy: "God hath numbered thy [Belshazzar's] kingdom, and brought it to an end; thou art weighed in the balances, and found wanting. Thy kingdom is divided, and given to the Medes and the Persians." In doing so, Daniel acts as a literary critic with an ethical bent and tells Belshazzar a story of reading.

Let us use the mysterious words that appear to Belshazzar and that require an interpretation as a parable of what readers must do. While Daniel's prophecy comes true, is it because Daniel knows and speaks God's will or because he is lucky? In any case, because most of us do not read texts with a sense that God has blessed our readings, we must draw upon our own intelligence, ethics, imagination, perspicacity, and experience. Whenever we read texts—or life experiences—we are a little bit like Daniel. Snippets of texts require that they be read, and yet they always remain partially understood or at least open to diverse interpretations. Texts—and our life experiences—cry out for understanding even as they resist our understanding. Since we cannot call upon Daniel, we have to be our own Daniel and do the work ourselves. To be sure, there are commentators and teachers—and theorists—who would be our Daniel, and we should make use of them. But, finally, we must interpret our words and experiences according to our own perspective and believe in our intelligence, imagination, and ethics. Occasionally, we have works like Joyce's *Ulysses* or *Finnegans Wake* or difficult poems like Wallace Stevens's *Notes Toward a Supreme Fiction* (or, for some of us, an organic chemistry textbook) that seem to require the presence of an external Daniel; but even these reveal their mysteries to an experienced reader. Words that we read may have never before appeared to us in the context in which we see them now; even if we have read them before, rereading puts them in a new context, for we have inevitably changed. As for Belshazzar, for us words may have no prior significance other than their own manifestation; or, more likely, they may refer to something with which we are familiar. But they must always be understood anew and brought within the ken of our experience and values.

Notes

1. Page numbers in parentheses refer to Elie Wiesel, *Night,* trans. Stella Rodway (New York: Hill and Wang, 1960).
2. Saul Rosensweig, "Freud, Jung and Hall the King-Maker," *New York Times Book Section* (24 January 1993), 1, 20.
3. I have explored these distinctions in depth in my book *The Case for a Humanistic Poetics* (London: Macmillan; Philadelphia: University of Pennsylvania Press, 1991). See also my "Culture, Canonicity and Pluralism: A Humanistic Perspective on Professing English," *Texas Studies in Language and Literature* 34 (spring 1992): 149–75.
4. Gerald Graff, *Professing English: An Institutional History* (Chicago: University of Chicago Press, 1987), 252.
5. Fredric Jameson, *The Political Unconscious: Narrative as a Socially Symbolic Act* (Ithaca: Cornell University Press, 1981), 21.
6. Graff, *Professing English,* 252.
7. Jameson, *The Political Unconscious,* 19–20.
8. Gerald Graff, "The Pseudo-Politics of Interpretation," in *The Politics of Interpretation,* ed. W. J. T. Mitchell (Chicago: University of Chicago Press, 1983), 153.
9. Dominick La Capra, "On the Line: Between History and Criticism," *Profession 89* (1989), 7.
10. Nadine Gordimer, "The Arts in Adversity: Apprentices of Freedom," *New Society* 24/31 (December 1981): ii–v.
11. Ibid.
12. Aristotle, *Poetics* (1451, chap. 9) trans. S. H. Butcher in *Criticism,* ed. Mark Schorer, Josephine Miles, Gordon McKenzie (New York: Harcourt, Brace and World, 1958), 205.
13. Aristotle, *Poetics,* 207.
14. Isaiah Berlin, "Philosophy and Life: An Interview," *New York Review of Books* 30 (28 May 1992): 50.
15. Quoted from Clifford Geertz, *Local Knowledge: Further Essays in Interpretive Anthropology* (New York: Basic, 1983), 161, in Martin Mueller, "Yellow Stripes and Dead Armadillos," *Profession 89* (1989), 30.
16. James Clifford, *The Predicament of Culture: Twentieth Century Ethnography, Literature, and Art* (Cambridge: Harvard University Press, 1988), 272.
17. Because of space limitations, my responses need to be limited, but I refer my readers to my "Teaching *Heart of Darkness:* Towards a Pluralistic Perspective," in *Conradiana* 24, no. 3 (1992): 190–206.
18. Chinua Achebe, "An Image of Africa," *Massachusetts Review* 18 (1977): 782–94.
19. Letter to Edward Noble, 2 November 1895, in G. Jean-Aubry, *Joseph Conrad: Life and Letters,* 2 vols. (Garden City, N.Y.: Doubleday, 1927), 1:184.
20. F. H. Bradley, *Appearance and Reality: A Metaphysical Essay* (London: Sonnenschein, 1893), 346.
21. Letter to R. B. Cunninghame Graham, 20 December 1897, in G. Jean-Aubry, *Joseph Conrad,* 1:215–16.

22. Page numbers in parentheses refer to Joseph Conrad, *Heart of Darkness,* Kent ed. (Garden City, N.Y.: Doubleday, 1926).

23. Patrick Brantlinger, *Rule of Darkness: British Literature and Imperialism, 1830–1914* (Ithaca: Cornell University Press, 1988), 271.

24. Martha Nussbaum, "Perceptive Equilibrium: Literary Theory and Ethical Theory," in *The Future of Literary Theory,* ed. Ralph Cohen (New York: Routledge, 1988), 61.

Relevant Publications by Daniel R. Schwarz

Narrative and Representation in the Poetry of Wallace Stevens. London: Macmillan; New York: St. Martin's Press, 1993.

The Case for a Humanistic Poetics. Philadelphia: University of Pennsylvania Press, 1991.

The Humanistic Heritage: Critical Theories of the English Novel from James to Hillis Miller. Philadelphia: University of Pennsylvania Press, 1986.

"Searching for Modernism's Genetic Code: Picasso, Joyce, and Stevens as a Cultural Configuration." *Weber Studies: An Interdisciplinary Humanities Journal* 10 (winter 1993): 66–86.

"The Ethics of Reading: The Case for Pluralistic and Transactional Reading." *Novel* 12 (winter–spring 1988): 197–218. Reprinted in *Why the Novel Matters,* ed. Mark Spilka and Caroline McCracken-Flesher, Bloomington: Indiana University Press, 1990.

"Reading as Moral Activity: Wayne Booth's *The Rhetoric of Fiction.*" *Sewanee Review* 93 (summer 1985): 480–85.

18

Literary History: Some Roads Not (Yet) Taken

Virgil Nemoianu

Virgil Nemoianu, William J. Byron Professor of Literature at the Catholic University of America, brings a knowledge of Western as well as Eastern European literature and criticism to his explorations of the place and functioning of literature. While maintaining a close acquaintance with the various trends and schools that have arisen since the advent of structuralism, he has gone his own way, investigating the questions that personally interest him. The result is often intriguing because he is able to enter an area of discussion from a perspective that cuts across the usual common arguments and oppositions; this is perhaps best shown in A Theory of the Secondary: Literature, Progress, and Reaction *(1989). His interest in the debate over the continuing canon debate is evidenced by his coeditorship of* The Hospitable Canon: Essays on Literary Play, Scholarly Choice, and Popular Pressures.

The present essay points to the dangers (and, retrospectively seen, absurdities) of allowing one's thought to become bounded by currently accepted paradigms and apparently dominating problems of the time, and proposes a variety of scholarly-critical pursuits likely to be more meaningful in addressing the injustices and sufferings of an inexorable modernizing process than continuing to march and countermarch across the same critical battlefields.

It is more frightening than amusing to observe the relentless scholarly stampede once a theoretical paradigm has been erected, along with the blind, unreflecting, allegiance that it comes to command. Thus the left-Nietzscheanism currently hegemonic in the literature departments of North America with its postulate that adversarial power is the center of human beings and relationships has been generating an enormous amount of research and has insinuated itself in virtually all of our reflections on literature, sometimes hampering other kinds of critical reading. It is in the nature of things that most of these materials will soon be obsolete and futile; some will seem ludicrous and unethical.

A good parallel to such paradigm worship is the following. In the last four decades (in America and elsewhere) vast resources in economics, sociology, and political science were applied to explore the best strategies for transition from "capitalism" to "socialism," or to devise paths for some convergence of the two. All this research effort was predicated on the proposition that Leninist-type societies were viable and justifiable constructs. Literally no research at all was dedicated to transitions from "socialism" *to* "capitalism"; indeed the mere exploration of such a possibility was sternly frowned upon by both intellectuals and officialdom. When, within a few short years, the illusion of a tenable utopian collectivism collapsed, hundreds of millions of people (not only in Eurasia, but also in Africa and in South America) found themselves devoid of the most elementary kind of guidance in coping with transition and progress and guiltlessly sentenced to uninformed, groping, blundering empiricism.

It seems chillingly probable that the current blithe complacency in an unreal world of "revolutionary" ivory towers in the humanities will have (if it is not having already) similar results. The humanities, as currently conducted, leave individuals and groups (above all minorities and postcolonial societies) disarmed and helpless in the face of emancipatory change and of its real, cruel, traumas. They fail at precisely the tasks they ostensibly pursue: preservation of otherness, and maintenance of a dialectic of local textures against unifying and homogenizing pressures; and they show themselves incapable of devising an authentic criticism of society.

Professional ethics should, of course, impel some of us to ruminate on the feasibility of an alternative orientation for the humanities, but this is not my purpose here. I shall simply outline some thoughts on alternatives to paradigm worship in literary history.

1. *Multidimensional realities.* It has been widely noticed that the breakdown of "New Criticism" and of the premise of aesthetic intrinsicality did

not bring with it a disappearance of textual analysis. On the contrary, if anything, it enhanced and intensified the dissective urge up to deconstructive dimensions (a super "New Criticism"). Likewise the subsidence of the Marxist family of thought generated an intensified historicism: a blending of the infinitesimal detail (or the insignificant context) with the grand unified theory, often under the sign of (how shall I say this?) well, aesthetic whimsicality. This, as I see it, is what we call "New Historicism," an enterprise behind which one always feels a slightly nervous grasping for a vanished certainty. Surely, it ought to be possible to provide a somewhat more balanced formula; that is, to place ourselves in an area equidistant from these two kinds of (almost morbid) intensification.

Human beings, under whichever shape history or geography presents them to us, are founded upon, and have to deal with, a few common tensions or polarities, among them: male versus female, old versus young, individual versus group (or society), self versus other, Godhead versus creatureliness, inborn versus acquired (and/or imagined) dimensions.[1] Simply keeping this indisputable fact in mind (without necessarily dwelling too much upon it) can protect us from the excessive burdening of *one* single oppositional axis with the entirety of human existence (e.g., the merely intersocial, the "never trust anybody over thirty" of yesteryear, gendering as of today, and others yet) or with all textual options. An initiative in literary history, more than a merely critical piece, ought to strive for the kind of complexity of polarities (or, to lower my pretensions yet more: awareness of such complexity) absent which it ends by quickly self-destructing.

The discourse of public-communication media is based upon binary adversariality, both in its relation to most other public institutions and in its own rhetoric. Binary modes of thinking are deleterious in many ways, but they also clearly respond to certain social needs of contemporary society. Our profession, however, by extrapolating from this type of media discourse and trying to replicate it faithfully, loses the nuance, complexity, and thickly layered organization that enables it or justifies its existence in the first place. Any genuine exercise in scholarly reflection, with all its qualifying, evasive, and refining strategies only subsists as a repudiation (or call it an undermining) of public-media communicative acts, even though in the long run it may help rather than wound the right functioning of the latter.

2. *Cultural morphology.* This is a mode on which authors as different as the early Jameson and the later Raymond Williams could at least in part

agree with Spengler and Friedell, with Sengle and Kenner, with Taine and Van Wyck Brooks. The obvious advantage of the method is that it allows for ample tumbling space to the multiple negotiations and metamorphoses of discourses and behaviors without necessarily privileging one factor over the other.

But there are two preconditions. One is that cultural morphology, to avoid becoming tedious and mechanical, must be quickened by asserting once in a while the diagnostic and therapeutic role of literature inside a given cultural model. I am optimistic enough to believe that literariness can be posited both as the mere symptom of a sociocultural matrix *and* (more arrogantly) as the playful *raison d'être* of that matrix: creation as the genetic code of human existence.

The other is the abundance of contextualization, on which, in principle, everybody agrees. And yet, what we get in practice is a kind of utopian allegory: What if a state of affairs obtained where the literary was an immediate consequence of socioeconomic materiality (power urges and economic and/or sexual acquisitiveness)? The veritable contexts of literary activity are, of course, different, whether negative (shame, fear, envy, and ambition) or positive (cognition and contemplation, generosity and gratuitousness, play and unsupressable creativity). Fashions and mentalities, giddy imitations, scientific hearsay, religious impulses, the grammar of sentiments, arbitrary subjectivity, hazy personal ambitions—these are the amniotic waters of the literary text. Bare socioeconomic and political-ideological events or attitudes are at one remove, and they are mediated as well as (usually) massively distorted, by these turbulent immediate contexts.

3. *Cognition over coercion.* Is it true that, as some historians of science say, humans are at bottom information-gathering and information-processing entities? Is it true at least in part? Can we read the history of mankind as a narrative of epistemological accumulation, expansion, and growth? I do not know the answer to these questions, but I do know that they are taken quite seriously in some quarters. If so, a literary history (*one* at least!) that would treat literature as the effort to package and transmit cognitive materials would be quite exciting. Umberto Eco has argued eloquently that it was the function of literature to cultivate abilities such as perceptual alertness, rapid induction, construction of hypotheses, positing of possible worlds, moral sophistication, linguistic proficiency, and value awareness.[2] Personally I would go a little farther and argue that the actual transmission of information (learning) in palatable forms would also be part of such a putative history.

Putative? It is the case already that some of the most exciting and promising critical writing (in America, in France, in Germany also, I believe) is one in which literature and science (sometimes with additions of eclectic spirituality) interact and teach each other: Michel Serres and Henri Atlan, Frederick Turner, Katherine Hayles and William Paulson, Mihai Spariosu and Paisley Livingston are just some names that come to mind.[3] I find in many of these a certain joyous agreement with the world and an exuberant, sassy, usage of its surplus of meanings.

But will this history not be just another "utopian allegory," another reductive game, merely hypothesizing about a state of affairs in which the beautiful is subservient to the true, rather than to the good, as in sociopolitical criticism? Not having read it yet, we have no way of knowing; perhaps it will, perhaps it will not. Presumably an epistemological history of literature will not shut out an awareness of the multiple definitional "axes" of our common humanity. Ernst Gellner writes precisely of the ways in which cognition, coercion, and production influence each other and interfere with each other.[4] There is no reason why a variant of this approach could not exist in literary history also.

4. *Reciprocity and gift-making.* An even more radical departure from current practices of literary history and criticism would be to interpret the gesture of literary production not primarily as part of the "market" or of "social command," but rather as an archaic survival of an earlier type of socioeconomic relationships, one based upon reciprocity and gift-making. (This would correspond to Karl Polanyi's first stage or type of economy.)[5] Suggestions of this type have been made by very different critics, from Wayne Booth (the friendship metaphor for books) to Raimonda Modiano, or, for those who prefer a more intricate and detailed model, to Georges Bataille.[6] This approach has solid factual bases in the large literature of direct address (dedications of poems and other works, the "I-you" insertions in works of fictions and others, and so forth). It is not difficult to imagine a more general model of literary history and criticism in which writing is deliberately taken as a gift to others (friends, "the neighbor," "the Other," or "mankind"), or as an exercise in generosity, and where this feature is energetically foregrounded. In such a reading the theme of communication (reaching out to those known and those unknown alike) interlaces in paradoxical and sweet ways with the theme of love.

Literary history would be on the one hand the record of loving gestures, but at the same time, critically, an exercise in love (whether as mere Diltheyan "Einfühlung," or as Susan Sontag's "erotics")[7] could become the preferred mode of approach to the text. The difference from the possessive and self-gratifying "desire" need not be elaborated here, I trust. The former as opposed to the latter is endowed precisely with those connotations of disinterestedness that are frowned upon by a good part of our current academic hierarchies. Values such as gratitude and praise, politeness and attention would receive their due, and the substantiality of leisure could be reconsidered.

5. *Taste.* There is, of course, something defiantly and vexingly old-fashioned or sentimental in the idea of gift-making, of "love," and of literature as survival of an older, discarded phase of human evolution. But why not? If anything, such a viewing mode can be only sharpened and vindicated in light of the widely circulating postulates of otherness and marginality. (David Perkins alludes to this in the last and best chapter of a recent book, and I have myself, elsewhere, outlined this mode of thinking.)[8] Without doubt, even a jaded and informationally overburdened public might sit up and listen to a literary history dedicated to bringing out, without squeamishness, the counterhistorical and the counterprogressive action of literary discourses.

The approach can be defended, briefly, as follows. The thickness of history, its substantiality, can only be rendered by acknowledging contrast and opposition. There is no more striking opposition to the ideological *topoi* of the present than the reading of Milton and Dante, for instance. By the same token, the education for otherness can find no more excellent foundation than a glance at the redoubtable values of aesthetic pastness. If multiplicity and adversarial virtues are qualities to be cherished and cultivated, as indispensable preconditions for the improved polities of the future, then it is precisely the dialectics of the unlikable and of the counterprogressive that must be studied and practiced. A "politically correct" attitude, honestly thought through to its true ends and complete implications, will result in a careful and loving study of the reactionary, not as an enemy, but as an indispensable co-actor.[9] By contrast, denying the dignity and the autonomy of the past (erasing the outrageous pastness of the past), is a very chancy enterprise: it opens the door wide toward any and all denials of otherness. Finally, a counterhistorical approach has the advantage of being less "elitist" and more democratic, by extending rights of participation (ideally: voting rights) to societies and human structures of the past.

6. *Hypocrisy.* I am not too much interested in or worried about the issue of the value of literary history (or of any history, for that matter), of

its mimetic merits, of its "possibility," or veridicity. Like any good neo-Leibnizian, I take it for granted that—in a strong and definitive sense—such pristine veridicity is quite impossible, but that in a much weaker epistemological sense (as plausibility, probability, credibility) it is readily available to us.

I also look with fatalistic indifference toward the overly much feared and denounced prejudgments of each and every literary historian. The recognition of such prior decisions does not prod me toward hopeless relativism and the embracing of blunt ideological constraints, but rather provides me with arguments in favor of such old-fashioned things as empathy, taste, and common sense. A literary history founded upon the latter will be no less (and no more!) biased than other histories, no less reliant upon gaps, guesswork, and arbitrary formulations. It will instead have the compensatory advantage of "talent," by which I mean an ability to perceive and to process more quickly associations and analogies; that is, to allow one's mind to function in ways derived from and more germane to the dynamics of literary production itself. In this sense, much like the skills and abilities of Olympic champions, critical talent is nothing more than the interface between some innate endowments and purposeful hard effort.

I am fully aware of the usual objection that what we call common sense and taste are nothing but internalized sets of prejudices and of received, unexamined values, but I respond to it in two ways. First, anybody who thinks that intuitive, "synthetical" responses of the mind are uncritical and simple betrays a woeful ignorance of how the mind works. Intuitive and "irrational" reactions are based upon thick and multifarious internal processings and are not less but more likely to be complex and dialectical than the "unpacked" and reductive explications of "critical" reasoning. The second is a consequence of my evaluation of hypocrisy, which differs from that of the objectors. Assuming that ideological bias is inevitable, it still remains true that an openly and cynically acknowledged tendentiousness in the guise of enforceable dogmatic imperatives is ethically inferior to and rhetorically less efficient than a coyly disguised or indirect form of prejudgment. The management of insincere discourse imposes refinements and counterbalances that limit the scope of pure ideological prejudice and allow a somewhat better access to factuality. Illusion, indirection, and yes, hypocrisy, can often be beneficial factors.

Should literary history be subordinated to the goals of social action, should it be a brave and disciplined soldier in the battle of social indoctrination, as is so often suggested to us nowadays? From all I have said above, it is clear that I do not believe so. Still, I do not find it hard to concede that ideological options ought to be part of any comprehensive reflection on literary history, albeit *only* a part of it. If such a reflection or debate is to be fruitful at all, it would have to be conducted in ways that are (mutually) beneficial to the discourses of postmodern societies, rather than bow to either the compulsions of utopian desire, or to a worldview in which the insistent presencing (no: the ontologizing) of negativity ensures a hopeless disorientation.

Among the circumstances of historical postmodernity two are most pertinent to the discourses that shape literary history. One is the globalization of human affairs. A "being-with-other-cultures" makes the Western literary past *more* rather than *less* relevant and immediate. An autistic Western civilization intent upon splendid isolation and supremacy could well be indifferent to Homer and Chaucer, and deal instead with its own contemporaneity. By contrast, a Western civilization aware of its synchronicity with and responsibility toward the southern and larger tiers of our planet (from Islam and China to sub-Saharan Africa and Catholic/Pagan Latin America) cannot possibly throw overboard a literary history the concern of which, of course, was never phallogocentrism but rather the pains, joys, and dilemmas of emancipation and transition. Attempts to allay the brutality of progress, dramatic enactments of options and scenarios in negotiating change—this is what the key patterns in Western literary history engage their readers in. (That is also, and overwhelmingly, though in infinite variations, the sociopsychological theme of non-Western and postcolonial societies.) Willfully to disremember them is to deliver younger generations (in the West, no less than globally) gagged and bound into the hands of the present and the future. My impression (and I wish I would be proved wrong) is that current discourses in literary history and academic criticism do nothing to soften the sandpaper harshness of postmodern history and to empower the individual in any transactions with it.

The second relevant ideological circumstance is the battle around the proper definition of liberalism. Even though it has not yet been noticed by many in literary departments, the major current political-economic debate in the real world is no longer waged among those that Lubac had once called "the spiritual posterity of Joachim of Fiore" (as it had been throughout much of the twentieth century).[10] We are dealing now with the "spiritual posterity" of Montesquieu. The conflict unfolds on a much narrower strip of ideological land, and it deals with how to set the landmarks and how to formulate the values of liberalism. Can the tradition that goes from Burke to Burckhardt be included in it? Should we bet on Mises or on Polanyi? Can Rawls or Nozick be a better adviser? Are Rousseau, are Herder and Cobbett indispensable to the canon of liberalism? How well is Tocqueville compatible with John Stuart Mill? These are some of the real ideological questions of the 1990s, when we are all inhabitants of a debating space outlined by Weber and Durckheim. At this point, of course, it becomes abundantly obvious that literary history, which had been dealing all along with these issues (not only in the last two hundred years, but for the careful reader earlier also), becomes—for this reason also—highly relevant. A literary history in which Fenimore Cooper, Manzoni, and Goethe, Mme de Staël, Scott, and Chateaubriand are principal actors is one that can intervene creatively in the real ideological debates of the late twentieth century. The insights of literary history are enormous and they can nurture and guide sociopolitical quandaries toward fuller, more flexible, and more compassionate social responses.

Notes

1. I take a page from George Steiner's splendid *Antigones* (1984; Oxford: Oxford University Press, 1986), 234–67.

2. Umberto Eco, *The Role of the Reader: Explorations in the Semiotics of Texts* (Bloomington: Indiana University Press, 1979). See the comments of Thomas Pavel in *Fictional Worlds* (Cambridge: Harvard University Press, 1986), 141.

3. Frederick Turner, *Beauty: The Value of Values* (Charlottesville: University of Virginia Press, 1992); Katherine Hayles, *Chaos Bound: Orderly Disorder in Contemporary Literature and Science* (Ithaca: Cornell University Press, 1990); and William R. Paulson, *The Noise of Culture: Literary Texts in a World of Information* (Ithaca: Cornell University Press, 1989) are just a few samples.

4. Ernst Gellner's *Plough, Sword, and Book: The Structure of Human History* (Chicago: Chicago University Press, 1988) is a truly seminal work as yet little read by humanities scholars. Gellner uses alternatively with "coercion" terms such as "predation" or the more habitual "political power."

5. Karl Polanyi, *The Great Transformation* (1944; Boston: Beacon, 1985).

6. Jean-Michel Heimonet, *Le mal a l'oeuvre: Georges Bataille et l'écriture du sacrifice* (Marseilles: Parenthèses, 1986).

7. Susan Sontag, *Against Interpretation and Other Essays* (New York: Farrar, Straus and Giroux, 1966), 3–14.

8. David Perkins, *Is Literary History Possible?* (Baltimore: Johns Hopkins University Press, 1992), 184–86. Virgil Nemoianu, *A Theory of the Secondary: Literature, Progress, and Reaction* (Baltimore: Johns Hopkins University Press, 1989), 3–25, 173–203.

9. In all fairness, it should be said that it was usually Marxist critics—Adorno, Bloch, and more emphatically Fredric Jameson (e.g., in *Fables of Aggression: Wyndham Lewis, the Modernist as Fascist* [Berkeley and Los Angeles: University of California

Press, 1979] and *The Political Unconscious: Narrative as a Socially Symbolic Act* [Ithaca: Cornell University Press; London: Methuen, 1981])—who have advocated and/or practiced this line of inquiry.

10. Henri de Lubac, in *La Postérité spirituelle de Joachim de Flore,* 2 vols. (Paris: Lethielleux, 1981), argues that modern secular utopianisms, as well as totalitarian, social, and revolutionary doctrines derive from Joachim's twelfth-century philosophy of history. The view that utopianism and totalitarianism are essentially secularized versions of religious vision is widely held in the field by quite various people, such as Karl Lowith, J. L. Talmon, Karl Mannheim, Frank and Fritzi Manuel, Thomas Molnar, and Norman Cohn, to name a few. Lubac differs from them chiefly in assigning the role of direct and essential source to Joachim's theory of the "third empire" (the phase or the *Reich* of the Holy Spirit).

Relevant Publications by Virgil Nemoianu

The Hospitable Canon (coeditor with Robert Royal). Amsterdam and Philadelphia: Benjamins, 1991.

A Theory of the Secondary: Literature, Progress, and Reaction. Baltimore: Johns Hopkins University Press, 1989.

The Taming of Romanticism: European Literature and the Age of Biedermeier. Cambridge: Harvard University Press, 1985.

"Learning Over Class: The Case of the Central European Ethos." In *Cultural Participation: Trends Since the Middle Ages,* ed. Ann Rigney and Douwe Fokkema, Amsterdam and Philadelphia: John Benjamins, 1993.

"Organizing Absence: The Usefulness of Romanticism as a Period Concept." *Comparatistica* 4 (1992): 53–64.

"Literary Canons and Social Value Options." In *The Hospitable Canon,* ed. Virgil Nemoianu and Robert Royal, Amsterdam and Philadelphia: Benjamins, 1991.

"Criticisms and the Coded Debate." *Times Literary Supplement* (19–25 January 1990): 59.

"Societal Models as Substitute Reality in Literature." *Poetics Today* 5 (1984): 275–97.

"Is Literature Always Reactionary?" *Georgia Review* 37 (summer 1983): 347–66.

19

The Literary Imagination in Public Life

Martha Nussbaum

"The Literary Imagination in Public Life" is one of a series of essays in which Martha Nussbaum, professor of law and ethics at the University of Chicago Law School and author of Poetic Justice: The Literary Imagination and Public Life *(1996), has affirmed and explored the value of literature in increasing the reader's understanding of human experience. Fifteen other such essays, informed by an unusual combination of philosophical sophistication and close acquaintance with a wide range of literary texts (especially in the novel) and literary criticism, appear in* Love's Knowledge *(1990). In the introductory essay of that volume, Martha Nussbaum emphasizes two claims she will be developing. "The first is the claim that there is, with respect to any text carefully written and fully imagined, an organic connection between its form and its content. Certain thoughts and ideas, a certain sense of life, reach toward expression in writing that has a certain shape*

This paper is the first of three Alexander Rosenthal Lectures delivered at the Northwestern University Law School in April 1991. I wish to thank the Law School for permission to publish it here before its (revised) publication in the book based on the series. The series as a whole has the title "The Literary Imagination in Public Life." The second lecture investigates the role of the emotions in literary experience on the one hand, public rationality on the other. And the third lecture describes a norm of legal judgment based on the account of rationality in the first two lectures, describing its implications for conceptions of judicial neutrality, the rule of law, and certain areas of constitutional interpretation.

and form, that uses certain structures, certain terms." "The second claim is that certain truths about human life can only be fittingly and accurately stated in the language and forms characteristic of the narrative artist." The present essay uses Dickens's Hard Times *as an example of the illuminating ethical power of literature.*

> "Bitzer," said Thomas Gradgrind. "Your definition of a horse."
>
> "Quadruped. Graminivorous. Forty teeth, namely twenty-four grinders, four eye-teeth, and twelve incisive. Sheds coat in the spring; in marshy countries, sheds hoofs, too. Hoofs hard, but requiring to be shod with iron. Age known by marks in mouth." Thus (and much more) Bitzer.
>
> —Charles Dickens, *Hard Times*

A child said *What is the grass?* fetching it to
me with full hands,
How could I answer the child? I do not know
what it is any more than he.

I guess it must be the flag of my disposition,
out of hopeful green stuff woven.

Or I guess it is the handkerchief of the Lord,
A scented gift and remembrancer designedly
dropt,
Bearing the owner's name someway in the
corners, that we may see and remark, and
say *Whose?*

Or I guess the grass is itself a child, the
produced babe of the vegetation.

Or I guess it is a uniform hieroglyphic;
And it means, Sprouting alike in broad zones
and narrow zones,
Growing among black folks as among white,
Kanuck, Tuckahoe, Congressman, Cuff, I
give them the same, I receive them the
same.

And now it seems to me the beautiful uncut
hair of graves.
Tenderly will I use you curling grass,

> It may be you transpire from the breasts of
> young men,
> It may be if I had known them I would have
> loved them,
> It may be you are from old people, or from
> offspring taken soon out of their mothers'
> laps,
>
> This grass is very dark to be from the white
> heads of old mothers.
> Darker than the colorless beards of old men,
> Dark to come from under the faint red roofs
> of mouths.
>
> —Walt Whitman, *Song of Myself*

Noting in his children a strange and unsavory exuberance of imagination, an unwholesome flowering of sentiment—in short, a lapse from that perfect scientific rationality on which both private and public life, when well managed, depend—Mr. Gradgrind, political economist, public man, and educator, inquires into the cause:

> "Whether," said Mr. Gradgrind, pondering with his hands in his pockets, and his cavernous eyes on the fire, "whether any instructor or servant can have suggested anything? Whether Louisa or Thomas can have been reading anything? Whether, in spite of all precautions, any idle story-book can have got into the house? Because, in minds that have been practically formed by rule and line, from the cradle upwards, this is so curious, so incomprehensible." (63)[1]

Mr. Gradgrind knows that storybooks are not simply decorative, not simply amusing—though this already would be enough to cause him to doubt their utility. Literature, he sees, is subversive. It is the enemy of political economy, as Mr. Gradgrind knows that science. It expresses, in its structures and its ways of speaking, a sense of life that is incompatible with the vision of the world embodied in the texts of political economy; and engagement with it forms the imagination and the desires in a manner that subverts that science's norm of rationality. It is with good reason, from this point of view, that Mr. Gradgrind teaches Sissy Jupe, the uneducated circus girl, to regard the storybooks she once lovingly read to her father as "wrong books" (99), about which the less said the better. And it is with good reason that he lapses into depression about the nation's future when he considers the citizens who, flocking to the public libraries of Coketown, "took DeFoe to their bosoms, instead of Euclid, and seemed to be on the whole more comforted by Goldsmith than by Cocker" (90). When idle storybooks get into the house, political economy is at risk. The world is seen in a new way, and uneconomical activities of fancying and feeling are both represented and, worse still, enacted.

I shall argue that Mr. Gradgrind is right: literature, and the literary imagination, are subversive. Literary thought is, in certain ways that remain to be specified, the enemy of a certain sort of economic thought. We are accustomed by now to thinking of literature as optional: as great, valuable, entertaining, excellent, but something that exists off to one side of political and economic and legal thought, in another university department, ancillary rather than competitive. The segmentation of the modern academy—along with narrowly hedonist theories of literary value—has caused us to lose hold of the insight that Mr. Gradgrind securely grasped: that the novel (for from now on I shall focus on the novel) is a morally controversial form, expressing in its very shape and style, in its modes of interaction with its readers, a normative sense of life. It tells its readers to notice this and not this, to be active in these and not these ways; it leads them into certain postures of the mind and heart and not others. And, as Mr. Gradgrind all too clearly perceived, these are the wrong ways, and highly dangerous postures, from the point of view of the narrow conception of economic rationality that is, in his view, normative for both public and private thought.

But if literature is, from the political economist's viewpoint, dangerous and deserving of suppression, this implies as well that it is no mere frill, that it has the potential to make a distinctive contribution to our public life. And if one should have some doubts about the texts of political economy—as to their adequacy as visions of humanity, expressions of a complete sense of human social life—one might then see in the very zeal of Mr. Gradgrind's repudiation a reason to invite idle storybooks into the house to plead their cause. And if they should plead their cause successfully, we might have compelling reasons to invite them to stay: not only in our homes and schools, shaping the perceptions of our children, but also in our schools of public policy, and government offices, and courts, and even law schools—wherever the public imagination is shaped and nourished—as centerpieces of an education for public rationality.

I shall focus, then, on the characteristics of the literary imagination as a public imagination, an imagination that will steer judges in their judging, legislators in their legislating, policymakers in measuring the quality of life of people both near and far. Elsewhere I have argued the case for the novel as an ineliminable part of personal deliberation; I have also made a beginning on the task of commending it in the public sphere.[2] This task is difficult, since many people who think of literature as illuminating concerning the workings of the personal life and the private imagination believe that it is idle and unhelpful when the larger concerns of classes and nations are at issue. Here, it is felt, we need something more reliably scientific, more detached, more sternly rational. But I shall now argue that here, all the more, literary forms have a distinctively valuable, and ineliminable, contribution to make. I shall make this case by focusing on the novel above all, as I have said—and, in particular, on Dickens's *Hard Times,* which takes as its explicit theme the contribution of the novel to the moral and political life, both representing and enacting the novel's triumph over other ways of imagining the world. The antagonist throughout will be not sophisticated philosophical forms of utilitarianism, and not the political economy of the greatest philosophical political economists, such as Adam Smith—but the cruder form of economic utilitarianism that is actually used in many areas of public policy-making, and is commended as a norm for still others. (Later I shall exemplify this with cases drawn from quality of life measurement in development economics.) I shall focus above all on the issue of measuring the well-being of a population, which happens to be a central theme of *Hard Times,* as well as an excellent place to see the contrast between the economic and the literary at work; and I shall be asking what activities of the personality are best for this task, what thoughts, what sentiments, what ways of perceiving. This will lead naturally to the question, what texts represent these desired activities, and call them into being?

My question, then, will be not just about what the novel represents, what goes on inside it. That is an important part of my project. But I want to ask, as well, what sense of life its form itself embodies: not only how the characters feel and imagine, but what sort of feeling and imagining is enacted in the telling of the story itself, in the shape and texture of the sentences, the pattern of the narrative, the sense of life that animates the text as a whole. And I shall ask as well, and inevitably, what sort of feeling and imagining is called into being by the shape of the text as it addresses its imagined reader, what sort of readerly activity is built into its form.[3] I shall ask, then, not only about the opposition within the story of *Hard Times* between Gradgrind and M'Choakumchild on the one hand, Sissy Jupe and the circus on the other, but also about the ways in which the sentences and chapters of the novel itself, and the activity of reading it, triumphantly enact their exuberant rebellion against political economy,[4] and against the "blue books" in which its view of the human world is encoded.

I. Nothing but Facts

Dickens's *Hard Times* contains a normative vision of a scientific political economy and of the scientific political imagination. It presents this norm, to be sure, as a target of withering satirical attack, a goal that cannot be truly described without being made to appear both ridiculous and sinister. But since the attack is a deep attack, the satirical target itself is described with insight, as the novel both depicts and shows the deeper significance of what is still today very often taught as normative in public policy-making, in welfare and development economics—and, recently, even in the law. What makes this norm appear so odd to the reader of the novel is that it is taken seriously all the way down, so to speak: understood not just as a way of writing up reports, but as a way of dealing with people in daily encounters; not just as a way of doing economics, but a way of defining a horse or talking to a child; not just as a way of appearing professionally respectable, but as a commitment that determines the whole content of one's personal and social life. But since this norm does in fact claim to be a norm of rationality, and not just a handy professional tool, and since, if it is really a norm, it seems fair to ask people to abide by it consistently, it seems perfectly fair to examine it in this way, asking what people who really and thoroughly saw the world in the way this norm recommends would be like, and whether such a vision does really seem to be a complete one. (And it seems reasonable, too, to suppose that the personal vision and conduct of committed social scientists *is* actually influenced at least to some extent by the content of the norm their science upholds, by the habits of perception and recognition it encourages. So in examining it this way we can expect to learn something about what we do *to* people by holding it up as a norm, and what we can expect *from* people so treated.) Dickens pays the economic utilitarian the tribute of taking him at his word and holding him to his word; of this treatment he can hardly, it seems to me, complain. Later I shall draw some explicit connections between the Gradgrind philosophy and some aspects of contemporary economic thought and practice.

But for now I need to set out the features of this norm, as the novel dissects it. (This will mean beginning to speak of its limitations as well: for in seeing it we see what the novel sees.)

What I am about to say here may seem in some respects obvious. For it is part of the novel's design that the economist's way of thinking, seen in the full context of daily life, should look extremely strange, and the opposing way natural. What I hope to bring out here, however, is that the economic opponent is not a straw man: it is a conception that even now dominates much of our public life, in a form not very different from the form presented in this novel. Once, focusing on the subtle modifications of utilitarianism that one finds in recent philosophy,[5] I felt that the satire of *Hard Times* was unfair. But now that I have spent time in the world of economics (see sec. IV), reading the prose and following the arguments, I am convinced that the criticisms in the novel are both fair and urgent. The simple utilitarian idea of what rational choice consists in dominates not only economic thought and practice, but also—given the prestige of economics within the social sciences—a great deal of writing in other social sciences as well, where "rational choice theory" is taken to be equivalent to utilitarian rational choice theory as practiced in neoclassical economics. Public policymakers turn to these norms to find a principled, orderly way of making decisions. And the allure of the theory's elegant simplicity is so great that it is having an increasing influence even in the law, which has traditionally reasoned in a very different way, using a different norm of the rational.[6] Recently the theory has even made its way into literary studies, where the prestige of neoclassical economics, Chicago-style, is evoked in defense of a broad application of its behavioral theory to all areas of human life.[7] To the reader who has no familiarity with the opposing position and the prose in which it is expressed, a short course in the writings of Gary Becker or Richard Posner might be recommended. (Their views are extreme—but only in the sense that, like the novel, they apply across the board a theory that economics treats as normative for rational choice in general. If it is indeed a norm of rationality, they are right to do so: and we are justified in examining their works as tests of the theory's normative appropriateness.)[8] To the reader I leave, then, the further investigation of the economist's position in contemporary life. For now I myself shall turn to Mr. Gradgrind—who at least ends the novel by expressing remorse, and revealing, in the process, a certain human complexity.

" 'In this life, we want nothing but Facts, sir; nothing but Facts' " (47). This famous demand, announced in the Gradgrind schoolroom in the opening chapter of the novel (a chapter entitled "The One Thing Needful"), states the essence of the Gradgrind philosophy. And the novel shortly characterizes it further, speaking for Mr. Gradgrind in the hard blunt confrontational sentences that seem well suited to express the quality of his mind: "Thomas Gradgrind, sir. A man of realities. A man of fact and calculations. A man who proceeds upon the principle that two and two are four, and nothing over, and who is not to be talked into allowing for anything over. Thomas Gradgrind, sir—peremptorily Thomas—Thomas Gradgrind. With a rule and a pair of scales, and the multiplication table always in his pocket, sir, ready to weigh and measure any parcel of human nature, and tell you exactly what it comes to. It is a mere question of figures, a case of simple arithmetic" (48). Gradgrind's political economy claims to be a science, to offer facts in place of idle fancy, objectivity in place of mere subjective impressions, the precision of mathematical calculation instead of the intractable elusiveness of qualitative distinction. "The reason is (as you know)," he remarks to Bounderby, "the only faculty to which education should be addressed" (62). And Gradgrind economics claims proudly to approach the world with reason rather than sentiment—and with the detached theoretical and calculative power of the mathematical intellect, rather than any more qualitative type of reasoned deliberation. Gradgrind intellect sees the heterogeneous furniture of the world, human beings included, as so many surfaces or "parcels" to be weighed and measured.

In this brief description we see four aspects of the economic-utilitarian mind, neatly encapsulated.[9] First, it reduces qualitative differences to quantitative differences. Instead of Louisa, Tom, Stephen, Rachael, in all of their complex qualitative diversity, their historical particularity, we have simply so and so many quantifiable "parcels of human nature." This effacement of qualitative difference is accomplished, we see, by a process of abstraction from all in people that is not easily funneled into mathematical formulas; so this mind, in order to measure what it measures, attends only to an abstract and highly general version of the human being, rather than to the diverse concreteness with which the novel confronts us. We see this abstracting mathematical mind at work in the Gradgrind school's treatment of its students, called by number ("Girl number twenty") rather than by name, and seen as an "inclined plane of little vessels then and there arranged in order, ready to have imperial gallons of facts poured into them until they were full to the brim" (47–48). We see it at work in the treatment of the workers of Coketown as so and so many "hands and stomachs"

(102–3), as "teeming myriads" whose destinies could be reckoned on a slate (131–32), their qualitative differences as irrelevant as those of "ants and beetles" "passing to and from their nests" (187).[10]

Second, the Gradgrind mind, bent on calculation, is determined to aggregate the data gained about and from individual lives, arriving at a picture of total or average utility that effaces personal separateness as well as qualitative difference.[11] The individual is not even so distinct as a distinct countable insect; for in Mr. Gradgrind's calculation it becomes simply an input into a complex mathematical operation that treats the social unit as a single large system in which the preferences and satisfactions of all are combined and melded. Thus, in Louisa's education, the working classes become:

> Something to be worked so much and paid so much, and there ended; something to be infallibly settled by laws of supply and demand; something that blundered against those laws, and floundered into difficulty; something that was a little pinched when wheat was dear, and over-ate itself when wheat was cheap; something that increased at such a rate of percentage, and yielded such another percentage of crime, and such another percentage of pauperism; something wholesale, of which vast fortunes were made; something that occasionally rose like the sea, and did some harm and waste (chiefly to itself), and fell again; this she knew the Coketown hands to be. But, she had scarcely thought more of separating them into units, than of separating the sea itself into its component drops. (187–88)

Lives are drops in an undemarcated ocean; and the question how the group is doing is a question whose economic resolution requires effacing the separate life and agency of each.[12]

Mr. Gradgrind does not achieve this goal perfectly in his school, where students, though numbered rather than named, retain their distinct levels of performance, their abilities to think and speak as separate centers of choice, and even some measure of qualitative distinctness. He does not achieve this goal perfectly, we are bound to observe, in his relation to himself: for his internal rhetoric, in the passage cited, insists on the separateness and the qualitative difference of his own mind from those of others: "You might hope to get some other nonsensical belief into the head of George Gradgrind, or Augustus Gradgrind, or John Gradgrind, or

Joseph Gradgrind (all suppositious, nonexistent persons), but into the head of Thomas Gradgrind—no sir!" (48). It is a subtle point in the novel that the measure of personal autonomy and self-respect that Mr. Gradgrind wishes to claim for himself requires him to view himself with a distinctness denied in his calculations—and even to indulge in a rare bit of (however crude) fiction-making.[13]

But within his immediate family, he fares better. For he does manage, most of the time, to perceive his own children in more or less the way that political economy recommends.[14] When Louisa, in inner agony about her impending marriage to Bounderby, bursts out: " 'Father, I have often thought that life is very short,' " her baffled father replies:

> "It is short, no doubt, my dear. Still, the average duration of human life is proved to have increased of late years. The calculations of various life assurance and annuity offices, among other figures which cannot go wrong, have established the fact."
>
> "I speak of my own life, father."
>
> "O indeed? Still," said Mr. Gradgrind, "I need not point out to you, Louisa, that it is governed by the laws which govern lives in the aggregate." (135)[15]

And in one of the novel's most chilling and brilliant moments, we see what it can be like to see one's own self through the eyes of political economy. Mrs. Gradgrind, subservient and with an always fragile sense both of her own qualitative distinctness and of her separate boundaries, her separate agency, lies on what will soon be her deathbed. " 'Are you in pain, dear mother?' " asks Louisa. The answer comes back. " 'I think there's a pain somewhere in the room,' said Mrs. Gradgrind, 'but I couldn't positively say that I have got it' " (224). Political economy sees only pains and satisfactions and their general location: it does not see persons as distinctly bounded centers of satisfaction, far less as agents whose active planning is essential to the humanness of whatever satisfaction they will achieve. Mrs. Gradgrind has learned her lesson well.

If we return now to the initial description of Mr. Gradgrind, we see in it a third feature of the political-economical mind: its determination to find a clear and precise solution for any human problem.[16] Mr. Gradgrind, we recall, is prepared "to weigh and measure any parcel of human nature, and tell you exactly what it comes to" (48). And his study, later on, is described as a "charmed apartment" in which "the most complicated social questions were cast up, got into exact totals, and finally settled" (131–32). Because it has from the start cast the human data into "tabular form," the economic mind finds it easy to view the lives of human beings as a problem in (relatively elementary) mathematics that has a definite solution—ignoring the mystery and complexity that are within each life, in its puzzlement and pain about its choices, in its tangled loves, in its attempt to grapple with the mysterious and awful fact of its own mortality.[17] The cheerful fact-calculating mind plays round the surfaces of these lives, as if it had no need to look within, as if, indeed, it "could settle all their destinies on a slate" (132). Gradgrind children are taught from an early age to approach the world of nature without any sense of mystery, awe, and depth. Thus Bitzer's definition of a horse, which gives a remarkably flat and abstract description of the surface features of that animal, refusing to imagine either its own complex form of life or its significances in the lives of humans who love and care for horses. So too with human lives. Mr. Gradgrind does not even understand the significance of his own child's outburst, when she speaks obscurely of a fire that bursts forth at night, and wonders about the shortness of her life (135). How much less, then does he feel a sense of mystery and wonder before the distant human beings who work in the factories of Coketown. In one of the most striking incursions of a first-person voice into this novel (whose narrative structure I shall describe more fully later), this habit of mind is described, and criticized:

> So many hundred Hands in this Mill; so many hundred horse Steam Power. It is known, to the force of a single pound weight, what the engine will do; but, not all the calculators of the National Debt can tell me the capacity for good or evil, for love or hatred, for patriotism or discontent, for the decomposition of virtue into vice, or the reverse, at any single moment in the soul of one of these its quiet servants, with the composed faces and the regulated actions. There is no mystery in it; there is an unfathomable mystery in the meanest of them, for ever.—Supposing we were to reserve our arithmetic for material objects, and to govern these awful unknown quantities by other means! (108)

If political economy does not include the complexities of the inner moral life of each human being, its strivings and perplexities, its complicated emotions, its perplexity and terror, if it does not distinguish in its descriptions between a human life and a machine, then we should regard with suspicion its claim to govern a nation of human beings; and we should ask ourselves whether, having seen us as little different from inanimate objects, it might not be capable of treating us with a certain lack of tenderness.

And this brings us directly to the fourth characteristic of economic rationality with which the novel acquaints us. Seeing human beings as counters in a mathematical game, and refusing to see their mysterious inner world, the Gradgrind philosophy is able to adopt a theory of human motivation that is elegant and simple, well suited for the game of calculation, but whose relation to the more complicated laws that govern the inner world of a human being should be viewed with skepticism. In accordance with Gradgrind's view of himself as a down-to-earth realistic man, a man of cold, hard fact rather than airy fancy, the theory has an air of hard-nosed realism about it, suggesting the unmasking of pleasant but airy fictions. Human beings, this unsentimental view teaches, are all motivated by self-interest in all of their actions.[18] The all-too-perfect Gradgrind pupil Bitzer, at the novel's end, reveals the principle on which he was raised. As the chastened Mr. Gradgrind attempts to appeal to his gratitude and love, Bitzer cuts in:

> "I beg your pardon for interrupting you, sir," returned Bitzer; "but I am sure you know that the whole social system is a question of self-interest. What you must always appeal to, is a person's self-interest. It's your only hold. We are so constituted. I was brought up in that catechism when I was very young, sir, as you are aware." (303)

Bitzer, the perfect product of political economy, refuses to acknowledge even those residual motivations of love and altruism that now deeply grip the heart of Mr. Gradgrind himself. For that is the philosophy on which he was raised. And this philosophy leads to odd and implausible interpretations of the world.

Earlier in the novel, when Sissy Jupe's father has left her, and her own first tendency is to impute to him altruistic motives, projects for her good, Bounderby will have none of it. She had better know, he says, the hard bad facts of her situation: she has simply been abandoned, her father has simply pleased himself and run off. The novel pointedly leaves this particular case unresolved; its function is to point up different behavioral assumptions, different ways of construing the world. The novel as a whole convinces the reader (and Mr. Gradgrind) that Gradgrind is wrong to deny the possibility of genuinely altruistic and other-regarding action. But if there exists this other possibility, then Bounderby has construed Sissy's situation hastily, and also ungenerously. The suggestion is that the economist's habit of reducing everything to calculation, combined with the need for an extremely simple theory of human action, produces a tendency to see calculation everywhere, rather than commitment and sympathy. "Every inch of the existence of mankind, from birth to death, was to be a bargain across a counter" (304). This tendency leads to crude analysis, and frequently to error. Even when it does not lead to error, it leads to an ungenerous perception of people and events. And, worst of all, taught from an early age, it produces pupils in its own image.

In short, the claim of political economy to present all and only the facts of human life needs to be viewed with skepticism, if by "facts" we mean "truths." And its claim to stand for "reason" must also be viewed with skepticism, if by "reason" we mean a faculty that is self-critical and committed to truth. For the "facts" of political economy are actually reductive and incomplete perceptions, and its "reason" is a dogmatic operation of intellect that looks, frequently, both incomplete and unreliable. The fact-finding intellect plays around the surfaces of objects, not even obtaining very adequate perceptual data—Mr. Gradgrind's study is compared to an astronomical observatory without windows, where the astronomer arranges the world "solely by pen, ink, and paper" (131) determined to perceive only those abstract features of people and situations that can easily be translated into economic calculations. From its own point of view it has positive motivations for this way of proceeding—in its determination to be realistic and not sentimental, its determination to be exact, and even its determination not to be biased in favor of what is near at hand. (For Mr. Gradgrind reflects that Louisa "would have been self-willed . . . but for her bringing-up" [57].) The novel permits us to see these positive goals.[19] Its very sentences express a commitment to be detached, and realistic, and unbiased—in their blunt square shape, their syntactical plainness, their hard sound and rhythm. (We must, however, note that the prose the novel imputes to the Gradgrind imagination is far more expressive, more succinct, more rhythmical, more *pleasing* in its odd squareness, than the flat unexpressive jargon-laden prose that is actually used by most economists of the Gradgrind type. Dickens has been able to make Mr. Gradgrind a lively character in a readable novel only by to this extent changing him.)

But, the novel shows, in its determination to see only what can enter into utilitarian calculations, the economic mind is blind: blind to the qualitative richness of the perceptible world; to the separateness of its people, to their inner depths, their hopes and loves and fears; blind to what it is like to live a human life and to try to endow it with a human meaning. Blind, above all, to the fact that human life is something mysterious and not altogether fathomable, something that demands to be approached with faculties of mind and resources of language that are suited to the expression of that complexity. In the name of science, the wonder that illuminates and prompts the most creative and deepest science has been jettisoned.[20] And we have, simply, a reductive charade of science, in which some small part of human life appears, as figures on a slate. We shall shortly see the political consequences of relying on such a picture.

But now we must pause to ask what sort of writing we are reading when we read this novel, how it differs from Mr. Gradgrind's economic texts, and how its own way of imagining and speaking shapes its reader's perception of the issues.

II. Mere Fables about Men and Women

Let us ask, then, how Dickens's novel differs from the texts in political economy that Mr. Gradgrind reads, with their "tabular statements" measuring social welfare. And we must begin with the most obvious facts: not taking for granted that we are reading a work in a different genre, but asking about the features of the genre itself, how they form the reader's imagination, and what sense of life they express.

First of all, then, we are reading a story. This story contains characters—men and women in some ways like ourselves. It represents these characters as very distinct one from another, endowing them with physical and moral attributes that make it possible for us to distinguish every one from every other. We are made to attend to their concrete ways of moving and talking, the shapes of their bodies, the expressions on their faces, the sentiments of their hearts. The inner life of each is displayed as having psychological depth and complexity. We see that as humans they share certain common problems and common hopes—and yet, as well, that each confronts these in his or her own way, in his or her concrete circumstances with the resources of his or her history. Even the utilitarians Bounderby and Gradgrind are rich and complex humans, whose abstract philosophy emerges from an inner world with which it is not always—as we have begun to see—in harmony. The exceptions to this general rule are Mrs. Gradgrind, so weak that she surrenders the boundaries of her selfhood to economic calculation, and, above all, the pupil Bitzer, that terrifying empty automaton of utilitarian calculation. Bitzer is the exception that proves the rule, the exception that invites us to notice what the instantiation of the economic portrayal of humanity really looks like, when consistently realized in a concrete human life.[21] We see the novel's abstract deliberations, then, as issuing in each case from a concrete human life, and as expressing only a part of the content of that life's inner richness. And although we do not always have extended and explicit access to that complexity, we are always invited to wonder about it, to imagine it—imagining the motives that drive Bounderby to deny his origins and Mrs. Sparsit to pursue Louisa, imagining, later on, with warmer sympathy, the complex turmoil in the heart of Mr. Gradgrind as he greets the collapse of his system with humble expressions of remorse. We wonder how to interpret their actions; and we wonder with a mixture of sympathy and criticism that is likely to vary to some extent from reader to reader, as attitudes do toward actual people in life. (Thus we can argue about what the correct interpretation of some element of the novel might be, and how justified our sympathies have been, without losing the fundamental concern that draws us together as readers.) All these things the novel, in its very ways of speaking to its reader, recognizes as salient, as worthy of attention and concern. This we take for granted, since we know what it is to read a novel. But we should not take it for granted. We should be aware at all times how our attention and desire are directed, and how differently from their direction in the course of reading a treatise on welfare economics.

If we want to become aware of this directedness in a more graphic way, we might focus on our relationship, as readers, to Mr. Gradgrind. If Mr. Gradgrind wrote an economics book, placing himself in it as an agent in a way consistent with his system, what would be interesting and salient about the Gradgrind character? How would it address the reader's imagination? Only, clearly, through the fact that his life was governed by the laws that govern lives in the aggregate, and through the fact that he exemplifies the so-called rationality of the economic bargainer. Only under these descriptions could Mr. Gradgrind appear in his own book. The "story" of such a book would be the story of transactions; and its reader would be held to it not by love or fear, but by a mixture of intellectual exhilaration and rational self-interest. Such is the moral content of the genre, if genre it is.

How different our own relation to Mr. Gradgrind here. What is it, in fact, that makes Mr. Gradgrind an interesting character for the reader, a gripping and ultimately a deeply moving character, in a way that Bitzer and Bounderby are not? It is, surely, his failure to be a consistent utilitarian. Bitzer is just weird; we cannot identify with him or wonder about him, for we sense that all within is empty. A novel peopled entirely by Bitzers would be a kind of science fiction, and would not grip its reader in the manner characteristic of the traditional novel, which relies on bonds of identification and sympathy. But we do, by contrast, find ourselves taking a sympathetic interest in Mr. Gradgrind; we are encouraged to wonder about him even as we criticize him, to care about what befalls him—in short, to experience him as an interesting and significant character in a compelling novel. Built into our aesthetic experience is a certain shaping of desire.

What in Mr. Gradgrind arouses this desire? It is, we have to say, the fact that we know early on that he is not consistent—that he is motivated by love, commitment, and plain decency in ways that do not find expression in his philosophy. We notice how he refuses to endorse Bounderby's crude dismissal of Sissy's father. We are aware of high-minded humanitarian motives in his preference for reason over fancy, motives that may have been misdirected but that are admirable in themselves. Above all, we notice a degree of love for his daughter, a hesitation in his implementation of his schemes for her, that make us think—so this man has a soul. All this, I want to say, this fancy and wonder, this respect before a soul, is built into the genre itself, into its modes of address to its reader. Without a certain number of characters to whom we can have this relation, we lose interest, and our pleasure ceases. But when we engage in such relations we are, from the economic point of view, acting badly.

This novel tells a story. In so doing, it gets its readers involved with the characters, caring about their projects, their hopes and fears, participating in their attempts to unravel the mysteries and perplexities of their lives.[22] The participation of the reader is made explicit at many points in the narration. And it is brought home to readers that the story is in certain ways their own story, showing possibilities for human life and choice that are, in effect, their own to seize. Thus their attempts to interpret and evaluate are encouraged to be both affectionate and critical: the text portrays them as social agents responsible for making a world that is either like or unlike the world depicted here, agents who must in life stand in some emotional and practical relation to the problems of the working classes and to the conduct of managers and leaders. In imagining things that do not really exist, the novel, by its own account, is not being "idle":

it is helping its readers to acknowledge their own world and to choose more reflectively in it.

In short, the experience of reading this novel has, not surprisingly, just the properties that it imputes to the experience of novel-reading, when (through the puzzled eyes of Mr. Gradgrind) it describes the tendency of the people of Coketown to prefer novel reading to the reading of government statistics: "They wondered about human nature, human passions, human hopes and fears, the struggles, triumphs and defeats, the cares and joys and sorrows, the lives and deaths, of common men and women! They sometimes, after fifteen hours' work, sat down to read mere fables about men and women, more or less like themselves, and about children, more or less like their own. They took De Foe to their bosoms, instead of Euclid, and seemed to be on the whole more comforted by Goldsmith than by Cocker" (90). As Mr. Gradgrind wonders about "this unaccountable fact," the reader of course notices that it is her own preferences and current activity that are being described.

So far we have spoken of features of the novel that it shares with numerous narrative genres: its commitment to the separateness of persons and to the irreducibility of quality to quantity; its sense that what happens to individuals in the world has enormous importance; its commitment to describe the events of life not from an external perspective of detachment, as the doings and movings of ants or machine parts, but from within, as invested with the complex significances with which human beings invest their own lives. The novel has an even greater commitment to the richness of the inner world than do many other narrative genres, and a greater commitment to the moral relevance of following a life through all of its highly concrete adventures in all of its concrete context. To this extent, it is even more profoundly opposed than other genres to the reductive economic way of seeing the world, more profoundly committed to qualitative distinctions.

But with Mr. Gradgrind's musings about the strange library habits of the Coketown working classes, we come upon a feature of the novel that sets it apart, to some extent, from histories and biographies and even tragic dramas: namely, its interest in the ordinary, in the daily lives and struggles of ordinary men and women. Think of the places we visit, as readers of this novel: a schoolroom, a middle-class home, a circus, a working-class home, the office of a manager, the factory in which working people toil, an abandoned mineshaft in which many working people have met their death. Not one of these places would have been judged fit for inclusion in tragedies of Sophocles or Racine. And even in political history and biography, the lives of the insignificant many appear, on the whole, only as classes or statistics, not too differently from the way they figure in books of political economy. But in reading this story we embrace the ordinary. It is made an object of our keenest interest and sympathy.[23] We visit these places as involved friends, concerned about what is going on in them. And this means that we have already as readers, if we read well, the moral experience that Louisa is represented as having when she visits the home of Stephen Blackpool, and is jolted out of all calculation by the perception that a Hand has a name, a face, a daily life, a complex soul, a history:

> For the first time in her life, Louisa had come into one of the dwellings of the Coketown Hands; for the first time in her life, she was face to face with anything like individuality in connexion with them. She knew of their existence by hundreds and by thousands. She knew what results in work a given number of them could produce, in a given space of time. She knew them in crowds passing to and from their nests, like ants or beetles. But she knew from her reading infinitely more of the ways of toiling insects than of these toiling men and women. (187)

This is one of the most striking of many self-referential passages in the novel. Coming well after much of the novel's own detailed description of the life of Stephen Blackpool, it reminds us that our own education and experience as readers have been and are very different from the economic education of the young Gradgrinds. The person brought up solely on economic texts is not encouraged to think of workers as fully complex human beings like herself, with stories of their own to tell. The novel's depiction of working-class life has some grave flaws. There is some sentimentality; there is an odd failure in basic literary technique, in that the mysterious promise of Stephen to Rachel is never explained and impossible to figure out—and yet it is permitted to determine the shape of the plot. Again, there is such great suspiciousness of all group or collective action that the work of trade unions is portrayed in a light manifestly unfair, even by the standards of Dickens's own nonfictional writing of this period.[24] And yet, the essential point made in this passage stands: the novel makes us acknowledge the equal humanity of members of social classes other than our own, makes us acknowledge workers as deliberating subjects with complex loves and aspirations and a rich inner world. It makes us see their poverty and their oppressive labor conditions in relation to those emotions and aspirations. It thus inspires compassion, wonder, and the passion for justice.[25]

If, then, from Gradgrind's viewpoint novels are bad economics, lacking in mathematical refinement, from the novel's viewpoint sophisticated economics is a bad novel—crude in its powers of representation and depiction, falsely detached toward the situations of fellow human beings, impoverished in the range of sentiments it recognizes and inspires. (Consider, too, the stories its utilitarian characters tell about themselves, and what crude fictions these are: Bounderby's cliché-ridden tale of abandonment and self-sufficiency, Grandgrind's plotless account of his victory over Joseph and George and the other Gradgrinds, the "leaden books' " account of the "good grown-up baby" and the "bad grown-up baby.") This fact can hardly, it claims, be politically irrelevant. For what one can do to ants and beetles is, morally, altogether different from what one can do to a being whom one sees as invested with the dignity and mystery of humanness. The social atrocities practiced in the novel are not unconnected with the vision of the Hands nourished by utilitarian education—by Gradgrind's mechanical vision, by Bounderby's equally impoverished vision of Hands as, all alike, longing to eat turtle soup and venison with a gold spoon. Dehumanize the worker in thought, and it is far easier to deny him or her the respect that human life calls forth.

The first principle of the science of political economy, according to Sissy Jupe the circus girl, miserably failing at her lesson, is "To do unto others as I would that they should do unto me" (95). (On which Mr. Gradgrind observes, "shaking his head, that all this was very bad; that is showed the necessity of infinite grinding at the mill of knowledge, as per system, schedule, blue book, report, and tabular statements A to Z" [96].)[26] I am claiming that Sissy Jupe's first principle is not merely represented *in* this novel; it is built into the novel's entire structure, as its guiding principle. For we are invited to concern ourselves with the fates of others like ourselves, attaching ourselves to them both by sympathetic friendship and by empathetic identification. When, then, we are invited at the close to think what we shall do, our natural response will be, if we have read well, to do unto other ordinary men and women as to ourselves, viewing the poorest as one whom we might be, and seeing in the most ordinary and even squalid circumstances of life a place in the most ordinary and even squalid circumstances of life a place where we ourselves have made in fancy our dwelling.[27] (And by "reading well," I do not mean coming up with one set of interpretive judgments rather than another, but something simpler and more basic: I mean, simply, reading with fancy and wonder, caring about the characters, being moved by their fate. This is compatible with many different interpretations. What it rules out is reading with disdain for them all, or viewing them all as inputs into a formula fixed in advance.)

And this brings me to one further feature of the novel, about which I have so far been silent: its capacity to give pleasure. For its moral operations are not independent of its aesthetic excellence. And it makes us bind ourselves to the workers because it causes us to take pleasure in their company. A tedious novel would not have had the same moral power; or, rather, the precision of attention that makes for interest is itself a moral feature. This is no incidental aspect of *Hard Times,* but one that it prominently stresses in its self-referential manner. The moral antitype of Gradgrind's school is Sleary's circus, whose capacity to please is closely linked to its moral superiority. And if we ask once again our obvious question about differences between this work and a text in political economy, we surely must answer that one of the greatest is that this book is fun to read. Like the circus, it contains humor and adventure, grotesqueness and surprise, music (note the frequent use of musical metaphors), rhythm, and motion. Its language is lyrical and full of poetic figures. Its plot is dramatically compelling; its characters inspire our trust and sympathy, or excite our laughter, or frighten us, or generate anger and disdain—or some complex combination of several of these. Its pleasure is more complexly critical, more richly moral, than the pleasure of the circus; and it depicts the circus as intellectually incomplete, insisting on a complex mixture of storytelling and social criticism that the novel as genre is well equipped to offer. But in all of its art, the novel acknowledges the importance of art—of the play of the imagination, the amusement of reading a good story.

It is the novel's explicit contention that this is an important aspect of the way in which it focuses the reader's attention and desire, and thus an important part of the moral and political action it expresses and generates. As Sleary twice observes, "People mutht be amuthed." Without play human life is drab and mean, all work and use, and no intrinsic delight. The capacity of this circus (this novel) to play, to give delight—inseparable, as in the circus, from the craft that informs it[28]—is part of what makes it a valuable part of human life, part of the generosity with which it speaks to and for its reader. For it expresses in its very artistry the wish that the reader should live a life of delight, of generous and liberal fancy, rather than merely the cramped drab life of political economy lessons.[29] And by forming with the reader a relationship rich in pleasure, as well as in moral reflection, it shows the reader a style of human relating in which deliberation is nourished by the exuberance of fancy, and moral attitudes are made more loving and more generous by the play of the imagination. Unlike Louisa, the reader of this novel "com(es) upon Reason through the tender light of Fancy" (223); this colors reason, making it, the novel claims, both more lively and more humane.

III. Fancy and Wonder

We have spoken of the novel, of this novel, as embodying in its form a certain sort of moral-political vision—radical, democratic, compassionate, committed to complexity and to qualitative differences. We have said that it does not merely *represent* a competition between fancy and political economy, but also enacts it in its very structure, in its ways of conversing with its hypothetical reader. But we must now go deeper, trying to say more about the fiction-making imagination itself, as the novel both represents and exemplifies it: above all, about *fancy,* that capacity to see one thing as another and one thing in another. For it is this activity of the mind that the Gradgrind school above all abhors and seeks to extirpate; and it is this capacity that the novel most centrally defends as necessary for good life, and triumphantly, exuberantly exemplifies in its every chapter.

Fancy is the novel's name for the ability to see one thing as another, to see one thing in another. We might therefore also call it the metaphorical imagination. It begins simply, as an almost instinctual reflex of mind (only Bitzer and Mrs. Gradgrind lack it totally). Even Louisa, forbidden its cultivation, sees shapes in the fire, endows perceived patterns with a significance that is not present in the bare sense-perception itself.[30] Things look like other things; or, more precisely, the other things are *seen in* the immediate things, as Louisa is aware at one and the same time both of the conjured images and of the fact that they are not present realities.[31] (With the good sense natural to fancy, she does not rush into the fire to grasp the images she reads there—a good sense, we might add, that eludes her father, who objects to a flower pattern in a carpet on the grounds that one does not tramp on flowers with one's boots. Sissy, objecting, knows that the flowers, being flowers of the fancy, will not be hurt by the boots of reality.)

Seeing a perception, then, as pointing to something beyond itself—seeing in the things that are perceptible and at hand other things that are not before one's eyes: this is fancy, and this is why Mr. Gradgrind disapproves of it.

In childhood, the novel reminds us, this ability is usually cultivated in countless ways—by games, stories, nursery rhymes—all of which are forbidden in the Gradgrind scheme for education:

> No little Gradgrind had ever seen a face in the moon. . . . No little Gradgrind had ever learnt the silly jingle, Twinkle, twinkle, little star; how I wonder what you are! No little Gradgrind had ever known wonder on the subject, each little Gradgrind having at five years old dissected the Great Bear like a Professor Owen, and driven Charles's Wain like a locomotive engine driver. No little Gradgrind had ever associated a cow in a field with that famous cow with the crumpled horn who tossed the dog who worried the cat who killed the rat who ate the malt, or with that yet more famous cow who swallowed Tom Thumb: it had never heard of those celebrities, and had only been introduced to a cow as a graminivorous ruminating quadruped with several stomachs. (54)

From the Gradgrind viewpoint, this is the omission of useless frills, leaving more time for the real stuff of education. But the novel announces, and shows (as we shall see), in its portrayal of Thomas and Louisa, that it is the omission of a morally crucial ability, one without which both personal and social relations are impoverished. As Louisa, chastened and empty, returns home, the authorial voice reminds the reader of the difference between her memories of home and the influences that home and the childlike imagination usually exert:

> Neither, as she approached her old home now, did any of the best influences of old home descend upon her. The dreams of childhood—its airy fables; its graceful, beautiful, humane, impossible adornments of the world beyond: so good to be believed in once, so good to be remembered when outgrown, for then the least among them rises to the stature of a great Charity in the heart, suffering little children to come into the midst of it, and to keep with their pure hands a garden in the stony ways of this world, wherein it were better for all the children of Adam that they should oftener sun themselves, simple and trustful, and not worldly-wise—what had

> she to do with these? Remembrances of how she had journeyed to the little that she knew, by the enchanted roads of what she and millions of innocent creatures had hoped and imagined; of how, first coming upon Reason through the tender light of Fancy, she had seen it a beneficient god, deferring to gods as great as itself: not a grim Idol, cruel and cold, with its victims bound hand to foot, and its big dumb shape set up with a sightless stare, never to be moved by anything but so many calculated tons of leverage—what had she to do with these? (223)

Here the novel makes some complicated connections, which the narrative as a whole has prepared us to see. We should pause to examine them. How exactly is Fancy connected with charity and generosity, with general human sympathy and a beneficent use of reason?

The man in the moon, the cow with the crumpled horn, the little star—in all these cases the child fancies that a form, which perception presents to it as a simple physical object, has a complex inner life, in some ways mysterious, in some ways analogous to its own. To see moon craters as a face, to speak to a star, to tell a story about a cow—these are things that the factual detached imagination of economic science is unwilling to do. But there is, as the novel says, a charity in this willingness to go beyond the evidence. And this charity is a preparation for greater charities in life.

Consider, now, what it is to see a human being. Perception represents a physical object, possibly in motion. It has a certain shape, rather like the one we ascribe to ourselves. Well, how do we really know what sort of physical object this is, and how to behave toward it? Do we ever have unimpeachable evidence that it is not a sophisticated robot or automaton? That it does indeed have a complex inner world of the sort that novels depict? How do we *know,* really, that this is a face before us—and not, say, a complex mechanical object with craters, a fiendishly clever machine? Where could such evidence ever be obtained? In this sense, Dickens suggests all of human life is going beyond the facts, an acceptance of generous fancies, a projection of our own sentiments and inner activities onto the forms we perceive about us (*and* a reception from this interaction of images of ourselves, our inner world). We are all of us, insofar as we interact morally and politically, fanciful projectors, makers of and believers in fictions and metaphors.[32] But the point then is that the "fact" school—which denies life to cows and horses, humanity to workers—engages in fiction-making as much as do the novel-readers and fanciers, in its adamant denials of life and humanity, which go, like the other's assertions, beyond the limits of the evidence. We never know for sure the contents of this perceived shape's heart; we have a choice, only, between a generous construction and a mean-spirited construction.[33] Seeing-in or Fancy, the great Charity in the heart, nourishes a generous construal of the world. This construal is not only, as the novel suggests, more adequate as an explanation of the totality of human behavior as we experience it,[34] but also a cause of better ways of living.

We see the difference, for example, in the contrasting ways of regarding workers: Bounderby seeing only self-interest, the novel seeing a complex variety of motives. We see it in the ways of contemplating possibilities for political change—for even when the ways of the world are "stony," Fancy can imagine a garden growing there. We see it too in the contrasting attitudes of the circus and of Tom Gradgrind toward the appetites of the body. The circus people are passionate in a romantic and tender manner, always seeing in one another a complex life, and delighting in that. Of Tom, the novel remarks, with heavy irony, "It was altogether unaccountable that a young gentleman whose imagination had been strangled in his cradle, should be still inconvenienced by its ghost in the form of grovelling sensualities" (165). Seeing bodies only as physical objects in motion produces an impoverished sexual life. It is by no means accidental that the utilitarians are depicted throughout with language at once phallic and military, as hard aggressive weapons conducting a pitiless assault on all that is tender. Mr. Gradgrind is a "cannon loaded to the muzzle with facts," a "galvanizing apparatus," directed against "the tender young imaginations that were to be stormed away" (48). By contrast, the approach of fancy is depicted as delicately, tenderly sensuous, as delighting in the dexterity of speech and gesture, the intricate rhythm and texture of words themselves. Gradgrind language sounds hard, intrusive, its cadences fierce and abrupt. As language, its body moves itself with a pitiless directness, combining aggressiveness with self-righteous complacency: "The M'Choakumchild school was all fact, and the school of design was all fact, and the relations between master and man were all fact, and everything was fact between the lying-in hospital and the cemetery, and what you couldn't state in figures, or show to be purchaseable in the cheapest market and saleable in the dearest, was not, and never should be, world without end. Amen" (66). By contrast, the speech of Fancy has, so to speak a supple and acrobatic circus body, a surprising exuberant variety. It loves the physical texture of language, and plays with it, teasing and caressing the reader. Even when it speaks about its adversaries, it cannot long restrain itself from treating them playfully and almost tenderly, as partners in a game of words, in which delight is taken for its own sake. Thus the many alliterative linguistic games in the depiction of the Gradgrind house, as the narrator enjoys the play of his supple speech around their blunter bodies—as in this passage, where an initially straightforward description becomes more and more joyously sensuous, until the play of the tongue quite takes over, defeating its own subject matter:

> The little Gradgrinds had cabinets in various departments of science too. They had a little conchological cabinet, and a little metallurgical cabinet, and a little mineralogical cabinet; and the specimens were all arranged and labelled, and the bits of stone and ore looked as though they might have been broken from the parent substances by those tremendously hard instruments their own names; and, to paraphrase the idle legend of Peter Piper, who had never found his way into *their* nursery, If the greedy little Gradgrinds grasped at more than this, what was it for good gracious goodness sake, that the greedy little Gradgrinds grasped at! (55)

Here the literary imagination opposes to the hard instruments of the *names* used by political economy its own very different language, and is carried away by its sensuous play. It does not stick to the subject, or move unswervingly to its goal. It thus deliberately embodies forms of desire and sensuality profoundly opposed to those it imputes to political economy. Imagine language as a way of touching a human body, Dickens suggests—and you have a good way of scrutinizing the claims of political economy to stand for us in the fullness of our selves.

(I should add here that Dickens has sometimes been represented as repressing sexuality, especially female sexuality. I believe that this reading cannot stand up to a close scrutiny of this novel's depiction of the ways in which tongue and mind approach a human form. It is not only that a crude aggressiveness is condemned while a gentler, more varied, and more playful sensuality is celebrated; it is also plain that this sensuous play is linked repeatedly with the influence of the female. What I have elsewhere argued about Dickens's feminization of the author-narrator in erotic contexts fits well here: the susceptible, playful side of life, the side lost, David Copperfield says, by most adult males, is the side out of which novels are generated.[35] This one is no exception, clearly.)

And with this mention of play, we come to a further element in Fancy, which we must now explore to complete our account of its social role. When a child learns to fancy, it is learning something useless. This is the Gradgrind school's main objection to it: storybooks are "idle." Facts are what we need, "the one thing needful"; and what use has anyone ever gotten from the man in the moon? But the child who takes delight in stories and nursery rhymes is getting the idea that not everything in human life *has* a use. It is learning a mode of engagement with the world that does not focus exclusively on the idea of use, but is capable, too, of cherishing things for their own sake. And this too it takes into its relations with other human beings. It is not only the ability to endow a form with life that makes the metaphorical imagination morally valuable; it is the ability to view what one has constructed in fancy as serving no end beyond itself, as good and delightful for itself alone. Play and amusement are thus not simply adjuncts or supplements to human life, but also exemplary in a crucial way about how to view life's central elements. In this sense, the reader's delight in this novel has yet a further moral dimension, and is a preparation for moral activities of many kinds of life.[36]

We can perhaps sum all this up by examining the two contrasting scenes of education presented in the two epigraphs to this paper. Both are scenes in which a request for a definition or account of something has been made. In the first, we have the orthodox Gradgrind answer given by the pupil Bitzer. The second passage is, of course, not from Dickens at all, but from Walt Whitman's *Song of Myself.* And I shall not pretend that I selected it simply because it is so apt as a contrast with the Gradgrind definition, and so much in the spirit of Dickens's novel, although it is both. In fact, I arranged the contrast around it, so that I could have an excuse for discussing it in this otherwise Dickensian argument—because I love it, and find it very beautiful. Perhaps this surprising circuslike declination from the straight path of my exposition will be found not out of keeping with the spirit of my argument.

Bitzer has never loved a horse, and has no interest in thinking what it might be like to be one. With an air of finality and certainty he recites the detached external description. The horse emerges as a useful machine, no more. How different is Whitman's speaker. First of all, he is motivated not by a mechanical urge to complete enumeration, but by the child's real curiosity, and by the sight and touch of the grass of which, lying in the grass, he speaks. His first response is to acknowledge that he does not finally know—to acknowledge, that is, a mystery in nature. All his ensuing answers are presented as *guesses*. He speaks first of his inner life, his hope; next, whimsically and not at all dogmatically, of a child's idea of god; then he tells the child that the grass is sort of like him, a young bit of vegetation—he asks the child to see it *as* like himself. He then shows the child that it can have, as well, a social significance: for one can see in it the equal vitality and dignity of all Americans, their equal rights and privileges across racial and ethnic differences. Then, turning in, we imagine, on himself, the speaker sees in the grass a darker set of significances, pondering in and through it about the beauty of dead men. He endows even their corpses beneath the earth with beauty, and speaks of them with a profoundly erotic reverence and tenderness—but in a way that does not exclude further thoughts of the grass as from elderly parents, or prematurely dead children. And yet, in its darkness—too dark to come from old mothers, or even from the mouths of those he has or might have loved, he sees an image of his own death.

Here we see all the abilities of fancy, deftly woven together: its ability to endow a perceived form with rich and complex significance; its generous construction of the seen; its preference for wonder over pat solutions; its playful and surprising movements, delightful for their own sake; its tenderness, its eroticism, its awe before the fact of human mortality. It is Dickens's view, as it is also Whitman's, that this imagination—including its playfulness, including its eroticism—is the necessary basis for good government of a country of equal and free citizens. For, as Whitman elsewhere writes, the literary artist "sees eternity in men and women, he does not see men and women as dreams or dots."[37] With it, Reason is beneficent, steered by a generous view of its objects; without its charity, Reason is cold and cruel.[38]

We can now understand that the persistent exuberant metaphoricity of the language of *Hard Times* is no mere game, no stylistic diversion; it goes to the heart of the novel's moral theme. Even while the novel portrays the Gradgrind schoolroom, it cannot help comparing one thing to another, seeing one thing in another: two dark caves, in Mr. Gradgrind's eyes; a plantation of firs in his hair; the crust of a plum pie in the bald surface of the top of his head (47). Even while it depicts the monotony and soul-crushing dreariness of the Coketown factory, it triumphs over it in language, comparing the coils of steam to serpents, the moving machine parts to "melancholy-mad elephants"—showing in these ways the human meaning of the inhuman. The novel cannot describe its opposition without doing battle with it, approaching it through Fancy and playfully surmounting it.[39]

I must now insist that in this novel—and in my own view—there is no disparagement of reason or of the scientific search for truth. What I am criticizing is a pseudoscience that claims to stand for truth and for reason. What I am saying about it is that it fails to stand for truth insofar as it dogmatically misrepresents the complexity of human beings and human life. It fails to stand for reason when it uncritically trusts half-baked perceptions and crude psychological theories in order not to complicate its elegant models. The novel speaks not of dismissing reason, but of coming upon it in a way illuminated by fancy, which is here seen as a faculty at once both creative and veridical. The alternative I am proposing is not Sleary's circus. The circus offers the reader essential metaphors of art, discipline, play, and love; but even within the novel its attitudes are shown as politically incomplete, too ill-educated and whimsical to govern a nation. The novel offers us an alternative: itself, its complex combination of qualitatively rich description with critical social reflection. And it indicates that political and economic treatises of a more abstract and mathematical sort would be perfectly consistent with its purpose—so long as the view of the human being underlying the treatises was the richer view available in the novel; so long as they do not lose sight of what they are, for efficiency, omitting. Government cannot investigate the life story of every citizen in the way a novel does with its characters; it can, however, know *that* each citizen has a complex history of this sort, and it can remain aware that the norm in principle would be to acknowledge the separateness and qualitative difference of each in the manner of the novel.

In one particular way the novel, as genre, is strongly in league with a certain norm of rationality: namely, in its insistence on the fundamental role, in its own construction, of a general notion of the *human being*. The description of the Coketown library speaks of "human nature, human passions, human hopes and fears," as the subject matter of the novel. In so doing it reminds us that the novel does not purchase its attention to social context and to individual variety at the price of jettisoning a sense of human community. It forges a complex relationship with its reader in which, on the one hand, the reader is urged to care about concrete features of circumstance and history, and to see these as relevant for social choice; but is, on the other hand, urged always to recognize that human beings in different spheres do have common passions, hopes, and fears, the need to confront the mystery of death, the desire for learning, the deep bonds of the family. Its hypothetical reader is explicitly addressed as one whose sphere of life is different from that of the author—with different concrete choices and possibilities. And yet it is assumed that the reader can still identify with the characters and events of the novel as with possibilities for human life in general, and think how "such things" can be instantiated in his or her own concrete life.[40] This complex movement of imagination and reason, from the concrete to the general back to the concrete, through both sympathy and identification, is built into the genre, as *Hard Times* correctly states. And in real life one does find that works of imaginative literature are frequently far more supple and versatile deliberative agents across cultural boundaries than are philosophical treatises, with their time-bound and culture-bound terms of art, their frequent lack of engagement with common hopes and fears.

In its engagement with a general notion of the human being, this novel (like many novels) is, I think, while particularistic, not relativistic. That is, it recognizes human needs that transcend boundaries of time, place, class, religion, and ethnicity, and it makes the focus of its moral deliberation the question of their adequate fulfillment. Its criticism of concrete political and social situations relies on a notion of what it is for a human being to flourish, and this notion itself, while extremely general and in need of further specification, is neither local nor sectarian. On the other hand, part of the content of the idea of flourishing is a deep respect for qualitative difference—so the norm enjoins that governments, wherever they are, should attend to citizens in all their concreteness and variety, and should respond in a sensitive way to particular historical and personal contingencies. But the point is, that is itself a universal injunction, and part of a universal picture of humanness. And it is by relying on this universal ideal that the novel, so different from a guidebook or even an anthropological field report, makes the reader a participant in the lives of people very different from herself and also a critic of the class distinctions that give people similarly constructed an unequal access to flourishing.[41] Thus the novel, in its structure and aspiration, is, I think, a defender of enlightenment ideals of the equality and dignity of all human life—not of traditionalism or parochialism. It is opposed to the perversion of that ideal in the name of the pseudoscience of economics, and also to its insensitive application with insufficient respect for stories told within a concrete historical context—not to the ideal itself.

IV. Sissy Jupe's Political Economy Lesson—And Ours

What does all of this mean for political economy? I shall conclude by telling the story of my own instruction in that science, in which I am no better a pupil than Sissy Jupe. For the past five years I have been affiliated with the World Institute for Development Economics Research, a research institute connected with the United Nations University, whose aim is to explore broader interdisciplinary approaches to the economic problems of the developing world. I have been a research adviser in a project that discusses how one should measure the "quality of life" of developing countries.[42] This is in fact the topic of Sissy Jupe's first lesson in political economy. And my interest in Dickens's novel was very much increased by the fact that it corresponds still, even in its broad satirical elements, to much of the practice of development economics, and to public policy as influenced by it.

This is how the Gradgrind school, then as now, proceeds (Sissy narrating to Louisa):

> "And he said, Now, this schoolroom is a Nation. And in this nation, there are fifty millions of money. Isn't this a prosperous nation? Girl number twenty, isn't this a prosperous nation, and a'n't you in a thriving state?"
>
> "What did you say?" asked Louisa.
>
> "Miss Louisa, I said I didn't know. I thought I couldn't know whether it was a prosperous nation or not, and whether I was in a thriving state or not, unless I knew who had got the money, and whether any of it was mine. But that had nothing to do with it. It was not in the figures at all," said Sissy, wiping her eyes.
>
> "That was a great mistake of yours," observed Louisa. (97)

Today in fact, when the prosperity of developing countries is compared in "tabular form," by far the most common strategy is simply to enumerate GNP per capita.[43] This crude measure, of course, as Sissy immediately recognizes, does not even tell us about the distribution of wealth and income. Far less does such an approach, focusing exclusively on the monetary, tell us about how the human beings who have or do not have the money are functioning, with respect to various activities that might be thought to be important for human life. It does not even tell us about life expectancy and infant mortality—far less about health, education, political functioning, the quality of ethnic and racial and gender relations.

A slightly more sophisticated approach measures, as Gradgrind would wish, the total or average utility of the population, amalgamating satisfactions. This at least has the advantage of looking at how resources work *for people,* in promoting human aims of various sorts. But it has a disadvantage that the novel makes all too plain: it ignores the fact that desires and satisfactions are highly malleable, and that people who are especially miserable can adapt to the circumstances in which they live—that one of the worst parts about deep deprivation is that it robs people of the aspirations and *dissatisfactions* connected with a robust sense of what is due to their dignity.[44] The Hands in the Coketown factory do manifest some discontent; but, given their exhaustion, the material and imaginative limitations under which they labor, they seem likely to welcome any small relief, and to accept a very inadequate and insensitive leadership, since they have not fully been able to form the ideal of full equality. Stephen can see that his life is "a muddle"; but he cannot clearly articulate the nature of his discontent, or fully feel its force. Gradgrind, on the other hand, is very satisfied with his life, which the novel shows to be spiritually impoverished; and his discontent at the novel's end is clearly a progress over his early equanimity. At the limit, the character Bitzer shows us the extreme unreliability of the feeling of satisfaction, when not linked to any more probing ethical evaluation. For whatever makes that empty vessel of self-interest feel pleased fills the reader with anxiety and even horror. And we know from the start that there is more worth, more humanity, in Sissy Jupe's misery and discomfort—a sensitive barometer of cant and injustice—than in Bitzer's empty self-complacency. "Whereas the girl was so dark-eyed and dark-haired, that she seemed to receive a deeper and more lustrous color from the sun when it shone upon her, the boy was so light-eyed and light-haired that the self-same rays appeared to draw out of him what little color he ever possessed" (49–50). By this eloquent symbolic description, the novel expresses the human richness of Sissy's response to life, including her unhappiness, and the ghastly mechanical quality of Bitzer's optimism.[45] Can utility give us the measure of these lives, of the education of which they are the fruit, and the human functioning they do and do not contain?

Such criticisms of utility as a measure—together with the other points I have mentioned about aggregation and qualitative differences, which have been much stressed in recent philosophical critiques of economics—have led a group of economists and philosophers, of which I am a part, to defend an approach to quality of life measurement based on a notion of human functioning and human capability, rather than on either opulence or utility.

(This approach was pioneered within economics by Amartya Sen, who is also a philosopher; and it has more adherents to date within philosophy than within economics.) The idea is to ask how well people are doing, by asking how well their form of life has enabled them to function in a variety of distinct areas, including, but not limited to, mobility, health, education, political participation, and social relations. This approach refuses to come up with a single number, reducing quality to quantity. And it insists on asking about the actual functional capabilities of each distinct and qualitatively different individual, rather than simply about how much in terms of resources an individual commands. This is so because the approach recognizes that individuals need varying amounts of resources in order to arrive at the same level of functioning: the handicapped person more resources to be mobile than the person of ordinary mobility, the large and active person more food than the small and sedentary person, and so forth.[46] Nonetheless, the approach does actually permit modeling and measurement: as when one studies the access that mobility-impaired people do and do not have to functions of various sorts in a given society; as when one studies the different food needs of people of different sizes, ages, and occupations; as when one studies the ways in which class distinctions impede access to political participation. The governments of Finland and Sweden actually use such plural quality-based measurements to study inequalities in their populations—proving, by doing so, that it is possible to measure in this way.[47] Such measures will indeed be plural and not single, qualitatively diverse rather than homogeneous. This, we argue, makes them better, not worse.

What I now wish to claim is that a novel such as this one is a paradigm of such assessment. Presenting the life of a population with a rich variety of qualitative distinctions, and complex individual descriptions of functioning and impediments to functioning, using a general notion of human need and human functioning in a highly concrete context, it provides the sort of information such an assessment requires, and involves its reader in the task of making the assessment. Thus it displays a kind of imaginative paradigm for public work in this sphere, to which any more quantitative and simplified model should be responsible.

Hard Times ends by invoking one of its most central characters: "Dear reader! It rests with you and me, whether, in our two fields of action, similar things shall be or not. Let them be! We shall sit with lighter bosoms on the hearth, to see the ashes of our fires turn gray and cold" (314). Addressing the reader as a friend and fellow agent, though in a different sphere of life, the authorial voice turns this reader's sympathetic wonder at the fates of the characters back on him or herself, reminding her that she too is on the way to death, that she too has but this one chance to see in the fire the shapes of fancy, and the prospects these suggest for the improvement of human life. The novel is right: it does rest with us whether such things shall be or not. I claim, with it, that it is not as economic utilitarians but as readers of novels that we should approach the social choices before us, trying, before our death, to consider our fellow citizens, our fellow human beings, with the wonder and the generosity that this imagination promotes.[48]

Notes

1. All citations from *Hard Times* are taken from the Penguin edition, ed. David Craig (Harmondsworth, 1969); hereafter cited in text. The studies of this novel from which I have learned most are Raymond Williams, *Culture and Society, 1780–1950* (London: Chatto & Windus, 1958), part 1, chap. 5; Craig's excellent introduction to the Penguin edition; and F. R. Leavis, *The Great Tradition: George Eliot, Henry James, Joseph Conrad* (New York: New York University Press, 1948).

2. See Martha C. Nussbaum, *Love's Knowledge: Essays on Philosophy and Literature* (New York: Oxford University Press, 1990), esp. "The Discernment of Perception," 54–105, and "Perception and Revolution," 195–219.

3. Compare the account of the reader's activity in Wayne Booth, *The Company We Keep: An Ethics of Fiction* (Berkeley and Los Angeles: University of California Press, 1988); the account of the ways in which narratives embody forms of desire in Peter Brooks, *Reading for the Plot: Design and Intention in Narrative* (New York: Knopf, 1984); and the account of the reader's acknowledgment in Stanley Cavell, *The Claim of Reason: Wittgenstein, Skepticism, Morality and Tragedy* (New York: Oxford University Press, 1979), part 4.

4. Today "political economy" is a term used (in self-description) primarily by the most critical and philosophical of economists (for example, Amartya Sen); so what I am criticizing here is not what would be so described in contemporary economics.

5. For example, see James Griffin, *Well-Being: Its Meaning, Measurements, and Moral Importance* (Oxford: 1986); and Richard B. Brandt, *A Theory of the Good and Right* (Oxford: Clarendon Press, 1979).

6. See above all the writings of Richard Posner, including *Economic Analysis of Law* (Boston: Little, Brown, 1977); *The Economics of Justice* (Cambridge: Harvard University Press, 1981); and *Law and Literature: A Misunderstood Relation* (Cambridge: Harvard University Press, 1988). In *The Problems of Jurisprudence* (Cambridge: Harvard University Press, 1990), Posner has modified his approach, espousing a kind of "pragmatism." For a good general critique of economic reasoning in public life generally, see the introduction to *Utilitarianism and Beyond,* ed. Amartya Sen and Bernard Williams (Cambridge: Cambridge University Press, 1988).

7. See Barbara Herrnstein Smith, *Contingencies of Value: Alternative Perspectives for Critical Theory* (Cambridge: Harvard University Press, 1988).

8. See Posner, *Economic Analysis of Law* and *The Economics of Justice;* Gary Becker, *The Economic Approach to Human Behavior* (Chicago: University of Chicago Press, 1976), and *A Treatise on the Family* (Cambridge: Harvard University Press, 1981). Especially instructive is the opening of Posner's *The Economics of Justice,* where he first introduces the "assumption that people are rational maximizers of their satisfactions," noting that "the principles of economics are deductions from this assumption"—and then goes on to use the word "rational," without further philosophical argument, as if it just *meant* "maximizers of satisfactions" (see 1–2). One trenchant critique of Posner, with regard to the worth of one's personal integrity, is Margaret Jane Radin, "Market-Inalienability," *Harvard Law Review* 100 (1987): 1849ff.

9. Some of these criticisms do apply, as well, to philosophical utilitarians, many of whom do treat values as commensurable by a single quantitative standard. See, for example, James Griffin, "Are There Incommensurable Values?" *Philosophy and Public Affairs* 7 (1977): 34–59, criticized in Nussbaum, "The Discernment of Perception."

10. The workers complain that their lives are constrained by an enforced "sameness" (180), an absence of qualitative variation. It is no wonder that a theory bent on eliminating qualitative distinctions would treat them in this way.

11. See the good account of this feature in Sen and Williams, introduction to *Utilitarianism and Beyond.*

12. Shortly after this, hearing of Stephen's misfortunes, Louisa remarks that she had previously heard them mentioned, "though I was not attending to the particulars at the time" (188).

13. For another example of crude economic fiction-making, see the account of the "leaden little books . . . showing how the good grown-up baby invariably got to the Savings-bank, and the bad grown-up baby invariably got transported" (90).

14. That this is no mere fiction can be confirmed by reading Becker's *A Treatise on the Family.*

15. Contrast 241, where Louisa now sees that her marriage failed because of "all those causes of disparity which arise out of our two individual natures, and which no general laws shall ever rule or state for me, father, until they shall be able to direct the anatomist where to strike his knife into the secrets of my soul."

16. This lies very deep in the motivation behind utilitarianism in general, and inspires some of its deliberate departures from ordinary belief. Henry Sidgwick, for example, conceding that to adopt a single metric of choice is to depart from ordinary belief, writes, "If we are not to systematize human activities by taking Universal Happiness as their common end, on what other principles are we to systematize them?"—and remarks that such departures are always found when a science is born (*Methods of Ethics,* 7th ed. [London: Macmillan, 1907], 401, 406, 425).

17. Just before we hear of the "leaden books," the narrator himself describes the people of Coketown as "walking against time towards the infinite world" (90).

18. For a trenchant documentation and critique of these behavioral assumptions, see Amartya Sen, "Rational Fools," *Philosophy and Public Affairs* 6 (1976–77): 317–44.

19. Indeed, if we bear in mind that one of utilitarianism's central claims on its own behalf is that it can take seriously the pain of the poor, we see the novel as offering, in addition, a devastating *internal* critique. I develop this argument further in the second Rosenthal Lecture.

20. At the same time, the utilitarian's particular conception of science owes something to the Cartesian conception of nature as a machine: this shows up especially clearly in the attitudes to animals in the Gradgrind schoolroom.

21. This is *one* way of reading Bitzer; but one might also *wonder* about him, and

whether he is not in fact a hypocrite, manipulating the education he has been given for his own ends. In this way, the curiosity inspired by the novel prompts one to try humanizing, in fancy, even the most inhuman of characters.

22. The reader's *emotional* participation is discussed in the second Rosenthal Lecture.

23. See Ian Watt, *The Rise of the Novel: Studies in Defoe, Richardson, and Fielding* (Berkeley and Los Angeles: University of California Press, 1957); and Charles Taylor, *Sources of the Self: The Making of the Modern Identity* (Cambridge: Harvard University Press, 1989).

24. See the excellent discussion by David Craig in the introduction to the Penguin edition.

25. This does not mean that there could never be an inegalitarian novel; it does mean that inegalitarianism is in tension with the structure of the genre, which invites concern and respect for any story to which it directs the reader's attention. See also Watt, *The Rise of the Novel* and Taylor, *Sources of the Self.*

26. See also 238, where Mr. Gradgrind proves that "the Good Samaritan was a Bad Economist."

27. In these ways, the novel constructs, in its imagined reader, an ideal moral judge who bears a close resemblance to the parties in John Rawls's Original Position (*A Theory of Justice* [Cambridge: Belknap Press of Harvard University Press, 1971]). But the faculties the reader is invited to use would not correspond to Rawls's account of "considered judgment"—on this see "Perceptive Equilibrium" in Nussbaum, *Love's Knowledge.*

28. Thus the novel also embodies a (rather Aristotelian) conception of pleasure according to which pleasure itself contains qualitative distinctions and supervenes on activities of various different sorts.

29. The utilitarian claims to be maximizing pleasure. Why, then, is novel-reading so opposed? Apparently the source of the opposition is Mr. Gradgrind's fear that this reading will cause people to behave in various nonefficient ways in the rest of their lives; thus, from his point of view, it will do more harm than good.

30. See 240, where Louisa contrasts the perception of "the shapes and surfaces of things" with the exercise of fancy.

31. On this, see Richard Wollheim, "Seeing-In and Seeing-As," in *Art and Its Objects: An Introduction to Aesthetics,* 2d ed. (Cambridge: Cambridge University Press, 1980), and *Painting as an Art* (Princeton: Princeton University Press, 1987), chap. 2.

32. See the wonderful account of this in Cavell, *The Claim of Reason,* part 4.

33. See 77, where the circus people are said to be "deserving" of both "respect" and "generous construction"; and also Sleary's famous injunction to "make the betht of uth: not the wurtht!" (83).

34. For it is part of the novel's claim that the simple economic model does not really reliably predict how people will behave: its formulas are not even in that sense useful. See Sen, "Rational Fools."

35. See "Steerforth's Arm" in Nussbaum, *Love's Knowledge.* This of course does not imply that Dickens is altogether free of contradiction on this point, as the harsh treatment of Emily shows. But in this novel it is noteworthy that the representative of the artistic imagination, Sissy Jupe, is also the only character to achieve a happy and loving marriage.

36. In the second Rosenthal Lecture I explore the reader's moral operations further, focusing on the connection between fancy and the emotions of love and gratitude.

37. Walt Whitman, "By Blue Ontario's Shore," line 153, in *Walt Whitman: The Complete Poems,* ed. Francis Murphy (Harmondsworth: Penguin, 1975), 369.

38. One might naturally ask, But can't one use Fancy to hate? I say more about this

in the second lecture, where I talk about the range of sentiments the reader is and is not invited, by the novel's form, to have; I connect this with Adam Smith's account of ideal emotional spectatorship. *Hard Times* urges us, further, to consider the nonjudgmental participation of the novel in each and every life, its recognition that each life does have its own story, its invitation to see each life from the person's own point of view. Here, I think, we see what Dickens means by "the great Charity in the heart": the novel, even while permitting and even suggesting certain criticisms of its characters, promotes mercy through its invitations to empathetic understanding.

39. Compare Mr. Gradgrind on 242, 244, where he is able to see a fire in Louisa's eyes, and begins to use metaphorical speech.

40. For more on this, see Nussbaum, "Aristotelian Social Democracy," in *Liberalism and the Good,* ed. R. Bruce Douglass, Gerald M. Mara, and Henry S. Richardson (New York: Routledge, 1990), 203–52; "Aristotle on Human Nature and the Foundations of Ethics," in *World, Mind, and Ethics: Essays on the Ethical Philosophy of Bernard Williams,* ed. Ross Harrison and J. E. G. Altham (New York: Cambridge University Press, 1995); and "Human Functioning and Social Justice: In Defense of Aristotelian Essentialism," *Political Theory* 20, no. 2 (May 1992): 202–46.

41. See Amartya Sen, *Choice, Welfare, and Measurement* (Cambridge: MIT Press, 1982); *Resources, Value, and Development* (Cambridge: Harvard University Press, 1984); *Commodities and Capabilities* (Amsterdam: North-Holland, 1985); and *The Standard of Living* (Cambridge: Cambridge University Press, 1987).

42. See *The Quality of Life,* ed. Martha Nussbuam and Amartya Sen (Oxford: Clarendon Press, 1991).

43. To some extent and in some contexts, inroads have been made by other approaches in terms of "basic needs" or, now, Sen's approach in terms of functioning and capability. But on the whole this remains all too true; see Sen, *Resources,* and the introduction to Nussbaum and Sen, *The Quality of Life.*

44. See Sen, *Choice, Welfare, and Measurement* and *The Standard of Living.*

45. See Leavis's account of this passage in *The Great Tradition.*

46. See Sen, *Choice, Welfare, and Measurement; The Standard of Living;* and his paper "Capabilities and Well-Being" in Nussbaum and Sen, *The Quality of Life.*

47. See the papers by Robert Erikson and Erik Allardt in Nussbaum and Sen, *The Quality of Life.*

48. This essay was delivered as a lecture at the Commonwealth Center in November 1990; I am most grateful to Ralph Cohen and to the Center for that opportunity to discuss my work in progress. I am grateful, as well, to Dan Brock, Kenneth Dornstein, Elliott Dunn, Jean Hampton, Linda Hirshman, Amartya Sen, and Cass Sunstein, all of whom made comments that contributed to my revisions.

Relevant Publications by Martha Nussbaum

Upheavels of Thought: A Theory of the Emotions. The Gifford Lectures of 1993, forthcoming from Cambridge University Press.

The Therapy of Desire: Theory and Practice in Hellenistic Ethics. Princeton: Princeton University Press, 1994.

The Quality of Life (coeditor with Amartya Sen). Oxford: Clarendon Press, 1993.

Love's Knowledge: Essays on Philosophy and Literature. Oxford: Oxford University Press, 1990.

The Fragility of Goodness: Luck and Ethics in Greek Tragedy and Philosophy. Cambridge: Cambridge University Press, 1986.

"Equity and Mercy." *Philosophy and Public Affairs* 22 (1993): 83–125.

"The Literary Imagination in Public Life." *New Literary History* 22 (autumn 1991): 877–910.

Select Bibliography

Brief selective bibliography of books containing relevant criticism of aspects of poststructuralist and related literary criticism and theory. This list does not include books listed in the individual bibliographies of contributors to this volume.

Abrams, M. H. *Doing Things with Texts: Essays in Criticism and Critical Theory.* Edited by Michael Fischer. New York: Norton, 1989. Although all the essays collected in this volume bear on the practice of literary criticism and theory, the six essays that make up the last section, beginning with "The Deconstructive Angel," are especially relevant in a time when literary study is still striving to emerge from poststructuralism.

After Poststructuralism: Interdisciplinarity and Literary Theory. Edited by Nancy Easterlin and Barbara Riebling. Foreword by Frederick Crews. Evanston: Northwestern University Press, 1993. A wide-ranging set of essays challenging various errors and confusions of the reigning "Poststructuralist Vanguard." Contains essays by Richard Levin, Robert Storey, David F. Bell, Paisley Livingston, Nancy Easterlin, William Cain, Carol Siegel, David R. Anderson, Barbara Riebling, and Gary Saul Morson.

Booth, Wayne C. *Critical Understanding: The Powers and Limits of Pluralism.* Chicago: University of Chicago Press, 1979. A clear argument for methodological pluralism as opposed to such alternatives such as monism, skepticism, and eclecticism.

Crane, R. S. *The Languages of Criticism and the Structure of Poetry.* Austin: University of Texas Press, 1953. An important mid-twentieth-century statement of a pluralist conception of criticism. Crane's concept of pluralism is equally distinct from poststructuralist indeterminacy and from belief in a master mode of analysis that will reveal the one sovereign meaning of the text.

Crews, Frederick. *Skeptical Engagements.* New York: Oxford University Press, 1986. The fourteen chapters are divided into three major sections: "I. The Freudian Temptation"; "II. The Theorized Academy"; and "III. At Closer Range," which explores a variety of contemporary practices.

Criticism in the University. Edited by Gerald Graff and Reginald Gibbons. Evanston: Northwestern University Press, 1985. The fourteen essays and four short responses by various hands focus largely on current problems and confusions in the academic study of literature. The contributors of the essays are Reginald Gibbons, Wallace Douglas, Gerald Graff, William E. Cain, Frank Lentricchia, Gene H. Bell-Villada, Morris Dickstein, Mark Krupnick, Donald Davie, Patrick Colm Hogan, E. D. Hirsch Jr., William H. Pritchard, and Wendell Berry.

Ellis, John M. *Against Deconstruction.* Princeton: Princeton University Press, 1989. A brief volume cogently responding to the fallacies and inconsistencies of deconstruction and related literary theories.

———. *Language, Thought, and Logic.* Evanston: Northwestern University Press, 1993. An analysis of problems and current endemic confusions in the theory of language, formal linguistics, epistemology, and logic. Although not focused on literary study, the positions critics or theorists consciously or unconciously take on the issues discussed directly affect their perspectives on literature.

Freadman, Richard, and Seaumas Miller. *Re-Thinking Theory: A Critique of Contemporary Literary Theory and an Alternative Account.* Cambridge: Cambridge University Press, 1992. Includes cogent chapters on Catherine Belsey, Althusser, Derrida, and Foucault; following the critique of "constructivist anti-humanism" in the first six chapters, the final chapter presents a literary theory intended to support a humanism that recognizes the individual and "emancipationist politics."

Graff, Gerald. *Literature Against Itself: Literary Ideas in Modern Society.* Chicago: University of Chicago Press, 1979. An early warning against some of the directions in which poststructuralist literature and structuralist theory was taking in the study of literature.

Hirsch, E. D., Jr. *The Aims of Interpretation.* Chicago: University of Chicago Press, 1976. Clarifies certain of the arguments of *Validity in Interpretation* and refocuses Hirsch's arguments more specifically toward major principles of poststructuralist theory.

———. *Validity in Interpretation.* New Haven: Yale University Press, 1967. Directed at the time of writing against what had come to be understood as the New Critical dismissal of authorial intention and the claims of the school of hermeneutics that denied the possibility of usefully reconstructing the historical situation in which a text was written, Hirsch's distinction between meaning and significance also challenges the central aspects of poststructuralism.

Livingston, Paisley. *Literary Knowledge: Humanistic Knowledge and the Philosophy of Science.* Ithaca: Cornell University Press, 1988. An argument for making literary knowledge more scientific that seeks at the same time to avoid confusing literature with science.

Merquior, José G. *From Prague to Paris: A Critique of Structuralist and Post-*

Structuralist Thought. London: Verso, 1986. An insightful critique by a close student of the structuralist/poststructuralist theory. The chapter titles provide a good summary of the book's content: "The Rise of Structuralism," "The Prague Crossroad Between Formalism and Socio-semiotics," "Claude Lévi-Strauss: The Birth of Structuralism in Social Science," "Literary Structuralism: Roland Barthes," and "Structuralism into Post-Structuralism: An Overview."

Parrinder, Patrick. *The Failure of Theory: Essays on Criticism and Contemporary Fiction.* Brighton: Harvester Press, 1987. The first half of the volume is devoted to critiques of the dominant role of literary theory and of particular theorists, with particular focus on Marxist theorizing.

Reconstructing Literature. Edited by Laurence Lerner. Oxford: Basil Blackwell, 1983. A very readable collection of essays criticizing various aspects of poststructuralist theory. The contributors are Cedric Watts, Roger Scruton, John Holloway, Gabriel Josipovici, Wayne Booth, Robert Pattison, Anthony Thorlby, and Laurence Lerner.

Vickers, Brian. *Appropriating Shakespeare: Contemporary Critical Quarrels.* New Haven: Yale University Press, 1993. Although focused on recent criticism of Shakespeare, the book's contents are broad; they are sketched by the seven chapter titles: "The Diminution of Language: Saussure to Derrida"; "Creator and Interpreters"; "Deconstruction: Undermining and Overreaching"; "New Historicism: Disaffected Subjects"; "Psychocriticism: Finding the Fault"; "Feminist Stereotypes: Misogyny, Patriarchy, Bombast"; "Christians and Marxists: Allegory, Ideology."

———. "Epilogue: The Future of Rhetoric." In *In Defence of Rhetoric.* Oxford: Clarendon Press, 1988. Includes insightful critiques of the thought of Jakobson and de Man.

Index of Names

Names cited in passing or simply listed are not included, nor are the names of authors of literary works cited as examples unless quotations are taken from the works. Notes are not indexed except that where the name of the author of a quotation is not provided in the text, the number of the note corresponding to the quotation is given (for example, "107n.6").

Index of Subjects

This Subject Index includes only material references to major terms and concepts. Thus the index listings for terms like "theory," "poststructuralism," "text," and "New Criticism" that constantly recur are restricted to passages that provide definitions or substantive discussions.